CONCEIVED IN CRISIS

Early American Histories

Douglas Bradburn, John C. Coombs,
and S. Max Edelson, Editors

Conceived in Crisis

The Revolutionary Creation of an American State

Christopher R. Pearl

University of Virginia Press
Charlottesville and London

University of Virginia Press
© 2020 by the Rector and Visitors of the University of Virginia
All rights reserved
Printed in the United States of America on acid-free paper

First published 2020

1 3 5 7 9 8 6 4 2

Library of Congress Cataloging-in-Publication Data
Names: Pearl, Christopher R., author.
Title: Conceived in crisis : the revolutionary creation of an American state / Christopher R. Pearl.
Description: Charlottesville : University of Virginia Press, 2020. | Series: Early American histories | Includes bibliographical references and index.
Identifiers: LCCN 2020004177 (print) | LCCN 2020004178 (ebook) | ISBN 9780813944548 (hardcover) | ISBN 9780813944555 (epub)
Subjects: LCSH: Pennsylvania—History—Colonial period, ca. 1600–1775. | United States—Politics and government—To 1775. | United States—History—Revolution, 1775–1783—Causes.
Classification: LCC F152 .P269 2020 (print) | LCC F152 (ebook) | DDC 974.8/02—dc23
LC record available at https://lccn.loc.gov/2020004177
LC ebook record available at https://lccn.loc.gov/2020004178

Cover art: "The Manner in Which the American Colonies Declared Themselves Independant of the King of England, Throughout the Different Provinces, on July 4, 1776," c. 1783, engraving. (Library of Congress Prints and Photographs Division, Library of Congress)

For Kelley, Ella, and Jackson

CONTENTS

	Acknowledgments	ix
	Introduction	1
1	"Perfect Strangers": The Problem of Community and Church Governance	11
2	"For Want of Power": The Search for Order and Government	39
3	The "Stupendous Machine": Imperial Pennsylvania and the Failure of Reform	70
4	"When the Thunder of the Law Sleeps": Regulations for "Liberty and Law"	101
5	"Usurping Powers": Resistance, Rebellion, and Revolution	128
6	"For the Security and Protection of the Community": Revolutionary State Formation	167
	Conclusion: New Constitutions and the Persistence of State	205
	Notes	221
	Bibliography	279
	Index	303

ACKNOWLEDGMENTS

Completing this book has not been a solitary adventure but a deeply collaborative one for which I am indebted to many faithful advisors, institutions, friends, and family members. First and foremost, this book could not have been completed without financial and intellectual support from numerous institutions. When I first started the research for this book, I was extremely lucky to receive support from the Robert H. Smith International Center for Jefferson Studies. It was there that I began to see the contours of this project. Similarly, research fellowships at the American Philosophical Society, the William L. Clements Library at the University of Michigan, and the David Library of the American Revolution were instrumental. At all of those places I made amazing friends who offered an endless supply of encouragement and research assistance. I especially want to thank Roy Goodman and Kathie Ludwig. Roy helped me find obscure sources at the APS, always had words of encouragement, and made my time in Philadelphia enjoyable with great food and baseball. Kathie has been indispensable to the research for this book. Over the years, the David Library has become a kind of second home, and I always look forward to walking into the library and chatting with Kathie. I cannot thank her enough for the assistance she provided, especially finding manuscripts and sending me digital copies when I could not make a trip to the library. Thank you, Kathie. You are awesome!

At Binghamton University, I was fortunate to work with outstanding faculty who provided endless support. My PhD advisor, Douglas Bradburn, nurtured a kernel of an idea into something a young graduate student never could have imagined, especially that that idea would one day become a book. I am deeply indebted to Doug, whom I pestered way too often, but who never turned me away and always found time to sit and talk through the project, pushing me to sharpen my arguments and recognize their significance. He made graduate school bearable with his generosity and humor. At Binghamton I also had the good fortune to work with Diane Sommerville, who read and commented on EVERYTHING. Her exacting red pen and critical questioning has saved me from many a blunder. Diane has been a supportive advisor and encouraging friend. I cannot thank her enough.

Trying to take the rough ideas from a dissertation and turn them into a book is no easy process. I am eternally grateful to the friends, colleagues, and students who made it possible. First off, I would like to thank my home institution, Lycoming College, especially Phil Sprunger, for the financial support to conduct further research and to hire student assistants. To my undergraduates, thank you so much. Miranda Beers, Sarah Donovan, Rebecca Reed, and Maggie Slawson were the best students a professor could ask for. They verified footnotes, tracked down sources, and helped me talk through numerous sections of this book. More importantly, their passion for early American history kept me enthusiastic about a project I have been working on for way too long. To my colleagues in the history department, Cullen Chandler, Laura Seddelmeyer, and Sarah Silkey, thanks for the encouragement, conversations, and research excursions. You all are the best. Throughout the research and writing of this book I met many excellent and generous people who helped refine my ideas through stimulating conversations and the critical reading of all or part of the developing manuscript, including the many participants in the Upstate Early American Seminar, Greg Brooking, Joshua Canale, Andrew Fagal, Matthew Spooner, Matthew Williams, William Tatum, Jessica Roney, Kenneth Owen, Paul Moyer, Patrick Spero, Max Edling, Robert Parkinson, and the late Bill Pencak. A special thanks to Owen S. Ireland, who sparked my interest in the American Revolution and Pennsylvania in particular, and who has been a constant source of support and encouragement.

Last but not least, I would like to thank my family. To my father and mother, thank you for nurturing and encouraging my passion for history from a young age, even if you do not find history as exciting as I do. To my wife, Kelley, you made this book possible with your encouragement and love. She has had to live with this project for most of our marriage, listen to me go on and on about the American Revolution, and even read the manuscript when we were both too tired to function as new parents. She can always see things that I cannot. To my kids, Ella and Jackson, thank you for "working on Daddy's book" and providing me with endless diversions. I will miss hearing small feet descend the stairs to bring me a late-night snack and good company while I worked on "the book."

CONCEIVED IN CRISIS

Introduction

THE AMERICAN REVOLUTION led to the creation of powerful, extractive, coercive, and regulatory *states*. Such a statement, while it may not reflect the thrust of histories about the American Revolution, certainly reflected reality for revolutionaries and budding nationalists—later known as Federalists—such as John Jay, George Washington, and Henry Knox. In 1786, after a string of dire letters from Jay expressing the crisis facing the American "nation" due to the power of the "states," Washington, trying to enjoy a semblance of retirement at Mount Vernon, responded that he shared Jay's concerns. His entire revolutionary experience led him to believe that a single "coercive power" needed to be "lodged" in a consolidated government. The states, as of that moment, had all of the "coercive power," and Washington wanted a general government to be as "energetic" and have the same "authority" as "the different state governments extends over the several States."[1] Jay and Washington were not alone. Henry Knox with a dramatic flair that Washington lacked thought the states had grown too powerful and therefore wanted to "smite them in the name of God and all the people."[2] Representing a dominant minority of Americans, these men hoped a revision of the Articles of Confederation with a new national constitution would achieve those goals, but after a grueling four months presiding over the Constitutional Convention, Washington sadly concluded that that he "despair[ed] of seeing a favourable issue to the proceedings."[3] The Constitution that convention created may have been "the best that can be obtained at the present moment," but it was far from what Washington wanted or imagined.[4] The final document did not achieve the national government's supremacy over the states. John Adams, who shared Washington's view, was still complaining during the War of 1812. Adams angrily asked Benjamin Rush, "ARE WE ONE NATION OR 18?"[5]

Considering the bulk of scholarship on the revolutionary era and the Early Republic, the frantic writings of Jay, Washington, Knox, and Adams seem irrational if not delusional. According to scholars, the American Revolution and the constitutional moment, that "Miracle at Philadelphia," created the United States with a national government buttressed by a budding national sentiment and identity.[6] Moreover, Federalist preoccupation with the power of the states seems doubly delusional considering interpretations of the American Revolution as a conservative process of continuation rather than change. The new American states, as some historians argue, merely continued long-held assumptions and visions of governance laid out in colonial charters and practiced over time.[7] If true, nationalists' worries seem mislaid. Those who experienced the colonial governments, such as Benjamin Franklin, Joseph Galloway, and Thomas Gage (representing much of the political spectrum of the late colonial period), viewed the colonial governments as anything but energetic, coercive, or powerful. Franklin saw them as "weak," having "scarce Authority enough to keep the common Peace."[8] Galloway dolefully predicted that "all Government was at an End and the very Design of Society destroyed."[9] Gage thought the colonies should not be considered governments at all.[10] Historians of the colonies have confirmed these contemporary sentiments. The colonial governments barely governed.[11] Due to the dearth of "permanent structural institutions" in the colonies that could provide "stable order," or as Michael Zuckerman puts it, their lack of "adequate agencies of enforcement," historians highlight community self-policing and the preponderance voluntary organizations created to fill the institutional void.[12] If the revolution marked the continuation of those governments, then it is hard to imagine why Washington and others were so worried about the "energy" and "authority" of the individual states.

Yet their fears were not imagined—they emanated from the transformations of the revolution itself. During the American Revolution, ordinary people entered into, interacted with, and sometimes resisted constitutional conventions and, later, legislatures, executive departments, courts, and other governmental institutions, and remade the colonies into states.[13] State formation was an intimate part of the revolution, and it is through that connection and process that we can understand the transformations of the American Revolution and make sense of the fears of some in the 1780s, 1790s, and beyond.[14]

This book, using Pennsylvania as an example, explains why and how those states were created. To be sure, each colony had its own distinct history and experiences, but all had to become states, and that process happened during the revolution. Looking at Pennsylvania's experience we can see two important aspects of the American Revolution. The first is that forming stronger governments was central to the origins of the revolution. The second is that the demands of the Revolutionary War and a continuing dialogue about republican governance during that war pushed the states to new heights of power and authority, challenging the autonomy of local spaces and centralizing power in the process. At the same time, republican ideology, with its focus on the "public welfare" helped imbue state law, officers, and institutions with significant police power in ways never imagined in the colonies. The needs of war and an emphasis on the public welfare went hand in glove, buttressing coercive and regulatory powers that allowed the states to project sovereign authority when that sovereignty was fledgling and fleeting at best. As a result, the states came into being and continued to dominate political life for much of the nineteenth century, challenging any notion that the United States was a nation, and, one could argue, setting the stage for the American Civil War.[15]

However, to understand the place of state formation in the American Revolution, the eighteenth-century colonial experience needs to be brought into sharper focus. It was there, in the factional bickering over policy, violent extralegal regulations, and the dreadful experiences of conducting an imperial war while governing a demographically growing and geographically expanding population that colonists and imperial officials began to formulate and popularize ideas about reforming the colonial governments into more powerful and coercive entities.[16] It was also in that period that colonists began pushing for their colonies to become distinct states, first under the king and then independent of the monarch entirely.[17]

Governance was a key issue that dominated much of the debate about the efficacy and viability of the empire in the 1760s and '70s. Historians of the revolution often see this debate about governance as a constitutional one between stable colonial polities and an increasingly assertive British Parliament over sovereignty, at once defining the "Imperial Crisis," while also explaining the causes of American independence and revolution.[18] But this view is far too narrow to capture a rather popular sense of "crisis" that permeated the debate about the empire. Governance, for colonists, was not just an experience with political power but was understood as the practice of governing. Colonists were just as quick to protest the failure of local market regulations or a defunct court as they were parliamentary sovereignty, and they viewed them as equally important to their daily lives.[19] Governance was as much about what governments do as about what they are.[20] This book expands the interpretation of the problem of governance during the Imperial Crisis to include the practice of governing, which requires taking seriously the massive outpouring of criticism leveled against a distant Parliament *as well as* the questioning of what the colonial governments did and should do, both of which were central questions that captured the attention of colonists in the years preceding American independence.

The governance debate was a product of dramatic changes taking place in eighteenth-century North America. The original colonies were built to govern rather small homogenous populations with shared community values upheld by a handful of political elites linked by blood, marriage, and business. However, through immigration and natural increase, the population boomed. Between 1700 and 1770, the colonial population increased eightfold.[21] Far from homogenous, the colonies became home to people of "different nations, different manners, different religions, and different languages." "Fire and water," a contemporary observed in 1760, could not have been "more heterogeneous than the different colonies in North America."[22] At the same time, the jurisdictions of the colonies moved westward, northward, and southward, straining the ability of the colonial governments to govern.[23] War with France and Native peoples further rendered the governments, particularly for colonists on the frontier, unpopular and, just as important, exposed them as "internally weak."[24] In response to a host of governing issues related to law, land, and war, extralegal regulations broke out in almost every colony; the most popular in the literature remain the regulations of North and South Carolina, but there were also outbreaks in New York, New Jersey, and Virginia.[25] All of them were part of a much larger and growing dialogue embroiling the colonies over the proper role of government and who should rule and why.

Although historians often remove Pennsylvania's history from this larger story of colonial dysfunction by emphasizing its overall stability, Pennsylvania experienced the mid-eighteenth century similarly.[26] Between 1700 and 1770, Pennsylvania's population expanded rapidly, more than doubling every twenty years.[27] As a major port of arrival for migrants to North America, the city of Philadelphia became a conduit for a heterogeneous people that quickly expanded the colony's jurisdiction, creating friction both within and without the colony. In the 1760s alone,

Pennsylvanians pushed the colony's border westward past the Susquehanna River and the Appalachian Mountains to near the confluence of the Allegany and Ohio Rivers. The colonial government, firmly in the hands of social and political elites either connected to the proprietors or the dominant Quaker establishment, faced a difficult situation that it had scarce the ability or desire to effectively deal with. By midcentury, only a handful of counties and governmental institutions existed, and they were understaffed, too far away from the people they were supposed to govern, and incapable of keeping up with the demands of a large and growing population.[28] As a result, as petitioners across the colony cried, "Justice is delayed" and "totally obstructed."[29] Pennsylvanians wanted more government, not less, and they wanted that government to be easily accessible and capable of regulating and protecting the interests and lives of "the Public." Yet, while ordinary Pennsylvanians detested their "being so very far removed from the seat of Justice" and could not help "considering the Insecurity of their Lives and Estates as worthy in some degree the Attention of the Legislature," little was ever done to solve the problem.[30] Justice in Pennsylvania, colonists argued, was "Just-Ass."[31]

The Seven Years' War exacerbated this feeling of discontent. Pennsylvania lacked a formal militia structure, and as the flames of war engulfed the frontier, colonists forthrightly declared that they felt "neglected by the Public." They were particularly angry at the mighty few who "have got the political Reigns in their Hands and tamely tyrannize over the other good Subjects of the Province!"[32] At the end of the war, and faced with a new conflict with Native Americans, Pennsylvanians swamped the press with treatises, diatribes, and satires that lambasted "the weakness of government." The phrase "weakness of government" became a popular expression in the 1760s utilized by political factions, imperial officials, and the public to demand some kind of change. Nevertheless, while politicians wrote much and argued more, they did little, alienating many in the process.

As people took matters into their own hands, extralegal regulations erupted across the colony. In 1763, inhabitants in the frontier county of Lancaster struck out, slaughtered peaceful Native Americans, and marched on the colonial government to demand institutional change. Almost simultaneously, a group calling themselves the Brave Fellows, but known to history as the Black Boys, formulated their own internal government in the back parts of the colony, regulating trade, the movement of people, and even the mail. They were so powerful that they could manipulate formal legal structures, and both the provincial and imperial governments were at a loss as to how to effectively deal with them. The situation was so bleak that Thomas Gage, the commander of British troops in North America, concluded that nothing could be done about the matter without effective colonial governments. Irritated, Gage questioned whether Pennsylvania could "even be called a government."[33] Nor was this experience a "frontier" phenomenon. In one of the oldest eastern counties of Pennsylvania, Chester, the late 1760s saw the rise of multiple violent vigilante gangs running roughshod over those they deemed "a common Nuisance and terror to the Neighbourhood."[34] Because of the "extreme weakness of our government," Deputy Governor John Penn concluded that he could do little but deem the situation out of his control.[35] The mid- to late 1760s, even without new imperial policies and constitutional questions about parliamentary sovereignty, should be considered America's real "Critical Period." It was a colonial crisis with vast implications for the future. According to contemporaries, a radical remedy needed to be applied to cure it. As Benjamin Franklin aptly put it in 1764, Pennsylvania had a "disease that shall finally produce its Dissolution."[36] Therefore, his compatriot Joseph Galloway publicly declared that same year, there needed to be "a Revolution" in the empire.[37]

By the mid- to late 1760s it seemed as if everyone had formulated ideas to fix the problems of governance. Ordinary colonists demanded political inclusion to give them the wherewithal to direct new policies. Franklin and Galloway, on the other hand, wanted to keep the exclusive status quo but sought to align Pennsylvania with the Crown, thus harnessing the empire's military might, while at the same time, they hoped, assuring the colonial legislature's ascendancy and autonomy. Even the proprietor and his supporters recognized "the weakness of government," but they feared and resisted change. They expected the problem to work itself out with time. None of those ideas squared with each other, let alone an emerging vision of an empire directed from the center with significant parliamentary oversight as articulated by members of Parliament, the king's Privy Council, the Board of Trade, and the numerous imperial officials on the ground in North America.

The sheer multiplicity of ideas as to the solution muddied the waters, exacerbated factional politics, and made any real change on the ground hopeless. The tangled if not baroque British imperial system and bureaucracy further stymied all attempts at reform. Although historians have viewed Pennsylvania's political problems as either the product of

Quakerism or proprietary disputes with the legislature, the Crown and its ministers significantly shaped both the politics of the colony and its ability to reform and govern. For example, making their way through the royal deputy governors, the Board of Trade, and, finally, the king's Privy Council, seven of eight laws to overhaul the judicial structure of the colony, popular initiatives, received the royal veto. The colonies may have existed in some kind of "salutary neglect," but that did not mean change was ever easy or even possible.[38] Some kind of consensus on both sides of the Atlantic needed to be achieved for lasting and, more important, significant change. Such a scenario was downright impossible.

The inability to fix what seemed to all a real problem of governance created what sociologists and political scientists term a "state crisis," where people perceive their government as "ineffective, unjust, and obsolete."[39] Such a scenario happened in Pennsylvania when both elites and popular groups deemed the government incapable of performing the basic tasks of governance. As this crisis deepened in the 1760s and '70s, petitioning drives, contested elections, and riots inflamed the colony, creating political chaos and politicizing the public. Aggressive parliamentary acts and Britain's new vision of empire aggravated this already contentious political climate. The confusion and clamoring for governmental reform with little official response coupled with the imperial dispute resulted in a cataclysmic breakdown—the dismantling of the imperial system, the toppling of the old regime, and the creation of a new independent state.

The creation of new states and American independence was one attempt and solution to the problem of governance experienced by many if not all colonists. In the spring of 1776, a vocal contingent of colonists, gathering in town meetings, county committees, and provincial conventions, embraced what contemporaries deemed "a spirit of innovation."[40] Trying to address the problems of governance, they vowed to "clear every part of the old rubbish out of the way and begin on a clear foundation." In the moment, it seemed as if "everything was to be altered."[41] The Declaration of Independence reinforced the idea that such change was in the offing. The declaration's list of grievances, for example, skewered the king for hampering basic functions of government. The Crown, representing, by that point, the entire imperial system, rendered the colonies weak and pathetic with ineffective courts and corrupt judges, which had "obstructed the Administration of Justice." Nor could colonists fix the problems, the declaration asserted, because the king refused "his Assent to Laws, the most wholesome and necessary for the public good." In its final paragraph, the document declared that by breaking away from the singular "State of Great Britain," new American citizens would rectify all of these problems by establishing "free and Independent States." It was on this idea that new American citizens would stake "our Lives, our Fortunes, and our sacred Honor."[42] This may not have represented the only or even most popular solution, as the existence and activity of loyalists, trimmers, and those who wanted to remain neutral during the Revolutionary War makes clear, but it was a solution nonetheless.

The colonial experience, bad as it was, only initiated the creation of states; the states were also conceived in the crisis of war. Divisions over independence, the existence of the states, and even the form and function of those governments proved serious challenges to the sovereignty of new transitional regimes in the midst of a war. The tenuousness of the states pushed revolutionaries to back regulatory and coercive policies that often blurred the lines between public and private to shape the social and moral order of "the people" that the states represented. In Pennsylvania, oaths of allegiance, affirmations of loyalty, and a myriad of new regulations to curb illicit market practices as well as "vice and immorality" abounded.[43] To enforce those policies, revolutionaries drew on the revolution's "spirit of innovation" and reconfigured and created governmental institutions that would bend to the will of central authority and direction. In the process, revolutionaries centralized their government and set crucial precedents for state police power that would remain a key component of state governance well into the twentieth century.

Republican ideology, too, proved a crucial factor in the creation of these powerful states. With an emphasis on the community's well-being, republicanism justified expansive police powers rooted in the language of "protection" that often placed individual rights and interests in a subservient position to the public welfare. The Revolutionary War breathed life into this activist side of republican governance. During that miserable and bloody conflict, divided loyalties, expressed neutrality, apathy, and economic self-interest vexed revolutionaries everywhere. Policing public morals and individual loyalty, revolutionaries in Pennsylvania declared, was necessary to protect "the welfare and happiness of the good people of this commonwealth," who "next under God, entirely depend on maintaining and supporting the independence and sovereignty of the state."[44] State sovereignty and the public's safety and happiness became wedded in the minds of revolutionaries, and both could be achieved, they argued, through a vigorous assertion of the state's "internal police."[45] The idea of *police* in republican thought was fundamentally linked to the promotion of "the pursuit of happiness," but, as revolutionaries in Pennsylvania articulated, that required institutional intervention through an active and energetic use of regulatory power.[46] Such a power, though calculated to serve the interests of the "public good," had a coercive side, especially for those who tried to work against socially and legally ascribed values, or those people the state defined as existing outside "the public," such as Native peoples, African slaves, loyalists, or anyone who refused to recognize the sovereignty of the states. By investigating the states' treatment of the latter during the revolution, we can see more clearly how the war and republicanism worked together in the shaping of the states and the way they governed.[47]

By the end of the war, the states were far different from where they started in 1776. In Pennsylvania, new laws, institutions, and officers proliferated during the war to maintain state independence and sovereignty. Through the legislature, the executive, and the judiciary, state leaders demonstrated the preeminence of state institutions and laws over local spaces and the lives of the people within them. Yet when the war ended, its impact on the formation of the state did not. Rebuilding from the destruction, healing from the violence, and reintegrating those the state marked as disloyal still needed to occur.[48] Of course individuals could try to restore their lives, but much more was required of the state to mobilize manpower and resources for rebuilding. Just as significant, legal definitions of the status of people would need to change for peacetime realities still reeling from the reverberations of war, penal laws would have to be reassessed, and institutions and officers created for war would similarly need reassessment, but many remained intact. Even the Constitution of 1776, it was popularly proclaimed at war's end, needed adjustment. The demands of war, both during and after the fighting, fundamentally changed the state of Pennsylvania, much as it did elsewhere, and that transformation, historians of the nineteenth century continue to make clear, had a lasting impact on American law and politics in the years to come.[49] Pennsylvania's revolutionaries, like colonists and would-be citizens elsewhere, created a state, conceived in crisis, that controlled, as Thomas Jefferson put it, the "principle care of our Persons, our property, and our reputation, constituting the great field of human concerns."[50]

Understanding how Pennsylvanians went about creating a state with such an encompassing jurisdiction requires an investigation of both the colonial and revolutionary periods. Both periods were perceived crises, and it was the debate about how to overcome those crises through governmental intervention and an expansion of its police powers that forged the state. For some, such as the Paxton Boys, Benjamin Franklin, and Joseph Galloway, the crisis or the "seeds of that Disease" had its origin in the creation of the colony itself, as the vision of governance laid out by William Penn and the colony's early Quaker leaders quickly foundered on powerful demographic and geographic changes sweeping the colony.[51] It is to that dilemma that we first turn.

1

"Perfect Strangers"

The Problem of Community and Church Governance

IN 1748, Henry Melchior Muhlenberg, a Lutheran pastor who came to America six years earlier, ruminated in his journal, "Some strange things go on here in Pennsylvania." No doubt reflecting on his experiences in this colony with few governing institutions, he ended his entry with a strong indictment of Pennsylvania, asserting that "the Book of Judges 17:6 expresses it well: 'In those days there was no king in Israel, but every man did that which was right in his own eyes.'"[1] Muhlenberg's choice of scripture points to a problem of governance at all levels: the community, the church, and the state. In the book of Judges, there was no central state authority, and individuals were left to their own devices, as their local communities could scarcely form sporadic unity and many ministers were incapable of enforcing the laws of God. In essence, Muhlenberg compared Pennsylvania to a story that epitomized utter anarchy at all levels of society and government.

The popularity of Penn's "holy experiment" to newcomers as well as Enlightenment philosophes like Voltaire, Montesquieu, and Chevalier de Jaucourt, who praised Penn's ideals to discredit the ancien régime, has tipped the balance in the historical literature in favor of the liberal benefits of the province, thus obscuring the severe criticisms of people like Muhlenberg.[2] While Pennsylvanians and visitors alike often lauded the religious liberty in the province and deemed it a "best poor man's country," they also noted its flaws. Acknowledging the colony was admirable if not desirable for being "a land of great liberties," Pennsylvanians also complained that "the People are not well restricted therein."[3] The Moravian brethren in Bethlehem, a sect noted for its liberality and peaceful qualities, read the *"constitution of the land"* and provincial *"rights and laws,"* and judged them too lax. The entire congregation approved their own regulations for everyone who wished to live on Moravian-owned land because they thought it "impossible" to concede "Pennsylvania liberties, which are so readily abused."[4]

Pennsylvanians regularly expressed such views in their observations about the province. The colony was far from a "terrestrial Paradise."[5] As early as 1701, Justus Falckner, a Swedish Lutheran minister who like many others noted the religious liberty of the colony also condemned it as a place that promoted the mantra "Do away with all good order, and live for yourself as it pleases you!"[6] Similarly, in 1736, another Swedish Lutheran followed up his appraisal of religious liberty by describing the province as a "sanctuary for all evil-doers from Europe, a confused Babel, a receptacle for all unclean spirits, an abode of the devil, a first world, a Sodom, which is deplorable."[7] Even prominent officials admitted that "Robberies, housebreaking, Rapes & other Crimes" were so commonplace that they feared going "to bed with our doors open."[8] Deputy Governor George Thomas ruefully commented that "Indians, who are left to the Law of Nature," were better off than the colonists, who were unrestrained from being "Thieves, Adulterers, Cheats &c."[9] Pennsylvanians after midcentury consistently complained about the "Insecurity of their Lives and Estates."[10] It seems, then, that the province's lack of order and good governance tempered its reputation for liberty.[11]

Pennsylvania's founder, William Penn, worried that such censures and observations would jeopardize his new "holy experiment," which he designed to prohibit unchecked licentiousness. Penn decried it as a "sort of anarchy" when an inhabitant did "that which he thought Right in his Own Eyes."[12] Penn's visions for Pennsylvania included community solidarity and mutual assistance in neighborhoods and towns where people formed strong social organizations that could act as centripetal forces in governing society. Religion too played an important role in providing moral guidance and discipline for the heterogeneous people that would make up this religious experiment. Penn's vision of governance did not rely solely or even heavily on a strong state but rather found its most powerful expression in extralegal spaces such as the community and church.

The Quakers who made up Penn's "holy experiment" and controlled the province's political, legal, and civic institutions and organizations until the 1750s embraced this decentralized vision of governance. While they disagreed with the founding proprietor on a host of issues related to the political and legal power of the executive, they adhered, sometimes against all odds and the needs and experiences of inhabitants, to a governing philosophy that placed the onus of responsibility on individuals and the communities they comprised to meet the basic needs and provide the essential services for day-to-day life. Throughout the colonial period public health, internal improvements, poor relief, and military defense remained in the hands of religious institutions and voluntary organizations rather than the state.[13]

The success of such a dispersed system of informal governance required the ideals of William Penn and the elite Quakers who controlled much of the policy making to match the reality of the province. Yet, almost from the beginning, this goal of making community and religion the cornerstone of governance fell short of expectations. Over the late seventeenth and eighteenth centuries, the ideals governing society and reality grew increasingly farther apart as changes in land policy, demographic growth, and economic change challenged the establishment of coherent communities and the effectiveness and reach of churches in the province.[14] In essence, human forces altered the social and natural landscape, and in turn, such alterations led to puissant instability for Pennsylvanians from all social strata, as life, liberty, and security of property hung in the balance.

Proprietary Land Policy and Town Settlement

To achieve community and neighborliness, Penn developed a land policy that promoted close-knit settlements in towns and villages.[15] Dubbed "the regulation of the Country," Penn's land policy dictated that towns precede settlements with precisely laid out village lots and town households. Each town was to be five thousand acres and initially composed of at least ten families situated every few hundred acres. Every town was also to have a centrally located five-hundred-acre village with a public space. This method of settlement and plan for "near neighbourhood" had in view "Society, Assistance, Busy Commerce, Instruction of Youth, Government of Peoples manners" and "Conveniency of Religious Assembling." Nevertheless, Penn's plans miscarried on multiple levels and thus failed as a form of governance for "the regulation of the Country."[16]

This is not to say that Penn did not try to implement his designs. During the early years of the colony, Penn made it clear that he wanted regularly laid out contiguous townships with centrally located villages. When companies like the Krefeld and Frankfort companies sought land for national group settlement in the early 1680s, Penn demanded conformity with his ideas for "the regulation of the Country." Penn felt so strongly about the creation of towns that he stipulated in land warrants that companies could lose their land if they did not comply with his directives for community settlement.[17]

Penn also attempted to achieve his ideal structured society by creating governmental mechanisms and procedures to provide for orderly settlement. He created a Board of Property that delegated authority to a land office, which included a surveyor general and numerous deputy surveyors. According to Penn's rules, no land warrant could be granted without an official survey, an important step, as land officers had to survey and lay out contiguous townships. Once surveyed, parcels in the township could be sold, thus limiting the choice of lawful settlement to specified areas. For Penn, mapping, surveying, and regulating the purchase of land literally and figuratively ordered the countryside.[18]

Penn's zeal for the carefully planned agricultural village quickly flagged due to his penchant for profit, political turmoil, and a rising frenzy of land speculation. In letters to his deputy governors, Penn often wrote of his pecuniary interests. Penn recognized that his position as "absolute Lord of the Soile" provided him the only means to attain a lifestyle beyond mere solvency. These private interests ultimately commingled with the increased interest of English speculators and ambitious colonists. By the 1690s, faced with extensive debts, Penn dropped any pretense of establishing agricultural villages. In 1699, for example, Penn sold sixty thousand acres to the Pennsylvania Company of London in widely dispersed parcels outside of the settled areas of the province. Not only were parcels scattered, but Penn granted the company warrants without surveys and removed the stipulations requiring community settlement.[19] Thus Penn sacrificed his ideal agricultural villages for the temptation of large sums of money through land speculation.

Penn's decision to eschew settlement stipulations significantly affected the size and layout of towns. In 1686, for instance, Penn granted Coxe and Company, a group of English speculators in the fur trade, thirty thousand acres in the back parts of Chester County. By 1705, Coxe and Company went belly-up and sold one-third of the acreage to Penn's friend Joseph Pike. Since Penn abandoned settlement stipulations, Coxe and Company as well as Pike could lay out townships and sell parcels at their discretion. The remaining twenty thousand acres of the Coxe and Company purchase thus became the large township of Vincent, and the ten thousand acres sold to Pike became the township of Pikeland. Without Penn's original guidelines, the town of Vincent was four times the size of the townships Penn had imagined and Pikeland double that size. Vincent Township proved so large that its own constables complained that it was "a very Great hardship To serve so Great a town as Vincent is."[20] Worse still, neither township had a centrally located village, nor were the parcels in any way symmetrical. In Pikeland, for example, where Pike and his heirs ruled as absentee landlords, parcels were demarcated only after a settler marked them off according to the goodness of the soil.[21] After 1700, oversized townships like Vincent and Pikeland became the rule rather than the exception.[22]

Bitter political struggles further compromised "the regulation of the Country." Penn predicated his rather idealistic visions on the belief that local Quaker leaders would not question his authority. However, Pennsylvanians, particularly those men in the assembly who were far from congenial and obedient, constantly questioned his ability to rule. According to Gary Nash, "By the end of the 1680s it was clear that the holy experiment, as originally conceived, was floundering in an atmosphere of recrimination, chronic friction, and struggle for position."[23] Penn, realizing he needed supporters, attempted to gain allegiance through political appointments and granting choice lands at discount prices. As early as 1685, Penn noted that for those people who were "of aid to me and Dilligent, I will be kind to them in land and other things."[24]

Penn's use of patronage also undermined his original plans for orderly settlement. The positions of surveyor general and deputy surveyor for the land office were proprietary-appointed and potentially lucrative, as they offered opportunity for indiscriminate land speculation. In 1717, a year before William Penn's death, the surveyor general and deputy surveyor marked off for themselves the choicest land in unclaimed sections of Chester County.[25] By the late 1760s, correlating the surveyor's office with land speculation became so entrenched that Deputy Governor John Penn believed it "impossible to put a stop to this trade of Land jobbing." The surveyor general, he noted, was often "very busy in surveying [for himself] when he goes into the back Counties."[26]

The commingling of patronage and land speculation continued long after Penn's death. His heirs parted with land at discount prices, handed out lucrative offices, and assisted their supporters' speculations in return for political allegiance. In the colonies, as in England, patronage linked social superiors and inferiors, clans and kinship groups together in promoting what they called "friendship," a euphemistic term for "interest." Patronage constituted a central component in Pennsylvania's social and political relationships, at least for the upper crust and those deemed useful to the proprietors and their supporters. William Penn's son, Thomas Penn, for instance, measured his "inclination" to bestow benefits in "proportion to the service" performed for him. If men proved loyal and useful, Penn returned the favor.[27]

Proprietary patronage and land speculation were all leaves of the same tree, and their connection is best evidenced in the success of William Allen, a staunch proprietary ally. Allen, who had supported the Penns since the 1720s and even arranged the marriage of his daughter to a Penn, received preferential treatment in land deals, news of potential purchases of Indian land, and appointive offices.[28] Between 1728 and 1774 Allen held or had occupied at one time the offices of common councilman, recorder, and mayor of the city of Philadelphia, justice of the peace for Northampton County, boundary commissioner during the Pennsylvania-Maryland border dispute, and chief justice of the supreme court. Allen also depended on proprietary allegiance for his speculative land ventures. In 1725, for instance, Allen bought ten thousand acres of rich alluvial land from William Penn Jr. for £741, well under the established £10 per hundred acres that everyone else had to pay. Not only did Allen get a deal, but the land purchased was above the forks of the Delaware River and still owned by Native Americans and therefore not surveyed. In addition, Allen purchased fifteen thousand acres near the Delaware and Lehigh Rivers for £1,000 from Thomas Penn and an additional five thousand acres in what would be part of Nazareth Township in Northampton County from Laetitia Penn Aubrey for £500. Allen sold this last purchase a mere five years later to George Whitefield for £2,200.[29] By 1770, Allen acquired no less than seventy-five thousand acres (exclusive of his holdings in the city of Philadelphia and other colonies), sixty-four thousand of which were unlocated lands (not surveyed) purchased from members of the proprietary family.[30] According to Allen, being "active and zealous" for the proprietors entitled him and others like him "to take up" large swaths of land.[31]

Proprietary grants of large tracts of unlocated land without the use of surveys had a trickle-down effect. Pennsylvanians took proprietary laxity as a license to dispense with proper procedure. By the mid-eighteenth century, selling warrants without a survey became the norm. Instead of laying out contiguous townships with similarly aligned properties in which the goodness of the soil made little difference, settlers and speculators bought what they thought was the best land. Doing away with Penn's original land procedures catered to the hopes and aspirations of many Pennsylvanians. As one Pennsylvania surveyor noted, "Every man" takes "what quantity [of land] he thinks fit" as "warrants are issued before the tracts are survey'd." Another surveyor argued that the whole process by which land was bought was "so contrived as to leave out every place that has the least appearance of being bad."[32] By the 1730s, surveyors were, according to a surveyor from Lancaster, "Strangers" to laying out land "according to the method of townships."[33]

Changes in land policy, while accepted and even well received, proved detrimental to the idea of a community governed by "near neighbourhood." Towns often exceeded the five-thousand-acre limit, and their structure with clearly defined boundaries, the symbols of order for William Penn, had lost importance. Towns were laid out according to the dictates of corporate purchasers; consequently, some towns went years without clearly defined boundaries. In Chester County, for example, it took over forty years and many complaints by inhabitants for Caln Township's boundaries to be established.[34] Town jurisdictions were sometimes so ambiguous that inhabitants were elected or appointed to offices in towns where they did not reside.[35]

Not only did the adapted land policy make for large townships being laid out, as one historian notes, like a "jigsaw-puzzle," but it also undermined Penn's idea for a tightly knit community.[36] Pennsylvania's settlement patterns often emerged indiscriminately, with long distances between neighbors. According to one country inhabitant, neighbors living less than one mile from each other were rather extraordinary.[37] Gottlieb Mittelberger, a German schoolmaster who traveled to Pennsylvania in 1750, remarked, "In the country the people live so far from one another that many a one has to walk fifteen minutes or half an hour to get to his nearest neighbor."[38]

A layout of "scattered" settlements without a centrally located public space undermined the formation of community and neighborliness. Germantown, Philadelphia, for example, was a long narrow township built around a single road. According to Stephanie Wolf, such a layout did not provide "the warm, close, almost claustrophobic life of a traditional village." It was quite possible that neighbors did not even know one another or have significant interaction. Wolf found that "one man on the Great Road could lose three cows and another a few doors away find them, and the fact would never be known until both advertised in the newspaper."[39] A young lawyer, Jasper Yeates, thought that "the want of society is the greatest evil to which a country life is generally subjected." Everyone seemed, he wrote despondently, "perfect strangers."[40] The experiences of the Germantown inhabitants and Yeates correlated to the layout of the towns. As James Lemon notes, Pennsylvania's townships, "lacking spatial regularity, appear to have done little to foster order and participation in community life."[41]

The observations left by Pennsylvanians and travelers through the colony during the middle of the eighteenth century speak to this lack of community development. Mittelberger found that relationships between members of a particular town or region were so weak that "many parents act as sponsors for their own children" during baptisms "because they have no faith or confidence in other people."[42] Muhlenberg thought similarly, noting that towns in the colony shouldn't even be called "townships." That appellation designated community and neighborliness, but in Pennsylvania the people were so "distantly situated," "isolated and do not live near each other," that they lacked "love and unity!"[43]

Colonial Pennsylvanians not only undermined community and town development by their settlement patterns, but they assaulted one another and defaced and defiled their neighbors' property with little in the way of deterrence. In West Nottingham Township the Reynolds family destroyed their neighbor's wheat field, tore down his fences, "ripped up the Belly of [his] Sows heavy with young," stole his cider and brandy, and then proceeded to break into the neighborhood church and "Bedaubed the Pulpit and Christening Bason with Human Dung," and yet never faced legal punishment.[44] Such instances, according to Muhlenberg, were common and had to be "tolerated to some extent," as

> the country people are isolated and do not live near each other. Their entire wealth consists of cattle and grain. The grain is stored in either barns or stacked in open fields. If the head of a house should give offence to some insolent Irishman or brutal German, he may very likely find that some harm has been done to his cattle or crops during the night, since everything stands out in the open, exposed to the revenge and spite of such callous people. Even before a man looks out of his house at night his barn and all his possessions may be completely

burned, and before he is able to summon the aid of a neighbor or the justice of the peace, the enemy may already have perpetrated the utmost damage and fled several miles away into the forest.[45]

Such a sentiment contrasted with the kind of settlement Penn and the early Quaker leaders imagined with cohesive communities that regulated their own social interactions and upheld community interests. Such relations between neighbors and the disinterest of many people in community development was not solely the result of the distances between neighbors. Surely the distance had an impact on the ability of neighbors to interact regularly with one another, but nonetheless it did not preclude them from establishing a connection in which expectations of neighborliness or even hospitality prevailed. There were other important demographic and economic changes, that, when combined with settlement patterns, strained and significantly affected "the regulation of the Country."

Mobility and the Fracturing of Communities

Eighteenth-century Pennsylvania also proved inhospitable to the development of strong social organization to regulate the country because it was marked by the impermanence of communities. The transience of people was due to three factors: land policy, demographic growth, and economic change. During the eighteenth century Pennsylvania's population increased by close to 50 percent per decade.[46] Such drastic population growth coupled with colonial land policy limited the ability of people to purchase land in the settled regions of the province, leading to widespread squatting, as well as acrimonious and sometimes violent disputes over property and high mobility rates. Explosive demographic growth and the development of commercial agriculture also produced a growing landless class of laborers, adding to the overall mobility that characterized Pennsylvania's countryside. All three together profoundly hindered the ability of Pennsylvanians to establish good and lasting relationships with their neighbors. Instead of neighborhood and neighborliness, then, these three human forces fostered a highly mobile community of strangers.

Such mobility challenged the informal methods of governance Penn and the early Quakers envisioned and depended on for social control. The communities they wanted required, at the very least, that people settling within them establish firm roots and long-lasting and complex connections with others in their community. In essence, they relied on forming strong social organizations. According to the work of sociologists, social organizations are "networks of people, the exchanges and reciprocity that transpire in relationships, accepted standards and norms of social support, and social controls that regulate behavior and interaction."[47] These scholars emphasize the importance of social organization as a process that develops over time through the shared experiences of a group. This understanding of social organization is a particularly useful way to view a colony made up of diverse peoples with different interests, beliefs, cultures, and languages. Because social organization is a process, it is adaptive and can change and evolve to establish new norms and common values to fit a heterogeneous community. Yet, because it is a process that develops over time, it requires lasting connections between people over generations. Such connections strengthen ties and help to develop a sense of fraternalism, thus providing the shared experiences that lead to the development of new or adapted social values and expectations.[48]

The high price of located lands (cleared and sometimes settled parcels) significantly challenged the creation of strong social organizations. Demographic growth contributed to the dramatic increase of land prices, pushing some Pennsylvanians to rent small cottages, squat on located lands, roam the countryside, or move to the massive portions of unlocated lands in the backcountry, much of which the Native Americans still owned. According to John J. McCusker and Russell R. Menard, the price of located land reached "ten shillings per acre in the 1730s, twenty shillings in the 1740s, and more than forty shillings per acre in the 1760s."[49] For land speculators the rise in prices promised quick monetary gain. In 1753, William Allen jubilantly wrote that "lands in this province that are located have risen very much in Value."[50] Similarly, one contemporary argued that "the Numbers of Foreigners," not to mention a new generation of Pennsylvanians looking to buy property, "has given the Proprietors of Land great expectations."[51]

Not all inhabitants benefited from the rise in prices for located lands. For incoming immigrants, servants released from their indentures, or Pennsylvanians looking to improve their circumstances, the rise in prices proved unfavorable. According to Gottlieb Mittelberger, "The price of land is increasing from year to year, especially because the English see that so many people, anxious to own farms or plantations are coming to the country every year." High prices, Mittelberger concluded, led many German immigrants to search out "uncultivated lands" or small parcels of land "to build a cottage."[52] Similarly, Pennsylvanians newly released from indentures could not find affordable property to either buy or rent. Often, recently released servants could not even find steady work in one particular community. William Moraley, like many common laborers, "roam'd about like a Roving Tartar," taking odd jobs for a few shillings and some victuals.[53]

For others, squatting in the vast sections of unlocated lands provided initial relief. Settlers, because the survey was unnecessary to the initial process of warranting land, often settled before they applied for a warrant or a survey, if they applied at all. Squatting proliferated even further when, between 1718 and 1732, the land office closed due to a debate over the terms of William Penn's will.[54] According to Isaac Norris Sr., the Penn family dispute fostered "Pyraticall Insolence & disregard to propertie."[55] The combination of demographic growth, both through immigration and natural increase, Penn's land policy, a dysfunctional decade in land administration, and rising land prices led to a rapid increase in the number of squatters in the province.

Despite the proliferation of squatters, their rights to the soil were essentially tenuous. In 1751, a group of squatters petitioned the Crown stating that proprietary officials kicked them off their land and burned down their homes. Such actions were standard practice in Pennsylvania. Government officials and private speculators deemed such people nothing more than criminals and "common trespassers."[56] Squatting, for many, then, provided only temporary habitation. The structure of the squatters' cabins or cottages and their ability to leave quickly speaks to this ephemerality. In May 1750, Secretary Richard Peters and a few magistrates, roused by Native American threats against the province due to the encroachment of squatters on their common hunting lands, traversed the countryside attempting to evict the intruders. Along the way, Peters noted several interesting facts about the squatters he encountered. Peters remarked that the "Families were not large, nor Improvements considerable." Their dwellings often consisted of "only a few Logs piled, and fastened to one another." When Peters and the magistrates demanded that inhabitants vacate the premises, it never took more than a few hours for an entire settlement to gather up its belongings and the cabins to be burned. It seems many of the settlers had prepared to leave at a moment's notice. In addition, some of the cottages they burned had long been "deserted before and lay waste," which equally speaks to the impermanence of such settlements.[57]

The choice to burn the cottages is equally revealing. Peters and the magistrates realized they needed to burn the dwellings, as leaving the structures standing would only "encourage others to come there" and therefore "signify nothing."[58] Such a rationale was likely based on the fact that squatters often sold their claims to land under the guise of "improvements." Isaac Norris Sr., ever ready to castigate the practices of "trespassers," noted that squatters had "No scruple" against selling their "Improvements as they call it" and moving on.[59] The combination of selling improvements and squatter transiency proved a nightmare for officials, as some land claimants were third- and even fourth-party purchasers who had only a rudimentary understanding of their claims' borders based on vague characteristics of the natural landscape. Maintaining legal boundaries, which conceptually ordered the countryside, was nearly impossible under such circumstances.[60]

Selling improvements to third or even fourth parties and the policy of issuing warrants without surveys made for confusing and often overlapping land claims, which resulted in endless property disputes that forced people to move to areas where they expected less internal strife and uncertainty. A land dispute between two inhabitants, Andrew Dunlap and John Black, graphically illustrates the problems conflicting claims caused and the mobility it inaugurated. Sometime during the mid-1720s, Dunlap squatted on four hundred acres in the "back parts" of Pennsylvania. Several years later, in 1732, Dunlap attempted to purchase a warrant for the land only to learn that a land speculator, Black, had recently done the same. Since neither party had surveyed the land, Dunlap claimed his right to the parcel because he "Settled upon and Improv'd the said Land."[61] So sure of his preemption rights, Dunlap sent petitions to the deputy governor and the king, both of which came to nothing, as each recognized Black's legal ownership.[62] Not only did this dispute eventually come before the deputy governor and the Crown, but it ended in violence, as Dunlap refused to give up his right and Black resorted to removing Dunlap with an armed posse. The misfortune and increasingly bad decisions of Dunlap did not end there, as he subsequently "settled and Improved some Land, further back" without title in the hopes that he might "enjoy the Same peaceably."[63] Dunlap, however, would not benefit from his labors, as Native Americans owned the land and the government forcibly removed him and burned down his home. In 1735, Dunlap left Pennsylvania for Virginia.[64] Conflicting claims in this case, as in others, resulted in confusion, violence, and considerable mobility, as Dunlap moved no less than three times in a decade.

Not only did people move because of such befuddling land claims that led to unbridled violence, but by the mid-eighteenth century land cost less in other colonies, especially Maryland, Virginia, and the Carolinas. In 1732, for instance, the price of land in Maryland was less than one-third the price of land in Pennsylvania, and this disparity continued well into the 1760s.[65] Moreover, ordinary Pennsylvanians were aware and upset that proprietary favorites like William Allen bought lands for "£5 per 100 Acres ... clear of Quit-rents," while everyone else had to pay £15 10s for the same. "Settlers say," Edward Shippen noted, "they will leave the Province and goe into Maryland if they [the proprietors] don't make a Considerable abatement."[66] The movement of people out of the province worried legislators who thought "the Excise will be lessened instead of being increased," as "People now leave the Province faster than they come into it" due to "cheaper" land elsewhere.[67]

The assembly's anxiety points to the fact that more than just squatters left their homes behind. In fact, Pennsylvanians, whether landholders or landless, frequently moved about. As a country farmer noted in 1773, "Farmers are, many of them, selling their plantations and going" elsewhere to "take up larger tracts."[68] By buying "larger tracts," farmers attempted to assure the landed inheritance and solvency of their progeny.[69] In West Nottingham, for example, a predominately agricultural region, the average acreage of farms in the early 1770s was ninety acres, with a mode of one hundred acres. Such an average acreage, with little probability of affordable land existing around or even close to a particular farmstead, especially due to speculation, severely diminished the ability of farmers to divide their holdings to provide for all of their children.[70] Farmers living on the West and East branches of the Susquehanna River, "induced by the Prospect of more commodious Settlements, and the agreeable Hope of providing advantageously for their Families, quitted the interior and more orderly Parts of the Province for their present Habitations" on the frontier.[71] The land requirements for partible inheritance cannot singularly account for mobility, as landholders were not the only transient inhabitants. After midcentury Pennsylvania experienced a rapid increase in the number of tenant farmers and other landless classes that proved highly mobile and therefore added to the ephemerality of Pennsylvania's community structure and through that, "the regulation of the country."[72]

Tenancy took root because it offered newcomers and others economic and social advancement. With a tighter land market, especially the rise in prices for located lands including a house, barn, stables, and some cleared farming acres, tenancy gave people the ability to reap the benefits of these options without paying exorbitant prices. Nor did some tenants have to come up with enough capital to pay for farm tools and work animals, as many landlords granted access to them in their leases. Because of these benefits, when immigrants came to Pennsylvania, they often received advice to rent land rather than buy property.[73]

Tenancy, however, did not lead to a situation in which an individual tenant put down roots in a particular town. Tenancy in and of itself was impermanent. Landowners granted leases from one to twenty-one years, but most often for just three to seven years.[74] From landowners' perspectives, tenancy provided certain flexibility in the short run to make gains on property and keep it in good repair while their family matured. Many leases had stipulations that the landowner could break the lease if needed for the family or to sell. Tenancy, then, served a particular function for many landowners; it held over the property in a lucrative fashion until they could either sell it or disperse it to family as an inheritance to sons or as a dowry for daughters. For example, Charles Grantham, who leased and improved the property of Andrew Henderickson, had to give up the property when Henderickson's eldest son came of age.[75]

Tenants were not the only temporary inhabitants. After midcentury, rural communities went through profound changes, both demographically and economically, which resulted in an increase of rural wage laborers. After 1720, Pennsylvania became a crucial exporter of wheat, flour, and bread to the British Isles, British West Indies, other mainland colonies, and after 1760, Europe, particularly Portugal.[76] Pennsylvania's involvement in the Atlantic economy not only shaped the development of Philadelphia as a major entrepôt but reached into the countryside and made a significant contribution to its economic development.[77] After 1720 and especially after 1740, commercial agriculture grew apace, and the number of cleared acres increased steadily each decade. Moreover, commercialization and its attendant profits brought a certain refinement of taste for rural inhabitants and an expanded domestic economy.[78] Imports sometimes outstripped exports, and in the countryside skilled craftsmen became increasingly in demand. In Berks County, for example, Karren Guenther found that by the 1760s tax lists "reflected a diversity of occupations, with more than two dozen vocations identified."[79] In Chester County, the number of skilled artisans also increased, and focusing on wheat production allowed for "bi-occupationalism" as farmers and laborers worked seasonally in the fields and then in the shops.[80] Inhabitants in the city as well as the countryside, then, relied less on neighborhood bartering and started to take part in a more impersonal market exchange.

One of the best indices to track the countryside's commercial development is the rise of a landless class of wage laborers, particularly people classified as "inmate" or "freeman" on tax lists. Between 1756 and 1775 the number of inmates and freemen nearly doubled in proportion to the rest of the rural community.[81] Inmates and freemen were landless wage-earning people. Inmates, according to the notes of a tax assessor in 1796, "are Such as live in Small cottages through the township and have no taxable property, except a cow, very few have a horse."[82] They were also heads of household who earned their living by working for wages. They often held short-term leases with resident landowners for two- to twenty-acre plots with a one-story eighteen- by twenty-foot dwelling. Freemen, on the other hand, were a landless class of single men over the age of twenty-one, who, like inmates, were wage laborers who lived on a small section of someone else's property or, more likely, in someone else's home.[83] According to Lucy Simler, inmates and freemen "made up a free labor force one step above bound laborers (Slaves and Indentured Servants)."[84]

While the economy increased the need for a larger labor pool than existed during the first half of the century, it did not lead to steady work. With the rise in immigration and substantial natural increase, competition for jobs was sometimes, but not always, fierce. The economy of the countryside had not altered in a way that could provide stable income in one township for all of Pennsylvania's wage laborers. Many laborers coped with intermittent and seasonal work by moving about. Two Irish immigrant brothers, Robert and Thomas Parke, moved to Chester County, rented a small parcel of land, and traveled about the county as farmhands, reaping and mowing for wages.[85] Similar to the experience of the Parke brothers, William Moraley, an indentured servant, noted that he had "no Abiding Place" and had to "skulk about" and "lay in a Hayloft," or out in the open air. He earned meager wages by sometimes acting as "the Blacksmith; at other times ... Work'd in the water" or as a "Cow Hunter" or even a tinkerer, and his chosen profession, a clockmaker.[86] The Parke brothers and Moraley would have been considered, at some point in their lives, freemen. Freemen and inmates were part of the same labor market that required flexibility and movement. They rented their cottages on a yearly basis, from April to April or as the season required.[87] Add to this reality of intermittent work, the search for better opportunities, especially land ownership, and you get a highly mobile class of people. Instead of putting down roots in a particular community, freemen and inmates moved about, and frequently.

The combination of squatting, rising land prices, and commercialization had a dramatic impact on community structure. Between 1756 and 1773, over half of the population regularly moved in and out of towns in Lancaster County. For example, 65 percent of Paxton Township's taxpayers in 1758 left the town by 1760, while 67 percent of the taxpayers were newcomers to the town in the same year. Taking into consideration the appearance, disappearance, and newcomers to towns in Lancaster County between 1756 and 1773, George Franz calculated that every two or three years about 55 percent of the population was mobile.[88] Stephanie Wolf found similar levels of mobility and a lack of family persistency in Germantown. Between 1734 and 1767 over half of taxpayer surnames disappeared from tax lists, while 86 percent of surnames in 1767 were completely new. In addition, only 35 percent of surnames in 1773 remained in 1793.[89]

Such mobility also occurred in the older eastern sections of the colony. In Chester County, one of the three original counties, long-established towns such as Chester, Charlestown, Goshen, West Nantmeal, and West Nottingham experienced similar levels of mobility as those frontier towns in Lancaster and Philadelphia Counties. Between 1740 and 1775 only 27 percent of surnames survived on the borough of Chester's tax lists for more than ten years. In Charlestown only 28 percent of surnames remained in the town for more than a decade, 30 percent in Goshen, 33 percent in West Nantmeal, and 30 percent in West Nottingham. As Wolf found in Germantown, only around 30 percent of family names in the townships of Chester could be classified as persistent or deeply rooted. Also, as Franz found in Lancaster, the percentage of individuals moving in and out of the towns in Chester County every two or three years hovered around 55 to 60 percent.[90]

The fact that mobility was a part of life did not make it any less jarring. Henry Melchior Muhlenberg expressed shock that within five years "scarcely one-half of the first members in the country congregations are left." While he recognized that some of them were "in eternity; most of them moved away from forty to one hundred English miles, to the borders of Pennsylvania, to Maryland, and to Virginia."[91] In 1747, Muhlenberg noticed that only three of the original parishioners from three different congregations "still remain."[92] More surprising was that his "congregations did not decrease, but much more increased."[93] Mobility, according to some ministers, created difficulties in defining church membership and shattered Old World concepts of a community with the church as the central and defining entity. At St. Michael's Lutheran Church in Germantown, a 1753 manifesto stated bluntly that the church would not accept "newcomers" as full church members as they had "no right to speak." According to the manifesto, such a punishment was necessary, as "those who move around a great deal gave no real interest in the community."[94] People in Pennsylvania moved in and out of towns regularly, creating what one scholar has called a "community of strangers."[95]

Early Pennsylvania was a highly mobile place, its people constantly in motion and communities in flux. Landholders moved to get more and sometimes better land to improve their circumstances and that of their progeny. Similarly, nonlandholders, looking to better their lot, rented farm land on a short-term basis, which provided mutual benefits for the lessee and the landlord but was nonetheless a temporary situation. As the population grew and the countryside commercialized, a growing landless class of laborers moved in and out of towns, ultimately adding to the overall impermanence of country communities. The arable town, with its tightly knit community structure that provided informal social control could not exist under these circumstances. The people in towns and counties were too far removed from one another both geographically and personally.

The community, or rather relationships between people in the community, was not, however, the only means to regulate the country that Penn and other early leaders envisioned. Religion and the church were also prominent fixtures, both to "govern the people's manners" and provide informal methods of mediation between neighbors.[96] Yet, here too, demographic forces challenged and strained these institutions and their effectiveness. Under stress, the churches and their ministers became embroiled in divisive disputes over their authority, particularly during the Great Awakening, which ultimately tore these loosely bound communities further apart rather than bringing them together.

Societal Transformations and the Crisis of the Churches

In colonial America, as in the Old World, social and spiritual order were conceptually bound. Whether an inhabitant was Anglican, Presbyterian, Lutheran, Reformed, or Sectarian, he or she learned and inherited a tradition that linked God to a well-structured society. Even libertines, deists, and philosophes of the late seventeenth and eighteenth centuries regularly expatiated on religion's social value. La Mothe le Vayer, a noted libertine, argued for the necessity of religion in society.[97] Similarly, Voltaire and other enlightenment philosophes, though they sought to discredit the institutionalized Christianity of the ancien régime, accepted religion as the most powerful enforcer of a moral order. While they believed that *they* could behave morally without the fear of punishment in an afterlife, they did not hold the same confidence for the bulk of society. Without religion to keep the masses in check, the common people would devolve into depravity and iniquity. In his *Dictionnaire Philosophique*, Voltaire deemed the idea of a society of atheists an "impossibility," as "men without some restraint could not live together." "It is necessary," Voltaire argued, "to have an avenging God, punishing, in this world or the next, such as escape human justice."[98] Like Voltaire, Montesquieu viewed religion as a tool for social control. In his *The Spirit of the Laws*, Montesquieu argued that "he who has no religion at all is that terrible animal that feels its liberty only when it claws and devours."[99] Benjamin Franklin saw religion similarly. "If Men are so wicked as we now see them with Religion," he wrote in 1757, "what would they be if without it?"[100] Religion, from multiple perspectives in the early modern world, was essential for maintaining an orderly society.

More than just faith instilled a social and moral order. Ministers held a prominent role in the lives of their parishioners. While Pennsylvania's ministers lacked the force of the state, inhabitants considered them important regulatory officers. Ministers catechized, baptized, confirmed, and married. They also served as community leaders, and people looked to them as authorities in spiritual, moral, social, and worldly affairs. The majority of Pennsylvania's inhabitants, whether immigrants from England, Scotland, Germany, or other mainland colonies, were accustomed to turning to their ministers for guidance and even arbitration in disputes with their neighbors.[101]

Upon arriving in Pennsylvania in the 1740s, Henry Melchior Muhlenberg became the minister of four Lutheran congregations, and his many congregants expected him to govern their communities. In his journal, Muhlenberg often recorded meetings where his parishioners came to him and "complained about their neighbors" in the hopes that Muhlenberg would resolve their differences.[102] In 1747, for example, Muhlenberg set off to deliver a sermon and offer communion to an outlying congregation in York. The inhabitants quickly used the availability of the minister to settle their rows. He was obliged to examine reports "that they had lived in strife and quarrels." Perhaps more suggestive of the authority of ministers was Muhlenberg's account that "even the *Justus of the Peace* presented himself and made a complaint concerning a bad, quarrelsome neighbor."[103] According to Muhlenberg, "both old and young . . . harbor everything until the pastor comes." "It is a pity" he wrote despondently, "that one cannot be nearer at hand and cultivate them better."[104]

Muhlenberg's gloom reflected his situation as a minister to a growing population of church Germans. According to Farley Grubb, "Pennsylvanians of German ancestry accounted for 50 to 60 percent of Pennsylvania's population in 1760."[105] Of this large population nine out of every ten Germans were "church people," meaning they were either members or nominal members of the Lutheran or Reformed churches.[106] By midcentury, however, both German Lutheran and Reformed ministers, spread thin, found it difficult to undertake their duties in the face of such an immense German church population. In the mid-eighteenth century there was only one Lutheran or Reformed minister for every five congregations.[107]

Many of the congregations serviced by one minister were not even in the same county or sometimes the same colony. In 1765, there were twenty-six Lutheran and Reformed ministers in Pennsylvania, and only three of them provided their services in one location. Eighteen of the ministers served two counties, and five ministers had congregations in three counties. Seven out of the twenty-six ministers served not only two or more counties but also ministered churches in a neighboring colony. One minister, for example, had congregations in Pennsylvania as well as New York and Maryland.[108] By 1775 the situation had not changed. Though there were eleven more ministers, the ratio of pastors to congregations was still one to four.[109] In sum, each minister had to provide for a substantial portion of the German population in disparately located places.

The tribulations of Muhlenberg serve as an excellent example of the strain placed on ministers and church authority by demographic growth and geographic expansion. When Muhlenberg arrived in Pennsylvania, he managed congregations in New Hanover, Providence, Philadelphia, and Germantown. Initially, he made weekly journeys to his congregations, traveling well over fifty miles each week, a burdensome load, as it took "great effort" to travel a little over three miles per hour on horseback, and he frequently complained of poor roads, impassable creeks, steep hills, rocky slopes, and perilous nighttime journeys.[110] Writing to his superiors, Muhlenberg protested that he could not adequately service all of these congregations, and he hoped they would send more ministers.[111] A year later, Muhlenberg wrote in his journal, "Only one thing gives me concern, and that is that I cannot preside over these three congregations indefinitely, for the work is too much and, besides, they are too widely separated."[112] The only solution was to cut back on his routes and favor one church over the rest. Subsequently, Muhlenberg limited his trips to Philadelphia to the third Sunday of every month and alternated his services in New Hanover and Providence. He realized that his decision would upset his parishioners, as his trips would be "too seldom and too little," but he could not do anything else. Even with these cutbacks, he "must surely sink under the burden."[113]

By 1749, superiors in Europe finally provided a minister for Philadelphia, yet that did not ease the burden. Over the course of the 1740s, particularly between 1742 and 1754, the immigration of German church people reached its peak.[114] As the population grew and new settlements developed, Muhlenberg received numerous requests to provide his services for those in need. When pleurisy broke out in the back parts of Philadelphia County, he received several pleas to come preach. While he was there, "a number of men got together" from several nationalities and religions and "entreated me with tears to take their condition to heart and resolve to serve them occasionally with God's word."[115] On another trip through the countryside, Muhlenberg met a "lame woman" who "wept and lamented that in Germany she had had a wealth of spiritual nourishment and now she had to starve here in this country," this spiritual "wilderness."[116] Muhlenberg's journal is filled with accounts of "supplications from the poor dispersed people to minister to them God's Word."[117] Due to these requests, Muhlenberg became the minister of at least seven congregations and numerous out parishes in Pennsylvania, New York, and New Jersey. "Thus we become involved beyond our ability," he wrote in his journal, agonizing that he could rarely "go to the aid of these abandoned little groups," as it was "too burdensome" and "impossible to keep up."[118]

Muhlenberg proved so overburdened that his congregations began to stir in anger "on the point of falling into confusion and faction." The congregations in New Hanover and Providence felt "forsaken" and sought to install a new "preacher, no matter where he came from," just as long as he stayed. In essence, they threatened to break with the church, as only superiors in Europe could provide ministers. Yet not everyone approved of such a drastic measure, and the two sides settled into factions, fighting over the propriety of turning out Muhlenberg and the Lutheran Church. Though Muhlenberg tried to assuage them by arguing that God's "servants cannot be in two or three places at the same time," it was of no avail. After his meeting with a few parishioners from Providence, he knew the dispute would result in schism. While parishioners in New Hanover and Providence looked for a steadier minister, the congregation in the borough of Lancaster revolted. According to Muhlenberg, their pastor, John Siegfried Gerock, administering to his congregations in New York, failed to return to Lancaster, missing two Sundays in a row. After these absences the parishioners resorted to "tumult" and tossed out Gerock.[119]

Even if the Lutheran and Reformed clergy could provide for all of the churches, a substantial portion of the population would still have to go without. Not every town with a population of German "church people" had church edifices. While there were "many churches built in the country," a lot of Germans had to travel, as Gottlieb Mittelberger averred, "2, 3, 4, 5 to 10 hours to get to church."[120] From the beginning of the eighteenth century, Germans in Pennsylvania complained that they were "destitute of altar and priest." Pennsylvania was a "Spiritual and Corporeal Wilderness," and this went unchanged throughout the eighteenth century.[121] One German Reformed clergyman even asked the proprietor for funds to establish ministers and more churches in the province. He feared "that the large body of Germans that inhabit your territory are in danger of growing savage, if there are not some quick methods taken to reclaim them: the want of a regular ministry, and of the instructions that are administered thereby, has such a desperate influence upon their morals, that they must in such a situation, by becoming bad men, become also very bad and troublesome subjects, of which we have some fatal instances already."[122] Without help some feared the province would further devolve into debauchery and depravity.

The only way to stem the tide was to either plead for more ministers from Europe or attempt to shake free from a dependence on Europe for ministers. Pleas for more ministers rarely worked, as few clergymen saw the benefits of working in a colonial backwater. Church leaders usually enticed ministers to travel to the colonies with promises of a short stay and an elevated status in Europe when they returned. Creating independent institutions in America to train and ordain ministers served as the only viable option. In this endeavor both the Lutheran and Reformed churches succeeded to an extent. By 1750, the German Reformed Church in America boasted its own coetus, and the Lutheran Church had a synod for ordination, yet scholastic institutions developed slowly. Even with these new church councils both found it difficult to staff their congregations and provide for parishioners.[123]

Like Lutheran and Reformed churches, Anglicans experienced similar problems. Since the beginning of the eighteenth century, the Society for the Propagation of the Gospel in Foreign Parts (SPG) controlled the administrative and logistical aspects of colonial Anglican churches. Overseeing the church and its ministry from across the Atlantic, the SPG lumbered along slowly and inefficiently, ignorant of the situation and needs of the colony. For example, the SPG created church "precincts" or circuit routes for its few ministers with an obvious disregard of geography, which had a detrimental effect. For nearly twenty years the Episcopal clergy in Pennsylvania complained to the SPG about these routes, pleading that they could not travel such distances and meet the needs of the population. Ministers found the "precincts" and the number of churches under their command "too heavy," and they argued that their failure to meet the needs of parishioners already resulted in popular consternation.[124] Missionary Alexander Howie complained in 1732 that he could not undertake the weekly "travelling for the greatest part of the year," as he would have to "run the hazard of losing my life in riding over Creeks between the two churches."[125] The SPG received and ignored similar requests dating back to the 1710s.[126]

While the SPG slowly fixed problems that had existed for decades, other issues cropped up that required immediate attention. As in the Lutheran and Reformed churches, demographic growth and geographic expansion strained the paltry Episcopal ministry in the province. Not only did ministers have to provide for their mandated congregations with troubling routes, but migration and demographic growth created pockets of Anglicans without churches and ministers. Like Muhlenberg, the Anglican missionaries had to care for their own congregations while also tending to the needs of others. Reverend Griffith Hughes complained almost immediately after gaining his post that he had to regularly visit "a great many Welch & English Gentlemen that lived far back in the woods" and were "entirely destitute of a Minister." "At their earnest request," Hughes traveled "there several times," and his most recent "journey to them," he grumbled, must have made his total travel since he gained the route, above "1105 miles besides my weekly attendance at Radnor &

Perquioma."[127] Obviously neither of these outlying settlements nor Radnor and Perquioma received regular attention.

Where the interior counties had some ministers, though stretched to their limit, the frontier counties often went without. By the end of 1760, there were only five Episcopal ministers outside of the city of Philadelphia. According to an "Account of the Missions in Pennsylvania" sent to the bishop of London, there were five ministers servicing at least fourteen congregations.[128] Three ministers served Chester, Bucks, and Philadelphia Counties, one provided services for the county of Lancaster, one for three congregations in York and Cumberland Counties, and none provided services for the congregations in Berks and Northampton Counties. Thomas Barton, who acted as minister in the borough of Lancaster, tried to visit the inhabitants of the other back counties but found the distance between the people difficult to overcome.[129] Barton complained that the "precincts of some Missions extend into two or more Counties, often making a Circuit (especially upon the Frontiers) of 160 miles."[130] Similarly, some of the interior ministers tried to provide for those in the back counties who had "no settled minister" but found the added work resulted in the neglect of their own congregations.[131] According to a petition of the "Inhabitants of the County of Berks" to the SPG, their "county is a very large and growing one . . . and hath never yet had any English Minister of any denomination settled in it, nor hath it had the happiness of being visited often by any of the Reverend Clergy of the interior counties." Parishioners lamented that their churches were in disrepair, their children did not have schools, and they feared that their offspring would be "brought up without any idea of public worship or religious Ordinances."[132] Even German Lutherans wished "that the nation of Great Britain might duly consider the condition of their brethren, both in spiritual and worldly aspect, and do for them what is necessary."[133]

The Presbyterian Church proved better poised to absorb the shock of demographic growth and geographic expansion. The church created three presbyteries in the early eighteenth century that provided a certain level of colonial self-sufficiency. While seminaries developed slower in the middle colonies, a few small schools, such as William Tennent's Log College, existed, providing a limited number of clergy. However, it was not until the creation of the College of New Jersey in 1746 that the Presbyterian Church became truly independent. With the founding of this college, the Presbyterian Church was better able to provide a ministerial force to meet the challenges of demographic growth. As Jonathan

Dickinson, the college's first president, exalted, the school would "raise up qualified Persons for the Sacred Service to supply the very numerous vacancies in all those provinces as far as Virginia, with qualified Candidates for the ministry."[134] These institutions did not guarantee all congregations would receive ministers, though, and churches still suffered from clerical shortage.[135] According to Janet Fishburn, "There was never a time in the middle colonies when there was even one pastor for every congregation. There were many small congregations visited by itinerating pastors no more than three or four times a year."[136] As a Presbyterian minister lamented in a 1752 sermon, "They have Difficulties in travelling and preaching to others as well as their own People, in this Day especially in these Parts, where there are so many Places vacant, thus trying to do Duty to their own People, and yet serve others, their Bodies are wore out with Toil and Labour: May we not think that this was the Occasion of the Death of several faithful Labourers of late?"[137]

The scarcity of Presbyterian ministers related directly to large-scale immigration and geographic expansion. From the 1720s through the 1770s, Pennsylvania experienced a steady wave of immigration of Ulster Scots, predominately Presbyterian, peaking in the late 1720s and again in the mid-1760s. After 1760 the number of Ulster Scots coming into the province reached an average of above fifteen hundred per year. Between 1766 and 1773 a total of 10,319 Ulster Scots immigrated to Pennsylvania.[138] These newcomers, often paying passengers arriving in family groups, moved through the city of Philadelphia westward, northward, and southward, challenging the ability of the presbyteries to provide ministers. Chester County, for example, had eleven Presbyterian churches to serve a large population of Scots-Irish Presbyterians. Only four of those churches had regular pastors between 1760 and 1775.[139]

For Presbyterians, like those of other religions, the lack of clergy threatened the good order of society. In the Old World, the church served a disciplinary function in the daily lives of parishioners.[140] The paucity of churches and ministers in the province led some Presbyterians to characterize Pennsylvania as a "Wilderness" of "Hardships and difficulties." Many of them, especially those on the frontier, thought they inhabited a "foreign world" where they were "among strangers not knowing how to trust any, [and] in danger by the heathen."[141] According to Patrick Griffin, while many of the Scots-Irish "settled among those of their persuasion," the lack of a "strong Presbyterian church" broke the "bonds that tied them together." They feared that the "Monstrous Swearing, whoring,

Sabbath breaking, [and] drunkenness," which were "all common," would remain unpunished and therefore increase. Such "Circumstances" left many "poor Souls ... under awful Danger of perishing for Lack of Vision" and "Gospel Ordinances." Continuing in such "circumstances of darkness," many feared, would "render both themselves and their posterity miserable Pagans."[142]

Demographic and geographic expansion often caused rancor within and without the church, most notably during the Great Awakening. At its core, the Great Awakening started as a vicious dispute over appointing and qualifying ministers for ordination. The Old Light ministers who adhered to a doctrinal rigor of their orthodox Scots forebears wanted to limit who could join their ranks, hoping to exclude those they deemed of inferior intelligence and understanding.[143] Old Light ministers who controlled the synod bemoaned requests to scale back the requirements for ordination, especially the examination of "useful learning, such as *Physicks, Ethicks, Metophysicks and Pneumaticks*." Removing requirements from the ordination process would lead, Old Lights argued, to a "disorderly licencing of Candidates."[144] In response to the Old Lights, Gilbert Tennent and those of his ilk demanded different criteria based on the heart to judge the fitness of ministers for ordination that would have alleviated the stress placed on the few ministers in the province.[145]

Simply increasing the number of clergy was not the sole driving force behind Tennent's attacks on the church, but the whole situation was deeply rooted in a feeling of disorder associated with the inability of ministers to govern a growing population. According to Patricia Bonomi, denominational infighting over "professional standards for clerical training, recruitment and practice—issues that were at the heart of the division of churches during the Great Awakening" were directly related to and "brought about by growth."[146] Martin Lodge likewise argues that the Great Awakening grew out of the "institutional failure of the churches," especially the "churches' inability to establish a clergy numerous enough, or effective enough" to serve the "elemental needs" of the people.[147]

In response to these needs, preachers like Gilbert Tennent, James Davenport, and George Whitefield moved through the countryside inspiring many others to join the ranks of the itinerant.[148] In the 1740s and 1750s, ordinary Pennsylvanians, many of whom were "private persons of no education and low attainments in knowledge" found a new calling and traveled about the colony inaugurating a "Spirit of Enthusiasm." Many people, who had gone without ministers now received intermittent services from traveling spirits of all ranks.¹⁴⁹

The Great Awakening, nevertheless, had wrenching consequences. The revival and the animosity it inaugurated tore more communities apart than it brought together. The revival movement affected, in some degree, every domination on the Eastern Seaboard. The Presbyterian Church, for example, was torn asunder with the fracturing of the Philadelphia synod in 1741 and the creation of a rival synod in New York. Though the two competing sides finally compromised in 1758, the animosity inspired by that split reverberated well into the late 1760s. The significance of the divide went beyond just the fracturing of the synod and reached deep within the countryside and communities where competing churches divided once homogenous congregations, pitting neighbors and even families against each other. Itinerant preachers, heeding the words of Tennent, Whitefield, and Davenport of the "Dangers of an Unconverted Ministry" moved into towns, excoriating the unregenerancy of ministers if they had them, and the entire church if they had not. Such messages did not appeal to everyone, and as some neighbors and family members broke off to form their new churches, others remained loyal to the old. According to one Quaker onlooker, "The Presbyterians are divided into Several sects mostly Dislikeing if not hating One another."¹⁵⁰ It is not surprising, then, to see pamphlets and newspaper articles from both sides decrying "divisions, separations, and confusions." According to one writer in the *South Carolina Gazette*, the "WHITEFIELDISM" of the Great Awakening "has raged and rioted" in the "Colonies to the Northward, particularly in Pennsylvania, the Jerseys, and the several Colonies of New-England; What *Evils* and *Mischiefs* it has produced in them! What *Divisions, Strifes, Hatred,* and *Animosities* in Neighbourhoods and private Families!"¹⁵¹

The Great Awakening also shook the foundations of other religions and churches. Anglicans were equally divided. After the Anglican clergy refused to admit Whitefield to preach in their pulpits, the exhorting preacher made powerful attacks on the church and its clergy. Whitefield's religious vituperations, the clergy believed, created "a confusion" in the province and "made a very great rent in all" the Anglican congregations.¹⁵² Likewise, the German Lutheran and Reformed ministers fought with itinerant "imposters" or "Zinzendorfers," a term used because of the itinerant preachers' association with Count Nikolas Ludwig von Zinzendorf, who occasionally, and at will, presented himself and the ministers he ordained as Lutheran, Reformed, and Moravian. The divisions created within the Lutheran and Reformed churches over the "Zinzendorfers" raged particularly hot in Philadelphia and Lancaster Counties, where violent "tumults" erupted and schisms threatened. Churches split into disputatious factions, where church edifices, cemeteries, and schools became violent battlegrounds. In many cases, one side would place locks on the church doors, only to be broken open by the other party. In both Lancaster and Philadelphia, the locking and breaking open of church doors resulted in violent disputes in which Lutherans, Reformed, and Moravians "trampled, pushed and knocked each other about."[153] It must have seemed the essence of chaos to see once united congregants shedding each other's blood while screams echoed through the streets.[154]

More than the threat posed by "Zinzendorfers" created divisions within the Lutheran and Reformed churches. As in the Presbyterian Church, the threat of an "Unconverted Ministry" and the power of the laity in deciding a minister's piety led to fractures and fissures within congregations. In 1763, for instance, the German Reformed Church in Philadelphia County split over adherence to Reverend Frederick Rothenbuhler, a recent Swiss immigrant trained and ordained as a Reformed minister. Almost immediately after his arrival, a storm arose over the doctrines Rothenbuhler preached. While not much is known as to the particulars of his doctrine, it is clear that it incensed many of the church elders and the Reformed coetus, who denied Rothenbuhler's application to join the coetus and disbarred him from the church edifice. In the press, the coetus publicly labeled Rothenbuhler "a Lunatic" who was "almost incapable of solid Thought."[155] In response, Rothenbuhler slung mud at the coetus, and each side settled into faction and vitriolic tirades.[156] Like many other religious disputes of the era, it was not just a battle between Rothenbuhler and the coetus but involved a now fractured and divisive congregation. Some of the congregants followed Rothenbuhler, and others sided with the coetus.[157]

Such faction resulted in tumult and violence. It seems not even cemeteries were off limits to rioters. After the death of a child in Rothenbuhler's new congregation, the members adhering to the coetus locked the church's cemetery gates to deny the opposing congregants access. A locked gate would not stop the mourners, and the women of Rothenbuhler's congregation simply "threw down the fence" and entered the cemetery.[158] During the service, the "old party" came to forcefully break up the funeral, which resulted in a "public tumult" where the "pastor himself was not spared and a great many were left bloody." To make matters worse, "there were perhaps a thousand onlookers, English and German, who gazed at the spectacle." Instead of a proper burial in which parents, family, and friends mourned the loss of a child, the divisions in the congregation led to a violent public exhibition. After the riot, the father had to the carry his son's corpse to the deputy governor to ask for protection so he could bury the child. The deputy governor provided for a private burial conducted by a Presbyterian minister, who did it quickly and "quietly" at night without mourners. According to Muhlenberg, such an event was "the work of Satan."[159]

Muhlenberg's comment suggests a certain amount of perceived disorder in the colonies. For ordained ministers like him, itinerant preachers who appealed to emotion and the schisms brought about by the Great Awakening comprised the very symptoms of widespread disorder and a decaying society. It was almost universally agreed among ministers of his ilk that the "freaks, frenzies," and "convulsions" of the Great Awakening brought nothing but "disorders and confusions," with "mobbing, disquiet, and disturbances to civil government!"[160] Nevertheless, the feeling of disorder and decay was not just the province of a "Conservative Attitude." The people involved in the "frenzies," the preachers who moved about the province, and the people who followed them and rioted with and against their neighbors viewed their society similarly. Their services were often broken up by tumult and violence, funerary rites were desecrated, and they learned through the teachings of Tennent, Whitefield, and other itinerant preachers that those working against them, their very neighbors, family, and their pastors, were the tools of Satan in a "wicked Vicious and Sinfull Age."[161] The two groups may have disagreed as to the origin of the disorder, but they both agreed that it existed.

Perceptions of disorder, both real and imagined, were symptoms of the tensions within society due to demographic and geographic pressures on communities and churches that challenged the informal mechanisms for "the regulation of the Country." After midcentury, such a scenario proved a real problem, especially since Penn and the early Quakers who created Pennsylvania depended on the success of these informal methods of governance, rather than the state, to govern the people.

2

"For Want of Power"
The Search for Order and Government

ON A COLD JANUARY MORNING in 1761, legislators sifted through a jangled collection of official papers and popular appeals. One of them was a carefully folded petition crafted by "divers inhabitants" in and about the town of Reading. This petition, like many others that made their way to the statehouse, articulated a scenario and set of grievances caused by dramatic changes taking place within the colony. Their local population, the petitioners impatiently noted, had grown significantly over the years. Just as pressing, the town and county had matured economically. In a few short years, Reading had become a bustling informal marketplace altering the everyday interactions of neighbors, kin, and strangers. Yet, unhappily, "for Want of Power to make By-Laws, or other Regulations" local officers could not provide "for the Government of so many People living together" and "great Inconveniences every Day arise." The situation had grown "dangerous in many places."[1]

From the colonists' perspective, the government needed to alter time-worn practices, traditional laws, and established institutions to meet the changing needs of communities. Though a significant amount of business came to Reading, inhabitants had little means to regulate it. Pennsylvania did not have strong town officials with ample governing powers. Instead, the leaders of the colony relied on informal social organization and meager governments based in county seats to police these vibrant communities. By midcentury community regulations had failed, and the county seats, like Reading, did not have enough "Power or Privilege" to govern.[2] Petitioners protested that even local magistrates, the most powerful of the county officers, were woefully deficient. For example, the deputy governor appointed John Potts, a prominent ironmaster, as Reading's chief justice, yet he did not live in the county, and he earned a reputation for refusing to attend court. For Potts, the office symbolized his accumulated power and authority, not his occupation.[3] Similarly, local notable James Reed treated offices as symbols of status and monopolized most of the county offices, which had a detrimental impact on the efficiency of government.[4]

Plural office holding and inactive officers aggravated a weak governing structure incapable of addressing community problems. Towns and counties lacked officers, institutions, and laws to regulate the social interactions of individuals. For example, Reading inhabitants complained that they did not have an officer to inspect and assure the quality of goods at the local marketplace, and thus they could not support the public economy with a well-regulated market. Though the province had laws to prevent illicit market practices, idle magistrates and the absence of regulatory officers resulted in monopolistic practices such as "Forestalling, Regrating and other Abuses," which omnivorous inhabitants "daily committed." Petitioners bemoaned similar deficiencies in preventing crimes unassociated with trade. Not even the county seat had enough power to keep the peace, which proved a "great Detriment of the People in general, both of the Town and Country."[5]

These complaints represent common yet substantial problems faced by Pennsylvanians. During the eighteenth century, demographic, geographic, and economic transformations weighed heavy on the fragile fabric of informal means of social control. With community regulations faltering, colonists groped about for cures to heal their communities and regain what they considered the stable and ordered nature of their lives. For many, the solution was clear. Government, created to embody the needs of civilized society, should provide the necessary palliatives. Nevertheless, the government, straining under the weight of societal change, proved a poor remedy. When that realization became clear, Pennsylvanians banded together, denounced the "Insecurity of their Lives and Estates," and pleaded with their representatives to make meaningful reforms for their future happiness and safety.[6]

In these protestations and in other public mediums, Pennsylvanians revealed the transformations they experienced and the limitations of colonial governance and articulated a vision of their ideal government that should be ever active, upholding public order and protecting the community through forcible regulatory policies. Contrary to historical assumptions, colonists demanded governmental services beyond the maintenance of a "negative" government because of their shared appreciation for civil libertarianism.[7] Instead, colonists looked to their provincial officials to provide "for the Good Order of Government" not only to defend individual property but to regulate individual passions to preserve the public good. Despite their ideals, crucial problems with the colony's police powers existed, and ordinary Pennsylvanians attempted to grapple with, define, and solve these governing complications. Together, the inadequacy of government and the search for order reveals the central element of the colonial crisis. While the crisis started with the breakdown of informal mechanisms of social organization and control, it was ultimately amplified by the harder-felt reality of the government's inability and outright unwillingness to provide services and build institutions that aligned with and represented the populace's visions and changing needs.

Eternal Truths: *Salus Populi Suprema Lex Est*

In Pennsylvania, ideas of government were crucially rooted in a particular understanding of man's social nature. For Pennsylvanians, and indeed many other early Americans, "the true Interest of every Man in Society, is the Welfare of that Society, upon which his own must absolutely depend." This statement cut to the heart of Anglo-Americans' belief in the subordination of individual desires and opinions to the needs, safety, and interests of the larger community. Such a conviction also powerfully shaped any conception of government and its regulatory powers. The public needed government, regulations, and laws to assure the "Welfare of Society" in the face of avaricious individuals. Ideally, government checked the detrimental effect of evil-minded persons by upholding the power of "the whole people."[8]

Pennsylvanians expressed and learned such thoughts in newspapers, petitions, and jury presentments. They debated them as petty politicians, petitioners, litigants, jurors, witnesses, and congregants. At the same time, they heard speeches about government and civil society on court days and sermons from the pulpit. They even read proclamations by the king and members of Parliament stating that only through "the maintenance of the public peace" could subjects have "the undisturbed enjoyment of their rights and liberties."[9] Law, order, and liberty, nouns seemingly at odds in the historical literature, were nonetheless intimately intertwined and mutually reinforcing for Anglo-Americans. Government protected the cornerstones of liberty, as "No man could with certainty call any thing his own, whether Possessions, Wife, Children, or even his Life" if society was left to the whims and prejudices of people without some restraint.[10]

These thoughts on society embodied the religious worldviews of many early modern Christians. Every person had a duty to God to obey the public good. As one minister proclaimed, God "fitted man's nature for society" and therefore individuals had "powers and faculties which could not be acted otherwise."[11] God created life with a "Beautiful Order"; everyone had his or her place in "the most perfect Arrangement." Yet an "inward Taint, some wrong Bias or Perversion of the Inclination" springing from a "hellish Source" threatened this "beautiful Order reigning in the Disposition of the Whole."[12] Irresolute people, Judge James Logan argued, often yielded to "natural Passions, such as Ambition, Lust and Revenge," which hurt society and transgressed God's law.[13] Other colonists argued similarly. In a speech reprinted several times between 1745 and 1775, Judge Samuel Chew told his audience that while God gave all people "Life and Liberty," after Adam and Eve's fall from grace "a Spirit of Rapaciousness and Corruption appeared in the World" and some "endeavored to find their own private Advantages and Happiness, by making a Prey of the Lives, Liberties and Properties of others, by Violence and a strong hand."[14]

To guard against such individuals, people entered civil society. "The natural Desire then of Happiness, and that Principal of Self-Preservation, common to all Men," Chew argued, "must first have inspired them, for their common Protection and Safety, with Notions of Compacts, of Laws, and of Government, as necessary, and without which it was impossible for them to be happy in any Degree."[15] Through civil society, individuals became part of a community and should not make private judgments but had to follow the "established Rules of the Society . . . for their common Safety and Happiness."[16] Presbyterian minister John Goodlet summed up such thoughts, writing, "Civil society consists of a number of men, as reasonable creatures, who have consented to unite their force together, according to the law of nature, for the safety of the whole; having a common established law and judicature to appeal to, with authority to decide controversies between them, and to Punish offenders."[17] In short, "government alone delivers us from that Savage and Barbarous State" where the strong ran roughshod over the weak.[18]

Even innocuous disputes easily erupted into full-fledged debates on the place, role, and importance of government. No less than a dialogue on the lawfulness of lotteries elicited such a conversation. From November 1758 through March 1759 two anonymous authors, one writing under the nom de plume Pennsylvanicus, debated the legality of lotteries. In his articles, Pennsylvanicus dubbed lotteries pernicious nuisances that endangered the public good since they swindled the people out of their hard-earned money. In this moment, the author touched on a central and indisputable point as to the role of government as the protector and promoter of the "public welfare." Government, Pennsylvanicus argued, must abide by the maxim "Salus populi suprema Lex esto" (the welfare of the people shall be the supreme law). Since lotteries threatened the public good, it made sense that the government should outlaw them.[19]

Pennsylvanicus's appeal sparked instant debate. Another anonymous author challenged Pennsylvanicus using similar political and legal reasoning. While the writer agreed that some lotteries defrauded the people, there were other lotteries, when regulated by the government, that promoted the public good. Through the prolonged debate the two writers came to agree on several points, the first being that government must uphold "that *Supreme Law, which is the Basis of all sound Policy*, namely the *Safety of the People*." Once the two authors came to this conclusion, they also agreed that those lotteries "found to be necessary *Where the public Safety has required them*" were lawful. Crucially, both authors used a "public safety" legal logic to pinpoint "private lotteries," those lotteries without a public good in view and without legal regulation, as detrimental to society.[20]

For colonists, public order trumped individual liberty. The period of expressive individualism, "the century of the *self*," remained more than a century in the distant future. Early Americans wholeheartedly believed that "*Salus Populi suprema Lex*, the Publick Good is the supream Law" was an "eternal Truth." Anyone who "shall dare contradict this eternal Truth," should be branded "with Infamy."[21] Colonists expressed, over and again, that they should "prefer the publick Good to their own private Inclinations and Opinions," as it was an "Absurdity" to think otherwise.[22] Such thoughts gave the government, theoretically, a supreme and powerful role in the everyday lives of inhabitants. The Latin phrase *salus populi suprema lex est* was not some master abstraction or empty phrase but served as the basis of police regulation, encapsulated the common law, and defined governance in a well-regulated society.[23]

The regulatory arm of government, particularly in upholding community values, was the criminal law. Although legislators and legal theorists divined a particular activity a crime, behind the law, above it, and encasing it was society. Before legislators considered a crime a crime, social reality had to transform the action into an unacceptable behavior, and it was that social context that gave law its real, lasting, and significant meaning. Criminal law in all its varied practices and with all its complexity upheld community interests by protecting the public from socially unacceptable behavior. In a grand jury address, Chief Justice Logan made this point clear. Crimes, he argued, were by their nature "altogether inconsistent with Society," and therefore it was "absolutely necessary for the Security of Mankind, that positive Laws should be provided against them." "Were it not for Laws," he concluded, "Mankind would no longer be safe in Society."[24] Similarly, ministers intoned that without laws and their enforcement colonists would be thrust into a state close to that experienced "in the Antediluvian age, when there was no civil government at all in the world" and "the wicked destroyed the righteous, till there was none left but Noah and his Family." In short, "the world needed government to keep it in being to this day."[25]

Nevertheless, law depended on the smooth functioning of local legal institutions and officers. Since law was the cornerstone of governance, its enforcers were every bit as important to the process. As an anonymous Pennsylvanian argued, "Laws give no security where they are not duly executed."[26] Without the due enforcement of the laws, magistracy would be "no more than an Empty Name, and Legislation itself no longer the free Voice of the People."[27] While legal maxims and state statutes might proscribe criminal acts, laws proved little more than words on paper if the government did not "industriously crush" criminals.[28] Pennsylvanians agreed that "all regular Government is founded upon Laws: Yet these Laws, tho' the only real Security of the Subject, are of no manner of Force or Use, but as they are executed, and as Justice, in pursuance of them, is duly administered."[29] Presbyterian ministers stated similarly that "civil government has no power, if it has not the sword, to be a terror to evil-doers, and a praise to them that do well."[30] Accessible and effective institutions and officers were central to any conception of government as the protector of the public good.

Using their own religious worldviews, many other Pennsylvanians came to similar conclusions. In a 1754 presentment, Lancaster County grand jurors argued that if "those who are in authority, who ought to be terrors to evil doers, do not use their utmost efforts" to enforce the law, "we are humbly of opinion, that this place will lie exposed to the Divine

Resentments."[31] Evangelical minister Gilbert Tennent put fire behind those ideas. In an open-air sermon, Tennent thundered that God sent and ordained magistrates; therefore, if any injustice passed unpunished, the forces of hell would reign supreme, the "Comforts of Society" would end, all property would become precarious, and "an Aceldama" would open, ushering in a "Scene of Rapine, Desolation and Blood." Ineffective magistrates, he railed, spelled the end of "civil Society" where "Men degenerate into savage Beasts of Prey!"[32] This powerful vision of government was projected, confirmed, and sought after by colonists from all walks of life.

Though individual farmers, artisans, laborers, women, and servants left few treatises and bombastic speeches, we can see their dependence on and belief in the institutions of justice through their actions at court.[33] Common people viewed the due execution of the law as the surest protection of their rights and liberties, not just as individuals but as members of a larger community. Ordinary folk entered their county courts and attempted to project the interests, values, and safety of their communities. Local courts, particularly the courts of quarter session, the main county court having criminal jurisdiction over offenses not considered capital, constituted the reality of governance in early America. They also provided common people with a participatory role in government. The courts only worked through and by the active participation of the inhabitants, whether through their service as jurors, their actions as local officers, or their attendance as victims, defendants, and witnesses. Upholding the public good necessitated a legal system that was enforced by colonial officials and, just as important, valued by and accessible to the people at large.[34]

The courts, the officers who staffed them, and the people who used them upheld social norms by guarding the community against actions considered "inconsistent with Society." They took neighbors to court and demanded public punishments and apologies. Rarely did inhabitants request or even receive private restitution. When their neighbors burned down their homes, barns, and farms, those places that housed "their entire wealth," individuals sought public justice first and, if necessary, private remuneration second. When two men burned down the waste house of James Pugh in 1760, the court deemed the act a public wrong and demanded public restitution and punishment. The court made no mention of compensating Pugh for his losses, nor did he demand it. Such a chain of action reflected the public interestedness of people and their place in upholding the will of the broader community.[35]

Over and over again, colonists used the courts to project community power and interests. Colonists brought numerous cases of fornication and bastardy before the court, making it the second-most prosecuted offense in counties such as Lancaster, Chester, and Bedford.[36] While such a crime challenged the moral sensibilities of some inhabitants, it also affected the public good. Children sired outside of marriage posed a serious public offense since the child and the mother often became a "public burthen" in need of support. Through the courts, a community not only punished offenders but ensured a father's aid of the child, thus relieving potential public harm.[37] Pennsylvanians also expected the court to punish offenders for public nuisances, such as throwing a carcass on a common road or constructing a dam that blocked travel up a waterway and fish from reaching the upper parts of a stream. Private interests, whether carnal lust, the easy disposal of a carcass, or the damming of a river for a mill, needed to give way to the public's welfare.

The crime of assault, one of the most prosecuted crimes, also reflected the colonists' belief in a legal and political philosophy centered on the "public welfare."[38] Though an offense against an individual, assault was considered a public wrong because it violated the personal security of the subject and therefore a breach of the duties individuals owed to their community. Since man was a social creature, it stood to reason that individual transgressions were socially felt, or so colonists believed. As a Presbyterian minister related to his congregants, "If any one openly breaks the law of nature, and injures his neighbor, he trespasses against the whole species, as to the peace and safety of it."[39] Prosecuted cases of assault ended in either fines or corporal punishment and in some instances, especially for assault and battery, a judge would assign both. Such punishments reinforced the idea that a criminal owed satisfaction to the public, not just the individual assaulted. When Charles Gallahan assaulted and attempted "carnally to know" ten-year-old Mary Saget, judge and jury deemed it a serious public offense. The court fined Gallahan fifty pounds and ordered that he be carted around two squares of the city. At each square Gallahan received a public whipping and read out an apology to the gathered community members, thus reinforcing the public dimensions of his pernicious act.[40]

Petitions, like the use of the courts, also provide a glimpse into the thoughts of ordinary people on the proper role of government. Petitions prove that average inhabitants were neither passive nor inarticulate about their government. Colonists believed it their "Duty" to present

"Grievances" to their representatives, and that it was their "Right, to ask for anything that may be for the Publick Good."[41] When aggrieved, or in need of governmental reform and help, colonists penned petitions and gathered signers for presentation to their representatives. Through the process of petitioning, Pennsylvanians asserted their desire to be included in the legislative process and that catering to their collective interest was crucial to good government. As one writer proclaimed, petitioning was the "undoubted Right of the People" and "it is certain, that in all Countries, the People's Misfortunes are greater or less, in proportion as the Right is encourag'd or check'd."[42]

Between 1740 and 1776, Pennsylvanians from all social strata and across the sexes took that maxim to heart and submitted over eleven hundred public petitions. In those petitions, inhabitants indicated that traditional methods of social control had fallen apart and that their communities had become deeply fractured. Demographic growth and economic change exacerbated those problems, and petitioners responded by clamoring for better laws, effective regulations, and procedures, officers, and institutions to enforce them. As their demands increased in urgency, colonists took pen to paper and emphatically expressed the necessity of a responsive government that adapted to challenges, met society's changing needs, policed communities, and provided order and stability during perceived turbulent times.

Pennsylvanians' demands for a more effective regulatory system to meet new conditions reflected decisive economic changes. During the first half of the eighteenth century, Pennsylvania developed a diverse agricultural industry that brought about a substantial growth of the economy through foreign trade. Augmentation of foreign trade also resulted in a burgeoning domestic economy for both the city and the countryside. The uptick of the local economy increased labor markets and commercialization and resulted in considerable market interaction among everyday people. Significantly, public policy encouraged this economic growth. For example, merchants and farmers only gained access to the profitable European flour trade by successfully lobbying for governmental regulations to guarantee the quality of flour for foreign consumers.[43]

Colonists demanded the same rigorous regulations of their growing domestic economy. Petitions requesting either the creation of new laws or enforcing old laws for a well-regulated market made up over 55 percent of those petitions regarding the economy (both foreign and domestic). In these petitions, Pennsylvanians demanded regulations of horses, cattle, deer, liquor, oysters, bread, wheat, Indian corn, and other grains brought by water and by land to their local markets.[44] They called for inspection and regulation of leather, hemp, gold, silver, and iron. Even manufactured goods did not escape public requests for scrutiny. Everything from shoes, buckles, and buttons to wagon wheels required, petitioners thought, regulation. Like the inspection of the quality of the goods, Pennsylvanians wanted laws governing the prices of goods sold and better laws to prevent illegal practices such as engrossing, forestalling, and regrating that manipulated the market by creating monopolies on certain goods.[45]

In all, colonists expected fair trade—the safety from buying inferior goods at inflated prices—in a well-regulated market. In 1755, for instance, tanners in Philadelphia, reveling in the increased demand for leather, cut corners using too much "Pitch in Lime," rendering the leather damp and unusable. Tanners also charged "very high Prices" for the inferior product. Some of the tanners attempted to maintain high prices by purchasing all the imported leather from "*Carolina* and elsewhere." Such practices, according to the cordwainers who relied on the leather for their own manufactures, harmed the public. By using expensive substandard leather the cordwainers could not make affordable quality shoes, edging them out of the market by forcing local consumers to buy from England or other colonies. As a result, money flowed out of the colony, and the cordwainers had to lay off workers who would become, because of the "Ruin of themselves and Families," a public burden. To "remedy the Evils," the cordwainers demanded regulations of the price and quality of leather.[46] Even the tanners, who stood to lose by such regulations, later agreed that "restraints upon Trade generally and laying Burthens of Expence and Trouble upon particular Occupations" were acceptable and "justified by apparent public Necessity."[47]

Petitioners consistently drew on the idea of the public welfare to demand legal means to regulate the interactions of individuals in society. Not only did Pennsylvanians see the law as the surest and probably most convenient way to regulate their markets, but they requested the government criminalize actions considered dangerous or contrary to the common good. Seemingly mundane issues such as hunting deer all year round or using large seines for fishing in the Schuylkill River elicited angry petitions claiming that nothing less than the public good was at stake.[48]

Petitions against commercial fishing serve as an excellent example of early Pennsylvanians' belief in the importance of regulations, law, and government. In the late 1760s, many inhabitants complained that unscrupulous companies looking to tap into a lucrative European and domestic fish market attempted to catch a large quantity of fish at the lower parts of the rivers using bulky nets, several at a time, spread strategically over the open pools. Inhabitants living up and down the Schuylkill River complained that such tactics resulted in the "great loss and inconvenience of the Poor, who depend in some Measure" on fishing "for Support."[49] Colonists on the upper parts of the river believed the assembly should pass regulations so that fish, which they considered a "Blessing, so bountifully bestowed by Providence, may be more extensively enjoyed."[50] They also argued that the government should criminalize private dams that obstructed both the trade of the province and fish from entering the upper parts of the river.[51] The interests of a few private fishing companies or those individuals constructing dams needed to give way to the needs of the community.

In due time, the colonial assembly responded to the petitioners' requests and enacted regulations. The new laws stipulated that only one seine could be used in the inlet's river pool on prescribed days, and anyone who broke this law faced a five-pound fine that would go toward the relief of the poor.[52] The assembly, noting that the inhabitants desired "to promote the welfare of the public," also passed several laws making the Schuylkill River navigable for rafts, boats, and other small craft. The laws provided for clearing the river and inspection and regulation of dams and other man-made obstructions. They also demanded that justices of the peace, constables, and new inspectors patrol the river and address any and all impediments. Anyone convicted at the local court for "erecting, building, setting up, repairing or maintaining any weir, rack, basket, fishing-dam, pound or other device or obstruction whatsoever within the said river" would pay a fine of twenty-five pounds or "suffer six months' imprisonment without bail or mainprise," a serious offense indeed.[53]

The positive statutory response meant little without sufficient enforcement. Despite the "good intent" of the law, inhabitants claimed it was "rendered fruitless" and "of little Advantage to the Public, owing to the Non-execution of the Law." The river, petitioners stated, "is now so full of Obstructions that Navigation is more dangerous, and more Fish destroyed than before the passing of that Law." Several of the inspectors died without any reappointments, several more officers did not patrol due to ill health, and the rest simply neglected their duty.[54] In short, law enforcement did not match the ideal of the law.[55]

The miscarriage of the fishing and navigation law represents a pervasive police problem in the province. The courts and the laws they enforced proved incapable of keeping the common peace. Take, for instance, the case of *King v. Samuel Meredith, Elizabeth Meredith, Margaret Collins, William Howell, and Thomas Hill.* These five men and women violently assaulted Barbara Shaver of Chester County and forcibly carried away her family's only gelding. While grand jurors judged these actions a severe offense "against the peace," Shaver's attackers went unpunished for their crimes.[56] Over the course of four court sessions, the judges called witnesses to give evidence and for the defendants to answer for their actions, yet neither the witnesses nor the defendants appeared at the same time, pushing the case farther down the docket until it faded from view or action.[57] Many cases, like this one, went unresolved and represented a serious problem in the administration of justice, a dilemma that Pennsylvanians petitioned about with increasing urgency as the century progressed.

A Clamor for Reform: Courts, Justices of the Peace, and the Colonial Crisis

Just as Pennsylvanians requested more and better laws to regulate their communities, they also sought to reform the institutions and officers in charge of law enforcement. The demographic, geographic, and economic changes taking place during the eighteenth century critically affected the government's ability to protect the people through law. Societal transformations, the demands for new laws, and the threadbare system of government stretched beyond its capacities mixed together and fomented a general feeling of hysteria, disbelief, and by the close of the colonial period, a deeply felt crisis. As one writer proclaimed during the heady days of 1776, Pennsylvanians "live under a species of government which has always been reprobated by good men as the worst in the world."[58] Such vehement censure marked the opening salvo of revolution after a hotly contested few decades when Pennsylvanians pleaded, to little avail, for better laws to govern their communities and improved methods of enforcement.

Explosive demographic growth was one of the most important developments in early America. It reshaped fledgling communities as well as the relationships between people. Between 1720 and 1770, Pennsylvania's population increased by more than 670 percent.[59] In 1720, an estimated thirty-one thousand people lived in Pennsylvania. By 1770, over 240,000 people called Pennsylvania their home. Such unprecedented growth tested and eventually overwhelmed existing legal structures.

Although the province's population had multiplied so rapidly, the institutions of justice and officers of the law had not; they were the same in 1722 as they were in 1770 and ultimately inadequate to the needs of a large segment of the population. For instance, in 1722, the assembly created two main county courts, the court of quarter sessions handling noncapital criminal cases and the court of common pleas for civil suits. However, the same three justices sat as judges for both courts, essentially separating the courts in name only, seriously challenging the efficiency of the local judiciary.[60] Further restraining the reach, scope, and impact of the law, both courts had to enforce the laws in often overextended counties. In Cumberland County, the court's jurisdiction stretched over thirty-five hundred square miles. While the county government sufficed for a small agricultural community clinging to the county seat, it proved completely insufficient as the economy diversified, the population grew, and the settlements moved westward. The central governing institutions of the counties were ill equipped to handle such change, and by the latter half of the century they began to falter, and it seemed, to many, that they were falling apart.

That Pennsylvanians saw problems in the nature, design, and implementation of government is visible in their petitions. Although historians have filled monographs, articles, and textbooks with colonial vitriol leveled at the inadequacy of military defense, paper money, and public transportation, Pennsylvanians drafted more petitions demanding better law enforcement than for those three categories combined. Between 1740 and 1776, 28 percent of petitions before the legislature requested reform of law enforcement, whereas defense made up 11 percent, paper money 7 percent, and public transportation 9 percent. No other category of petitions, such as internal improvements (banking and damming marshland, erecting dams, docks, and lighthouses, and installing sewers and sluices), taxes, and land policy, came close to the number of petitions about law enforcement.[61]

Many of the problems with the dispensation of law had to do with unwieldy judicial jurisdictions in bloated counties. By 1776, Pennsylvania's settlements extended westward over 280 miles from the Delaware River to the Ohio but had only eleven counties that served as the law enforcement and administrative hubs for its inhabitants. In short, the county jurisdictions in Pennsylvania proved nearly unmanageable. As an exasperated Deputy Governor James Hamilton stated bluntly to Thomas Penn, governing this extensive province with the tools at hand "is beyond my comprehension."[62]

An increase in a county's population and expansion of its geographic jurisdiction had a negative impact on the internal police of the entire colony. In response, petitioners urgently advocated founding new counties, a step they viewed as necessary for the maintenance of public peace. In 1729, for example, Chester County stretched from the banks of the Schuylkill and Delaware Rivers all the way to the western limits of the proprietary grant. The people, like the geographic jurisdiction of the county itself, sprawled westward and away from their county government. Nevertheless, these migrants expected continued access to those institutions. In a petition to the deputy governor and assembly "a great number" of irritated migrants complained that they could not "secure themselves against thefts and abuses almost daily committed upon them by idle and dissolute persons, who resort to the remote parts of the Province, and by reason of the great distance from a Court or Prison, do frequently find means of making their escape." Living "near one hundred miles" from the government, petitioners bemoaned their "want of a sufficient number of Justices, Constables and other officers." Such a reality threatened "the security, peace and good order of the whole Government."[63] Chester County inhabitants continued to complain about inadequate access to justice well into the century. In 1766, for example, county residents sent twenty-eight petitions to the assembly demanding easier access to the courts. Such petitions echoed the grievances of their provincial cohorts. Near 30 percent of petitions deriding law enforcement complained about insufficient access to legal institutions and officers.[64]

The swollen size of county jurisdictions and the growth of the population within them also resulted in a significant increase in the number of court cases. The county courts, however, could not keep up with such activity. Petitioners from Bucks County put it best in 1753, noting that at the time the courts were created they proved "suitable and sufficient, but those circumstances being since much altered, both with respect to the Number of Inhabitants, and Increase of Business at those Courts, it has now become impracticable." Even local justices realized the difficulty of providing their services to a mushrooming population and complained that "much business comes before us, which cannot be accomplished." When the government did not act, petitioners from the county of Bucks again remonstrated in 1764 that "justice is delayed" and "totally obstructed." In the same year, Lancaster County petitioners protested that they "suffered" from "unruly disobedient servants, idle strolling Vagrants, drunkenness and profane swearing, breach of Sabbath, Tumults, robberies and many vices." These problems, the petitioners explained, "so much prevail, that it is scarcely in the power of the Magistrate to suppress them."[65]

Mounting caseloads led to delays in the courts, hampering attempts to administer justice and establish order. For one, subpoenaed jurors and witnesses had to travel nearly insurmountable distances to attend court without knowing if their particular case would be heard that session, potentially wasting valuable time better spent on the farm or in the shop. Eventually, this judicial problem became more acute, and jurors and witnesses refused to attend, further hindering legal processes. Jasper Yeates, a lawyer from Lancaster, often complained about "unfavorable appearances" of jurors at the courts. In Carlisle, Yeates found that "the Country People are wholly ingaged with getting in their crops ... so that the Prospects of the Court are not very pleasing."[66] Even in Philadelphia, as a young lawyer lamented, "very little Business has been done, on account of the Non attendance of Jurors."[67] In Northampton County, the failure to attend trials at quarter sessions produced a continuance docket in 1776 that included 140 cases dating back nearly a decade.[68] In Bedford County, between the county's creation in 1771 and the closing of the court in 1776, only 41 percent of indictments ended in any type of settlement. The court simply pushed most cases off into oblivion since jurors, witnesses, and even defendants refused to attend trials.[69]

Such outcomes are not surprising since many colonists lived a good distance away from the courts. For example, "a considerable Number of the Inhabitants of Bedford County" complained that "the most inhabited part of the said County" was "upwards of Fifty miles" from law enforcement officials and "upwards of an Hundred" from the county seat. These distances, combined with the "extreme Badness of the Roads," made going to court nearly impossible.[70] In Lancaster County, more than 30 percent of the taxable residents lived on the periphery and far away from the court. Like colonists elsewhere, they refused to attend trials, and it became common practice to push cases off the dockets with at least an intervening term. From one lawyer's perspective, such practice "deprived" a defendant "of his Liberty by being detained so long in Prison without having an Opportunity of making his Defence."[71]

If witnesses and jurors did attend the sessions, judges attempted to push through verdicts on paltry evidence and refused requests for appeals. In 1768, for example, the court convicted Matthew Neel for horse stealing on the "slightest circumstantial evidence." The jury based Neel's conviction on a third-party witness, or mere hearsay. This verdict "gave surprize to every one who attended the trial, and even the gentlemen concerned for the Crown acknowledged the testimony insufficient for a conviction." Neel's counsel immediately motioned for an appeal, as Neel faced time in the pillory, public whipping, and the cropping of his ears. The judges, however, denied the appeal "being cautious of invading" not only the "province of the jury" but their time.[72]

When jurors failed to attend the supreme court, which occurred often, the court resorted to passing judgments without using juries. In 1764, Richard Peters Jr., a Philadelphia lawyer, noted that the nonattendance of jurors pushed judges to make decisions on cases that "turned on matter of fact." In English law, matters of fact were specifically for jurors because they relied on evidence given in testimonies and witness statements. Only in matters of law, which required applying statutory rules and common law precedents, could judges pass judgment without jurors. Even then the failure to use juries was hotly contested. Chief Justice William Allen believed acting without juries, while technically unconstitutional, was necessary. From the bench, Allen justified ruling on matters of fact by asserting that the legal maxim "*communis error facit jus*" was "the Pole Star that must direct us." Allen's reasoning is just as revealing as the action itself. *Communis error facit jus* means "common error, repeated many times, makes law." In essence, Allen argued that his court must adapt its legal proceedings to the circumstances of the times and adjudicate without juries.[73] For many, that seemed a dangerous precedent.

Pushing through trials did not make the courts more efficient. Pennsylvanians realized that cases brought before the courts would take too long to settle and cost more than the worth of the trial. Colonists "would rather sustain" their losses "than spend the whole Principal, with the additional Expence of much Labour and Time, in the Means of obtaining Justice."[74] If they did not wish to sustain their losses, some Pennsylvanians requested other methods of mediation. For example, when the court asked Richard Baird to gather his evidence and witnesses for the next county court session in the winter of 1770, he grew extremely wary. "It was above three years since I brought the Action," he complained to his lawyer. If he gathered all the evidence and summoned witnesses only for the judges to push his case off to the next session again, he feared the worst. The witnesses would outright refuse to attend, and he would lose his case. Instead of taking it to court, Baird asked his lawyer to attempt an outside settlement if possible. The experiences of Baird and many other Pennsylvanians, then, proved the old adage "Justice delayed is justice denied."[75]

Regardless of the courts' Band-Aid practices, the entire judicial system, especially at the provincial level with the high court, had practical and logistical issues that aggravated the legal maladies of the province. With original jurisdiction in capital cases and trying appeals from the county courts, the supreme court stood at the apex of a theoretically integrated judicial system and therefore constituted the most powerful court in the province. Moreover, its weight and jurisdiction assured that its problems would have local and provincial reverberations. As with the county courts, demographic growth, economic change, and geographic expansion took a toll on the reach and effectiveness of the high court. Because of these transformations, the court's business, as Chief Justice William Allen complained, was "thirty times as much as it was." By 1774, the court faced a docket over eighty pages long listing more than two hundred cases. Yet the court rarely went on circuit to carry justice "to the peoples doors."[76] Instead, the court demanded most trials take place in the city of Philadelphia, making it, as even the proprietor argued, "a Second Star Chamber."[77] The failure to ride circuit became so notorious that when Allen spoke of holding court in the back counties to his friends, they deemed it nothing "more than talk."[78] In essence, by the close of the colonial period two problems with the judiciary stood out: overworked courts and a greatly inconvenienced populace, both of which proved detrimental to governance in Pennsylvania.

After midcentury, an onslaught of petitions reached the assembly demanding the supreme court judges ride circuit for better access to the law. Residents in Chester County argued that "holding all the said Courts at the City of Philadelphia" constituted a "great Inconveniency not only of the Petitioners, but of the Inhabitants of the other Counties in the Province, as they are by that Means put to considerable Expense in attending the said Courts as Jurors, Witnesses, &c." Likewise, Lancaster petitioners complained that traveling great distances to court proved "very detrimental to Persons" since they often had to travel on substandard roads and over impregnable creeks "at the Risk of their Lives." Over twelve hundred Cumberland County residents blasted holding the court in the city as "a Burden so unreasonable and oppressive."[79] As one county inhabitant argued, colonists could barely travel to their county seats without great hardship, let alone all the way to the city, especially the "poorer Sort, many of whom" could not "bear the Expences of so long a Journey."[80] Even residents who lived closer to Philadelphia than frontiersmen found traveling to the city arduous and expensive. The trial of cases in Philadelphia required people to "expend large Sums of Money" due to court costs, lawyer fees, and the added expense of travel and lodging. Because of these geographic and economic barriers, the supreme court could not oblige "Suitors, Jurors, Parties and Witnesses" to make the onerous journeys to attend court sessions.[81] "Justice," because of these realities, "is often delayed, and sometimes totally obstructed."[82] Chief Justice Allen conceded the necessity of reform, but he still could not justify riding circuit, as he believed he "could not on account of age, undergo the fatigue of fourteen or fifteen weeks in a year traveling about the Province."[83] Unsurprisingly, though, his status in proprietary circles would not result in removal from such an important office for the sake of a circuit.

Logistical barriers, while burdensome for travelers, also proved detrimental to the peace, order, and safety of the colony. The most heinous criminals ran willy-nilly throughout the province, terrorizing inhabitants without much fear of the law. Because capital offenses had to be tried in the supreme court, capital offenders had to be captured and then conveyed, sometimes many miles, to the distant court. Constables, sheriffs, and justices of the peace unfortunately learned that the route to that court was a dangerous one. Fearing the violence of the road, some local officials simply refused to capture and convey criminals—with good reason, as captives and their accomplices routinely assaulted officers during the trek to the city.[84]

The failed attempt to convey a known serial outlaw, wanted for multiple murders, several assaults, arson, and inciting a riot, to Philadelphia in September 1770 exemplifies the difficulty local officials faced and its peril for ordinary citizens. On the fifteenth of that month, the constable of Lebanon Township in Lancaster County, Frederick Buhlman, arrested Lazarus Stewart for the crime of arson on a warrant issued by the supreme court. Knowing that "Stewart was a dangerous, turbulent Man, & apprehending a Rescue might be attempted," the constable hired three men to aid in transporting Stewart to Philadelphia. Stewart, though, succeeded in intimidating the three deputies, leaving "the Constable to do as he could," which did not bode well for that officer. Not yet out of Lancaster, some of Stewart's accomplices waylaid the convoy, handed Stewart the handle of an axe, and watched as the recidivist knocked "down the Constable & beat him in a Cruel and Unmerciful manner."[85]

After learning of the violent escape, justice of the peace John Philip De Haas tried to gather community members to overtake Stewart and his rescuers. The people in the community refused. If they helped, they argued, more of "Stewart's Friends" would come and wreak havoc on the town. Stewart and his growing coterie of cutthroats confirmed community fears. They milled about the town, terrorizing townsfolk and local officials alike. For example, Stewart and his posse followed De Haas home and with a "Pistol in one hand and a Club in the other" dared the JP to make an arrest. De Haas did not test the odds and retired to his chambers. Reveling in the successful intimidation of a local magnate, the gang made their way to the tavern and threatened the innkeeper and his imbibing clientele. Stewart strutted about the bar, swearing he would cut the innkeeper "to Pieces, and make Breakfast of his Heart" if he or anyone else in the establishment helped local officials. After this violent bravado, "Stewart and his Company Rode off in Triumph."[86] Such a scenario was not an isolated incident; violence against constables comprised over 30 percent of assaults in those cases where the victim's occupation could be identified.[87]

By the close of the colonial period, Pennsylvanians understood and readily complained that the institutions of law and justice did not live up to basic expectations. Crimes went unpunished, victims did not receive justice, and the ideals of the public welfare proved unattainable, especially for those Pennsylvanians who did not live near the county courts, not to mention the high court in the city of Philadelphia.

The courts, however, were not the only instruments at the disposal of Pennsylvanians to achieve a legal means of justice, order, and stability. Local justices of the peace were designated to meet those needs and police communities. Nevertheless, as the Stewart episode vividly illustrates, local officers all too often could not and sometimes would not take on that weighty responsibility. The reason for their inability or unwillingness was both personal and political. JPs were local magnates who gloried in the status enshrined by their office, but rarely did they relish the day-to-day duties of that station, and many simply shirked it. Moreover, many of the JPs domiciled on landed estates and ornate town homes in eastern towns and county seats. Like the problems with the courts, societal transformations easily overwhelmed the few active officers and undermined the effectiveness and usefulness of others who lived far away from the broader community.

In the ideal, the near totality of law enforcement rested on the shoulders of the justices of the peace. Local JPs provided vital civil, regulatory, administrative, and law enforcement functions for local communities. They handled small debt cases and disputes between masters and servants and supervised the erection of bridges, roads, and highways. They appointed viewers of partition fences and persons to receive the claims for bounties offered on animals. They issued writs of replevin (writs to repossess property wrongfully attained) and attachment (writs to seize persons or property) and awarded processes for taking lands in execution and to recover on mortgage. They recommended applicants for tavern licenses, collected fines, and acknowledged deeds and probated wills. JPs also handled all criminal cases not capital, took recognizance and sureties, and imprisoned, ordered the corporeal punishment of, and amerced inhabitants with fines or forfeitures. In short, the JP was the most powerful officer in the county and "to him was referred all such controversies as arose among his neighbors."[88]

The elevated status this office guaranteed to its holder assured that local grandees monopolized appointments. As royal officials, the JPs held their offices at the will and pleasure of the Crown. They were appointed and removed for their work by the only representative of the Crown in the colony, the deputy governor. Through the control of these offices the deputy governor and other local notables directed, shaped, and even manipulated local politics. The county seats, the only place of election, turned into hubs of special interest. Deputy governors and prominent locals worked together and strategically chose officers to galvanize allegiance. Such was the politics of an early modern monarchical world. As one contemporary noted, "As to your Lancaster Politicks, they are like those of every other Place, quarrelling for Straws." Nothing mattered beyond obtaining offices for friends and kin, establishing power and place; everything else, he concluded, "is Goats-Wool."[89]

This political framework created a situation where politicians and local officers were, as one historian noted, borderline "incestuous."[90] William Allen and his extended family serve as a perfect example. Allen married into the prominent Hamilton family; his brother-in-law, James Hamilton, served as deputy governor for nearly two decades. His daughter, Anne Allen, married proprietor John Penn and because of these ties, Allen received prominent judicial positions. Likewise, Allen's son Andrew Allen, became the attorney general, and his other son, James Allen, held the positions of JP and legislator for Northampton County, though he did not live there.[91]

Similar to the Allen clan, the Shippen family monopolized politics in Lancaster County. Edward Shippen, a close friend of Deputy Governor Hamilton and an in-law of William Allen, simultaneously held the positions of prothonotary, clerk of orphans court, clerk of quarter sessions, recorder, deputy register, and justice of the peace. His son Edward held prominent offices as the prothonotary of the supreme court and a member of the provincial council. His younger son, Joseph, succeeded Richard Peters as secretary of the province, and his son-in-law, Colonel James Burd, received an appointment as a justice of the peace. Edward Senior as patriarch of the family positioned himself to dominate Lancaster politics. Because of Shippen's connection to key political figures in Philadelphia, seekers of local offices pursued his support first. In his personal papers, Shippen held lists of potential JPs he felt optimistic he could get appointed since the deputy governor should make moves for the "satisfaction of his old friends."[92] It seemed, as one man groused, that the blue bloods "at the head of affairs, have in many instances behaved as though they thought they had a sort of fee simple in them and might dispose of all places of Honour and profit as pleased them best."[93]

This politically charged system of nepotism and patronage resulted in an unequal geographic distribution of magistrates in the counties. Elites like the Shippens and Allens lived or owned extensive land close to the county seats or in other older eastern sections, the same locations created by a select few landowners and speculators. Turning a large tract of land into a bustling county seat almost immediately increased the land's value. Therefore, many families at the top of a county's social, economic, and political ladder were either involved in the creation of those areas or settled there to benefit from the potential and proven lucrativeness of those places.[94] Such a geographic concentration of the gentry with large patronage networks and political clout obviously limited the geographic pool from which to appoint potential JPs.

As a result, Pennsylvania did not have enough magistrates equitably distributed throughout the province. In Bucks County, for example, nine out of the seventeen justices in 1775–76, a little over half, resided in the three oldest townships surrounding the borough of Bristol.[95] This geographic distribution proved especially problematic for the administration of justice. Bucks County petitioners had argued since the early 1740s that the population around Bristol was "by no Means proportionable to the Number of People" in the rest of the county, yet most magistrates resided there, making the rest of the county "suffer" from "frequent disorders."[96] In fact, according to tax lists, the ten towns with the largest number of taxable citizens had only four JPs, and they resided in three of the ten towns. The six most populated towns, representing the central part of Bucks County, had no JPs.[97] The clustering of justices of the peace in the southeast left the rest of the county without these important officers of the law.

The problem of unequal distribution of justices of the peace plagued other counties. In Cumberland County eleven of twenty-one JPs resided in and around the county seat of Carlisle. Out of twenty-three townships, only twelve had JPs.[98] In Lancaster County, seven of fourteen JPs lived in and near the county seat. Justices of the peace resided in only ten of the thirty-three townships. The entire western section, made up of ten townships with more than 30 percent of the county's taxable residents, only had three JPs.[99] In Chester County, 76 percent (sixteen of twenty-one) of the JPs lived on the northeast side of the Brandywine Creek, closest to the county seat, leaving sixteen towns in the southwestern corner with only three magistrates who lived in the towns bordering the creek. The southwestern corner had five of the most populated towns in the county, yet those five towns had no JPs.[100] A similar geographic concentration of JPs existed for the rest of the counties in the province.

Regardless of their place of residence, JPs had a legal obligation to police the entire county, but most JPs rarely traveled beyond the jurisdiction of their own towns and sometimes their own homes. James Burd, one of the justices of the peace residing in the borough of Lancaster, often issued writs and subpoenas by carriers for those offenses that occurred outside of the borough, including small offenses he could settle himself. In his personal docket book for 1764, which functioned as both a record and reference book, Burd noted only one instance of traveling beyond the borough to settle a dispute, and this was in the adjacent town of Lampeter.[101] Henry Melchior Muhlenberg, too, complained of a German justice of the peace, who, because of his "remoteness" from the rest of the population, required colonists to travel to him for arbitration.[102] Even Chief Justice William Allen noted acidly and hypocritically that the JPs "rather chose the whole Country should attend them at their dwellings."[103]

Even if JPs traveled, geographic obstacles made traversing long distances difficult and therefore bridled their ability to govern much of the population. According to historian James Lemon, a typical equestrian colonist, on flat land, could undertake a thirty-mile round trip in a day. However, in much of the country, which consisted of creeks, rivers, and hills with inadequate roads, an average person could only ride eighteen or twenty miles in a day. That estimate might be optimistic.[104] Muhlenberg, an able and avid itinerant, noted that it took "great effort" to travel a little over three miles per hour on horseback. A thirty-mile trip, then, might require ten hours in the saddle and traveling at night, which many people deemed perilous.[105] The conditions of rivers, creeks, and roads, some of which were impassable in the winter or a wet spring, significantly diminished the radius a JP could cover. If a JP could not or would not travel, the onus fell to the inhabitants, which proved especially troublesome because at least 27 percent of southeastern Pennsylvanians did not own a horse.[106] For those men and women, traveling beyond six or seven miles was a herculean task. As Muhlenberg noted in his journal, the "poor folk" often suffered because they "did not have the convenience of riding like others."[107]

The difficulty of traveling coupled with unequal distribution of JPs posed a serious threat to the common peace. In the realm of criminal law, geography often meant the difference between the success and failure of the magistracy to uphold the law and defend the public peace. As early as the 1620s, the English Privy Council recognized the threat geography posed to upholding the king's law and demanded the placement of magistrates throughout England's counties every six or seven miles to create a regional system of law enforcement.[108] Pennsylvania's deputy governors and provincial councilors, however, did not hold the principal of magisterial distribution in the same regard, and they simply perpetuated the dominance of a geographically confined elite with familial pedigrees.

The residences of local JPs and therefore the politics of the colonial world had a real impact on the competency of law enforcement. The geographic distribution of cases before the quarter sessions of Chester County between 1740 and 1776 reflects the influence JPs had on the administration of justice. In Chester County the majority of justices lived on the northeast side of the Brandywine Creek.[109] It should come as no surprise, then, that over 50 percent of the cases brought before the court between 1740 and 1776 came from that same northeastern section. Even more telling, 32 percent of the cases before the court came from the towns immediately surrounding the county seat, where 38 percent of the magistrates domiciled. In stark contrast, residents from four towns constituting the northwestern corner brought less than 9 percent of cases before the court. Similarly, fewer than 6 percent of cases before the court came from the heavily populated townships in the southwestern corner, such as West Nottingham, East Nottingham, and Oxford. The county seat, which was geographically and demographically smaller than many other towns in the county, produced more cases than those three southwestern towns combined.[110]

Residents living at some distance from a JP were thus greatly disadvantaged and often complained about the matter. Some, like Captain Lewis Ourry of Cumberland County, simply settled their disputes and policed their communities extralegally. In a letter to the deputy governor, Ourry grumbled about "the want of a magistrate to enforce the Laws of the Province." "The barefaced Frauds openly committed here with impunity," Ourry wrote, "increase daily, and the aggrieved are obliged to set down with their Loss & Damages, because the Remedy is too far & expensive for them to procure."[111] Ourry also argued that without magistrates "frequent Riots & breeches of the Peace" troubled the county. Like Ourry, petitioners protested that limited access to a JP resulted in unchecked crime and violence. In 1769, Cumberland petitioners complained that the absence of JPs resulted in "Vexation and Terror" since "Rapine, Violence and Injustice are suffered to pass unpunished, and the Lives as well as the Properties of the Inhabitants are rendered insecure."[112]

The colonial rumor mill exacerbated this fear of unbridled crime. Articles in the local newspapers constantly informed people of jail brakes, cutthroats, thieves, highwaymen, violent assaults on women and children, robberies, and sometimes the most horrendous sociopathic crimes imaginable. Colonists read about decapitated bodies on the road in Chester County and victims of some heinous experiment floating in the river "cut open from the Collar Bones to the lower part of the Belly, and sewed up with double Ozenbriggs thread."[113] Illiterate inhabitants heard similar garish stories in the taverns. In the winter of 1764, on his way to Philadelphia from Lancaster, Jasper Yeates noted that at every tavern he "baited" the people obsessed over a string of violent crimes perpetrated on the highway. The stories were "exaggerated by a different relation at every Tavern" and he found them so frightening that he regretted "leaving Lancaster at all."[114] If Pennsylvanians did not go to the tavern, they heard verses belted out by the printer's lad on the streets about "thieves desp'rate," "Rogues," "Vice and Robbery," and that not even "Providence" kept people "secure."¹¹⁵ We can see in these words and stories a mixture of hysteria, anger, and alienation that the colonial government, involved as it was in the quarrel for straws, proved ill equipped to manage. The situation required a stronger palliative than anyone at the head of affairs could or would administer.

"Labour in Vain": Corrupt Judges, Petitions, and the Limits of Politics

The demand for responsive JPs willing to provide for the common good also meant that those officers should undertake the tasks laid out in their commissions without respect to their own private emolument. Magistrates should not, for instance, exact excessive fees or otherwise abuse the power of their office. The very definition of a "bad Government," one contemporary argued, was one "wherein Magistrates commit those Crimes themselves, or Encourage in others the Mischievous Practices which is the whole Intention of their Office to Restrain." In "such a State," the author went on, "the oppressed Cry and no Man delivers them, Violence sits in the seat of Judgment, and Extortion and Rapine are establish'd as [if] it were by Law."¹¹⁶ Ordinary Pennsylvanians, believing in the rule of law and that the due execution of law guaranteed their liberty and prosperity, thought magistrates needed to represent collective interests and protect the people.¹¹⁷ Yet magistrates existed outside of the people's control, and many were uninterested in their concerns, further angering and alienating Pennsylvanians.

Between 1740 and 1776, inhabitants presented numerous petitions to the provincial government complaining of unjust and abusive officers of the law. Widows in Bucks County demanded the removal of extortionate sheriffs, and inhabitants accused commissioners and assessors of embezzling tax revenue and court clerks of squeezing undue fees from the people. The majority of the petitions, though, were leveled at local magistrates. Inhabitants charged magistrates with holding "arbitrary and oppressive proceedings," exacting excessive fees, and simply fleecing the people. The assembly received so many complaints about misconduct that it created a committee to sit and hear grievances against such officials.¹¹⁸ Despite the assembly's intentions, none of the petitions blasting magistrates resulted in a formal charge or a removal of a person from office. Politics, as it often did, got in the way.

The charges against a justice of the peace for Chester County, William Moore, serve as a poignant example of the limited protections for common people from official abuse and the detrimental effect of provincial politics. Moore, one of the wealthiest and most politically prominent men in the county, held the office of justice of the peace and president judge for over thirty years.[119] Moore believed himself superior in all capacities of life, judgment, and station. Whether dealing with his servants, tenants, claimants, suitors, or others he judged beneath him, Moore confidently pursued his own gain, dictated his own terms, and sought to promote his own interest. According to inhabitants, he also used his official position for nefarious ends. Between 1756 and 1758, fed up with Moore's thralldom, nearly one hundred residents of Chester County complained to the colonial government that Moore "intimidated and frightened" them into paying excessive fees and turning a blind eye to actions they considered "extortionate and unjust."[120]

In one complaint, Judge Moore called Christian Everhart, a small farmer in Chester County, before him for a debt owed to Samuel Humphreys. Since Everhart did not deny the debt, he struck a deal with his creditor to settle his arrears without the force of a legal command given by Moore. When Moore learned that the two men had settled their dispute and that the constable confirmed the payment, he grew angry. Moore yelled at the constable, "You Fool! You should not let the People make it up, that does not bring Grist, or Water, . . . to our Mills." Moore made the constable haul the two men back to his mansion house, where he threatened to charge Everhart with perjury if he did not pay him three shillings in fees. Legitimately, Everhart owed Moore nine pence, as the judge did fill out a warrant. However, by demanding fees for, as Moore stated, "entering bail," even though, as the constable attested, "no Bail was taken" nor judgment passed, Moore effectively used his office to extort fees from Everhart. In the end, Everhart, fearing the consequence, paid the fees.[121]

Many more instances existed where Moore "illegally, extortionately, and, by Colour of his Office" fleeced the people of the county. And there were many colonists like Everhart who simply paid the fees because they "thought it in vain to contend" with "powerful Opponents." Inhabitants charged Moore with creating fictitious creditors to line his pockets, rigging auctions to buy goods for a fraction of their value, and threatening local artisans with jail unless they worked on his mansion. Such a narrative of "the fraudulent and extortionate Acts of William

Moore, Esq" could go on for pages, since he had an insatiable appetite for corruption.[122]

It took the assembly nearly two years to take any action against the cormorant judge. Month after month, from January 1756 through February 1758, colonists from Chester County implored their representatives to do something about the "divers arbitrary and oppressive Proceedings of *William Moore, Esq.*"[123] Only after receiving over a dozen petitions did the assembly finally make a move. However, instead of leaving the impeachment proceedings to the discretion of the deputy governor, legally required according to the tenure of Moore's office, the assembly instigated a battle over executive prerogative and attempted to use the petitions against Moore to establish a precedence to gain power over judicial tenure. Such a motive was not lost on the deputy governor, who stated that all the legislators wanted was to make judges hold their offices "during your Pleasure, and be continued or discarded agreeable to your Directions."[124] Further aggravating political animosity, the assembly ignored the deputy governor and held its own impeachment proceedings with a large show trial.

Regardless of the assembly's maneuvers, Moore remained secure in his office. The assembly, as the deputy governor and finally the king made clear, had no power to impeach royal officials who held their offices at the pleasure of the Crown. While the assembly argued that its trial conclusively demonstrated Moore's guilt and that, like the House of Commons, it had the "power of determining such impeachments," the deputy governor thought otherwise. The legislators, he stated, correctly assumed that the House of Commons had such authority, but they incorrectly supposed that those rules applied in Pennsylvania. "Neither the Branches of the Legislature of this Province," the deputy governor argued, "have any other Powers or Jurisdictions but those which are expressly delegated and granted them." Since the charter made no mention of the power to impeach a royal official, the deputy governor judged the assembly's actions void. Only the deputy governor, the Crown's representative, had the power to remove a JP. The king affirmed the deputy governor's argument by rebuking the assembly, noting his "high Displeasure at the unwarrantable Behaviour of the said assembly, in assuming to themselves Powers which did not belong to them, and invading both his Majesty's Royal Prerogative and the Liberties of the People."[125]

Now that Moore's impeachment had turned into sparring between the assembly and the deputy governor over power and prerogative, Moore could rest easy that he would keep his office. The deputy governor could not order the impeachment on the demand of the assembly since it would validate the legislature's claim to a share of executive power. Instead, the deputy governor held his own trial, largely for show, as he never intended to convict Moore. The deputy governor and his council, Moore's friends and political allies, instantly moved to assure the trial ended in Moore's favor by refusing to hear grievances that did not have to do with Moore's actions as a public official, and therefore "many of the Petitioners, who had been greatly injured and defrauded, returned Home unheard."[126]

Such a step "defrauded" petitioners because many of Moore's deceitful practices, while technically carried out unofficially, depended on his status as a justice of the peace. John Carl, a recent German immigrant who rented a small farm in Chester County and one of the petitioners who went away unheard, complained that Moore was able to defraud him because he trusted Moore as a magistrate. It all started with a small debt Carl owed his neighbor. Carl hoped that his yearly crops would cover the debt, but he feared his creditor would demand payment before the end of the growing season. Without the crops to pay off his creditor, Carl might lose most if not all of his meager property to a sheriff's auction. In search of advice, Carl went to the local magistrate and was quickly assured he would not lose his property. Moore told the unsuspecting debtor that he would protect Carl's property by taking it in his possession. All Carl had to do was sign a fifty-pound bond for a fictitious debt to make the transfer look official. When Carl questioned the bond, since he "owed him ... nothing," Moore told the small farmer that he "must have something to shew the People why I hold these Goods"; otherwise they would be susceptible to seizure and sale. Carl trusted the wrong magistrate. Moore almost immediately demanded Carl pay back the fake debt, and when Carl failed, Moore seized the young man's property. To add insult to injury, when Carl challenged the judge, Moore demanded the recent immigrant leave his wife and children behind and "go to Germany and be seen here no more." When Carl refused to leave, Moore sent constables to harass him, threatening him with "Warrants or Writs." Finally, Carl fled to Virginia.[127]

The deputy governor and his council also denied the validity of grievances by petitioners who, though they had witnesses, could not produce documented evidence of fraud or extortion, effectively making the people's words and grievances illegitimate. The council, on the other hand, took Moore at his word. Besides, Moore had evidence to back up his claims of innocence, his docket book, which witnesses (such as the local constables) claimed he forged.[128] Moreover, delegitimizing grievances by challenging the credibility of petitioners played right into Moore's plans for his defense.

In the public papers, Moore depicted the suit as a conspiracy concocted by Isaac Wayne, an angry neighbor, and an irate assembly upset at a petition Moore signed in 1755 with thirty-five other inhabitants pleading for a "well regulated militia." Moore publicly declared his innocence of all the charges brought about by the machinations of a few assemblymen who conspired among themselves to elicit petitions from "ignorant and weak Persons," many of whom, Moore claimed, could not read or write. After all, who should be believed, Moore, one of the "creditable and substantial Freeholders" of the province, or the "sundry Persons of mean and infamous Characters," those "wicked and idle . . . poor ignorant People" who signed the petitions with "one trifling Complaint" or "another"? Moore believed that weighing his and the petitioners' social status would answer such a question.[129] The deputy governor used a similar scale and acquitted Moore of all charges. In a public letter addressed to Moore, the deputy governor stated that "the Petitions appear to me to be entirely groundless" and that Moore acted in his "Office with great Care, Uprightness and Fidelity" and so deserved "the Thanks of every good Man, and Lover of Justice."[130] In the end, the people's complaints went "disregarded, and their Injuries [remained] not only unredressed, but unheard."[131]

Moore's acquittal sparked instant anger. The assembly, slighted and challenged, published the affidavits against Moore in the papers, publicly exposing his actions and the deputy governor's decision to scrutiny. With this information in hand, the public had a field day with the deputy governor's judgment. Pinned up all over the city and countryside, a broadside entitled *Labour in Vain* criticized the deputy governor for leaving this "Foe of God and Man" free to spread his "Oppression round the Land." The real losers in this drama, the broadside concluded, was the "the Lab'rer fainting with the Toils of Day" who went home empty-handed because Moore "stopp'd his Pay," the "poor Orphan" whom Moore "plunder'd of his Right," and the widow who mourned the fate of "her mate." The "Widows Cries" and the "Orphans Tears" were futile, since Moore escaped with impunity.[132]

The broadside exposes a deep cynicism about the colonial government and its responsiveness to its citizens. Not only did the broadside proclaim Moore a thief and the deputy governor and council complicit in his treachery, but a visceral engraving depicted the judge as a "Black-Moor" sitting in a tub as the deputy governor, attorney general, and other proprietary supporters tried "in vain" to "wash the BLACK-MOOR *white*." The engraving suggested that the deputy governor and council could not wash away Moore's crimes. Moreover, by portraying the judge as a "Black-Moor" the author effectively drudged up a common racial and cultural trope equating blackness with evil and corruption.[133] In addition, the title of the broadside, *Labour in Vain*, worked as a double entendre. Not only did the deputy governor and his supporters "Labour in Vain" to wash Moore, but the laborer, orphan, and widow found their charges against Moore's rapacious actions equally, if not more, ineffectual. As the broadside put it, "But vain the Widows Cries, the Orphans Tears, The ruthless Verres [Moore] wants both Eyes and Ears."[134]

More than the title itself, the names the author gave to Moore and his supporters are particularly revealing of this underlining contempt for the colonial government. The author dubbed Moore "Verres" after the corrupt Roman official tried for his crimes by Cicero. Though, unlike Verres, Moore escaped punishment and exile, the name does reveal how some obviously learned thinkers judged Moore's corruption and the action taken by the government. The crushing weight of Verres and his excessive fees, imposts, and bribes brought the economic epicenter of the Roman republic, Sicily, to its knees.[135] Like the Sicilian farmers who suffered under Verres, Chester County farmers had to endure the extortionate and corrupt practices of Moore. Instead of a Cicero triumphing at court, the attorney general, named ingloriously Bigamio (bigamist), with his rancorous crew, Ardelio, a class of people known for idleness and vice, handled the Moore case.[136] The government, according to this construction, was morally bankrupt and ineffective.[137] The deputy governor's and council's actions in the Moore case and their refusal to take the grievances of the people seriously must have made it clear to most that they could expect little support and far less protection from the government.

"Labour in Vain" is an apt metaphor not only for the petitions against William Moore but for the entire corpus of petitions concerning law enforcement and the judiciary. During the colonial period, the government rarely redressed the inhabitants' grievances. To be sure, through the seventeenth and early eighteenth centuries, elite Quakers who controlled the legislature shouldered some of this blame. They made it clear that they supported minimal government with few laws and regulations. However, by the 1750s the legislature became increasingly more active in trying to rectify pervasive police problems, but a combination of factional and imperial politics stymied most attempts at reform. The government's shortcomings and official unresponsiveness crucially intertwined with the growing imperial dispute of the 1760s and 1770s. To understand how and why these seemingly local issues turned into imperial problems and ultimately revolution, we need to turn our attention to the interplay of provincial and imperial politics.

3

The "Stupendous Machine"

Imperial Pennsylvania and the Failure of Reform

IN 1738, AN ANONYMOUS WRITER took aim at the provincial government and the nature of politics in the province by describing a curious yet fictitious event. According to the pseudonymous A.B., five thousand people gathered for a show outside the chamber of the colonial legislature to see that "stupendous Machine" in motion. From morning until night the "mighty Croud" waited in "tedious Expectation," but nothing happened. No motion. Nothing. Soon observers began to "murmur, then to cry out Shame at such glaring Impudence." Finally, the crowd roared that the show was "no better than a downright Cheat." Understanding what was "in the Wind" the "*Grand Maitre*," a satirical pseudonym for the president of the provincial council, blustered, "stamped and cursed," and told the crowd that they "were a Pack of willful positive Illiterate Puppies." They could not use their "Eyes and Fingers" to detect the propulsion of the machine. The onlookers had to believe him that "By G-d the Machine is now in its most violent Motion." Then the Speaker of the House, the "*Petite Maitre*," stepped up and with all the cunning he could muster, explained that "not one amongst you all ever did, ever could or ever will rightly understand what Motion is, and what are its various eccentrick, concentrick, retrograde, oblique and other its manifold Laws and Powers." The machine, he assured the crowd, was moving. It was "Reviving, Re-enacting, Repealing, and Re-repealing Laws" as he spoke.[1] What better evidence of motion could there be?

The crowd was not so easily duped. "A plain Fellow" interrupted the Maitre and argued that such actions did not denote motion. "For his

Blood, he could not perceive any, and to his Eyes and Fingers it stood as stock still as his Grandma's Spinning-Wheel that had been thrown by these fifteen Years past." He could not feel the workings of the machine, as nothing that affected his daily life had changed. Reenacting and repealing laws did not constitute motion. Only by creating new laws to more effectively govern the province could the masters of the contraption prove the machine worked. In the end, the Maitres swindled the crowd for "no less than 40,000 English Shillings" (taxes) to watch a machine stand "stock still."[2]

The question remains: Why had this "stupendous Machine" become so motionless? Why could it only reenact, repeal, and re-repeal laws? Why was there "but too little done"? These questions are important, as they cut to the heart of the problem of politics in colonial Pennsylvania and the inability of the government, at all levels—imperial, provincial and local—to address the needs and interests of its citizens. The pseudonymous A.B., like many other Pennsylvanians, had an answer to these crucial questions, executive "PREROGATIVE," that "Vegetable stunted in its native Soil, and about half a Century ago, transplanted into this warmer Clime, hath here brought forth the truly *Golden* Fruit, here cherished by the warm Dung and Hotbed of COUNCIL OF STATE." The buds of this pernicious fruit bloomed forth in Pennsylvania with the royal "WE, and grows luxuriant with the spreading Branches of OUR WILL AND PLEASURE." Prerogative proved so potent in Pennsylvania that "even the DEAD must feel the Effects of its powerful Influence." Prerogative invaded the machine, stalling legislation through factional politics, the endless disputes between the legislature and the executive, with the Crown, through the proprietor, and sometimes more directly looming in the background and other times completely pulling the levers of the machine. In this way, factional politics and the empire served as the external forces that hindered the propulsion of the machine.[3]

Since the inception of the colony the fight over executive versus legislative powers colored most if not all political debates and major policy decisions. For much of the late seventeenth and early eighteenth centuries, that dispute pitted elite Quakers in the legislature against the proprietors and their supporters over the growing authority of the executive. The result, the Charter of 1701, begrudgingly signed by William Penn, gave the legislature ample tools to restrict the executive's reach and remit. At the same time, however, the king and his ministers slowly set in place policies, procedures, and precedents to extend royal prerogative through the executive over the province, which, after fits and starts, came to fruition in the 1730s. By that decade the fight was no longer simply between the legislature and the executive or the Quakers and the proprietors but rather over the place and power of the empire in the proprietary colony. Ultimately, it was this changing history rather than just Quaker principles and proprietary self-interest that shaped the everyday realities and inadequacies of governance in Pennsylvania.

After 1730, political factionalism over the king's prerogative thwarted the ability of the government to react to the petitions of Pennsylvanians demanding new laws, better courts, and more officers to correct problems of governance and alleviate the feeling of crisis. Laws that provided necessary reforms were so caught up in factional politics that little ever came of them. Internal bickering stalled the passage of some laws, the deputy governor's attempts to uphold the prerogative of the Crown resulted in the veto of others, and still more laws made it back from across the Atlantic branded with a royal disallowance. The legislative system needed a mechanic.

The British Empire inspired much of this internal colonial factionalism, played a large role in retarding the legislative activity of the colony, and therefore had a negative impact on institutional development and day-to-day governance of the province. The influence of the empire on provincial political and institutional development is a significant point. As a proprietary colony, Pennsylvania has often been viewed as a buffer of empire that shielded colonists from the dreaded consequences of the royal prerogative and therefore differentiated the experience of colonial Pennsylvania from the political problems and developments in the other mainland colonies.[4] However, focusing on the governing structure, political atmosphere, and legislative process of the province demonstrates that the empire contributed to and shaped the internal factionalism that raged throughout the latter half of the eighteenth century and acted as sand in the gears stopping up the "stupendous Machine."

Establishing Empire in a Proprietary Colony

The roots of empire and the royal prerogative in Pennsylvania went back to the creation of the province. William Penn received the colony as payment for a debt the Duke of York owed Penn's father, Admiral Sir William Penn. By gaining the land as an individual, not only did Penn receive private emolument but the Crown vested him with political powers. Extending the English empire through the creation of private colonies was not a new course of action. The North American colonies began as offshoots of trading companies and petty corporations chartered by the Crown. The early colonies represented, in many respects, commercial endeavors for adventurous merchants. Commerce alone cannot explain the motivations of individuals or English officials in creating colonies. Religion and European politics had as much to do with forming England's overseas empire as trade, but the main point is that private individuals and corporate entities settled, created, and ultimately governed these colonies.[5]

Pennsylvania, however, did not receive the same autonomy as these earlier corporate endeavors. Much had changed between the charter granted by James I to the Virginia Company in 1606 and establishing Pennsylvania in 1681. A civil war rocked the English world and ultimately transformed the outlook of England toward its colonies. The hands-off approach of the early Stuarts had no place in Cromwell's Western Design or Parliament's understanding of the breadth and reach of its own power. The invigorated vision of empire only increased after the restoration of the Stuarts in 1660. Charles II and James II, influenced by their advisors and councilors, thought differently about the empire than their father and grandfather. For the Stuarts and their advisors, the empire as it existed, the mishmash of constitutions with no central direction and no clear linkages to the Crown, seemed a confused mess in need of reform.[6]

The emergence of a newly conceived and invigorated imperial authority coincided with news of widespread disorder in the colonies, validating for some imperial officials the need for greater royal involvement. After 1660, Indian wars threatened colonial stability, boundary riots wreaked havoc in New England, imperial officials uncovered treasonous activity in Jamaica, and rebellions erupted in the Carolinas, Virginia, Maryland, New York, and Massachusetts.[7] Such episodes confirmed all was not well. In 1679, imperial official William Blathwayt, a man with enormous responsibilities and power in the empire, complained that the Crown's lack of control in the colonies had "lately produced a Rebellion and other unhappy effects." According to Stephen Saunders Webb, such a realization made "stronger political control . . . necessary to meet the expectation of monarch and minister that investment in the colonies would be repaid."[8]

Amid this imperial reimagining, Penn petitioned the Crown for a colony. Although Penn tried to draft a patent to put his province on the same footing as the other charter and proprietary colonies, particularly Maryland and Rhode Island, he dealt with a new imperial government with different imperial goals. Charged with reviewing, amending, and approving all colonial patents, the Committee of Trade and Plantations, a committee of the whole Privy Council charged with upholding the king's interest and bent on establishing a stronger royal presence in the colonies, would never allow a patent like Penn originally conceived.

Undergoing several rounds of reform, imperial managers changed the whole scope of the patent and considerably extended the power of the Crown over the province. On the recommendation of the king's attorney general, the plantation committee denied Penn ecclesiastical authority and mandated that colonial laws had to conform to English law and "English precedents in cases of property, felony, and inheritance." No such stipulations appear in the Maryland grant. The plantation committee also brought Penn's patent in line with emerging imperial trade restrictions, specifying that exports required a royal custom duty, and it insisted that Penn's colony observe the Acts of Navigation.[9]

Lord Chief Justice Francis North and secretary to the plantations committee and imperial auditor general Blathwayt further augmented royal power in the proprietary colony through another round of reforms. In January 1680, the Committee of Trade and Plantations charged North with the task of taking "the said Patent into his consideration" to make sure that it "bee soe drawn that it may consist with the King's interest and service."[10] According to North, such a task meant that he would not grant Penn "all the benefits" that the "others enjoy."[11] North was well suited to the task of reforming the patent to protect and exert the king's "interest." After all, it was North who famously commented "that a man could not be a good lawyer and honest but he must be a prerogative man." According to his biographer, throughout his career Lord North "labored as much as he could to set up the just prerogatives of the crown."[12] Penn's final patent reflected that labor.

North significantly circumscribed the power and autonomy of the proprietor and his colony by increasing the authority of the Crown. He included provisions demanding the colony follow English legal standards, limited the proprietor's pardoning power, reserving the crimes of treason and willful and malicious murder to the king. He expanded the economic and military provisos to include stipulations against trading with any state at war with the king or "to war with any state at peace with the king." North further mandated that if twenty or more colonists applied to the bishop of London for clergy, the bishop could send his nominees without Penn's approval. Such stipulations further tightened the reins of royal authority on the proprietary colony and assured a royal presence.[13]

While North drew the reins tighter, he dug the royal spurs deeper into the province's sides by placing the colonial government, particularly in its civil and military capacity, in a subordinate position to the royal Privy Council and plantation committee. He demanded that the Crown's Privy Council had the power to review all colonial legislation and allow or disallow laws at its discretion. Moreover, colonists had to direct all legal appeals to the Privy Council rather than an English judge, making the Crown the court of highest appeal in the proprietary colony.[14] Through these revisions North guaranteed that the "Ecclesiasticall Civill and Military" powers "within the said Province" would "be subordinate and Subject to the Power and regulation of the Lords of the Privy Council."[15] Private property remained the realm of the proprietor; effectively all else belonged to the Crown.

The imperial connections established and the relegated status of the colony in the final Penn patent also reflected the labors and visions of Secretary and Auditor General Blathwayt. In his oath of office in 1680 Blathwayt promised "to do all that may honestly and justly tend to the King's advantage and profit and to the augmentation of the Rights and Prerogatives of His Crown."[16] Taking his duty to heart in revising the patent, Blathwayt reserved the power to declare martial law to the king and mandated that Penn appoint an "attorney general or agent" to register with the Privy Council who could answer for any challenges to the royal interest. Further circumscribing the autonomy of Pennsylvanians, Blathwayt crossed out the famous clause that promised religious freedom as well as a clause conferring to colonists the status of "natives and liege men . . . of our Kingdom of England and Ireland," effectively denying Pennsylvanians all the attributes of subjecthood.[17]

After all of these revisions, Penn's patent looked far different than he originally imagined. Through the labors of imperial managers, the Crown could exert significant authority over the colony. Penn's province settled on a precarious balance, not quite completely royal, yet not fully proprietary. Nevertheless, the expansion of imperial authority did not end with the Penn patent. Over the course of the late seventeenth century and into the eighteenth, imperial managers consistently assailed the autonomy of Penn's province, particularly by altering the role, responsibility, and allegiance of Penn's deputy governors. At the same time, however, that internal control created a deep political rift in Pennsylvania that had a dramatic impact on the ability of the government to govern effectively, thus creating the "stupendous Machine."

Creating and Controlling Royal Governors

Sixteen ninety-six was another year of imperial reimagining and reorganization. In that year, William III, who ushered in the Glorious Revolution of 1688, created a new Board of Trade as an advisory board for his Privy Council and as a manager of day-to-day imperial affairs. In part, the creation of the board served as a check against trends in Parliament to reform the empire to bring it in line with the revolution's constitutional arrangement. The strength of the monarchy in North America, from William III and many of his ministers' perspective, needed to be protected and enhanced, rather than denuded for more popular control. From its inception, the Board of Trade fulfilled those goals. It exercised a careful supervision of colonial laws and extended the power of the Crown in North America by assaulting the independence of both proprietary and charter colonies.[18]

In the same year that William III created the Board of Trade, imperial officials on both sides of the Atlantic began examining and pushing for the reform of the great lumbering beast that was the English Empire. Part of the problem was the autonomy of many of the colonies and the weakness of the Crown. Edward Randolph, an arch imperial administrator in charge of enforcing the Navigation Acts, stirred many in England to action in 1695 with a report on the deficiencies of imperial authority over colonial trade. In that report, not only did Randolph catalog the many instances of colonial negligence and corruption, but he also outlined a plan to fix the problem of empire by centralizing royal power in the colonies. According to his plan, South Carolina and the Bahamas should become a single Crown colony. Virginia should subsume North Carolina, and Delaware should come under the jurisdiction of a royalized Maryland. New York should annex Connecticut and East Jersey, Massachusetts should annex Rhode Island, and the Crown would control all. Only one colony remained in the hands of a proprietor, Pennsylvania, because it had sufficient imperial influence written into its patent and only needed "an active governor there appointed."[19]

While many in England did not see the necessity for the totality of Randolph's reform initiatives, his plan did highlight the severe disconnect between some of the proprietary patents and the ability of the home government to exercise its power in those colonies. In December 1695, the House of Lords, spirited into action by Randolph's report, found there was not "sufficient Power in *Carolina, Maryland, Pensilvania,* and other Plantations where there are Proprietors."[20] In Pennsylvania, although the patent gave the Crown significant authority over the province, there was no royal officer in the colony to exercise that right. As of 1695, the royal status of proprietary deputy governors was still ill defined, undermining the empire's internal control.

To remedy that deficiency, the House of Lords conducted a hearing in March 1696 and assailed the autonomy of the proprietary colonies by reinterpreting the position of the proprietors and their deputy governors. Directing attention to William Penn, the lords stated flatly, "The Governors for the Proprietors should receive the same instructions from the King as his Majesty's Governors," and "the Proprietors shall be under obligation that those instructions be observed by their Deputies, and be liable to answer for their misbehavior." Ending ominously, the lords told Penn, "If there be further complaint against the Proprietors after this, the Parliament may possibly take another course in this matter, which will be less pleasing to them."[21] William Penn, aghast, blamed the "most fals insinuation of a little officer [Randolph]" for the recent efforts "to examine our Patents" and "arraign our Powrs." "The King is never the farther off from all we have, if we misbehave," he continued, and now it seemed that there would be further "checks, & retrenchmts to frighten us."[22] Penn was right to be shaken. The House of Lords had crucially reinterpreted the role of the proprietor and his deputy governors. In the lords' hands, proprietors became similar to royal governors responsible to the Crown with deputies in the colonies who equally had to abide by royal dictates.

Within a month of the hearing, Parliament enshrined the opinion of the lords in positive law. In April 1696, Parliament passed an "Act to Prevent Frauds and Abuses in the Custom," which transformed proprietary deputy governors into royal officials. According to the law, "all governors nominated by proprietors" required the approval of the Crown and his councilors. In addition, the deputy governors had to pay the Crown £2,000 security and had to obey royal instructions.[23] The newly empowered deputy governors, charged with upholding the royal interest and armed with a veto, became powerful agents of empire.

Regardless of this change in the deputy governor's status, Pennsylvanians experienced imperial power in fits and starts after the first few years of the colony's existence. From 1697 to 1715, the Board of Trade and the Privy Council acted diligently in their duties, but between 1715 and 1730, the two bodies experienced numerous internal problems with personnel and overall outlook. Compounding this problem in the imperial bureaucracy, Pennsylvanians resisted imperial control. Deputy governors often refused to recognize their status as royal officials, and the assembly evaded the Privy Council review of laws. The actions of the deputy governors and tactics of the legislators did not last long, however. Once the Board of Trade overcame its own internal issues and the Privy Council took more interest, the ability of Pennsylvanians to circumvent imperial authority simply ended.

Irritated by the truculence of the provincial government, the board and council went on the offensive in the 1730s. The lords rebuked the deputy governors for failing to uphold the king's interest and for not reporting to Crown officials the inner workings of the provincial government.[24] Since the proprietor acted as "Chief Governor" of the province, imperial officials also brought the proprietor, now William Penn's son, John Penn, to task, threatening the future of his province if he did not whip the deputy governors into shape.[25] The board and council even went so far as to request a parliamentary act to demand the colony comply with the imperial dictates of its patent. In response to these threats, the deputy governor sent his apologies and assurances of his future goodwill, the proprietor sent instructions to the deputy governors demanding compliance with imperial directives, and the assembly ended its evasive tactics.[26] Additionally, after 1730, every deputy governor received over seventy pages of royal instructions.[27] Most of the time instructions included tedious lists of the trade laws the Crown bound the deputy governors by duty to uphold. Sometimes, however, the Crown sent general instructions, such as those dealing with defense initiatives or attaching a "suspending clause" mandating that no paper money law could take effect until the Crown expressed approval.[28]

Not only were the deputy governors guided by royal instructions, but they were also under directives from the proprietor. It would, however, be a mistake to interpret Penn's instructions as a product of his own independent actions and beliefs. Imperial managers treated the proprietor as a royal official, the chief governor, charged with protecting the royal prerogatives entrusted to him. Although historians often interpret the proprietor as an independent actor who tried to rule the province through private instructions to the deputy governors, Penn existed as another agent of empire that the Crown, through his ministers, controlled.[29] Penn's private instructions, while certainly intended to protect the revenue arising from proprietary land and the taxation of proprietary estates, were nonetheless written under the guidance and in consultation with imperial managers and Crown officials. Moreover, there was much more to proprietary instructions than just protecting Penn's landed estates. In those instructions, Penn demanded the deputy governors resist and refuse any law that challenged executive power, a critical component of the royal prerogative. As Proprietor Thomas Penn wrote Deputy Governor Hamilton in 1749, "In passing all Bills you must take care to preserve the just Authority of Magistrates" and other officers that constituted "the Executive part of the Government."[30] Such instructions were crucially directed by imperial managers, especially the president of the Board of Trade, Lord Halifax, and his secretary, John Pownall.

The Second Earl of Halifax, president of the Board of Trade from 1748 to 1761, kept a tight rein on the proprietors during his tenure. He held regular meetings with Thomas Penn, sent his staff to Penn's home with further instructions, and was ever ready to upbraid the proprietor when he found him lax in his duties.[31] During these encounters with Halifax, Penn received opinions and warnings from one of the most prominent, ambitious, and powerful men at the head of imperial affairs. Halifax guided Penn in writing his instructions on everything from paper money bills to the appointment of executive and judicial officers, and he often pushed Penn to make strong declarations against giving up any executive power to the assembly. If Penn did not listen, Halifax cautioned, he would be challenging the trust reposed in him to guard the king's interest. For example, during a colonial dispute over the passage of paper money bills, Halifax told Penn that while Pennsylvania's currency was not in a state of ill health and therefore under "no necessity for restraining," Penn needed to inform the deputy governors of the "mischief that attended the assembly having the power of disposing the interest Money," which should not happen in "the Kings' Colony's."[32] In this and many other instances, Penn had received "my Lord Halifax's sentiments" and had to act accordingly.[33] As he later pointed out, if he and the deputy governors did not conform to imperial directives, they would "undoubtedly highly deserve his majestys censure."[34] "Thus you see," Penn wrote, "I do not act without the knowledge of those to whom under the King my Family is accountable."[35]

The demands placed on the proprietors and the deputy governors by imperial managers created a scenario where the colonial assembly and the deputy governors were completely at odds. The deputy governor had to abide by royal dictates that the assembly refused to acknowledge, and the two settled into long periods of faction, resulting in legislative paralysis. That political stasis only existed because of the Crown's successful control of the deputy governors.

The Crown's success was in part due to a crucial shift in the attitude of governors. Beginning with the administration of Deputy Governor George Thomas in 1738, deputy governors proved far more attached to the royal interest than ever before. A West Indian planter from Antigua, a colonel in the army, and a man of royal inclinations, Thomas was radically different than those deputy governors who came before him. Where Patrick Gordon, deputy governor from 1726 to 1736, rarely kept imperial managers abreast of colonial developments, resulting in several reprimands, Thomas communicated "knowledge of every thing done in the country."[36] Thomas had "kissed the king's hand" and felt it his duty to fight for the royal prerogative in the colony.[37]

Thomas's diligent adherence to the royal interest affected Pennsylvania lawmaking. Between 1740 and 1742, for example, the colonial government passed no laws. Thomas, excessively headstrong, proved unwilling to brook the rancorous attacks of the assembly on executive prerogatives. He told the secretary of state, the Duke of Newcastle, that he would never submit to an assembly that made a "prostitution of His Majesty's Name." The legislators had "so little Regard to government, the interests of their mother Country, or indeed common Justice."[38] In the face of incredible opposition, Thomas regularly demanded recognition of the Crown's prerogative and after 1740 used royal instructions, particularly the "suspending clause," to back up his executive vetoes. From Thomas's perspective, he represented the king and therefore had to uphold the royal interest.

Issues of duty, power, and prerogative colored most if not all of the political disputes between the two branches of the government in the province. Faced with a truculent legislature and an unyielding ministry, deputy governors had little choice but to frame their interactions with both bodies around their duty as royal representatives, no matter the cost. James Hamilton, who succeeded Thomas, lost a great deal of popular respect due to his insistence that he was the Crown's representative bound to uphold royal instructions.[39] The mere rumor of prerogative set the legislature on edge. Hamilton's successor, Robert Hunter Morris, had not even arrived in Pennsylvania before legislators labeled him "the Devil" because they heard he was a "great stickler for the prerogative."

Rumors swirled around Philadelphia, particularly among those "little barking snarling Currs [legislators]," that Morris had met with "the Lords of the Board of Trade and King's Council" to assure them that he would uphold the king's interest. Assembly members would "cut his throat for it cou'd they do it with impunity."[40]

This new royal attitude of the deputy governors exacerbated the most innocuous of colonial disputes. The appointment of an officer to inspect the health of recently arrived German immigrants, for example, embroiled the province in a controversy over the power of the Crown in Pennsylvania. In 1741, the assembly removed a doctor appointed by the deputy governor and replaced him with its own physician. The assembly's usurpation of executive power irritated the deputy governor and his council, who believed the assembly could not "direct or control any magistrate or Officer, not even a Constable," because the "Government of this Province" was "unquestionably in his most sacred Majesty the King & those who have Authority under him." Therefore, the assembly had acted "illegally."[41] Although legislators disagreed, the deputy governor, reflecting on his position, flatly told them, "My Duty to the King is prior and paramount to any Obligations I am, or can be laid under, to any persons whatsoever; and where an inferior Duty interferes with a Superior, the Superior is to be prefer'd."[42]

The political problem was so acute in Pennsylvania because the assembly and deputy governor fundamentally disagreed on the colony's governing instrument and therefore Pennsylvania's place in the empire. For the deputy governors as well as imperial officials across the Atlantic, the original royal patent dictated the terms of governance as the founding document. For the legislators, a charter they received from William Penn in 1701 was the immutable constitution of the province. It reflected a political settlement and, they believed, superseded the original royal patent. When the assembly refused to recognize the deputy governor as a royal official, thereby denying the legality of royal instructions, it relied on the Charter of 1701. According to the legislators, the charter made no mention of royal instructions or the position of the deputy governors as royal representatives; therefore the governors were merely the proprietary's deputies, and the province had an "Exemption" from imperial directives. The deputy governor, using the original patent, could not understand what could "induce" them "to think that the Words of the Royal Charter may be construed in Favour of such Exemption?" While the Charter of 1701 did not reference the Crown, the original patent, still in force, provided significant royal "Jurisdiction over its Subjects."⁴³ Therefore, the deputy governor was duty bound to the Crown and could not "disobey . . . His Majesty's Instructions" without "disregarding my own Honour and Safety."⁴⁴

Like the deputy governors, the home government, time and again, made it perfectly clear that the Charter of 1701 did not exempt the colony from royal control. In 1753, for instance, the king's chief justice Sir Dudley Ryder submitted a legal opinion to the proprietor and the deputy governor that they both must adhere to the original patent and royal instructions. According to Ryder, the assembly's position "that although his Majesty might issue such Instructions to *his own* immediate Governors, where there are no Charters, yet, that in *Pennsylvania*, where such a Charter subsists, such Instructions had no Force," had no legal basis. Ryder cited both the original patent and the 1696 act making deputy governors representatives of the Crown as evidence. Ryder therefore concluded, "I am of Opinion it is by no Means safe, or advisable, or consistent with his *Duty*" for the deputy governor to disregard royal instructions.⁴⁵ If Ryder was not clear enough, Penn entertained "A Visitor" sent by the president of the Board of Trade who told the proprietor, "Lord Halifax and others are firmly of opinion that" royal instructions "should be observed and must not be given up by the Governor."⁴⁶ Within a few months of this visit, the Board of Trade issued a strong warning to the deputy governor and the legislators that they must obey all royal instructions.⁴⁷

The efforts of imperial managers to dictate the terms of the debate through instructions to the deputy governors and the legal opinions of Crown counselors stunted the ability of the colonial government to act. This proved especially true since legislation was the only means at the assembly's disposal to challenge executive power and the royal prerogative. When creating bills for the dispensing of interest money, establishing public institutions, reforming legal structures, or creating a militia, all reforms Pennsylvanians pleaded for in their petitions, the assembly often tried to gain power over the appointment or tenure of provincial officers. The deputy governors would rarely accept such an innovation, and many of the bills died a slow and insignificant death.

The stubbornness of both sides did not bode well for ordinary Pennsylvanians. Although they had petitioned time and again for reform of the laws and institutions that governed their daily lives, very little could actually be accomplished. A twenty-seven-year-old George Bryan, speaking for many ordinary people, noted in his makeshift journal in 1758 "that it is for power and influence our folks contend."[48] From Bryan's perspective, the assembly, the deputy governor, and their cronies filled their days with "lying, misrepresentation & false reports" for the sole purpose of gaining "the right to appoint offices, which you know gives a mighty influence to the persons or party who enjoy it."[49] As for the "consequences to others or the body of the people," Bryan ruefully wrote, "Politicians who have self interest in view, cannot be expected to attend to them."[50] The people's public petitions, representations, and remonstrances had limited possibilities to actually produce reform in this antagonistic political environment.

Although historians often ignore the place of the Crown and the empire in Pennsylvania, royal authority was quite literally wrought into the fabric of Penn's patent and evolved in power and scope over the course of the seventeenth and eighteenth centuries. By the middle of the eighteenth century, imperial administrative and advisory boards could shape the internal governance of Pennsylvania through the deputy governors, whether the medium of exchange be royal or proprietary instructions. While those instructions often successfully circumscribed the actions of the deputy governor and stymied the initiatives of the assembly, there were times when they failed. Nevertheless, when deputy governors faltered, the imperial government could and did take direct control.

Direct Control from the Center

The mid-eighteenth century also witnessed a reinvigorated colonial legislature. Faced with a destructive imperial war and severe difficulties governing a geographically expanding, economically diversifying, and demographically growing colony, elite Quakers who had controlled lawmaking in the province since its inception found it increasingly difficult to align their religious beliefs with the policies necessary to address changing circumstances. As a result, many left formal politics, leaving the legislature in the hands of a new generation of politicians such as Joseph Galloway and Benjamin Franklin, who were far more interested in expanding the reach and remit of the government to fill critical voids. Nevertheless, old animosities over the extent of executive and legislative powers still remained, shaping any initiative, no matter how necessary, the legislature attempted.[51] With the Crown and imperial administrators ever more attentive to upholding and, in some instances, extending executive prerogative, legislators found it extremely difficult to achieve basic reforms and secure basic services for the people they supposedly represented.

Regardless of the number of times colonial legislators heard the opinions of the deputy governors, proprietors, or other imperial officials, they refused to alter their disposition and goals. They searched for any opportunity and imperial weaknesses to achieve their ends, and sometimes they proved successful, at least initially. The assembly became adept at using exigencies and small advantages to circumvent the empire's control of deputy governors. However, deputy governors were only the first line of imperial defense. When that bulwark failed, there were other significant checks that the home government could martial to defeat the fleeting victories of the assembly and stifle the colony's institutional development.

During the omnipresent reality of war after 1750, the assembly cultivated a useful political tactic. The legislators realized that necessity rather than political ideals could open a window to challenge executive power. When people on the frontier and commanders in the field implored the assembly to provide militia laws and provisions, the legislature would stall, delay, and withhold bills until the deputy governor would agree to give up the executive privilege to appoint militia officers or dispense the interest money arising from the supply bills granting funds to the "king's use." According to one historian, "That men froze in the streets or were scalped on the frontiers was secondary to the security and privileges of the assembly itself."[52]

Despite the efforts of the assembly to take advantage of such wartime necessities, the imperial bureaucracy and the royal constraints on the power of the provincial government acted as a significant check on legislative authority. While the deputy governor under pressure to produce something may have begrudgingly accepted laws mitigating executive authority, these laws did not fare as well across the Atlantic before the Board of Trade and the Privy Council. The council, for example, quickly repealed a militia law in 1755 because it challenged the royal prerogative, effectively denying Pennsylvanians of crucial military defense during a time of chaos and war.[53]

The crumbling status of civil government in the province provided other moments to test the deputy governors' insistence on the superiority of ideals over necessity. As petitions rolled into the assembly demanding institutional and legal reform, the assembly tried to use those urgent pleas to its advantage. It crafted judicial and land record laws, both popular reform issues, with direct attacks on executive power. The assembly's actions, however, contravened royal instructions and therefore were often deeply affected by factional politics and very rarely were passed by the deputy governor. Despite gubernatorial vetoes, the assembly kept up the game and in 1759 found an imperial weakness, a corrupt deputy governor, that it could exploit. Yet, while seemingly victorious, the assembly's actions instigated a critical imperial dispute that changed Pennsylvania's world for the remainder of the colonial period and exacerbated the sense of governmental crisis due to the failure of reform.

To pass bills attacking executive power, legislators needed a malleable, indolent, and indifferent deputy governor, which they received in 1756. That year began with a rather precarious predicament faced by Thomas Penn. Prince William, the Duke of Cumberland, firmly urged Penn to appoint Captain William Denny as deputy governor. Penn, who had requested the duke recommend a ranking military man, was, to say the least, disappointed at the duke's suggestion of this relatively unknown captain without any actual leadership experience. However, Penn was in no position to argue with a prince.

Denny's obscurity turned out to be the least of Penn's problems; Denny cared little for heeding instructions and even less for conducting the business of his office. The new deputy governor, whom Penn would come to call "the Creature" and that "miserable Wretch," was, as his biographer points out, "venal, lazy, and inept."[54] According to Secretary of the Province Richard Peters, who had to prod Denny into any sort of action, the deputy governor was "a trifler, weak of body, peevish and averse to business and, if I am not mistaken, extreamly near if not a lover of money."[55] Denny proved so avaricious that history knows him for his near fire sale of flags of truce during the Seven Years' War.[56] From the perspective of one political outsider, "Denny seems not calculated for either the King's or the people's service."[57] The legislators found such a man as Denny perfect prey, and as Penn noted, they would have "what the worst of them wished done" with little resistance from the deputy governor.[58]

Denny did not possess the stomach for disputes with the assembly. During his tenure as deputy governor, he faded into the gubernatorial mansion where he kept "no company," dining alone and rarely venturing out. The only thing Denny really cared about, according to ex-governor Morris, "seems to be money." Since the legislators controlled his salary, Denny learned to court them and cater to their wishes. According to Morris, "His inclinations are in favour of the Assembly" and he "frequently complains of having his hands tied by instructions." Denny made his favoritism of the assembly known by refusing to take the advice of his council and making assemblymen his confidants. Soon Denny began articulating those "unmeaning distinctions between the Kings' affairs & the Proprietors as if the Proprietary government was not the Crowns," a division the assembly made for years.[59]

Denny most likely favored the assembly because its members satisfied his pecuniary interests. In 1759, behind closed doors in the deputy governor's retreat on the falls of the Schuylkill River, Denny and Speaker Isaac Norris held meetings where they must have come to some sort of agreement.[60] Between Norris's initial conference with Denny in April to the end of September, the deputy governor and the assembly passed a slew of bills that would have never seen the light of day had a deputy governor such as Hamilton or Morris been in charge. During that period, the assembly also paid Denny £3,000. The dispersal of the £3,000 strongly suggests that Denny received this money to pass certain bills. After Denny approved a few bills, the assembly parsed out £1,000. Within three months, Denny made more money than Morris did during his entire gubernatorial tenure.[61] Typically, each deputy governor received between £500 and £1,000 a year, well under the £3,000 given to Denny. Writing a bit deviously to Benjamin Franklin, Norris noted that "the Governors Finances" were "at present in good Order."[62]

With Denny in its pocket, the assembly passed several bills that challenged executive authority. The House passed a supply bill that taxed proprietary estates, giving the assembly power over the dispensation of funds and the officers in charge of appraising proprietary land. Even more shocking, the bill stipulated that if Penn failed to pay his portion of the tax, the government could seize and sell his lands. Such a bill obviously ruffled the proprietor's feathers. Not only did the legislators pass bills taxing proprietary estates but, up to "their old Leaven," they resumed their "old pretences of appointing officers Independent of the Governor."[63] What was more, legislators tried to gain control of the judiciary.

Fights over the management of the judiciary or even the mere reform of the courts had a long history in the province. The administration of justice, the control of officers, and the creation of courts were functions of the royal prerogative that the Crown proved unwilling to give up. In granting William Penn a patent, the king did not simply surrender such a power; instead, he put Penn in charge, as any royal governor, of maintaining and protecting the royal interest. Because the king did not relinquish his prerogative, local law enforcement officials such as sheriffs and justices of the peace held commissions granted by the Crown, not the proprietor. According to the commission for Joseph Breintnal, sheriff of Philadelphia County, "George the Second, by the Grace of God, King of Great Britain, France & Ireland, Defender of the Faith & so forth ... nominated, constituted and appointed" the new sheriff, and the Crown empowered him to keep "our Peace."[64] Justices of the peace and supreme court judges, both appointed by the deputy governor, were even more under the control of the Crown. Not only did the king "constitute and appoint" judges, but the judges held their offices at the king's pleasure.[65] If judges failed in their duty, only the king, through his representative the governor (the proprietor) or deputy governor, could remove them.

In the first half of the century, the royal prerogative also clashed with the need for the constitution of courts and the creation of other law enforcement mechanisms. Setting up and organizing courts, like the power over officers, was a crucial factor of the prerogative. Royal prerogative was the sole reason that the king gave Penn and his heirs, not the legislative arm of government, the power to create courts. The mere fact that an assembly might legislate a court that upheld the "king's laws" into existence constituted a challenge to royal authority. The Privy Council and Board of Trade made that point of prerogative clear before 1725 by vetoing four of five judiciary bills.[66] The one act that survived in 1722 slipped through the system because the board actually lost the bill during a decade of imperial ineptitude. In the future, especially after 1730, the Crown vigorously protected its powers over the administration of the king's law and limited the negative repercussions of neglect.

The Crown, however, had few direct chances to display its vigor regarding the courts. Under the close supervision of Deputy Governors Thomas, Hamilton, and Morris, the assembly could barely legislate for day-to-day necessities, let alone an overhaul of the courts. This is not to say the legislators did not try. In 1749, for example, the assembly attempted to pass a bill to reform the judiciary. Though some of the reforms were necessary, the real purpose of the bill was "calculated to curtail the Power of the Magistrates." Deputy Governor Hamilton would have none of it and simply "got clear of it."[67] The bill never left the legislature nor did the debate over it make it into the printed minutes of the assembly.

However, in the same year that Denny became deputy governor, the old Quaker elite had left the legislature in the hands of new more energetic politicians willing to push the issue. After their success passing bills taxing proprietary estates and wresting away control of officers, assembly members felt confident they could get away with reforming the judiciary and gaining control of judges and justices. The assembly also had an urgent need, claimed by petitioners, to institute reforms. According to the assembly, the judicial system as it existed, bogged down by the growing number of cases, needed a complete overhaul. Like most legislation aiming at large-scale reforms, the assembly wanted the bill to conform to its visions for the future, which meant an increase of the legislature's control and power at the expense of the deputy governor's.

The judiciary bill drastically renovated the courts in the province. In an attempt to make the courts more efficient and effective, addressing popular concerns, the new bill designated different types of judges with separate duties and powers. Five judges would sit as judges of the court of common pleas, and they could not hear cases in the court of quarter sessions, effectively separating civil and criminal judges as well as judges that could rule on matters of law and matters of fact. In addition to this change, local magistrates would act as "Conservators of the Peace only," in that they would serve as a police force rather than simply an umpire at court.[68] Legislators, however, did not stop with these structural reforms but demanded that the tenure of office for judges and justices change from the pleasure of the Crown to "good behavior," challenging the royal prerogative.

From many of the legislators' perspectives, the notion that judges held their office at the pleasure of the Crown was an archaic and potentially tyrannical relic of the past. In England, the Glorious Revolution, particularly the 1701 Act of Settlement, had made judges independent of the Crown, and Pennsylvania's legislators argued they inherited that revolutionary settlement. Yet in the present situation, legislator Joseph Galloway argued, Pennsylvanians fared little better than English subjects did before the Glorious Revolution, when the kings of yore tyrannized the people through their control of judges whom Galloway dubbed "murderous weapons of perverted law." In a pamphlet distributed to the public, Galloway proposed a law that eradicated this vestige of monarchical tyranny. The judges needed to function *"independent of power,"* and the people needed to stand behind the legislature in its attempt to "show that an increase of prerogative, a perversion of the laws, a suspension of your natural right, and a violation of the fundamentals of an *English* constitution" equaled an "undue and *illegal influence* on the courts of justice."[69]

Galloway failed to mention, however, that the assembly never intended to make the judges truly *"independent of power"* but simply sought to shift authority over judges away from the Crown to the assembly. Under the English system, judges gained their independence not only by a change in their tenure but through a guaranteed salary. The bill proposed by the assembly only sought to change the judges' tenure from the pleasure of the Crown to "good behavior" while retaining the right of the assembly to grant or withhold the payment of judges at its pleasure. Moreover, the bill never stipulated the procedure to remove the new judges for bad behavior. By making the impeachment proceedings perfectly ambiguous the assembly no doubt sought to gain control over impeachment without exposing this pretension to power to the scrutiny of royal officials. The fight over William Moore's impeachment, however, made the assembly's goal particularly clear.

The judiciary bill was part of a two-pronged initiative to make the legal system efficient, while also mitigating the power of the executive. During Denny's tenure, the assembly also attempted to create a new public institution for the recording of land records in an effort to meet the needs of a province experiencing dramatic demographic growth. Legal cases regarding disputed titles, nonexistent documents, and overlapping claims overwhelmed both the local courts and the supreme court. Such was the outcome of a poorly supervised office contending with major population growth. While a public institution proved necessary, the assembly used this need to steal power away from the proprietor. Since the colony's inception, proprietary officials had conducted the recording of warrants and surveys. The new law obliterated proprietary control. The responsibility for recording basic documents transferring proprietary lands to individuals shifted from officers representing the proprietors to a new officer, the recorder, responsible to the assembly.[70]

While the assembly could never count on previous deputy governors to approve of blatant attacks on the executive prerogative, they could rely on Denny. When the Judiciary and Land Records Acts came before the deputy governor, Denny ignored the advice of his council and gave his approval. Enraged, all but one councilor boycotted a meeting to set the seals to the bills. Denny's actions so "greatly alarm'd" one councilor that he "did not sleep for three nights."[71] Another councilor wrote that Penn needed to do something to stop "the Vilest Practices, and still Viler Intentions of the most worthless of men."[72] Denny and the assembly colluded together to effectuate a complete "Prostitution of power."[73] According to Chief Justice William Allen, "all good men among us" despised Denny, that "poor mercenary Creature," for what he did.[74]

As councilors and others ranted about these flagrant attacks on government, most of the legislators basked in their recent triumphs. Writing from London, agent for the assembly Benjamin Franklin gloated that the passage of bills seizing executive power "gives me great Pleasure" and the "Firmness of the Assembly ... pleases me much." Such crowing seems a bit premature, as these laws still had to pass through the imperial bureaucracy and receive the royal approbation. Legislators and the assembly's supporters, however, never believed the Crown would veto these bills because they did not think the laws challenged the royal prerogative. From the legislature's perspective, the bills only defied a proprietor who sought "to oppress us." Drawing on the Charter of 1701, legislators consistently dissociated proprietary from royal interests and therefore argued that if imperial managers had a "clearer Knowledge and truer Notion of our Disputes" they would support the assembly over the proprietor. Franklin went as far as to claim that even the proprietor would not "dare to oppose" the bills because the home government would "decide against him."[75] Franklin's optimism proved contagious. From Philadelphia, Isaac Norris jubilantly wrote, "The Bills the Governor has passed this Year makes us all pretty good Friends here," and he could not wait for the "Confirmation of them at Home." Norris, brimming with confidence, concluded that the king's imminent approval of the recent laws would finally bring the proprietors to a "Sence of their true interest."[76]

Unlike the assembly, imperial officials made no distinction between the affairs of the Crown and those of the proprietor. In fact, they often complained that the proprietors thought of themselves as "Landholders only" instead of governors in charge of upholding the "prerogative of the Crown."[77] In 1758, Penn tried to explain this imperial relationship to Franklin, but he refused to listen. Penn told him "that it was as unsafe for the People, as it was for us, to claim priviledges by my Fathers Charter [Charter of 1701], that could not be warranted by the King's Charter to him [royal patent]." Franklin clearly disagreed. In a letter to Isaac Norris, Franklin argued that the royal patent made little difference, as William Penn granted the assembly "all the Power and Privileges of an Assembly according to the Rights of Freeborn Subjects of England" in the Charter of 1701. Thomas Penn, according to Franklin, was nothing more than a "low Jockey" who tried to cheat the people out of their hard-won privileges.[78] Penn received a copy of Franklin's letter to Norris, deemed it "a most imprudent Paper," and gave it to "Lord Hallifax and some other People" who agreed with the proprietor's explanation of affairs to Franklin and equally agreed as to Franklin's impudence. After the meeting with Halifax and others, Penn, obviously vexed, warned his correspondents in the province that "great care" needed to be taken "to keep close to the Kings Charter" as "the present Charter [1701 Charter] was not a means of settling the Province." The imperial response to the recent acts passed by the assembly and Deputy Governor Denny would provide a valuable lesson as to the merits of Penn's cautionary warnings about the power of the original royal patent over the 1701 Charter.

The laws passed by the assembly and Denny sparked instant anger in England. When Penn received some of the bills, especially the Judiciary Act, he could not believe the glaring insolence of the deputy governor. Penn argued that the bill altering the tenure of judges constituted "such an unheard of breach of Instructions as I could not have conceived would have entered into his head."[79] The laws equally perturbed imperial managers. Imperial officials so thoroughly disdained the province's attack on executive power that the actions of the assembly and deputy governor became a part of general conversation. Thomas Penn reported hearing that during a dinner at "a Cabinet Ministers Table" the discussion turned to the recent bills, and those at the table denounced the Pennsylvania legislators as a "most infamous corrupt People." The assembly's actions triggered similar censures at a dinner of "several Lords of Trade."[80] Penn also learned that "the Assembly are looked upon in so unfavorable a light by our Judges" that the legislature would receive nothing "more than what they are in the strictest justice entitled to."[81] Such general animosity proved to Penn that he would "find no difficulty" procuring a repeal of laws usurping appointment or impeachment powers for the assembly. "When this is done," Penn hoped, "that Point of Prerogative will be settled."[82]

Penn had good reason to expect the Crown's disallowance of the objectionable bills. Almost immediately after the arrival of the new laws, the Board of Trade sent them to the king's attorney general and solicitor general, as well as the board's own attorney, Sir Matthew Lamb.[83] Lamb subsequently submitted a legal report stating that the judiciary and land records acts proved that the assembly aimed "to seize the whole Government into their hands."[84] In addition, Alexander Forrestor, barrister and MP for Oakhampton, who preceded Lamb as the Board of Trade's attorney, sent a similar report to Penn and President Halifax.[85] Halifax's secretary, John Pownall, also investigated the bills. Citing the precedent of a Jamaican law, he informed Penn that the Privy Council would definitely veto the "Judges Bill."[86] Even the king's attorney general and solicitor general agreed to speak against the bills at a scheduled hearing before the Board of Trade. The solicitation of numerous legal opinions combined with the attorney general's and solicitor general's presence "contrary to their usual practice" signified the importance imperial officials placed on the repeal of colonial bills challenging the royal prerogative.[87]

Over the course of four sessions between May 21 and June 3, the Board of Trade heard the arguments for and against each bill. Penn's own lawyer, Henry Wilmot, whom the proprietor labored with to craft justifications to reject several of the assembly's recent laws, did not even speak. The king's attorney general and solicitor general dominated the entire four sessions and made any argument Wilmot could muster superfluous. The attorney general and solicitor general, as royal officials, had a power and authority beyond that of Wilmot. The officers came, they averred, as officials entrusted to "support the Rights and Prerogatives of the Crown." Both officers, in long speeches, castigated the assembly not only for its lawmaking but also for its bald assertions denying the force of royal authority in the province. The laws they passed, according to both officers, merely confirmed a "general tendency and disposition ... to encroach upon the rights of the Proprietaries, the prerogative of the Crown, and the sovereign Government of the mother country." The attorney general, Charles Pratt, rebuked the assembly for repeatedly "asserting that the Lieutenant [Deputy] Governor was not the Governor of the crown" and for its "rebellious declarations" respecting royal instructions and "other acts of avowed democracy." Similar to Pratt, solicitor general Charles Yorke castigated the assembly and its laws as "arbitrary" and detrimental to not only royal power in Pennsylvania but "the Peace, Order, and Good Government" of "the several others of his Majesty's Plantations in America." The Crown, Yorke argued, needed to repeal the laws and demonstrate the authority of the Crown in that "rebellious" province before it spread.[88]

By firmly connecting proprietary and royal interests, the attorney general and solicitor general put the assembly's legal counsel in an awkward and ultimately indefensible position. The defense used an interpretation that relied on the Charter of 1701 to deny royal power in the colony. They argued that the proprietor existed independently of the Crown, and therefore laws diminishing proprietary authority did not challenge the royal prerogative. The defense, then, as the assembly had done for years, based its argument on the supposition that the charter superseded the original royal patent. In essence, the assembly's counsel offered a defense and line of reasoning that the attorney general and solicitor general, royal officials with significant political clout, had just denied had any legal basis.[89]

Though the defense's statements might earn the applause of Franklin and other assembly members, they did little good in front of the Board of Trade. After the trial, the board adjourned, debated the bills behind closed doors, and finally agreed on a report to the Privy Council that replicated, almost verbatim, the speeches made by the attorney general and solicitor general. In the report, the board played up the presence of Pratt and Yorke, stated that the bills and votes of the House confirmed a "uniform system of Collusion between the Governor and Assembly," and recommended the repeal of seven laws. Significantly, the Board of Trade also denied the central arguments of the assembly's counsel as to a separation of proprietary and royal interests and prerogatives. According to the board's report, Penn served as an important royal official "intrusted with some of its [the Crown's] most valuable Prerogatives." Penn had a duty, the board argued, to uphold and maintain those prerogatives, and that is why Penn issued instructions to the deputy governors and took an interest in the repeal of several laws. To the board and many other imperial managers, there existed little difference in the government of proprietary and royal colonies.[90]

Once the board confirmed the place of Pennsylvania in the empire, they had a firmer base with which to attack provincial laws and request action by the Crown. The board demanded the royal veto of any law that even remotely usurped executive authority. The Lords of Trade judged the bill taxing proprietary estates as "unjust" and calculated to assume to the assembly a "great Part of the Executive and in Effect the whole Legislative Power." In addition, although the lords agreed that the provincial laws reforming legal structures and creating new public institutions constituted a public necessity, they refused to approve the bills because they challenged executive power. From the board's perspective, experience proved "that it is in vain to negotiate away His Majesty's Prerogative; every new Concession becomes the foundation of some new demand, and that, my Lords, of some new dispute." In short, it did not behoove the king to approve of laws "fatal" to "the Prerogatives of the Crown." Instead, the Crown needed to return the "Constitution of the Colony to its proper principles" by checking "the growing Influence of the Assembly" and restoring "to the Crown, in the Person of the Proprietors, its just Prerogatives." If the Crown did not act now by repealing the laws under question and rebuking the assembly for its insolence, the Lords of Trade argued, it could lose all authority in Pennsylvania as well as the rest of the colonies.[91]

The imperial officers' arguments and strong reprimand of the assembly pleased Penn. Summing up the trial, Penn jubilantly wrote that "Mr. Franklin heard so much said, by both the Attorney & Solicitor General of the Assembly's intention to establish a Democracy, if not an Oligarchy in the place of his Majesty's Government, and of the Duty we were under to oppose it, and of our intentions steadily to pursue that Duty, and at the same time that they should think it their Duty, while they remained Servants of the Crown, to assist us therein."[92] Penn hoped, as he wrote in a second letter, that Franklin now realized "the difference between a Representative of the People of England, and that of a Colony only by a Charter from the Crown." In the future, he should "not dare to patronize such schemes for raising the power of Assembly to so great an height as he and his friends have done."[93]

Despite Penn's jubilation, the board also reproved the proprietors. The lords, "in a manner" Penn did not "so well like" lectured the proprietors for failing to protect "the Rights of his Majesty."[94] The lords could not "help lamenting that" the proprietors had "not been more consistent and uniform in the Support" of the prerogatives entrusted to them. "For it is Observable," the lords argued, that although the proprietors "profess to be very sensibly affected at any Encroachment on the Prerogative of the Crown, and state themselves very properly as intrusted with its Preservations," they acted as nothing more than "Landholders in the Province." The lords ominously concluded that if the proprietors failed to check the machinations of the assembly in the future, the board would obtain a "constitutional Interposition of the Crown, to restrain the Powers of the Assembly" from "becoming exorbitant" and thereby "protect... the Rights of His Majesty, which have been gradually departed from by the Proprietaries."[95] The board offered a strong censure and even more threatening warning. If Penn did not consistently uphold the rights of the Crown, he stood to lose everything.

The trial before the Board of Trade and Privy Council shaped future debates between the assembly and deputy governor, constrained Penn still further, and made clear, to some, that the empire would act as a formidable force in the colony. The importance and ultimate meaning of the event for the future of Pennsylvania was not lost on Benjamin Franklin's son, William, who went with his father to the hearings as his secretary. Writing to Joseph Galloway a few days after the trial, the young Franklin argued, "The Plan of Attack must be chang'd from the Proprietors to the Board of Trade." "Till the iniquitous System of

Government which they would establish in the Colonies, for their own selfish Purposes, is fully expos'd," he went on, "I think we can hope for no good from that Quarter."⁹⁶ A Franklin had never before written truer words about imperial managers.

The Inability of Reform: The Post-1759 World

The hearing before the Board of Trade, particularly the board's report criticizing Penn's efforts to protect the royal interest, set Penn on edge. The trial, however, also gave him confidence that he would receive imperial backing in his future dealings with the colonial legislature. To his new deputy governor, James Hamilton, Penn wrote, "I believe we shall be supported by the Government here, in exercising its Just rights, for which purpose I shall always endeavour to act in concert with the Ministers here." Not only would Penn "act in concert," but he would seek imperial advice for the future, carefully watch the imperial manager's dealings with other colonies, and make sure that his government did not replicate other colonial mistakes.⁹⁷

The colony immediately felt the reverberations of the Board of Trade and Privy Council hearings, which had long-term repercussions. Not only did the Crown repeal necessary laws, but the Board of Trade's report to the king's Privy Council set up entirely new instructions for the deputy governors. After the hearing, both the attorney general and solicitor general advised Penn to use the Board of Trade's report as general instructions to his deputy governors. On July 5, less than a month after the report by the lords, Penn sent the deputy governor a copy of the report as "the best Instruction we can send you." Penn hoped that by using the report as instructions, the deputy governors would be more obliged to obey them and the assembly would have little room to argue or delineate proprietary from royal commands. "I heartily wish," Penn wrote, "it may convince the People, that the points we have insisted in refusing to give up to the Assembly, are, according to our present most happy Constitution [the royal patent], such as we have a Legal right to the possession of."⁹⁸

The firmness and particularity of the new instructions and the stubbornness of the assembly inevitably clashed and thereby affected the institutional development of the colony. In 1762, for instance, the deputy governor used the report by the Board of Trade against the assembly to quash an attempt to create a public land office that challenged executive power. In February of that year, the assembly created another land records act that mirrored the 1759 act. After receiving the bill, the deputy governor sent it back with an executive veto. In a message to the assembly, Deputy Governor Hamilton stated that he was "sorry to find that the present bill is formed on the same plan, and liable to the most material part of the same objections for which your late law respecting these offices, was, after a full hearing, repealed by His Majesty in council." Though he tried to amend the bill to meet the stipulations in the Board of Trade's report, he could not. The "necessary alterations and amendments," Hamilton argued, "would be so numerous and perplexing" that any revision of the bill as it existed would be impossible. Any bill creating such an office, he argued, had to make sure that the officers gave "sufficient security to the King or to the proprietaries." The assembly would in no way agree to Hamilton's recommendations, and therefore the bill died a quick death.[99]

The new instructions similarly thwarted any possibility for future reform of the judiciary, desperately needed in the growing colony. In 1761 and early 1762, the assembly attempted to make important and much-needed reforms to the courts and its office holders. In April 1761, Chief Justice William Allen complained to his fellow assemblymen of the "difficulties and Delays" faced by the "Courts of Oyer and Terminer." Since the court conducted most of the trials in Philadelphia, the court had problems "collecting Jurors," which resulted in cases being "repeatedly put off from Time to Time, to the Obstruction of Justice, and manifest Injury of the Public."[100] For over five months legislators debated, sometimes rather violently, the particulars of a new judicial bill. According to Samuel Foulke, a representative from Chester County, no sooner did the assembly begin debating the law than "a Violent Storm arose in ye House" between William Allen and Joseph Galloway over the tenure of judges. Even the Speaker of the House, Isaac Norris, "Uhappily join'd" the dispute "and shew'd not only marks of great impatience but even rage." Foulke "was not a little Chagrined to See in that Honorable House so great a departure from that decency Decorum & Solemnity" and lamented that "too many of the Members seem'd to forget where they were situated and what their Country Expected of them by placing them in that Station."[101]

After the prolonged "debate," the assembly finally passed a bill that offered significant judicial reform. The act created separate supreme court justices to sit in each county to hear appeals and carry out oyer and terminer functions, which redressed popular grievances by establishing new courts closer to the people and increasing the number of supreme court justices to meet the demands of a burgeoning population. However, as had happened in 1759, the new bill altered the tenure of judges and therefore was doomed to fail. The deputy governor, armed with the report by the Board of Trade against changing the tenure of judges, demanded alterations and amendments that the assembly refused to acknowledge, so the bill died stillborn.[102]

The Board of Trade's report combined with Penn's new vigor to appease imperial managers further affected necessary reform of the judiciary. In 1761, while Lord Halifax and Penn vacationed in the country, the proprietor learned that Robert Hunter Morris had earned Halifax's disfavor because he approved of "during good behavior" judicial tenures in New Jersey. According to Halifax, Morris acted "in opposition to his Majesty's Commission" and therefore "must expect nothing from him."[103] In the same year, Penn heard that the Board of Trade rebuked New York's lieutenant governor for simply thinking he could grant a judicial act that changed the tenure of judges.[104] By December 1761, the Crown issued general instructions not to pass any bill that changed the tenure of judges "upon pain of being removed from your government."[105] In March 1762, the Crown followed through on its warnings after New Jersey's governor Josiah Hardy issued three commissions "during good behavior" and the secretary of state, on the "strong representation" of the Board of Trade, removed Hardy from his office.[106]

This cavalcade of events resulting in sharp retributions by the imperial government prompted Penn to make a strong declaration against "any such Bill" to the deputy governors. On the morning of March 6, 1762, Penn had a meeting with Undersecretary of State John Pownall where he learned of Governor Hardy's removal. Immediately after this meeting, Penn sent off a quick letter to Pennsylvania's deputy governor demanding a strict compliance with the general instructions issued by the Crown. He wanted the governor to "tell the Assembly positively that you have our directions not to pass any such Bill." In fact, Penn found that he did not want the deputy governor to "pass any Bill to regulate the Courts further," as the assembly "cannot want to regulate them but for bad purposes."[107]

The assembly could never reform the judiciary with the Board of Trade's report and the new Penn directions. Where the assembly faced difficulties before, at least there was room for compromise, however small.

After March 1762, there existed no such potential. The deputy governor made this point sufficiently clear the following January. In that month, the assembly tried again to reform the judiciary. Not only did the legislators angrily debate the bill within the legislative chamber for over a month, but their efforts came to nothing, as the deputy governor did not even send it back with proposed amendments; he simply vetoed it. Whatever "exigency or circumstance" compelled the passage of this bill did not matter; the deputy governor could not approve it.[108] He made similar declarations against attempts to reform the courts in 1764 and again in 1765.

The popular demand for the reform of the courts, growing more urgent as the century progressed, made Penn's instructions refusing any future reform of the courts untenable. Adding to the popular requests, Chief Justice William Allen regularly informed Penn of the inadequacies of the courts. In response to the urgent need for reform, Penn relented on his instructions a bit, allowing the deputy governors to approve bills that provided much-needed reform. However, Penn still maintained that any bill had to conform to the Board of Trade report by not changing the judges' tenure of office. Moreover, Penn demanded that the deputy governor could only approve a court bill if it maintained all executive power. In effect, Penn's new instructions, while providing the possibility of reform in theory, would never actually result in court reform in reality. The future good governance of the province was held hostage for points of power.

Struggles over executive prerogative thus continued. The battle over judicial reform in 1767 serves as an excellent example. On the heels of petitions demanding a bill to establish a supreme court circuit to better govern the province, the assembly and the deputy governor squabbled over particulars of a new bill and ultimately put together a piece of legislation that changed little in terms of a circuit court. The new bill added only one new justice to the supreme court, never stipulated a compulsory circuit, and augmented the fines for nonattendance of jurors and witnesses. In terms of the circuit court, the only aspect of the bill different from the 1722 act was that the assembly deleted the mandated dates for holding circuit courts in Chester and Bucks Counties (which the judges ignored anyway) and left the times, dates, and places for holding courts to the discretion of the judges. Such a change did not bode well for the circuit court. At the same time the assembly debated particulars of their "circuit bill," the chief justice wrote Thomas Penn that he could not undertake riding the circuit. Nor could Justice William Coleman travel on circuit, as he "would not travel." If left to the discretion of the chief justice or Justice Coleman, the high court would continue to conduct most of its business in the city of Philadelphia, and it did.[109]

During the debates over the "circuit bill," however, there existed a potential for significant reform. The deputy governor, now Thomas Penn's nephew, John Penn, offered two amendments to the bill on the advice of Chief Justice William Allen that would have brought important changes to the colonial court system by making the circuit mandatory and less burdensome on the supreme court judges, particularly the chief justice. In his first series of amendments, the deputy governor suggested an increase in the number of supreme court judges from three to five and the establishment of two circuit districts controlled by two judges each, and he mandated that the chief justice should remain in Philadelphia to handle cases there and offer advice, through post, to his associates on the road. The assembly, however, refused. Therefore, Penn sent a second set of amendments stipulating the assembly should establish that one supreme court judge could convene the high court in each county assisted by two local men "of ability and integrity" that the deputy governor would commission as deputies. Together, the deputy governor argued, a supreme court judge and his two deputies could carry out all the functions of the supreme court "for the complete execution of justice."[110]

In this instance, as in many others, neither side would relent and therefore nothing was accomplished. The assembly, "acting from interested motives," wanted to use the opportunity a circuit bill offered to oust proprietary supporters and "to have all offices filled by their own creatures," which the deputy governor would never approve.[111] Deputy Governor Penn, for his part, wanted to use the bill to augment executive influence through patronage by increasing the number of judges, which the assembly would never accept.[112] Nevertheless, the provincial government needed to pass a bill, as neither side could publicly come out against a circuit court or be charged with the responsibility for its derailment. As Allen noted, no side wanted to be "put in the wrong in the opinion of the whole province," as a circuit court was a popularly demanded reform.[113] The bill that the assembly and deputy governor passed, then, constituted a political artifice to save face in front of the populace and, as Deputy Governor Penn noted, was "so very inadequate to the purposes intended by it."[114]

Throughout the eighteenth century the assembly adhered to a simple political principle: if gaining significant reform or obtaining relief for the inhabitants required giving power to the executive (even powers legally belonging to the executive), the members would rather do nothing at all.

As the legislators argued in 1767 to their agents in London, they would rather "suffer all the Mischiefs, however great," than "give up a Point so absolutely necessary to their future Liberties" by granting power to the deputy governor.[115]

Likewise, on the other side of the Atlantic, it was Thomas Penn's duty to the Crown to "insist on . . . the Rights of Government," and "never give up the appointment of officers." Penn knew he had to uphold this simple principal on pain of royal disapproval.[116] Moreover, Pennsylvania's deputy governors were unequivocal as to their position and their duty to the Crown. As Deputy Governor John Penn noted in 1769, "the Governor, who is the King's Representative here," had a right, "by the English Constitution," to uphold the nomination and ultimately control of government "Officers, which is a Prerogative of the Crown."[117]

It was this mentality and struggle, on both sides, over prerogative and power that ultimately inhibited both the imperial and provincial government from addressing the needs of Pennsylvanians. Courts remained unreformed due to fights over executive power. Land records remained in a state of disarray because of a dispute over control of officials. Initiatives for defense came too little and too late due to arguments over the appointment of officers. Paper money bills were stymied while many inhabitants languished in prison due to the scarcity of cash to pay debts because the assembly wanted the sole right of appropriating public funds.[118] In many ways, the "stupendous Machine" had not moved much since the crowd gathered to see it in 1738.

4

"When the Thunder of the Law Sleeps"

Regulations for "Liberty and Law"

THE STRUGGLE OVER PREROGATIVE AND POWER that prohibited the government from addressing the needs and requests of its citizens had grave consequences. One lawyer and popular essayist, Isaac Hunt, who detested the "poisoning Fountain of Faction and Revenge," understood the potential disaster awaiting the colony.[1] He warned that "when the Thunder of the Law sleeps, or when Men are afraid to call for it (whether their Fears be well or ill grounded) they are easily led, to consider themselves as in the State of Nature; and to take the Remedy which the Laws of that state dictate."[2] Hunt was not alone. A young George Bryan also noted that many ordinary Pennsylvanians "look on themselves as deserted by the government here & seem to be setting up for themselves. Necessity indeed has no law."[3]

Both men wrote during a time when the confluence of imperial and provincial politics collided with the hard realities of war and ongoing, yet still jarring, societal transformations. It was a state in crisis. Over the previous twenty years, Pennsylvanians complained that governing institutions and their officers did not keep up with expansive societal changes and the ever-present reality of war. The military was nonexistent, courts were too far away, officers of the law too few, and many people judged the entire government, when it could not fix these problems, as broken, prejudicial, and even corrupt.[4]

By the 1760s, irritated colonists, as Hunt and Bryan imagined, had "waited long enough on government" and readily mobilized to police their own communities and correct the government if it did not work in the way expected, if the wheels of justice did not turn, or even worse, if the law seemed compromised, biased, or partial.[5] They banded together, meted out their own brand of justice, and justified their actions by criticizing the government for failing to uphold what they considered first principles and protecting the public. By relying upon themselves instead of the normal legal course of justice, Pennsylvanians showed a serious lack of confidence in the ability of the government to govern, undermining the reigning political order and transforming the colony's political dynamic forever.

The Paxton Boys, well-trodden ground in Pennsylvania's history, was the first important expression of this extralegal mobilization. Through their explosive actions, they embroiled the province in political turmoil that shone a spotlight on the inadequacies of the government and thereby paved the way for other inhabitants to take what they considered the law into their own hands. So complete was their association with the outbreak of popular justice in the 1760s that by the end of that decade most extrajudicial actions or violent challenges to the government were assumed their doing.[6] Even some riotous Virginians, the Augusta Boys, were rumored to be in league with the Paxton Boys. Within Pennsylvania, there were plenty of groups to label "Paxton Boys," and not all of them were frontiersmen, which shows the ubiquity of the crisis in the colony. There were black-faced regulators in Cumberland County, masked vigilantes in Bedford County, "Fair Play Men" who created their own government in Northumberland County, and "yellow wigs" and paramilitary vigilante groups in Chester County.[7] This chapter explores the actions and motivations of several of these popular assemblages, including the Paxton Boys in Lancaster County, the Black Boys in Cumberland and Bedford Counties, and the West Nottingham uprising of the "yellow wigs" in Chester County. Though the particular situations of each group and their targets differed, the underlying motivations for their actions did not. A crisis of law and governance served as the common thread in these episodes of popular justice where men and sometimes women took a shared set of political and legal principles to extremes.

Gathering Story: The Paxton Boys and the Violent Push for Reform

In the winter of 1763, an armed gang, known to history as the Paxton Boys, massacred peaceful Indians and then, at the height of their fury, marched on Philadelphia to murder still more and demand an overhaul of the provincial government. Their actions and their causes instantly transformed the political discourse of the province. Members and supporters of the Paxton Boys permeated the colony with political tracts and petitions elucidating a common set of grievances highlighting the sheer extent of perceived crisis in Pennsylvania and a budding move for governmental reform.

While some contemporaries, principally Benjamin Franklin, labeled the Paxton Boys merciless murderers motivated by racism, the members of that gang as well as their supporters obviously, though dishonestly or just blindly, disagreed. Matthew Smith, onetime leader of the Paxton Boys, believed "Necessity compelled us to do as we did." Lazarus Stewart, another ringleader, thought he acted "for the security of hundreds of settlers on the frontier." "No man, unless he were living at that time in Paxton," could pass judgment, as they "could have no idea of the sufferings and anxieties of the people." The "blood of a thousand of my fellow-creatures called for vengeance." Smith and Stewart insisted their actions were just, rational, and utterly necessary.[8]

Less than a month after that fatal event, John Elder, a Presbyterian minister and prominent local leader of inhabitants near Paxton, noted, "The storm which had been so long gathering, has, at length, exploded." Like Smith and Stewart, Elder viewed the actions of the Paxton Boys as the climax of a much older dispute over the government's failure to preserve the public peace while inhabitants experienced a significant amount of loss, devastation, and fear. The government, Elder argued, drove frontiersmen "to madness." Had it responded to their "urgent" pleas, "this painful catastrophe might have been avoided."[9]

The accounts of Smith, Stewart, and Elder offer important perspectives. While their fears and desires for protection were certainly a product of growing racial tensions on the frontier,[10] their actions, when viewed in the context of disorder and poor governance also show the significance of a general sense of "state crisis" to the movement. As Smith, Stewart, and Elder recognized, the event was the product of unimaginable wartime experiences and significant disillusionment with a government that didn't provide for a people in need. The event, from that angle, was part of an important phenomenon developing in Pennsylvania after midcentury when government and law broke down and colonists lost confidence in the government's ability to protect the public.

Frontier settlers' understanding of what they should expect from government and how they should respond if it didn't meet those expectations was crucially shaped by religion. The people living in and around

Paxton in Lancaster County were a religious lot. Most the inhabitants were recent immigrants. They were, mainly, Scots by ethnicity, Irish by birth, and devoted to the Presbyterian Church. In those churches, their ministers often conveyed a message that conflated civil, philosophical, theological, and ecclesiastical doctrines into a workable image of society and government. Their message was simple. God made man "a sociable creature, to promote not only his own but the *public Good*." Anyone who placed individual interests over community needs was guilty of "*Self-love*, which is criminal and vicious."[11] Since man was made for society, government, a product of man, reflected this public welfare mentality. Government acted for the "Publick Good," protecting the collective liberty of the community by being a "Terror to evil Doers & an Encouragment & Protection to all those who do well."[12]

This message, while promoting the rule of law, also sanctioned an underlying rebelliousness. "When man joins himself in civil society with others," one minister argued, "he, as well as every one with him, gives up his rights which he has naturally, to be regulated by the laws made by the society, and to which he consents; at least so far as his own safety, and that of the *rest of society*, shall require."[13] That limit, according to Reverend Gilbert Tennant, set the parameters of political obedience. If the government did not punish criminals and protect inhabitants from a foreign enemy it becomes "an empty Name, a meer *Cypher*, of no Moment and Consequence to Society" and so could not expect "Obedience."[14] Another minister, "Sounding the Trumpet of Liberty and Truth," argued people owed "*Caesar* the Things that are *Caesar's*," while Caesar upheld the "Agreement made when we threw off the State of Nature" for common protection. Therefore, "when I am not protected" the government could not expect submission, and this, for him, was "the Truth of Christ."[15]

Ministers also taught that people should act for the public good when government failed. While government protected and promoted liberty by upholding the duties individuals owed to the community, people could not sit idly by. As Reverend Elder lectured, "Liberty does not consist in an Absolute Indifference."[16] All people, a minister born in Paxton surmised, should "make use of such means as God and Nature hath put in our hands" for their common protection and safety.[17] If people did not use the "means in our power" when government did not "observe its original design," Minister John Carmichael argued, they "then tempt God, and rebel against his government."[18] As told by Presbyterian ministers, God sanctioned resistance and the forcible regulation of a failing government.[19] The politics of Pennsylvania, the breakdown of local government, and the experience of war tested this political theory.

Throughout the 1750s and 1760s, British North America experienced considerable disruption due to two wars that rocked the colonies. The first war pitted the British and their allies against the Bourbons of France and Spain, as well as Russia, Austria, Sweden, Saxony, and the Mughal Empire. In North America, the French and their powerful Indian allies were the principal antagonists. The second war erupted in the wake of the first. Instead of a struggle between European nations, this second war found the British confronting a confederation of over a dozen Native American polities loosely led by the Ottawa war chief, Pontiac. Both wars brought with them a significant amount of loss, devastation, and ruin.

During the early years of the French and Indian War and most of Pontiac's, the Pennsylvania frontier was a war zone. "Our Country," a contemporary wrote from Fort Augusta, "is now become a Land of Murder & Rapine."[20] Lurid scenes dominated the letters of inhabitants, military men, and the public papers. In a typical report, Captain George Mercer recounted that just outside Shippensburg he came across an inhabitant "kill'd & his body inhumanly mangled, and his wifes tracts going off with the tracts of an Indian on each side & the House burn'd."[21] Likewise, the public newspapers published letters from the frontier with visceral descriptions of mutilated bodies with their intestines ripped out and their hearts missing.[22] In conversations and in the press, inhabitants learned of the slaughter of colonial families—women and children, husband and wives, aged and lame. Homes lay waste, farms were decimated, and families were scattered, captured, or killed.[23]

The brutality of war and the extensiveness of suffering hardened the minds of many colonists against all Native peoples. The grisly scenes of war, the grotesque mutilated bodies, the misery of the fleeing settlers witnessed, lived, and experienced by people and expressed, most often exaggerated, by writers in private and in public produced what historian Peter Silver calls an "anti-Indian sublime." This language and imagery were also magnetic; they brought people together to commiserate in their common suffering and deepened the lines between "white people" and "bloody Savages."[24] It also strained the relationship between colonists and the government.

The way colonists described Native American warfare elucidates just how far the war years strained that relationship. Colonists rarely labeled Native American warfare as anything other than "murder." While such a distinction surely helped colonists separate themselves from "the other," though they would often use the same tactics against their Native enemies (and even their friends), labeling Indian warfare as "murder" escalated the gravity of grievances and influenced how some Pennsylvanians understood the ability of the government to provide the proper functions it owed to the governed. Indian war, or at least the reporting of and gossip about it, shocked Euro-Americans. Schooled in the law of nations by European thinkers such as Hugo Grotius and Emerich de Vattel, American colonists consistently declared that while women and children could be enemies, they should not be the focus of war. Noncombatants were supposedly off limits, and Indian war sharply contrasted with this ideal.[25] For many colonists, a steady stream of reports describing dead families and "mangled Carcasses" did not equal casualties of war; they were victims of merciless murderers.[26] This shift of nomenclature marks a psychological state of mind that altered the severity of grievances. Seeking governmental protection from murderers considerably differed from appeals for defense initiatives against a foreign enemy. Labeling Indian war murder, therefore criminal, put the martial wherewithal of the province as well as the ability of the government to offer basic necessities into question. The government, even outside the spectrum of war, proved, to many inhabitants, incapable of protecting the public good.

The provincial government offered Pennsylvanians ample opportunities to experience such governmental shortcomings. Inhabitants routinely requested that "protection be provided for their borders."[27] They wanted the government to arrange "for the Safety and Gard of the frontiers" because they believed it hard "to have not only our Lives Endangered but also to have our Building, Stock, and all our Crops Wholly Destroyed."[28] They urged the government to drop the internal political disputes to "unite in the Fear of the Almighty God" and "take such Ways and Measures as may be most agreeable to his divine Will, for our Preservation in this Time of imminent Danger."[29] Nevertheless, "They received empty promises and had to remain exposed to the plunder of the enemy."[30] One small farmer thought, "The Degree of Care that our government heath for the Back parts of the province I am afread will appear more affuly ere Long."[31]

The failure of the government to respond incensed many inhabitants. In Paxton, John Elder expressed this exasperation: "Such shocking accounts we frequently receive, and tho' we are careful to transmit 'em to Philadelphia & Remonstrate and petition time after time, yet to no purpose; So that we seem to be given up into the hands of a merciless Enemy."

He complained that Indians daily "murdered" or captured inhabitants while "unreasonable Debates between the two parts of our Legislature" discouraged a "probable Scheme for the Protection of the Province and the preservation of its Inhabitants."[32]

While the assembly and deputy governor ensconced themselves in political factions, ordinary Pennsylvanians looked on in disbelief as neither side seemed to represent their interests. The problem of faction became so acute that inhabitants demonstrated their opposition to both sides in violent protests. In 1756, residents of the "Back Counties" resolved to meet in Lancaster and "proceed to this City, to make some Demands of the Legislature now sitting."[33] Another group warned that they would "tear the whole members of the legislative body Limb from Limb, if they did not grant immediate Protection."[34] Even the eastern counties expressed their anger. Over "2000 inhabitants" from Chester County prepared "to come to Philadelphia . . . to compel the *Governor* and the *Assembly* to agree to pass Laws to defend the County and oppose the enemy."[35] Not long after, between three hundred and seven hundred German inhabitants trudged to Philadelphia and took "the Bodies of some of their Countrymen who had been just scalped by the Indians, and threw them at the *Stadt-House* Door, cursing the *Quakers* Principles, and bidding the Committee of Assembly to behold the Fruits of their Obstinacy."[36]

In sum, war engendered distrust and confusion. Settlers, stoked by garish stories of Indian "murder," suspected all Indians of harboring some malevolent design and conveyed a similar cynicism about the provincial government. By the early 1760s, inhabitants did not think the government would or could protect them from either external or internal threats to the common good. Deep distrust of an unresponsive government and the hatred of Indians made for a combustible mixture, one easily ignited.

The conflagration came soon enough. As war enveloped the countryside during Pontiac's War, frontier inhabitants turned their sights to those peaceful Indians living among them. After the "murder" of several people near the Moravian Indian missions in 1763, for example, settlers pinned the crime on the local Christian Indians. Frontier inhabitants also mistrusted the peaceful Indians of Conestoga, who had lived in harmony with Pennsylvanians since the colony's inception. During the French and Indian War, inhabitants near Lancaster suspected the duplicity of this small group. Some colonists came to believe the Conestoga Indians harbored unsavory characters who supported the enemy and that at least one of them, Will Sock, was a murderer. Suspicion of Sock proved damaging for the Conestoga community. As historian James Merrell notes, "Most thought Sock a treacherous killer, his home town the enemy's lair." These peaceful Indians who made a livelihood selling homemade brooms and baskets now feared "to go any distance to sell their wares, as people began to threaten them with what was likely to be their fate."[37] Whether the Conestoga Indians and Will Sock were a real threat or not made little difference. People around Paxton imagined them as such and so the threat posed by the small group to their common security represented reality. As Francis Hutcheson so aptly stated about human behavior in his *System of Moral Philosophy*, "Whoever imagines himself miserable, he is so in fact, while this imagination continues."[38]

Inhabitants initially turned to the government for help and protection from this supposedly murderous tribe. Frightened inhabitants demanded the "Basket & Broommaking Bandittey" removed, and those suspected of "murder" brought to justice.[39] People in the backcountry had "frequently, but without success, urged" the government to remove the Indians.[40] The Conestoga, well aware of such ill will and the potential for violence, also requested governmental protection. Sheehays, a Conestoga elder, reminded the deputy governor that they "have always lived in Peace and Quietness with our Brethren & Neighbours round us during the last & present Indian Wars" and now needed the government's "favour and protection."[41] Although settlers and the Conestoga appealed to the government for defense, neither received it.

Frontiersmen, trying to make sense of what they considered glaring unresponsiveness, used the political language they best understood. The government should preserve the public good, and it should attend to the security and protection of the whole; anything less equaled a breach of trust. Frontiersmen found the cause for such a violation not just in Quaker pacifism but in the popularly understood self-interest of prominent officials who threatened the security of the public for the sake of an Indian trade that lined their pockets. As Elder noted, the "minds of the Inhabitants are so exasperated" because a "particular set of men, deeply concerned in the Government" put their private interests before the community's. Frontiersmen despised the "Singular Regards they have always shown to Savages" to support the Indian trade for the benefit of "individuals" without "any prospect of advantage to his Majesty or to the province."[42] Lazarus Stewart thought mercantile self-interest undermined the province's ability to offer military protection and the value of local legal structures. Accentuated by his racial animosity toward all Native

Americans and his negative view of the colonial government, Stewart argued that it was a "notorious fact" that local courts, controlled by interested men, did not represent colonial interests, as they "secured from punishment" all those Native Americans who "treacherously murdered" families on the frontier.[43] Such was the inhabitants' "unhappy Situation, under the Villany, Infatuation and Influence of a certain Faction that have got the political Reigns in their Hands and tamely tyrannize over the other good Subjects of the Province!"[44]

From this perspective, the whole purpose of the present government proved flawed, fundamentally off center. The government supported the interest of a few instead of the needs of the province. While people in the east "ate, drank, and were merry," frontier inhabitants suffered the ravages of war and "murder" without the help of government. The military arm of the government proved insufficient and the legal system compromised, leaving the frontier exposed to external enemies and internal threats. Frontier inhabitants, believing they had "waited long enough on government," now left "our cause with our God, and our guns."[45] Pursuing what they considered "lawless murderers" and "imbittered Enemies," anywhere from fifty to one hundred mounted men "equipped for murder" (a striking irony) cruelly decimated the Conestoga Indians in Lancaster County.[46]

The government's actions following the Conestoga Massacre further inflamed the minds of frontier inhabitants and strengthened the extralegal movement. Because many frontiersmen considered the Christian Moravian Indians in Northampton "known murderers," the deputy governor moved them to Philadelphia under the watchful eye of a small detachment of Royal Highlanders. The government's outward protection of Indians that many thought were "concerned in recent murders" exacerbated tensions in the province and swelled the ranks of the Paxton Boys.[47] Emboldened by numbers, the Paxton Boys marched on Philadelphia to either kill all the Indians in the city or remove those they suspected of murder. If the scene at Lancaster is any sign of their design, they intended the former rather than the latter. In addition, the Paxton Boys, now believing they represented all the frontier counties, sought to use that representation as leverage to force an overhaul of the provincial government.

The Paxton Boys, however, never made it to Philadelphia. While at Germantown, they learned that General Thomas Gage had sent the king's troops to guard the Indians in the city. They also discovered that the deputy governor had read the Riot Act, and the streets bustled with half-cocked citizen-soldiers. Supposedly, even younger Quakers took up arms in the defense of the city. The deputy governor and assembly, looking to stave off the effusion of blood or even worse and just as likely, civil war, sent a delegation to Germantown to deal with the rioters. News that the city was under arms and the delegation's promise to redress frontier grievances quieted the Paxton Boys and ended their design of entering the city. Instead of fighting their way through Philadelphia, the angry frontiersmen presented the deputy governor and assembly two petitions, one penned before they entered Germantown, and the other composed by Matthew Smith and James Gibson while in town.

In these two petitions, the Paxton Boys articulated grievances and initiatives for reform that agreed with their vision of the proper role and responsibility of government to uphold the public welfare. The requests of the Paxton Boys did not exclusively focus on the defense of the frontier but highlighted important and long-standing animosities that were at once political, legal, and martial. The disgruntled frontiersmen rebuked the legislature as unrepresentative and unresponsive, blasted the judicial system as inadequate and corrupted by special interest, and condemned the negligible martial power of the colony. In sum, they argued, the frontier had been "neglected by the Public." To correct this situation, they demanded equal political representation in the assembly for frontier counties, the reform of the judicial system to bring the courts closer to the people for fair and regular trials, and the institution of wartime measures, principally a bounty on scalps and the reinforcement of frontier forts.[48]

The actions and grievances of the Paxton Boys inspired a large-scale push for reform. People from all over the colony sent petitions to the government. At the heart of those petitions rested the salient notion that government should work for and represent the whole people. Self-interest, petitioners exclaimed, destroyed government. With that vision of government in mind, petitioners demanded equal representation in the legislature, a restructuring of the county and supreme courts, new policies and officers to regulate the local economy, and defense initiatives. These reforms would finally make the government work for more than just "a Part of the Inhabitants." As over twelve hundred petitioners from Cumberland County put it, the structure of government, both provincially in the legislature and locally in law, favored the few and left the many to suffer, which "inconsistency" inflamed "the Minds of his Majesty's other good Subjects," increased "public Disturbances," and threw "the province into the most violent Convulsions."[49] The actions of the Paxton

Boys unleashed a popular hostility to the established government, provided a common language of opposition, and paved the way for further extralegal mobilizations. They opened a Pandora's box.

Law and Government in Their Hands: The Black Boys' Regulation

Less than a year after the turmoil over the Paxton Boys, Deputy Governor John Penn and General Thomas Gage received reports of armed men who disguised their faces with black paint in Cumberland County, Lancaster County, and near the Monongahela River. Mixed groups of "Irish, English, Dutch and Welch" patrolled the countryside inspecting trade goods and rifling through official mail "from the Potomack to the Kittatinney hill."[50] To the dismay of many government officials like Penn and Gage, this disguised "banditti" policing the Indian trade and the mail quickly enlarged the scope of their movement. Like the Regulators of North Carolina, these black-faced men, popularly known as the Black Boys, targeted imperial policy, the provincial government, and a legal system they considered inadequate to their needs and unrepresentative of their interests.[51] They attacked unscrupulous traders, threatened local justices of the peace, kidnapped British officials, besieged imperial forts, and manipulated legal structures to meet their needs. The regulation of the Black Boys, some thought, was the Paxton Boys returned.[52] While not accurate in reality, the link makes sense. Not only did these groups mobilize within a year of each other, but they both were a response to and result of a local, provincial, and imperial crisis of governance that, by the mid-1760s, dominated much of the public dialogue.

Their initial leader, James Smith, a well-known Presbyterian in the backcountry, had been captured by the Mohawks in 1759 when a teenager. After his return home and amid another war, he and other westerners were angered by the blatant self-interest of a few who traded with the Indians during wartime. Frontier settlers were also angry at the government. It seemed as if provincial and imperial officials discounted the law and the people's welfare to support the unlawful trade. The Black Boys, then, believed they had to work outside the "channel of the civil law" because they received "no assistance from the state."[53]

Echoing these sentiments in verse, George Campbell, an Irish emigrant from Dublin, cast the Black Boys as "brave souls" who acted "for their king and their country's good" at a time of governmental negligence.

The song highlights many grievances of the people, their motivations for extralegal actions, and where the Black Boys fit in the larger political context of colonial Pennsylvania after the Paxton affair. Using language and ideas similar to the proponents of the Paxton Boys a year earlier, Campbell applauded those "patriot souls" who triumphed over a "party interest" that "strove what it cou'd to profit itself by public blood." This "party interest" represented the contentious and nepotistic politics of Pennsylvania and pinpointed how some Pennsylvanians viewed it.[54] Where the assembly and deputy governor judged their fight a constitutional struggle, others considered it a contest for power and self-interest, a "quarrelling for straws" for friends and kin.[55] This competition for power and place threatened the people's liberty as it unbalanced the government in favor of a few to the harm of the many. In Campbell's song, the Black Boys served as patriots who righted this wrong by preserving the law for "their country's good."[56]

The Black Boys believed they upheld the law in part because of the king's Proclamation of 1763. The proclamation, well known to history for its creation of a geographic dividing line that marked the limits of Euro-American settlement and Indian country, also, as Smith later remembered, banned "any person from trading with the Indians, until further orders."[57] According to the proclamation, any person who wanted to partake in the Indian trade needed to receive a license from the deputy governor. Potential traders also needed to "give Security to observe such Regulations" as the Crown thought fit. Additional stipulations outlawed traders from plying their wares out of defined regions and specified forts and forbade trade with all but allied Indians. During Pontiac's War, the Crown placed a moratorium on the Indian trade. Only the governors could reopen the trade when they judged it safe to do so.[58]

Nevertheless, within a year of the proclamation "such quantities of [illegal] goods" daily made their way to the frontier.[59] Large firms looking to corner the market of the lucrative Indian trade in the Illinois Country vied for passes or even semiofficial backing. In Philadelphia, the firm of Baynton, Wharton, and Morgan did just that. The firm received the legally questionable backing of George Croghan, the deputy superintendent of Indian affairs, and became the first and near exclusive traders to the Illinois Country.

Under instructions from General Thomas Gage, Croghan was to make his way to the Illinois Country and "Engage some of the Principal Chiefs" in a bid for peace. Gage also directed Croghan to procure supplies for the troops and "such presents as shall be necessary for your Expedition."[60] Under these orders and using passes from Colonel Henry Bouquet, Croghan contracted with Baynton, Wharton, and Morgan for supplies, gifts, and, importantly, Indian trade goods. Croghan went beyond his official orders because he expected peace and believed opening the Indian trade would solidify reconciliation by showing goodwill; he also stood to make a pretty penny. Sweetening the pot for the firm, Croghan told Baynton that if he promptly shipped the goods "he would purchase of him preferable to any other."[61]

Regardless of the motivations, such conduct was, as General Thomas Gage argued, "Contrary to Law."[62] Colonel Henry Bouquet condemned Croghan's "dark cloud" of "new and strange management" as the pass he gave Croghan "extends only to such Presents as he might want for the Execution of his Orders."[63] Gage, equally miffed, supposed "Many Pretences will be made and Story's told to conceal the truth, but it appears pretty plain" that Croghan and the mercantile firm sent the goods to "open the Trade at Fort Pitt before Permission should be given."[64] An irritated Deputy Governor Penn assumed the contract for the Crown to supply the expedition served as "a Cover for a private Concern."[65]

Equally angered, frontier inhabitants demanded the government act against the illegal trade. In a long petition to Deputy Governor Penn, Cumberland County residents wrote of their "alarming apprehensions" that they would experience a long and destructive war because of "the unseasonable supplies of cloathing & warlike stores" to the Indians. Such a trade defied "all the laws of God & man," as a few men "bent upon enriching themselves" threatened the welfare of the public. They begged Penn to "interpose your Authority" and bring to justice those people "who contrary to his Majesties royal proclamation & that of his officers, as well as to the laws of Great Britain, are concerned in this unlawful commerce with our enemies." If Penn did not act, "the People" might foment "disagreeable disorders."[66]

Such supplications did little. Pennsylvania's government, lacking a militia or any sort of coercive power, could not stop the illegal trade. Nor did the empire have enough officers to enforce regulations. Sir William Johnson, superintendent of Indian affairs, consistently noted that "additional officers . . . for the Department are very much wanting, and in fact there is no doing without them," as traders, despite the proclamation, used "every artifice to trade where they please without being restricted."[67] With an incapacitated government, Cumberland valley residents watched as Croghan's Philadelphia firm confidently sent "a number of waggons loaded with Indian goods, and warlike stores" into the backcountry unchallenged by the government.[68]

The traders also felt assured that their goods would make it to Indian country because of the extensive local and official networks Croghan and the firm cultivated. Croghan and Baynton, Wharton, and Morgan partnered with a Cumberland County justice of the peace, Robert Callender. A large mill owner, militia captain, and successful fur trader, Callender had substantial local, provincial, and imperial connections. He was the son-in-law of the surveyor general, a regular correspondent with Pennsylvania's deputy governors as well as General Thomas Gage, and a close friend of Colonel Henry Bouquet. During the Seven Years' War, he served as a captain in the First Battalion under Cumberland County justice of the peace Lieutenant Colonel John Armstrong, with fellow justice of the peace John McKnight. Additionally, he had business and friendly ties with Justice James Maxwell and sheriff and justice of the peace John Holmes, all of whom played a role in the movement of goods to the Illinois Country.[69]

Working with local elites like Callender protected the goods from the prying eyes of some local officers. County justices of the peace had a duty to uphold imperial laws such as the Proclamation of 1763 and to aid the deputy governor, who had not yet opened the Indian trade. Partnering with a local magistrate and the firm's stature in elite political circles in Philadelphia assured the complicity or apathy of some of those prominent county officers. Justice John Armstrong and Sheriff John Holmes, for instance, knew of the undertaking and sympathized with the grievances of the frontier inhabitants but, most likely because of their connections to prominent provincial officials and their friendship with Callender, did little to deter the trade.

While Armstrong's and Holmes's inertia suggests tacit acquiescence, some officials were more forward in their involvement. Justice James Maxwell actually worked with Callender to move the trade goods. Callender wrote Maxwell in December that a "quantity of goods were soon to be sent up to Conecocheague and that he should want pack horses," men, and storehouses to transport the goods to Fort Pitt. Cementing official collusion in the illicit trade, the two justices worked together to hide over a quarter ton of gunpowder and four or five horse loads of lead, some of which they concealed in Maxwell's barn when they heard of the hostility brewing in the valley.[70] Official complicity in the illegal trade served as a significant source of contention for Cumberland County residents.

Only one local justice of the peace, William Smith, the brother-in-law of James Smith, proved willing to actively deter the trade. Nevertheless, Smith did not completely work within the law to discourage the trade; rather, he encouraged the people of the valley to regulate the illicit traders. Smith most likely realized that with extensive political connections, Robert Callender, George Croghan, and Baynton, Wharton, and Morgan would never receive a fair trial, especially since it would involve provincial and imperial officials, thus ushering in all the power of patronage interests. There was much truth in such a realization. Though prominent men in power, such as Thomas Gage, William Johnson, Henry Bouquet, and John Penn, considered the trade illegal, they did little more than exchange angry words and inquire into the affair. They never contemplated legal action or punishment. That Justice Smith, commanded to uphold the king's law, encouraged extralegal measures is telling.

The Smith brothers found it easy to mobilize people in the valley. The passage of a large convoy of Indian trade goods, contrary to law, without legal opposition confirmed that many in the government had little interest in their concerns.[71] This instance was not the first time valley inhabitants experienced this hard reality. Just two years earlier, residents of Great Cove and Conococheague, believing themselves "in very imminent Danger," asked the assembly to fund a group of rangers commanded by James Smith. The assembly unanimously rejected the request, and, petitioners later fumed, "the *Indians* fell on the Inhabitants of the *Great Cove*, and butchered and carried into Captivity some of the Settlers, while the rest were compelled to abandon their Habitations, and are now in great Distress and Poverty, becoming a Burden to their Neighbours and Friends." The "Compassion of the House" could have saved them from this painful tragedy.[72]

With this negligence seared into their memory, armed and disguised men, scattered in pairs over "forty rod" waited for the more than eighty packhorses to snake their way into Great Cove. When the convoy reached them, the Black Boys opened fire on the horses, threatening one man that they would "blow his brains out." Within moments, they waylaid the convoy and destroyed the goods.[73] A few days later, disguised men with blackened faces broke into Justice Maxwell's home, searched his house and barns, found the hidden gunpowder, and destroyed it.[74] With signature bravado, James Smith remarked, "We then heard nothing of these trader's merriment or burlesque."[75]

During this initial stage of the movement, the Black Boys, though acting extralegally, tried to work with rather than against the law and hoped that the government would recognize that fact. Nevertheless, they found that however hard they tried, they could not make the government acknowledge their extralegal actions as in any way rooted in law. Later events powerfully proved this point, making all lawful authority appear partial, unjust, and obsolete. The resulting dilemma threw the province into deeper turmoil and further divided the people from the government, both imperial and provincial. By 1769, the breach seemed beyond repair. No amount of ointment could cure the ills of governance, and the people stood ever ready to enforce their will and act as a check on what they viewed as corrupted government.

The provincial government certainly fostered this negative image. After the events near Great Cove, Deputy Governor Penn did not act as the inhabitants hoped. Instead of recognizing that the frontiersmen tried to uphold the law, he held an inquest to scrutinize the activities and involvement of Justice William Smith. To the Black Boys' dismay, Justice Smith, who had tried to cloak their actions in legal garb, had failed miserably in the process. Equally unsettling, Deputy Governor Penn asked for Justice Maxwell's help to investigate Smith and even used Maxwell's testimony as sufficient evidence to remove Smith from his office. It was a peculiar and bewildering scenario. Those traders who Penn earlier argued acted contrary to law never received formal punishment, not even a reprimand. Justice Smith, on the other hand, who tried to uphold the law, had to travel to Philadelphia and undergo impeachment proceedings where a JP complicit in the trade served as one of the primary witness.[76] "Governor Penn," inhabitants later argued, "turned against us."[77]

The imperial government similarly seemed to support the illegal traders and corrupt local officials. British officers, siding with the traders, refused to recognize the Black Boys' legal arguments, considering them common robbers and a lawless banditti. Thomas Gage summed up the official reaction to the Black Boys when he argued that "the gallows must be the fate of many of them."[78] To make matters worse, Lieutenant Charles Grant, commander of a nearby British garrison at Fort Loudon, worked with Justices Maxwell and Callender to punish the "rioters" under the color but not the rule of the law. As Maxwell later sheepishly pointed out, they issued no writs when they captured and imprisoned suspected Black Boys. For example, on the night of March 7, Justices Maxwell and Callender as well as two of their associates burst into the house of suspected Black Boy Rees Porter, ransacked it for evidence, tied him up, and dragged him to jail at Fort Loudon.[79] In addition, a detachment of the Forty-Second Regiment of Highlanders, stationed at Fort Loudon, hauled six more suspected Black Boys to the fort. This was a new and, many colonists argued, dangerous innovation. Typically, British soldiers left civilian affairs alone and relied on local officials to carry out arrests. Now officials and soldiers worked together without true "civil authority" in the form of official writs to punish frontiersmen for stopping a convoy carrying illegal goods.[80]

The imprisonment of suspected Black Boys by illegal traders, justices of the peace, and royal troops combined with the later removal of William Smith from office exacerbated tensions and altered the Black Boys' movement. They no longer sought to deal through and with lawful authority. They tried to use Justice Smith's official status to secure legal formality, but events in 1765 and 1766 challenged the usefulness of such an approach and highlighted the inadequacy and complicity of the government. As a result, the Black Boys moved beyond the Indian trade and set themselves up as regulators of the government in the valley. They waylaid the mail, controlled the movement of troops and citizens, intimidated officials, and manipulated local and provincial legal structures. In an advertisement, which mocked government and served as a crass lampoon, they bragged that they could do "what we pleas for we have Law and Government in Our hands."[81] So complete was their takeover that one onlooker noted that Pennsylvania had "two kinds of Governments on the East and West . . . that to the West is Absolutely Republic" as the frontier settlers "are all Governors, and Claim a Superintendancy over the Whole."[82]

With that power, James Smith and near two hundred men surrounded Fort Loudon to release prisoners and bring corrupt officials to task. Justices Maxwell and Callender, in the fort, panicked because the Black Boys "openly avowed their design of rescuing the said prisoners and taking the Lives of this deponent [Maxwell] and the said Callender." The Black Boys' intimidation tactics had great effect. Maxwell and Callender, in an extraordinary turn of events, released the prisoners to the armed leader, James Smith, irritating the commander of the fort, Lieutenant Charles Grant, who refused to give the prisoners their weapons. The event left such an indelible mark on the mind of Maxwell that, "understanding that some threats had been made of doing him a personal injury," he "did not think proper to go among" the people—for good reason, as the Black Boys continued to harass the justice. One night they came "armed and disguised" to his home and demanded that he appear before them; Maxwell hid in fear.[83]

The Black Boys threatened and punished other provincial and imperial officers they considered corrupt. They threatened George Croghan to the extent that he was afraid to run the "unnecessary Risque" of traveling beyond Lancaster without a detachment of troops to protect him.[84] The Black Boys also targeted Lieutenant Charles Grant who, James Smith argued, unlawfully used his military power to apprehend suspected criminals and detain their private property, their guns. Smith additionally charged Grant and several other royal officers with receiving large bribes to shield the illegal trade.[85] Unlike their dealings with Croghan, the Black Boys actually kidnapped Grant and dragged him "into the Woods" where they taunted him with their plans to carry him "away into the Mountains & keep me there & that in the mean time the Country wou'd Rise & take the Fort by force of Arms." With renewed threats of tying him to a tree and leaving him for dead, they convinced Grant to "give Security" to surrender the weapons he still kept in the fort.[86] In this instance, as in many others, the Black Boys followed their own legal procedure. They demanded "security," issued commissions, and handed out trade passes, all legal documents. By using a kind of legal formality, the Black Boys made themselves a governing body granted quasi-sovereignty through its foundation in the will of the people.[87]

With popular backing, the Black Boys exercised near complete control of the valley. They effectively cut off Fort Loudon and Fort Pitt from the outside world and kept themselves abreast of all developments in the valley. Lawful passes and proclamations from government officials now had no weight. "The Solders of the garrison," a colonel complained, "are not safe to go any where about their Lawfull affairs by a Pass from their own Officer."[88] When a group of men refused to surrender liquor and gunpowder they carried under a pass from Colonel John Reid, the regulators "tied them up and floghed them severely, killed five of their horses, wounded two more, and burnt all their saddles."[89] The Black Boys also "plunder'd Liquors and Necessarys going up for the Officers, tho with a Pass" from Captain Murray, and now the officers "are reduced to drink Water," never good in a garrisoned fort.[90] Beyond trade goods, the Black Boys also stripped troops and other official runners naked and tied them to trees in the search of letters and dispatches. No person was "safe from their Insults."[91] The regulators, Thomas Gage argued, acted "without any reserve, and with as much Confidence as if their Actions had been legal and Warrantable, keeping Regular Scouts and Guards upon the Roads."[92]

Though the high-water mark of the movement occurred between 1765 and late 1766, the Black Boys exercised considerable control over the valley well into the late 1760s.[93] For example, one citizen noted in 1768 that the "The Black Boys" were still very much active and that he heard plans that they intended to do some harm to George Croghan. In recognition of the Black Boys' continued power in the country, the citizen refused to sign his name to the letter and implored his correspondent not to tell anyone where he received this information; "Otherwise I shall be altogether unsafe in my Family and Property."[94]

Despite all of this violence and intimidation, the government proved ill-equipped to deal effectively with the Black Boys. In large part, that inability had to do with the utter magnitude of the movement. The Black Boys did not just regulate trade, but they had enough coercive power to manipulate the law and bend the courts to their will. In 1765, for instance, Deputy Governor Penn traveled to Carlisle to gather depositions to prosecute some of the Black Boys, especially James Smith. Penn believed that through his presence he could garner plenty of evidence for prosecution, a reasonable assumption considering that Justice James Maxwell had previously taken several depositions in which men such as packhorse driver Robert Allison named several members of the Black Boys. When Penn reached Carlisle, however, intimidation and fear had altered memories. Alison now had no clue who was "concerned in the said outrage."[95] Similarly, Justice Maxwell only related that the rioters spoke German. Maxwell's friend, Richard Brownson, who had been at Maxwell's house when the Black Boys destroyed the hidden gunpowder, declared they came from Maryland and therefore were not those men under indictment.[96] With this evidence, the grand jury ruled there was "not sufficient testimony to convict a single person charged."[97] Penn, in despair, argued he could do little because of the "extreme weakness of government and the resolution of those desparate people, who it seems are determined at all events to oppose the authority of the Magistrates."[98]

That spirit of opposition ossified divisions in the valley. On one side stood the Black Boys, representing a bulk of the population, and on the other the government. This division furthered the distinctions between the people's perceived interests and the government's, undermining whatever remaining respect ordinary people had for the law and those who upheld it. If the government acted contrary to what inhabitants expected, they either took matters into their own hands or forced compliance. Either way, the people of the valley stood ready to mobilize at a moment's notice to check the government and enforce their own conception of the public welfare.

Events in 1769 proved that point. With renewed threats of Indian war, the Black Boys took to the roads and commenced their inspection regime, stopping traders, and demanding obedience and acceptance of their authority. Sometime in early September, royal troops and justices of the peace caught some of the men and imprisoned them in Fort Bedford. Like what happened in 1765, "James Smith, Thomas Paxton, and one Jameson . . . all Blackened on their Faces in the same Manner as the Rest of the Black Boys" took over the fort and released the prisoners.[99] Emboldened by their escape, the Black Boys continued to regulate the Indian trade. Interestingly, they especially targeted Justice Robert Callender, who again partnered with local magistrates and royal troops to trade with the Indians.[100]

The violence at Fort Bedford and the persistent plundering of Callender's goods escalated tensions in the backcountry. Rumors swirled around the province that "the *Black Boys* intended" to attack one of Callender's pack trains heading out to the Alleghany Mountains. To deter the regulators, Callender put his goods under the care of royal troops and kept official guards on the roads. When Justice John Holmes, a longtime friend and business associate of Callender, encountered James Smith and two other men during his rounds, he hurriedly made his way straight to Callender and "gave an alarm."[101]

On the order of Justices Holmes and Callender, four armed men caught up with Smith and "immediately pulled out their pistols" and demanded he come with them peacefully or he "was a dead man." Smith refused, presented his rifle, and in the intensity of the moment two shots rang out and Smith's traveling companion lay dead. The justices' four men charged Smith with murder, clasped him in irons, and imprisoned him in Fort Bedford. With Smith ensconced in jail, Justice Holmes assembled an official inquest, which included himself and one of the very men he summoned to capture Smith. Obviously, the inquest declared Smith "guilty of willful murder." Fearing inhabitants would conduct a rescue, local officials then sent Smith "privately through the wilderness to Carlisle, where" they laid him "in heavy irons."[102]

Frontiersmen quickly labeled official actions as "beyond all Bounds of the Law or Government" and complained that the inquest "was not so fair as it ought to be." Reports also reached the backcountry that the government conspired with the traders to move Smith from Carlisle for an unfair trial at the supreme court in Philadelphia. The whole affair, ex-justice William Smith told the public, was a "truly unlawful and tyrannical" "scheme" concocted by interested men to undermine the "Liberties of Englishmen."[103] Such rumors were readily believed because the Black Boys exacerbated the political divisions in the colony after the Paxton affair. Inhabitants did not trust the government, and therefore any notion of official corruption, no matter how absurd or trivial, had the aura of truth; the divide was too wide for anything else.

To ensure the government did not carry out its prejudicial designs, over 150 inhabitants blackened their faces and marched on Carlisle. According to several accounts, the marchers intended to force a "fair" local trial and short of that, to rescue Smith from jail. One correspondent from Carlisle noted that "a large Party of armed and disguised Men, were within ten Miles of this Town, in order to take the Prisoner out of this Gaol, alleging that we wou'd send him to Philadelphia." "To prevent the Effusion of Blood," officials guaranteed that Smith would receive a fair trial in the county.[104]

Even with these assurances, the inhabitants refused to disperse. In fact, over the course of a few days, the mob grew in number. The reinvigorated Black Boys situated "spies on every Road" to assure the government upheld their agreement. They proved their willingness to act and their continued apprehension that Smith "would not get a fair trial" when a large group "rushed into Town" demanding his release.[105] A severe lack of confidence in the provincial government pushed people to such extremes. They had no faith that the government would conduct a fair trial without collective action and intimidation.

Their efforts, as they had in 1765, prevailed, forcing the deputy governor to call for a special court of oyer and terminer in Cumberland County. In addition, the Black Boys applied enough pressure on local officials to force another coroner's inquest. Many Cumberland County inhabitants believed the first inquest was unjust, carried out by the "opposite party," who would use any artifice to secure Smith's prosecution.[106] William Denny, the coroner of Cumberland County, had to travel to Bedford, exhume the victim's body and reexamine it with a new jury made up of men from the valley. On examining the body, the inspectors discovered the cloth around the bullet hole had burn marks, intimating that someone shot him at close range. Based on this discovery and testimony about Smith's distance from the victim, the new inquest judged Smith not guilty.[107]

At the trial, the supreme court judges tried to evade any use of contrary evidence so Smith would be "severely prosecuted." The judges acted, according to Smith, in a "very unjust and arbitrary manner" and "rejected several of my evidences." However, the judges had to use both official inquests, and therefore, with the second coroner's inquest and some "corroborating evidence," the jury judged Smith "NOT GUILTY." Visibly annoyed, Chief Justice Allen lashed out and "declared that not one of this jury should ever hold any office above a constable."[108] His anger stemmed from the fact that the applied pressure of a mobilized and politically charged people suspicious of the government's motivations trumped official, and in Allen's view, legitimate opinion.

Looking out at the colony from his quarters in New York City, Thomas Gage remarked bitterly that "the Factions in the Government of Pennsylvania, if it can be called a Government, seemed to have favored the Infamous Riots of the Banditti upon the Borders of the Province." For Gage, the failure to punish any of the Black Boys was the result of a deeply flawed and weakened government. In an odd way, the Black Boys might have agreed with the words but not the spirit of Gage's remark. Neither Gage nor the Black Boys believed Pennsylvania had a government, at least not a working one.[109]

"Terror to the Neighbourhood": Regulations in the East

In the same year the Black Boys besieged Carlisle, Deputy Governor Penn had to deal with another potentially damaging uprising, but this time it came from the oldest eastern county in the province. In a letter to Maryland governor Horatio Sharpe, Penn complained that masked banditti roamed Chester County southwest of the Brandywine Creek and closest to the Maryland border committing atrocious crimes "attended with very aggravating Circumstances." What was worse, they acted with impunity and, like the Black Boys, with popular approval.[110] Some even speculated that this unruliness had its origins "in Paxton."[111]

The southwestern corner of Chester County, where a bulk of these extralegal mobilizations occurred, was, as Penn imagined, a lawless zone. Inhabitants there quarreled among themselves. They fought over property, debt, and the very core of good neighborliness. Yet not much in the way of official or even informal authority existed to negotiate those disputes. Few magistrates resided in the area; the high sheriff lived over thirty miles away on the other side of an often impenetrable creek, and the few local town officials had little means to uphold the law. In response, locals took matters into their own hands. During the 1760s, the southwestern corner had a documented "riot" that could be considered an instance of extralegal justice at least once a year.[112] In 1768, the Reynolds family felt the brunt of this penchant for popular justice, and their experience serves as a perfect example of the limits of law enforcement, the use of extralegal justice when all else failed, and the ubiquity of state crises in colonial Pennsylvania.

The Reynoldses were a large prosperous family living in the townships of West and East Nottingham, Chester County. William Reynolds, the family patriarch, owned a large plantation and had notable social and political connections, including the famous lawyer and politician Andrew Hamilton and the justice of the peace in New London, Alexander Johnston. Nominal Quakers, few of the Reynolds family members subscribed to Quaker ideals. They used guns, sometimes against people, owned slaves, and caused much trouble.

According to county residents, William Reynolds and his family "gathered frequently into Clubs," assaulted neighbors, ravished their wives, burglarized homes, and destroyed livestock and crops. In one instance, William Reynolds and his cousins broke into their neighbor's cellar, drank "at Pleasure Cyder and Brandy," and then killed his cattle and "Hogs by Ripping up the Belly of Sows heavy with young." They also raided the local Presbyterian churches, where they drank sacramental wine and stole a "tankard" that they ran "down into Spoons." They even "Bedaubed the Pulpit and Christening Bason with Human Dung." Petitioners complained the infamous family cut bridles, bred quarrels, and deprived "People of Property in lesser Matters frequently."[113]

County residents tried to use the local government to enforce order on the Reynolds family. From 1727 through the mid-1760s, the court heard an array of charges against the Reynolds family including theft, fornication and bastardy, forcible entry and detainer, assault, battery, and riot. Despite these charges, the family rarely received punishment. For example, between 1740 and 1765, the court heard cases charging William Reynolds with fornication, misdemeanor, bastardy, assault, battery, and riot. The court, however, never convicted Reynolds for these crimes. In one case, Reynolds's lawyer used a legal technicality to have the charges thrown out. In another, the court pushed the case off the dockets because family members rescued Reynolds from the constable's custody.

The court ruled the rest of the cases groundless because of insufficient evidence due to the lack of witnesses.[114]

The ineffective judicial system was only part of the problem. Corruption, inhabitants argued, was rampant. The sheriff supposedly witnessed the Reynoldses commit an attempted murder yet did nothing. While they inferred corruption with the sheriff, residents outright charged Justice Alexander Johnston with colluding with the Reynolds family to sell stolen goods. These rumors of corruption exacerbated the fact the Reynolds family broke known laws with minimal legal repercussions.[115]

Due to these circumstances, the courts and its officers lost the respect of the populace, resulting in the increasing use of collective violence and extrajudicial punishment. In 1768, when William Reynolds, using a tactic his family perfected over the years, manipulated an estate sale and made off with four or five slaves without the administrator of the estate's permission, a group of six men ransacked his home, assaulted him, and took three slaves.[116] They would have recovered all the slaves if it had not been for the timely arrival of several of William's family members. This dispute over the legal possession of slaves that inhabitants negotiated with violence outside the law quickly escalated four days later into a full-scale episode of popular justice where neighbors violently punished the Reynolds family for their past misdeeds. The leaders of the initial raid, Francis Baker and Robert Porter, looking to recover the other missing slaves, organized a second invasion and had little trouble mobilizing over thirty men from the area.

They drew from a population already acting beyond the law to police their communities. It seems that inhabitants regularly patrolled the countryside punishing suspected criminals and settling both debt and property disputes using fear and violence. These were not simply ad hoc mob actions but calculated and organized affairs. In 1763, for instance, John Harris of West Nottingham, who encroached on his neighbor's land by strategically placing fences and partnered with the Reynolds family to displace tenants, faced a paramilitary gang of at least ten armed, disguised, and mounted men with an "Ensign Bearer" who "Cary'd a Red Silk Handkerchief on a pole" representing the ominous 'No Quarter Given.'[117] These armed men tried to use formal legal channels first, but the courts dismissed the cases.[118] When that avenue failed, the group forcibly removed the fences and assaulted both Harris and one member of the Reynolds family. Just a few months before the Reynolds affair in 1768, a similar group left one West Nottingham resident "in great fear."[119]

Several of the men from both incidents joined Baker and Porter; one was the "Ensign Bearer," James Gamble.[120]

While Baker and Porter capitalized on this growing extralegal violence in Chester County, they also harnessed the notoriety of the Reynolds family and recruited from a population with a lot of old scores to settle. John Carmichael and John Cavenah, who joined the second raid, consistently had their livestock and crops destroyed by the Reynolds family.[121] In addition, in a seeming reference to rape, Henry Reynolds "evilly treated" Carmichael's wife while William, Jacob, and Elisha Reynolds held Carmichael at gunpoint. When Carmichael brought this heinous act to the attention of officials, they could do little. The constable tried to take the men to jail, but two Reynolds family members, Isaac and Jesse, assaulted the officer and rescued their kin, and the court threw the case out.[122] As far as local officials were concerned, the Reynolds family would never stand trial because officials were tired of carrying out warrants against a family that would "not suffer themselves to be taken."[123] This instance surely altered Carmichael's trust in the law.

Events and circumstances like these compelled men to join Baker and Porter, and on the night of August 19, 1768, over thirty men, described as "yellow wigs," disguised with handkerchiefs and armed with an assortment of cutlasses, guns, clubs, and staves, descended on William Reynolds's "Mansion House." Waiting for the family to wake, several of the men broke into the cellar and feasted on bread and an assortment of liquor. Possibly these men were the victims of similar cellar raids carried out by the Reynolds family. In any event, their merriment aroused William and his wife, Prudence, from their sleep. Getting out of bed and looking out his second-story window, Reynolds remarked that the moon and starlight revealed a "great Number" of men "all under Arms." Reynolds acted quickly. He stole downstairs, grabbed his rifle, walked outside and shot in the air to alert his brother and his nephew. The gunshot also alarmed the masked men outside, and when Reynolds tried to glimpse the group by pulling back the sashes on the windows, he heard someone cry out, "There is the Son of a Bitch, Shute him, Shute him." The entire armed posse opened fire and shot out more than sixty panes of glass. Then a collection of men broke open the door and others swarmed into the house through the now wide-open windows. They went "over all the House opening the Doors of the Rooms and went into the Garrett and brought down four Negroes."[124]

The gang looked not only to recover the slaves but to institute some rough justice. Instead of leaving after they had gained the other slaves—after all, that was the stated goal of leaders Baker and Porter—several of the men attacked the Reynolds family and threatened their lives. John Cavenah found William Reynolds and attacked him with a short naval sword. According to Reynolds, Cavenah cut him several times and then "with a Cutlass in his hand after they had got the Negroes swore he would Split his Brains out." While Cavenah threatened Reynolds, John Carmichael and Robert Porter called Reynolds's wife, Prudence, a "Dam Bitch" and "struck her" on the head, tore her clothes off, threw her over a stump, and "pulled the Skin off her Arms." While "five men" held her down, Stephen Porter, a local lawyer, "came up to her with a Pistol in one hand and a Club in the other" threatening to "Murder her that Minute." Four or five men also attacked Reynolds's frightened daughter, who tried to hide in the apple orchard. Cavenah held his cutlass above her head, "Damd her for a Bitch," and threatened to "Split her Brains out." Elisha and Jacob Reynolds likewise received a severe lashing. Several of the masked men even wanted to murder the entire family and be done with them. Cooler heads prevailed, and they left the family seriously injured yet still alive.[125]

In a striking case of irony, the battered Reynolds family took their case to the courts in an effort to prosecute the gang. When neighbors and others heard that Reynolds intended to press charges, over 120 locals sent a long petition to the county court, deriding the criminality of the Reynolds family and praising the character of the gang members. Moreover, this mixed group of petitioners consisting of laborers, "jobbers," artisans, farmers, tavern keepers, freemen, and two Presbyterian ministers, signifying the ubiquity of the problem of law and order in the county, condemned the government for its ineffectiveness and failure to bring William Reynolds and his family to justice.[126] The Reynolds family, according to petitioners, was "a common Nuisance and terror to the Neighbourhood" who colluded with local officials and evaded the law. Therefore, they argued that the family deserved the violent vengeance of the people.

Such a petition, while excellent for the historian, was rather unnecessary. The government did not have the power to capture the gang. Symbolic of the entire problem of governance in Pennsylvania, after months of failing to apprehend the "rioters," local officials could do little more than state that the gang still "lurks and wanders" about the county.[127] Deputy Governor Penn, disowning the matter, claimed the rioters lived in Maryland and thereby passed the problem on to that colony. The petitioners were most likely ecstatic when the government failed to capture the gang.

The Reynolds affair, as well as the extralegal actions by the Paxton Boys and the Black Boys, which occurred in both the east and the west, marked a breaking point. Pennsylvanians had, over the course of the 1740s and '50s, tolerated ineffective government to a certain extent, but in the 1760s they did not. By taking the law in their own hands, Pennsylvanians expressed their disdain for this problem with governance in a very vivid and violent way. An armed, organized collection of people with ensigns carrying colors and defying legal authority to uphold their own brand of it does not speak to a well-governed society and a people enamored with the status quo. It spoke instead to an extreme state crisis where Pennsylvanians viewed their government as ineffective, unjust, and, ultimately, obsolete.

The intersection of this crisis with popular upheaval changed the political dynamic of the colony forever. Jasper Yeates, ever mindful of such developments, noted that the Reynolds affair and those other "strange events" that "happened amongst us" had "given rise to much politics." Ordinary people, Yeates mused, were stirring, realizing their own political importance and demanding significant change.[128] This moment was so powerful that Pennsylvanians in the late 1790s and early 1800s were still talking and writing about its significance. In 1797, one "Country Correspondent," reflecting on the "different stages of democratic phrenzy," thought the "first blaze of sans-cullottism" that "illumined the pacific province of Pennsylvania" was "conducted by the Paxton Boys."[129] In 1800, another Pennsylvanian reveled in the idea that all "ye enemies of Liberty" still fear the cry "PAXTON BOYS! AWAKE!"[130]

5

"Usurping Powers"

Resistance, Rebellion, and Revolution

REFLECTING ON THE "REMARKABLE" EVENTS of his past, James Smith could not help but connect the actions of his Black Boys with the American Revolution. For Smith, the local problems he and his neighbors faced, the government they judged ineffective, and the perceived corruption they violently resisted were part of that revolution. They were "American rebels" fighting against "arbitrary" power.[1] Smith's understanding of the revolution should give us pause. After all, his view of colonial resistance and independence does not reflect the standard narrative of the revolution. Not once did he mention the aggressive parliamentary acts of the 1760s and early 1770s. This is not to say that those imperial measures were not a crucial factor in the coming of the revolution; they definitely had their place. But, as Smith reminds us, they do not explain everything.

Local experiences powerfully influenced the American Revolution, both the motivations that drove people to resist and their effort to topple governments in the formation of new ones. James Smith serves as a case in point. Not only did Smith, a rather obscure fellow and political outsider, lead a popular resistance against local, provincial, and imperial authority, but when popular forces gained ground over the legally constituted government, he became a political insider, representing local interests in the revolutionary committees and shaping the future of the state as a member of the 1776 Constitutional Convention and the legislature it created. When serving in those capacities, Smith carried with him, just as other delegates did, his past struggles with the colonial system, and he sought to effectuate change, something he could never do without the revolution. In Pennsylvania, the fights for, as Carl Becker famously labeled, "home rule" and "who should rule at home" were seamless and simultaneous; one couldn't exist without the other.[2]

The place of local experiences in the coming of the American Revolution becomes clearer and more important when one views aggressive parliamentary acts as a trigger for rebellion instead of the sole cause of it. The coming of the revolution was the result of a cataclysmic breakdown after a long period of crisis encapsulating local grievances and struggles, which was exacerbated by imperial measures that gave oppositional focus to a large swath of the colonial population. As sociologist Jack Goldstone argues, revolutions are the result of a "state crisis" where people, both elite and ordinary, perceive their government as "ineffective, unjust, and obsolete."[3] Such a crisis does not inevitably lead to revolution; there are multiple contingencies at play. If the government changed popular and elite perceptions, if it reformed to meet new demands, it could ultimately end such a crisis and thus stave off breakdown and revolution. Yet this did not happen.

The significance and impact of that crisis came to a head in the 1760s. During that decade, Pennsylvania entered a new political age that dramatically altered the face of popular politics. Local and isolated grievances became more collective, more general, infiltrating the public political dialogue, politicizing and mobilizing political outsiders. Violent tumults by the Paxton Boys, Black Boys, and vigilantes in Chester County symbolized this mobilization and created a scenario where issues of law and order, the proper role of government, and the failure and weakness of Pennsylvania's government came crashing into the political scene, threatening to tear the province asunder. The imperial center added to this turmoil with new colonial policies, taxes, laws, and coercive military structures. By the end of the decade, ordinary Pennsylvanians, politicized and mobilized, began associating their grievances with one or another or all of the political organizations that ruled them. By the mid-1770s, that same populace consolidated all political power in their own hands and thus began a revolution.

The coming of the revolution is best understood through an exploration of these three processes—politicization, mobilization, and the consolidation of power. Without any one of these, the revolution would have taken a dramatically different course or would not have happened at all.[4] The first and second processes expose fundamental ingredients for revolution; they demonstrate a crisis; the colonial and imperial government lost both their perceived effectiveness and justice, producing divisions and defections. The last process provided the third and most important ingredient—the effort to force change through extralegal institutions that undermined existing authority and consolidated power within a new ruling group with substantially different visions for the future. This process, in short, produced critical breakdown in the legally constituted government. Together, all three provided for a fundamental transition from an effort to reform the existing political system to a revolution that sought change outside it.[5]

Politicization of Grievances

The politicization of grievances started with the march of the Paxton Boys. When they threatened the safety of Philadelphia, they sounded the bell of terror and confusion. Colonists who may not have considered how the province was governed before surely did in this moment. The assembly remained deadlocked, and the deputy governor stood helpless. He seemed to run around aimlessly, lamenting his inability to "strengthen the hands of Government." In the end, all that stood in the way of a large group of supposedly armed and angry frontiersmen was a meaningless riot act, a collection of untrained and frightened citizens who nearly killed each other with cannons, and, thankfully, the arrival of some British regulars.[6] If such a scenario did not reveal the problems Pennsylvanians faced, the aftermath of those frightful few days did. The presses boomed, churning out pamphlets and newspaper articles that whipped up the province and exposed deep wounds. Whether individual colonists agreed with the Paxton Boys or not, the event left an indelible mark on everyone's mind, revealing a provincial crisis of governance.

It was not just the physical havoc the Paxton Boys caused; their *Declaration and Remonstrance* was equally important for Pennsylvania politics. Their demands for a government that protected and promoted the public welfare spoke to many inhabitants who also thought the government did not perform its proper role. As historian Gregory Evans Dowd points out, the Paxton Boys started a serious political debate where Pennsylvanians "fought over the virtues and deficiencies of taxes, Quakers, Presbyterians, proprietors, Royal government, the representative system, the history of defense of the province, and a host of issues that had little to do directly with the shooting and tomahawking of unarmed innocents."[7] The sheer scope of those topics highlights the nerve the Paxton Boys touched. By assailing politicians for failing to uphold the central purpose of government, they opened a political door for those inhabitants who deemed their own situations intolerable and saw the government as responsible.

Inhabitants representing the eastern and western sections of the province inundated the assembly with petitions stating their agreement with the Paxton Boys' declarations. Just as important, these petitioners attempted to use the moment to precipitate change. While petitioners demanded the "Redress, during the present Sitting, of certain Grievances . . . of Matthew Smith and James Gibson," they also expanded on those demands to encompass their own local situations and experiences. Petitioners from Cumberland, Northampton, York, and Chester Counties pushed the assembly to provide equal political representation and a militia law and demanded the reform of local and provincial legal structures, particularly the supreme court and the creation of a judicial circuit. They wanted the government to work for and defend the province through an effective judicial system that efficiently upheld the law for the betterment of the whole instead of just "a Part of the Inhabitants."[8]

Like these petitioners, writers swamped the province with political tracts applauding and condemning the actions of the Paxton Boys to forward their own criticisms of the present and their hopes for the future. Anglican Minister Thomas Barton, for example, latched on to the Paxton Boys to vent his frustration with the political system. Barton, a frontier inhabitant and Irish immigrant from Ulster, argued that the government's unresponsiveness revealed a fundamental problem of governance. According to Barton, the "Neglect of the *Legislative Part* of this Province" during the Seven Years' War and Pontiac's War was just the tip of the iceberg. Factionalism was rampant, public measures "clogg'd," and the government seemed to suffer from some sort of "CACHEXY." Barton contended that extralegal actions should be expected under such a government; after all, people "never assemble in any riotous or tumultuous Manner, unless when they are oppressed." The government's refusal to respond to grievances symbolized that oppression. The assembly treated the people "like *Asses*" who were unworthy to have the "*Privilege* or *Authority* to complain of their Sufferings or remonstrate their Grievances." In short, the legislators trod a "highly imprudent, not to say dangerous" path.[9]

For Barton, the government's unresponsiveness violated the fundamental obligation of government and threatened the liberty of the subject. Like the Paxton Boys argued, Barton viewed the public welfare as the sole purpose of government. "*Salus Populi suprema Lex esto*," he wrote, "is a Sentence that deserves to be written in Letters of Gold—It is a Sentence that should be the MOTTO of every Government, where LIBERTY and FREEDOM have any Existence." This political creed spoke to more than just the lack of defense initiatives and the protection of the frontier; it highlighted the core of political ills in the province. Not only did the assembly fail to provide timely defense, but some members put their own private interests and the protection of "their *darling* [political] *Power*" before the needs of the public. This private interest muddied the governance of the province by leaving the executive branch weakened, the frontier without equal political representation, and even worse, "Murderers and Robbers" (by which he meant friendly Indians) free from any punishment by the government. Only by responding to the needs of the people and upholding the public interest could colonists "feel the happy Effects resulting from LIBERTY and LAW," central elements of the "Good Order of Government."[10]

Like Barton, other writers assailed the government for failing to adequately govern the province. They too attacked rampant factionalism, the protection of lawless Indian "murderers," and a government that could not keep all in order. Even those Pennsylvanians who found the actions of the Paxton Boys detestable saw in the situation a real problem of governance. Benjamin Franklin, for instance, very different politically from Barton, wrote similarly about what the Paxton affair represented. For Franklin, the failure to stop or even apprehend the Paxton Boys proved that "the Government that ought to keep all in Order, is itself weak, and has scarce Authority enough to keep the common Peace." Using language eerily similar to Barton, Franklin reasoned that the province suffered from riots and a government that could not act in the people's interest because factionalism clogged and embarrassed all the "Wheels of Government," which threatened "common Security."[11]

Where Barton and Franklin placed responsibility for those troubles reveals the difference between the two. For Barton, the obstinate assembly was to blame, and for Franklin it was the proprietor. Nevertheless, both political partisans presented a picture of the current government as severely limited if not broken. "As some physicians say," Franklin wrote, "every Animal Body brings into the World among its original Stamina, the Seed of that Disease that shall finally produce its Dissolution; so the Political Body of a Proprietary Government, contains those convulsive Principles that will at length destroy it."[12] Unsurprisingly, such a statement mirrored the vision of illness or "CACHEXY" that Barton offered the public. Through these two writers and many more like them, one can envision a shift in popular politics characterized by a deep questioning of the ability of the government to govern.

Because the popular politics swung in the direction of problems with governance, the political factions, ever ready to take up a cause to use as a political cudgel, appropriated the debate, used it for their own ends, and engulfed the province in treatises, diatribes, and snarky satires that explored the "weakness of government." It proved a popular issue. According to one historian, the political debate was a "compelling one for large numbers of Pennsylvanians. The number of observer/readers grew from a few hundred to a substantial portion of the colony's populace, and pamphlet sales were huge."[13] It was a peculiar political reality where Pennsylvanians wrote openly of their detestation of the current government in which no group, governing body, or politician escaped unscathed. Moreover, in their effort to popularize problems of governance in a push for political dominance, politicians offered a revolutionary rhetoric that they could not contain.

A powerful faction in the assembly led by Benjamin Franklin and his younger political partner Joseph Galloway struck first and attempted to utilize the central grievances fueling popular outrage to undermine the proprietors. Since at least the 1740s, there was a growing movement among that faction to wrest control of the province away from the proprietor by making Pennsylvania a royal colony. In their vision of past and future, these legislators blamed all problems of governance on the proprietors because they controlled the deputy governors, judges, and even the land. Under a king's government, these legislators surmised, all problems would disappear; the Crown would appoint worthy officers and the assembly would rise in power and importance, unshackled by the restraints of proprietors seeking their own ends. Such a vision had little basis in reality, but it nonetheless shaped the assembly's political actions. The Paxton Boys enhanced this movement by giving legislators a justification to transform the government into a Crown colony. As Franklin noted well before the Paxton affair, his faction needed "tumults and Insurrections, that might prove the Proprietary Government insufficient to preserve Order, or show the People to be ungovernable" to "do the Business."[14]

Following Franklin's lead, members of his faction used the "weakness of government" to push forth their agenda. It all started on March 24, 1764, when the assembly adjourned to "consult their Constituents" on the merits of petitioning the Crown "to take the People of the Province under his immediate Protection and Government."[15] Over the next month and for the next several years Franklin, Galloway, and their faction undertook a vigorous campaign to persuade Pennsylvanians of the necessity for a change of government. In order to prove that point, they announced that the "present Insecurity of Life and Property" and the "imminent Danger" of the people due to the "weakness of government" should be blamed on the proprietors, who put their own private interests ahead of the people's. Politicians spoke and wrote as if Pennsylvania faced an extreme crisis. "Look around," one author enjoined, and see the failure of government that threatens "your Welfare." "Is it unjust" to demand that the "Peoples Warrants, Surveys and Estates should be secured? That distributive justice should be impartially administer'd?" In nearly the same breath, the author demanded the people to "see the Felicity enjoyed under the several Royal Governments! Are there any Disputes there that impede Protection, or obstruct the People's Welfare?" Obviously, the author thought not.[16]

Pennsylvanians read and heard speeches that proclaimed over and over again that under the present government the people had "no Prospect of enjoying either Security of Person or Property, the grand and important Objects of all Government." Pamphlets castigated the proprietor as the "supreme oppressor" and the judges and justices of the peace as a product of "Dependence and Corruption," loyal only to the proprietor and bent on doing his will to the detriment of the province.[17] Writers singled out Chief Justice William Allen for abuse. Through his office, Allen "grew rich, proud, saucy and uncivil," and they hoped he would ride his ornate "Coach and Four" to "the Devil."[18] The same writer went so far as to argue that "Every Man *in his Wits,* who has any Dispute with the Prop—rs about Property, chuses, tho' he may have the Law ever so clear on his Side, rather to leave the Matter to *Arbitration,* where he has *Half a Chance* of a favourable Decree, than run the Risque of a Decision from a *Pr—ry C—f-J——ce.*"[19] Broadsides pervaded the countryside depicting Lucifer rising from the ashes to control the proprietor and his appointees.[20]

Only a few in the assembly, writers urged, had "an honest Regard to the Public Weal." In opposition to the proprietary "State-Jobbers" who lived off the "Posts of Honor and Profit," the legislators were "Men of Merit" and the "Friends of Liberty, and Lovers of Order and Government."[21] Yet these few "virtuous men" could not liberate Pennsylvania as it existed. According to Joseph Galloway, "nothing" short of "a Revolution" could "save" the province from corruption and the "Confusion and Violence" it bred. Everyone, Galloway urged, should harbor "great

Disrespect and Contempt for a Proprietary Government" because "there was no longer any Security under it, whence his Majesty's good Subjects were not only deprived of those invaluable Blessings so fully granted and confirmed to them, but that all Government was at an End and the very Design of Society destroyed." This discouraging depiction represented the present and future prospects of Pennsylvania without, as Galloway noted, "a Revolution."[22]

Not only did writers and speechmakers deride the government in general terms, but they provided rather specific critiques that harnessed a decade's worth of popular grievances over land, law, and defense. The overarching criticism was that proprietary instructions to the deputy governors hamstrung the government and inhibited necessary reforms. Under such restraint, legislators could not provide the "Protection to the People committed to our Care, which it is our Duty to give, and their Right to receive." Proprietary land policy would continue to threaten the security of property, and the judicial system (crippled by special interest) would forever undermine the public welfare. The same, they argued, could be said about military defense. It was not Quaker pacifism that derailed the formation of a military power in the province; rather, it was proprietary instructions that made the creation of a militia impossible. The government could not offer "Protection of the Subject from internal Tumults and Insurrections at home, or from the common Enemy abroad" unless legislators caved to the "the most arbitrary and unjust" demands of the proprietor "that will surrender both the Lives and Properties of the People to the Will and Mercy of the Proprietors and their Deputies." In sum, under proprietary rule, the government would sit "Month after Month, spending and wasting our Constituents Money, fruitless and ineffectual."[23]

The solution was to petition the king to put the government in his and his ministers' capable hands. With such a change, a public officer and not an individual corrupted by the proprietor would administer the province's land policy, and judges would be "Men of Merit" who held their office during "good behavior" and susceptible to removal if they failed in their duty. Pennsylvanians would finally have an efficient and effective judicial system controlled by virtuous men who willingly provided their services to the rest of the people. They also argued that Pennsylvania would finally have a "Military Force" controlled by the Crown and capable of offering security and protection. According to these partisan writers, Pennsylvanians could expect such reforms because existing royal colonies had none of Pennsylvania's proprietary "Mischiefs." "We find in them a full Freedom and Power of Legislation:—No Obstructions to his Majesty's Service, a perfect Administration of Justice, no legally established Source of Vice and Immorality, and a sufficient Protection against all Tumults, Insurrections, and Invasions." "Why then," writers asked, "should we dread a Change?"[24]

Franklin, Galloway, and their faction put any opposition in a difficult situation. Denying that there were problems with the governance of the province would never persuade the populace; it was agreed on all sides that the government in its legal and military capacity was fundamentally flawed.[25] However, if the opposition accepted that governance was a real issue, they needed to shift blame away from the proprietor. As one of the opposition pointed out, "It is granted on all Hands that we are in a wretched Situation," but, he asked, "What Cause the Weakness of Government proceeds?"[26] Franklin and Galloway wrongly assumed that the opposition would not dare answer that question by blaming the Crown, though they had sufficient evidence to prove that point. They hoped that popular patriotism, which erupted after the ascension of George III and the end of the Seven Years' War, would deter such a move.[27]

Popular patriotism was not much of a deterrent. Opponents of royal government quickly and vehemently shifted responsibility to the Crown. For them, the "weakness of government" did not "proceed from the Proprietaries"; they "were not to blame." As recently as 1759, the "Proprietary Governor" and the assembly passed the same reforms that supporters of royal government touted would be the result of the Crown's takeover. In that year, they attempted to change the tenure of office for judges to good behavior, create a new public land office, and even form a militia "in the midst of war." Such reforms "have always been wished for," but they amounted to little after they crossed the Atlantic for royal review.[28] It seemed absurd to think such laws would pass in the future. "Perhaps indeed," one author argued, "we may get some King's Governor" to pass such legislation again. "But what shall we gain by that? Since the laws will certainly be repeal'd. For it is demonstrable, that none of these laws which they praise so much, can ever be obtained in any form of government. The Ministry, and all his Majesty's Council can hardly be chang'd along with our Charter."[29] The power of the Crown over legislation prompted John Dickinson, a formidable opponent of both the proprietors and the majority of the assembly, to ask the public to remember how "the Crown" was already "*fully enough exerted* over us."[30] As another author argued, if "a change of government should happen," the "*King's little finger we should find heavier* than the Proprietor's whole loins."³¹

Aggressive parliamentary acts of the 1760s fueled this ongoing dispute. Although historians argue that the Stamp Act received less attention in Pennsylvania than in other colonies, its place in the political debate cannot be ignored.³² The Stamp Act came at a critical time. Just as the majority in the assembly contended that a firmer connection to the empire was the only option to assure the future happiness and prosperity of Pennsylvania, Parliament passed a Stamp Act that taxed printed materials such as newspapers and legal documents. To enforce this act, the Crown appointed stamp agents and increased the authority of the remote and often inaccessible admiralty courts.

Not only did the Stamp Act challenge fundamental constitutional assumptions about representation and taxation, but it touched with a heavy hand on the issues the colonists debated at the time, the administration of justice and access to the law. For instance, Galloway argued that the proprietary government created an unnecessarily expensive system of justice loaded with fees and other mechanisms to fatten the coffers of proprietary appointees. By making the courts and law expensive, Galloway reasoned, it also made them inaccessible and therefore ineffective. Under a royal government, he argued, the Crown would only appoint "Men of Merit" who would provide for a less expensive and by extension more accessible legal system. Yet the Stamp Act challenged that assumption by placing duties on the documents necessary for the courts. As Grenville himself noted, the tax was "intended to act as a Regulation" to "discourage by a high Duty" a "Spirit of unnecessary Litigation."³³

The opposition seized on these aspects of the Stamp Act. For one, they argued, the use of admiralty courts proved that the empire wanted "weak or wicked" men to be judges "to render Us the most sordid and forlorn of Slaves," a far cry from the virtuous men of Galloway's predictions.³⁴ Moreover, they argued that the tax placed on paper for legal proceedings would ruin "multitudes," disproving that greater imperial control would provide better judicial access. A new Currency Act already made it difficult for the colonists to pay their debts, and now Parliament saddled colonists with a Stamp Act that made suits and debts an onerous financial burden at court. As Dickinson pointed out, "The Stamp Act, therefore, will be severely felt by those, in whose welfare the prosperity of the state is always so much interested," particularly "the lower ranks of people" who "are frequently engaged in law suits; and as the law is already a very heavy tax on the subject in all parts of the British dominions, this act will render it destructive here." The Stamp Act, he reasoned, would draw off "the last drops of their blood."[35]

As elsewhere, the opponents of royal government also saw in the Stamp Act a deeply laid conspiracy to undermine the liberty of the province. As Dickinson proclaimed, resistance to the act hinged on whether or not colonists wanted to "be Freemen or Slaves."[36] However, the originators of the conspiracy, so they argued, did not exist across the Atlantic. Rather, Benjamin Franklin, Joseph Galloway, and other proponents of a royal takeover concocted and advanced the plot; "the Cup of their political Iniquity" had "run over."[37] Franklin, they claimed, instigated the act, a horrible treachery that revealed his duplicity. Similarly, Galloway was portrayed as an imperial lackey looking to ingratiate himself and his supporters with the seat of power to "job matters into each others Hands."[38] That a vocal supporter of royal government, John Hughes, was commissioned a stamp agent confirmed the conspiracy, and he was "held in the most sovereign Contempt."[39] The evidence was so persuasive that a mob paraded the streets with "Muffled Drums," besieged Franklin's home, and threatened Hughes that "my House should be pulled down and my Substance destroyed."[40] Fueling popular violence, the opposition to a royal takeover deemed such actions as "inspired by the generous Love of Liberty."[41]

Parliamentary acts intertwined with Pennsylvania's internal political debate, solidifying connections between problems at home and across the Atlantic and adding to a political atmosphere that questioned all levels of government—imperial, provincial, and local. The political debates of the 1760s made it clear to all that there were real problems of governance and that local grievances constituted more general issues that required "a Revolution" or at the very least significant reform. But therein lay the importance of it all; the political debate hinged on the fact that the government could not provide for the public welfare and that it never would unless some kind of change were possible. To many people, as they looked on at the political wrangling and an invigorated empire, that possibility seemed slimmer by the day.

The politicization of grievances and the questioning of government at all levels had other consequences for the nature of Pennsylvania politics. Over the course of the eighteenth century, the assembly and proprietary factions only called on the public to fit their own electoral agendas. In most cases, the proprietary side did not even do that, as it rarely ran candidates or developed a significant platform to reach a wide audience. The 1760s changed that to some extent. By politicizing the "weakness of government," both sides struck a chord with the populace, galvanizing politics and political dialogue on the streets, in homes, and even in the pulpit. Neighbors, family members, and friends who used to live "in great Harmony, cannot now spend an agreeable Evening together" if they did "not jump together in political Judgment."[42] Ministers gave political speeches from the pulpit and even made signing petitions "a *Sabbath's Day Exercise*." The consequences were clear. Politics gave the people's grievances political legitimacy and oppositional strength. Moreover, those people were roused and ready to become part of the political system in more ways than just as a passive audience. It seemed as if "many of the meanest rank, and inferior capacities, are puffed up with pride that is almost become past dealing with. Some of the most contemptible creatures among us yet think themselves sufficient to direct Statesmen, dictate to Legislators, and teach Doctors and Divines."[43]

That people "of the meanest rank" were more politically active proved a legitimate concern, especially considering the nature of politics in the 1760s. Writers and speechmakers not only exposed the government as extremely ineffective, but by lampooning all the people who held positions of authority, they placed the entire governing structure on both sides of the Atlantic in contempt. As one politician asked, "If all the Thoughts and private Vices of you, and me, or of the best Men, were to be laid open, and displayed to the World, how contemptible would we appear?"[44] The actions of Pennsylvanians during the next few years answered that question.

Mobilizations of the People Out of Doors

As politicians found, horrifyingly in some instances, ordinary people, once politicized, refused to sit by and act as spectators during this time of perceived crisis. Pennsylvanians, by and large, were also aware of the problems of governance that both the assembly and proprietary factions wrote so hysterically about, and they demanded reform. When it became all too clear that reform was not forthcoming and that the politicians were, as often described by both sides, corrupt, lascivious, and conducting a politics of self-interest, many people looked to include themselves in the political process through persuasion if possible, by force if necessary. Some petitioned for equal representation and legislative transparency;

others took to the polls and attempted, against great odds, to vote in new candidates; and still others disregarded the government and acted on their own. In the 1760s, not only were local grievances politicized, but the people were stirring, mobilizing to effectuate change.

Achieving such change proved an uphill battle; colonial Pennsylvania's political system was not an inclusive one. A majority of the assembly no more wanted ordinary people, "those wretched Rabble" who believed "themselves intitled to a Vote," as Franklin put it, to gain a sense of their own voice than they desired the proprietor to retain control of the province.[45] For much of the eighteenth century, a strong core of eastern elites controlled the legislative arm of government. Between 1756 and 1775, a majority of the legislators came from the merchant and professional classes, and nearly 60 percent of assemblymen shared familial connections.[46] That men of wealth, birth, and status naturally occupied most seats in the legislature was perfectly captured by Benjamin Franklin, who, reflecting on his first election to the assembly, made it a point to note how "flattered" he was "considering my low beginning."[47] While Franklin's story shows the upward mobility for some, by midcentury such "promotions" were nearly impossible to obtain.[48]

Men of "Merit and Virtue," sardonic euphemisms for the rich and well born, achieved political prominence through the electoral process and by excluding growing sections of the province from political access. The suffrage in Pennsylvania, though greater than in England, was still significantly circumscribed. To achieve the right to vote, an inhabitant needed to be at least twenty-one years of age, white, male, a naturalized subject who had resided in the province for at least two years and who owned either fifty acres of land or fifty pounds worth of personal estate, free and clear. As a result, no more than a little over 50 percent of adult white male inhabitants were eligible to vote. In Chester County, for example, only 56 percent of the adult white males were eligible, and of them, barely 30 percent actually voted. While logistical barriers certainly dissuaded some from making the trek to the county seat to cast ballots, likely the limited choices of candidates deterred many others.

By the mid-eighteenth century it was the established norm for the "great men" of the counties to gather together and establish tickets listing the names of a handful of eligible candidates for election. Using distributers, election managers assured each voter had the available ticket, and more often than not, attempted to deprive rival tickets from making their way into the hands of voters. More to the point, rarely did candidates face any opposition at the polls. The lack of contested elections in no way symbolizes an apathetic acceptance and approval of those in power. It merely represented a political reality; there were rarely any rival choices to create a dispute.[49] Take, for example, the creation of the *only* election ticket in Lancaster County in 1769. Several leading men from the "upper part of the country" met at a local tavern, established the ticket, and declared if anyone disliked their choices, they should "stay at home" during the election.[50] Some potential voters detested "the unhappy way that a man must have eight men crammed down his throat at once" on these tickets.[51]

Out on the frontier, in counties such as Lancaster or Bedford, where land was far more plentiful and access to it a bit easier, over 60 percent of white males were eligible to vote, and the county of Northampton surpassed them all with over 70 percent. However, the collective voting power of the frontier counties could not change the makeup of the legislature. In 1765, for example, the assembly consisted of thirty-six seats. The eastern counties of Philadelphia, Chester, and Bucks held twenty-four of those seats, leaving the city of Philadelphia with two, Lancaster County with four, the counties of Cumberland and York with two, and Berks and Northampton Counties with just one representative. It should be no surprise that legislators were extremely reluctant to add new counties and even more hesitant to give the frontier equal seats in the legislature with those of the longer-settled eastern counties. Moreover, it is hardly difficult, given this political context, to see why it was so rare for more than 35 percent of eligible voters on the frontier to even be bothered to vote.[52]

To be sure, both proprietary and assembly factions sought to represent "the people," but they did so in a limited way. Like the assembly elections, both factions gave inhabitants a set of choices; one side wanted "new wine in old bottles," the other desired the status quo, and neither represented the wishes of inhabitants.[53] In sum, popular representation was a chimera that both sides claimed in order to buttress particular policies but just as easily abandoned as inconsequential when it got in the way. For instance, assembly leaders sought to popularize the push for royal government, and they set out garnering signers to a petition for that purpose. Between March 24 and May 14, 1764, they gathered about thirty-five hundred signatures. Once completed, they congratulated themselves on gaining popular acceptance. Joseph Galloway calculated that these thirty-five hundred signers represented men of wealth and interest or, rather, those members of society who could "with any Propriety be Petitioners."[54]

Congratulations came to a screeching halt when they learned that almost fifteen thousand people signed petitions opposing the change of government. When pressed by demands for a more unanimous referendum of the people, Galloway and others shrugged it off, asserting that no government in history "has been changed by the expressed universal Consent of the People." Besides, it was "the Right in this House to petition for a Change, whenever they think it necessary for the Welfare of their Constituents," and they could do this "without consulting or taking the Opinion of the People." He and the assembly would decide what "is right and necessary for the Safety of the People . . . tho' Millions and Mountains oppose."[55]

While many inhabitants bristled under the logic of such sentiments, it did not increase the power of the Penns. Those who may have detested the push for royal government still remembered past animosities and detested the proprietors. As the enthusiasts for royal government liked to point out, many of their opponents "had within a Fortnight before declared the Proprietaries to be as arbitrary as a Mogul."[56] It seems that people simply refused to accept the assembly's solution to the problem of governance and, quite realistically, questioned the possibility for change as espoused by both ruling groups. "All Things they'll *change*, yet keep the *same*," was a critique leveled at both factions.[57] The proprietors never gained in popularity, nor did their supporters. Political newcomers, like John Dickinson and George Bryan, who publicly railed against the proprietors, the assembly, and the idea of royal government, were a case in point. These men were not part of either of the two ruling factions, and they challenged both.

Trying to make sense of this new reality, historians channel this political activity into party politics, labeling this new assemblage of people the Presbyterian or Whig party. However, no one definition or nomenclature can adequately represent what was going on. The problem of definition lies in the fact that there was not really a collection of people at all; instead, what historians notice is a popular opposition with no common purpose, no collective identity, and really no platform to gather people together under one moniker, let alone in a "party." People floated in all directions, often splitting on craft, ethnic, religious, and sectional lines and attempting to work both within and outside the political system in ways they thought best and open to them. Nevertheless, we can see in this moment the emergence of a popular opposition that, because it was fractured, rarely achieved the changes so ardently sought.[58]

Extralegal groups that embodied local interests and resisted local, provincial, and imperial political realities were among the most popular organizations of the 1760s. Those groups worked against the grain of the political structures that ruled them and demonstrated the willingness of some to push beyond the circumscribed limits of political inclusion and representation to take "Law and Government in Our Hands." As historian Terry Bouton argues, such groups represented "a model of an organization far different—and, one could argue, far more revolutionary" than what existed in the past. They exemplified a "model of organization that ordinary folk would repeat throughout Pennsylvania—and America—in the years to come."[59] For the 1760s, they demonstrate that the old political system of exclusion and oligarchic dominance was splitting along the seams under new popular pressures.

Popular mobilizations, however, were not always violent. In 1764, Presbyterians united their congregations with a committee of correspondence to enter a colonial political system they found closed to them. According to a circular letter signed by twenty-seven prominent Presbyterians, both ministers and the laity, "Notwithstanding we are so numerous in the province of Pennsylvania we are considered *as nobody*, or a body of very little strength and consequence, so that any encroachment upon our *essential* and *charter privileges* may be made by evil-minded persons who think that they have little to fear from *any opposition* that can be made to their measures." The committee would combat this political exclusion and "promote the *union and welfare of society*, and the general good of the community, *to which we belong.*" While the Presbyterian committee embodies the inroads traditional political outsiders attempted to make, it also highlights the fractured nature of the opposition. This was, after all, a committee only for Presbyterians.[60]

Resistance to imperial initiatives such as the Stamp Act and the Townshend duties started to break down these barriers. In resisting the empire, committees and associations sprang up overnight, collecting together diverse peoples of different regions, ethnicities, religions, and vocations. Merchants, artisans, shopkeepers, and farmers, Germans, English, and Scots-Irish, Presbyterian, Anglican, Reformed, and Lutheran all mobilized together. These bodies not only brought together people who rarely worked together in the past, but they provided a critical political outlet. They promoted economic boycotts, attempted to intimidate people into compliance and political solidarity, and, importantly, challenged the representativeness of the existing government. When the assembly, trying to gain royal favor, refused to take direct action in opposition to the Stamp Act and later the Townshend duties, these committees took on new and important powers that furthered the disconnect between legal political institutions and the people fortifying the importance of popular mobilizations.[61]

While the committees had a sense of purpose—resisting imperial measures through economic boycotts—they did not completely eradicate the fractured nature of popular opposition. Committee members clashed, stunting their overall effectiveness. The prolonged dispute between artisans and the dry goods merchants over control of the committees is a well-known representation of this fact. While this internal fracturing would change over time as the groups matured through the resistance effort, as the goals for the future gained more shape with seemingly tangible results, and as the committees received a semblance of legitimacy through the continental struggle, they would then have force and power representing a collective resistance. But for the 1760s, they remained ad hoc and ephemeral.

Extralegal groups and committees were not the only methods of popular mobilization available to ordinary people. Petitioning campaigns, too, required organization, development, and sense of purpose. Petitions provided an outlet for ordinary people to express their grievances and include their voices outside of elections and extralegal movements. Moreover, petitioning campaigns increasingly drew on the politics of the day, mobilizing people in local communities to take action. For example, in 1765 and 1766 Pennsylvanians sent the assembly eighty-eight public petitions, 57 percent of which demanded better law enforcement by reforming both the supreme and county courts.[62] Petitioners wanted better access to those institutions and more officers in their locales. In essence, solicitors demanded the same reforms that both the proprietary and assembly factions said would fix the "weakness of government." These petitions show the impact the political dialogue had on the thoughts and actions of many Pennsylvanians. In addition, such petitions elicited little response from the government, and as the disconnect between the polity and the people widened, Pennsylvanians began to demand a greater level of political inclusion and representation.

During the first half of the eighteenth century, political inclusion and equal representation always existed on the margins of complaint and were rarely explicitly requested. Instead, a host of other issues related to a lack of governing institutions and officers remained the primary focus. It was not until the early 1760s that the number of seats in the legislature gained in importance. It seems that as people saw their petitions for reform rarely acted on and their voices muffled, they sought political inclusion.[63] In 1764, for example, over twelve hundred frontier inhabitants sent a rather long list of grievances to the assembly reiterating past complaints and ridiculing the government for its failure to act. Therefore, they argued, it only made sense that they should be equally represented. "What lies at the Bottom of all their Grievances and must be complained of as the Source of all their Sufferings is there not being fairly represented in Assembly," which they judged "contrary to the Design and Letter of our excellent Charter, contrary to the Rights of *British* Subjects, contrary to Reason and common Sense."[64]

Some eastern colonists also sent petitions backing frontier settlers' request for "equal representation." Still more eastern inhabitants, while they could not complain of underrepresentation, demanded essential reforms to the nature of that representation that would have altered the relationship between the government and the governed. Seeking representative accountability, colonists requested the assembly print the decision of each representative on all votes and provide "better explanations" of the laws it passed and their impact on the public. They also demanded the assembly reverse the "absurd and tyrannical custom of shutting the Assembly doors" so that the people could "be admitted to hear the Debates in the House, and thereby be informed of the true State of such Matters under the Deliberation of the *Representatives of the People*, as may in any wise affect the Interest and Welfare of their Constituents."[65] In all, Pennsylvanians pressed for changes that would have offered ordinary people greater inclusion in the legislative process.

Besieged on all sides with petitions for better representation, the assembly continued a time-worn practice and simply ignored them, letting the petitions "lie on the table" scattered amid messages, letters, and crumpled notes. Its refusal to provide for popular political inclusion seriously undermined claims that the assembly represented the interests of the province. It also produced a deep disenchantment and alienation among the colonial populace. Shocked, one visitor to Pennsylvania in 1773 noted that "the House of Representatives are but thirty-six in number" and "as a body held in great, remarkable and general contempt." One of the reasons for this public disapproval, the writer explained, was that "their debates are not public, which is said now to be the case of only this house of commons throughout the continent. Many have been the attempts to procure an alteration in this respect, but all to no purpose."[66]

Regardless of the legislature's effort to hold on to the political status quo, by challenging the oligarchic nature of government, ordinary people made a few inroads, especially at the polls, where they successfully turned out elected officials who held seats of power for years. However, these moments were fleeting. The election machinery was intended to maintain the oligarchy, not to allow popular forces to upset its hold of the political reins. Nevertheless, there were several moments when that machinery failed; 1764 proved one of those years.

In that year, the number of voters dramatically increased, in some areas reaching well over 40 percent, and five prominent assemblymen lost their seats to some rather obscure upstarts. Benjamin Franklin, Joseph Galloway, Samuel Rhoads, Plunket Fleeson, and Rowland Evans, five of the most important and vocal legislators, lost their seats to George Bryan, Thomas Willing, Henry Pawling, Amos Strettle, and Henry Keppele, who embodied different political forces. Only one of them, Henry Pawling, had held a seat in the legislature before, and that was more than ten years earlier. Moreover, they represented diverse ethnic and religious interests—Bryan was a Scots-Irish Presbyterian, Willing and Pawling were Anglicans, Strettle was a disowned Irish Quaker, and Keppele a German Lutheran. After the election, Samuel Wharton, a strong supporter of the oligarchic assembly noted disparagingly that these men only won because they catered to the "lower class of people," those "Presbyterian and Dutch Tinkers, Cobblers & c."[67] Despite the gains made in 1764, Franklin, Galloway, and their supporters assured such an upset could not happen again, and it rarely did. Out of the five new men, only Henry Pawling and Thomas Willing served in the assembly again, and Willing barely made it through 1765.[68]

Although the ruling elite did everything in their power to retain control in the face of popular pressures, events transpired that further discredited the government. Nearly one hundred miles north and west of Philadelphia, Connecticut settlers moved into the Wyoming valley, claiming territory for that colony. Over the course of the 1760s, the area around Wyoming became a sort of war zone. Colonists from both Pennsylvania and Connecticut fought over land and government. Homesteads became forts, settlers erected palisades, and law seemed to vanish from the valley.[69] At the same time near Fort Pitt, Virginians under the direction of Governor Dunmore seized large tracts of land, and like the Connecticut settlers, declared the colony of Virginia as their lawful government. Law enforcement officials from both colonies attempted to claim jurisdiction in the same area, most times imprisoning opposing officials and turning a blind eye to violent land disputes to garner favoritism with land-hungry settlers. According to one dismayed onlooker, both governments created an "asylum of the lawless."[70] It should not be surprising that the majority of ordinary people living in these areas went "Liberty mad" in their support of the American Revolution.[71]

While Pennsylvania struggled over jurisdiction with Connecticut and Virginia, Indian war seemed imminent. The fight over land in Wyoming threatened a delicate peace with the Seneca, and the violent push for land by the Pennsylvanians and Virginians near Fort Pitt inflamed the minds of the Shawnee, Delaware, and Mingo nations. To make matters worse, in the back parts of Cumberland County, a German named Frederick Stump and his servant John Ironcutter murdered ten Indians—four men, three women, two young girls, and a female infant—burned their homes and hid their bodies. The Pennsylvania authorities, fearing Indian resentment and war, attempted to bring Stump and Ironcutter to trial in Philadelphia, letting loose sectional tensions over the failure of the court to go on circuit and adhere to the principal of conducting trials by a jury of peers. Inhabitants rescued them from jail, and they escaped punishment.[72]

The chaos inspired by jurisdictional fights between colonies, the fear of a renewed Indian war, and Stump's escape signified that nothing changed over the course of the 1760s; in fact, they seemed to get worse. Although politicians guaranteed some kind of reform, the province still struggled under an ineffective government that could not keep the peace or defend the colony. As the assembly explained, there was "a manifest Failure of Justice, either from a *Debility*" in government "or inexcusable Neglect." Nevertheless, legislators went on, they could not rectify this scenario. That inability, they well knew, might spell disaster for their own political positions, but they did not seem to know what to do or how to respond.[73]

Part of the problem was that the controversial imperial policies of the 1760s accomplished several goals of Galloway and other proponents of a royal takeover, yet things seemed to either get worse or remain the same. In the same year as the disturbances on the frontier, royal authority was manifest. The King-in-Parliament decreed that new taxes would be implemented and, moreover, that they would pay for troops on the frontier, local judges, and even the governors. Then the imperial secretary of North America, Lord Hillsborough, issued a circular demanding legislative compliance with the empire's wishes or dissolution. These new policies eradicated any doubt that the empire exercised supreme authority in Pennsylvania, but that control seemed unlikely to fix the "debility" of government. Moreover, if legislators still moved for a royal takeover, what more could they give the Crown to control? They would, as some argued, move Pennsylvanians "from the frying-pan into the fire."[74] Realizing the failure of his plans, all Galloway could do was complain that "we have the Name of a Government but no Safety or Protection under it. We have Laws without being executed, or even feared or respected. We have Offenders but no Punishment." In short, Galloway believed that Pennsylvania had "no Government" at all and that nothing could be done about it now.[75]

Such a realization meant that a majority of the assembly politicized and popularized a problem that they now claimed they could not solve. Obviously, this scenario frustrated ordinary citizens, and they, in turn, as one contemporary pointed out, "foam with politics" displaying an "an eternal rage."[76] In Lancaster County, the news of Stump and Ironcutter, combined with the "fresh insults" to government by Virginia and Connecticut, "has given rise to new flames in government & a torrent of abuse on those in authority."[77] Many ordinary inhabitants believed that those events demonstrated the "*evident* Debility of the present" government "enfeebled by an Union of Power & Property." As Jasper Yeates noted, politics seemed to "ingross" the "heads ... of many who could much better employ themselves in attention to their families," particularly the poorer sorts of people who questioned the ability of the government to provide for the welfare and happiness of the colony.[78] William Goddard, printer of the *Chronicle*, represented that renewed questioning, and to the public he described Pennsylvania's government as "*toothless* and *precarious*." In a series of letters from the editor in 1768, entitled *The Political Tattler*, which ran simultaneously with John Dickinson's *Letters from a Pennsylvania Farmer*, Goddard wrote extensively on the failures of government. He chided undutiful local law officers, rued the lack of a "coercive power," and complained that the government rarely brought criminals to justice. Goddard doubted whether even good laws could cure the ills of governance; "for it is not how *laws* are *made*, nor how they are *interpreted*, but how they are *used*." The government, he concluded, "neglected" and "discountenanced" the execution of the law.[79]

The prospects for the future were frightening. "Should Crimes of the first Rank, of the deepest Dye, remain unpunished, wicked Men will never be wanting, in any Country, to take Advantage of the Times, and the Debility of Government, to commit the like and other Crimes." The government, in "feeble Hands," proved too "weak to support Order in the

Province, or give Safety to the People."[80] Such deplorable circumstances, according to one observer, "more and more convinces the thoughtful part of the Inhabitants . . . that Unless a Change of Government takes place We shall be totally Undone and the Lawless and Abandond will do as they please."[81]

In sum, the train of events in the 1760s confirmed that something was hopelessly wrong and that the government, for all politicians proclaimed, could do nothing about it. Humble petitions requesting reform became, after 1768, more direct and unabashedly critical of the existing government. Petitioners could not help "considering the Insecurity of their Lives and Estates as worthy in some degree the Attention of the Legislature," and they were patently upset that the government ignored them. In crafting their petitions, inhabitants proclaimed with renewed urgency that "Lawless Murderers and Robbers" and "disorderly and wicked Persons" tormented them. Yet their remoteness from "the Seats of Justice and public Officers" left them susceptible to the crimes of people who easily escape "after perpetrating Crimes and Offences against the good Laws of the land." However, petitioners could not "see how the Evil is to be remedied while Courts of Law and Places for the Administration of Justice continue at Distances of Eighty Miles and upwards from them;— indeed they expect an Increase rather than a Diminution of those Evils." Such circumstances were, according to petitioners, "scarce to be paralleled in the History of any civilized Country."[82]

The combination of anger over the problems of governance and the exclusionary tactics of the assembly strengthened popular mobilizations to include more people in the political system. In Lancaster, for example, the rise of popular animosity toward the colonial government had an important impact on local politics. In 1768, James Webb, the chief burgess of Lancaster and ardent supporter of the assembly stepped down, inaugurating a new election where popular forces put an obscure shopkeeper, James Ralph, into the vacated chair. It was a stunning scenario and even more spectacular victory. Some elites, however, were mortified. The "butchers, barbers, taylors, blacksmiths & etc," a "class of plebeians we don't approve of" and who poured "a torrent of abuse on those in authority," entered local politics, sounded "Ralfe & Liberty . . . through our streets" and elected a man who made it known that the assembly and all who supported that body "may kiss his a[ss]."[83]

Popular outbursts transpired to some extent everywhere. One author noted in 1768 that "town meetings" in imitation of "well ordered republics" sprang up around the colony to instruct their representatives.[84] Similarly, artisans, challenging the governing structures that ruled them, explained in an open letter to Benjamin Franklin that "though the mechanics are censured and despised for attempting to judge or intermeddle in any public affairs, yet we are determined to pursue one steady plan ... [and will resist] every attempt made to oppress us or violate our [rights and liber]ties."[85]

By 1770, artisans, shopkeepers, and small farmers defied the political hierarchy on two fronts—extralegal and legal. Although many of these vocational groups participated in extralegal committees to resist imperial policies, these bodies grew increasingly factionalized as the dry goods merchants tried to direct the resistance effort. As a result, artisans, shopkeepers, and small farmers demanded to be looked on as more than "a rabble" and "totally disregarded!" They argued that "every man is part of the public" and it "cannot be deny'd that the emolument, and the preservation of liberties of the people is a universal maxim in government" and therefore it was "arrogant" and arbitrary for "a few individuals" to "insist that they only have a right" to rule. Ending rather threateningly, they stated, "The security and emolument of the people is the primary law of nature and nations," and whoever "acts contrary to this law should be considered a usurper and punished accordingly." Such violent language made statements such as "Stand forth ye famers, manufactures, mechanics and tradesmen ... in the defence of your Liberties," an ominous call to arms indeed.[86]

In the same year, ordinary citizens also wrote extensively against the "haughty" and "imperious" assembly that cared "but little of the midling Sort of People."[87] Artisans, for example, were upset that the assembly only represented elite merchants and lawyers, while everyone "avoided putting the Name of a Mechanic" up for election as they would "a Jew or a Turk." It infuriated them that a "Company of leading Men" had the power "to nominate Persons, and settle the Ticket for Assembly-men, Commissioners, Assessors, & c. without ever permitting the affirmative or negative Voice of a Mechanic to interfere." The legislators treated the mechanics as if they "have no Right to be consulted; that is, in Fact have no Right to *speak* or *think* for themselves." While middling folk may have "cautiously avoided" upsetting the oligarchy in the past, they were now determined to create their own election tickets; no one would act as "our Lord and Masters, and us their most abject Slaves."[88] Pennsylvanians everywhere called for their peers to "Rouse!" and "assert your Freedom at the Expence of your Fortunes and your Blood."[89]

Such sentiments when combined with the committee movement in the 1760s did have substantial effects. For example, through the committees, artisans, who had often separated on craft lines, started to see themselves as a group sharing some ideas and common political enemies. In the 1770s, they ran their own election ticket to oppose the "old corrupt Junto" and to gain an "equal right to agreements and resolutions with others for the public Good."[90] Even the rather conservative "White Oaks and Mechanicks" who used to support candidates like Galloway and Franklin "left the old Ticket." Striking out on their own, artisans seriously disrupted the political culture. The usual suspects in the legislature looked around them and agreed, "As to our Election, we are all in Confusion."[91]

In the end, however, the election machinery did not allow for a full-scale victory; the door to political inclusion did not swing open by the demands of artisans and others. Only one man on the mechanic ticket, Joseph Parker, a successful artisan tailor, won a seat in the assembly. It was nonetheless a huge victory and a substantial change in the political dynamics of the day. Opposing popular forces offered their own ticket and managed, against great odds, to elect one of their own. However, as happened in the past, oppositional groups won a fleeting victory, and Parker lost his seat in 1772, never to return.[92] Nonetheless, popular opposition frightened Galloway, who could not understand these "discontented ... mad people," who would leave the province to be "managed by the very Dregs" of society.[93]

Victory and defeat, progress and retrenchment, these polarities represent the reality of popular politics in the 1760s and early 1770s. Regardless of the roadblocks to inclusion, many who were spectators in the past attempted to enter politics by any means necessary. But their efforts represent a kaleidoscopic mobilization with no one pattern, no one identity, no one purpose or platform. As a result, collective pressure was ephemeral, fractured, and lacking the force necessary to make real change. However, as that mobilization through the Continental Congress took greater collective shape, it ultimately altered an effort for inclusion to one of exclusion or, rather, to a move to fashion a government that represented the people and their interests and that was not the current government.

The Consolidation of Power and the Beginning of Revolution

The developing colonial resistance effort in the 1770s and the imperial reaction radically transformed the popular mobilizations and political activity of Pennsylvanians. It gave focus, collective purpose, and legitimacy to new oppositional forces that substantially differed from those of the past. Pennsylvanians with considerably different ideas for the future came to power in extralegal spaces during these years and offered a plan of action to redress both imperial and provincial concerns. In the months before American independence, the committees and conventions birthed in the resistance movement became the popularly accepted government, and they set Pennsylvania on a path to governmental reform that had been demanded for decades, except now this reform would be enacted and created by a new government with a new constitution existing on an entirely different calculus, the sovereign authority of the people. Revolutionary forces waxed strong in the 1770s, and the colonial government, try as it did, could not contain or resist them.

With the partial repeal of the Townshend duties in 1770, opposition ebbed but did not completely disappear. A duty on tea remained and provided enough animosity to keep resistance afloat. In Pennsylvania, internal problems kept colonists extremely active and ever questioning the government. For example, it did not take much in 1773 with the Tea Act, which gave the East India Company a monopoly over the North American tea trade, for popular forces to materialize and violently deter the landing of tea and the tea agents from carrying out their office. The popular threat was so menacing that one onlooker remarked, "Any further attempt to enforce this act must end in blood."[94]

Those in power frowned upon such popular gatherings. Earlier that same year, the Virginia House of Burgesses suggested that the legislatures throughout the continent create committees of correspondence, and the Pennsylvania assembly balked. Creating committees remained a nonstarter for someone like Speaker of the House Joseph Galloway. After all, the control of those committees shifted over the course of the 1760s into the hands of artisans, shopkeepers, and farmers who openly challenged the representativeness of the legislature. By February 1774, every colony except Pennsylvania and North Carolina had established committees, which left the resistance effort in the hands of what politicians considered illegitimate groups and assemblages of people.[95] Resisting the landing of tea, for instance, was carried out by artisans and others working within town meetings and through published calls for action. The old committees and the legislators were nowhere to be found.[96]

As a result, broadsides, pamphlets, and newspaper articles shot from the presses blasting the legislature. One article noted that the assembly's failure to establish committees in the face of parliamentary attacks confirmed that Galloway and "his Junto" conspired "against the Liberties of their Country." They should "lose the Power they have so arrogantly assumed." Moreover, Pennsylvanians began to turn the "weakness of government" argument back on the political leaders. The strong government that those politicians promised in the 1760s, writers claimed, could only occur if new people took the helm of government. Such a move, a writer in Philadelphia noted, would bring "Law to this opulent City and County." Pennsylvanians needed "Men to represent them, who have, in addition to Integrity of Heart, Heads to plan, Spirit to execute, and who can feel for such of their Constituents who stand most in need of their Care and Protection."[97]

However much the assembly under the direction of Galloway sought to curb these popular challenges to its authority, imperial measures propelled matters forward faster than he or anyone else could effectively deal with them. Over the course of 1773 and 1774, the Crown acted vigorously to project its own power in the face of colonial intransigence. The Tea Act inspired collective action and tumult up and down the Eastern Seaboard, coming to a head in Massachusetts. The Bostonian response, dumping tea into the harbor, sparked imperial reactions with the ingloriously dubbed Coercive Acts of 1774. The Boston Port Bill, the Administration of Justice Act, the Massachusetts Government Act, and their combination with the Quebec Act created havoc throughout the colonies. As historian Pauline Maier has noted, they "seemed to prove beyond all doubt the existence of a despotic plot."[98]

Almost immediately after news of the Coercive Acts, colonial North Americans clamored for renewed and concerted resistance with economic boycotts. However, they planned their resistance differently than they had in the past. The committees that enforced the boycotts before, those factional entities without common direction and lacking any type of legitimacy, proved leaky vessels and largely ineffectual. The individual colonies acted independently and therefore the demure of one meant, in reality, the end of boycotts for all. In order to assure a continent-wide resistance effort and to demonstrate colonial solidarity, several colonies called for the formation of a continental congress.[99]

Pennsylvanians joined the chorus for a congress. Yet they attempted to use the moment to address *both* imperial and provincial political realities. On May 20, 1774, mere days after news of the Coercive Acts, Pennsylvanians came together in a mass public meeting at City Tavern to discuss the merits of a continental resistance. The leaders of the meeting—Joseph Reed, Charles Thomson, and Thomas Mifflin—were new to the political world, excluded by the assembly, and looked to use this meeting to challenge the colonial government. At the tavern, these men spoke openly for a concerted resistance, demanding that Pennsylvania join Boston in a complete embargo of British trade. They capped off the day with a speech by John Dickinson in which the famous Pennsylvania farmer proposed forming a petition to the deputy governor and Speaker of the House to convene the assembly to choose delegates for the proposed congress, thus garnering the approval of any moderate-leaning members of the gathering. This seemingly moderate move was part of a plan to challenge the colonial government. Reed, Thomson, and Mifflin did not expect the deputy governor or the Speaker to comply with such demands, nor did they want them to. According to Thomson, "They had no confidence in the members of the Assembly, who were known to be under the influence of Galloway and his party. They, therefore had another object in view." That "object" was to use the assembly's inaction to gain popular control of the resistance and the choice of congressional delegates, thus propelling opposition and undermining the government in one fell swoop.[100]

Seriously miscalculating the gravity of the situation, the deputy governor and Galloway acted as expected, refused to convene the legislature, and played right into the hands of Read, Thomson, and Mifflin. Soon after, colonists supported popular control during well-attended public meetings in Hanover, Lancaster County, York Town, York County, and various other places throughout the province.[101] On June 15, for example, over twelve hundred artisans met on the statehouse yard to proclaim their support of a continental congress and a convention to direct the colony's resistance efforts. Just a few days later, nearly eight thousand inhabitants attended a town meeting and created a forty-four-member committee of correspondence to coordinate with all of these other committees and meetings to form a provincial convention. Achieving their goals, the convention was called, met, and swiftly acted by choosing popular delegates to Congress and drafting instructions to both the new congressional delegates and, importantly, the assembly.[102]

This popular action stunned Pennsylvania's politicians. New extralegal bodies claiming to derive their power from the people demanded the representation and political inclusion the assembly had resisted for decades. According to one legislator, the convention's drafting of instructions to the assembly proved that Pennsylvanians wandered "into the maizy labyrinths of perplexity and disorder." He urged his fellow assemblymen to ignore such directives because if they gave them "any weight," these new extralegal bodies "will supersede you" and thus "incur a dissolution of our charter.""Setting up a power to control you," he went on, "is setting up anarchy above order; IT IS THE BEGINNING OF REPUBLICANISM." In short, the government must "nip this pernicious weed in the bud, before it has taken too deep root."[103]

In a belated move, Galloway and Deputy Governor Penn tried to salvage the government's control and convened the assembly. But some damage had been done, and a committee from the convention greeted the assembly with a list of delegates to Congress and instructions demanding Pennsylvania act in concert with the rest of the colonies. Its choice of delegates was just as galling to the legislators as the instructions. The convention wanted Thomas Willing, John Dickinson, and James Wilson to represent the province, none of whom held seats in the assembly, though two of them, Dickinson and Willing, had served as legislators for a short time in the past.[104] By offering up these three candidates, the public meeting defied the representativeness of the assembly, especially Joseph Galloway. All three openly despised the Speaker, and many remembered that Dickinson actually got into a fistfight with Galloway in 1764. Nevertheless, the legislators met this challenge as they did all popular representations in the past—they ignored it and chose delegates for Congress from among their own members, and Joseph Galloway was one of them.[105]

Approving the Congress, no matter the selection of delegates, made any attempt to nip popular mobilization and power in the bud an impossible task. The Continental Congress forever changed politics in Pennsylvania and elsewhere. The first Congress addressed salient issues related to the resistance by declaring colonial rights as British subjects and providing a concerted plan of opposition to imperial measures. The most important accomplishment proved the creation of the Continental Association that placed nonimportation on a quasi-national footing. Signed by all members of Congress, even Joseph Galloway, who opposed the move from the beginning, it bound all colonists in mainland North America to obey the articles of association, stipulating that on December 1, 1774, colonists could not import certain articles from Great Britain, and in September 1775 a full embargo of British trade would take place. To enforce the association, Congress recommended the creation of new committees throughout the colonies that would derive their power from the people and the new Congress.[106]

Refusing to wait for the assembly to act, Pennsylvanians set elections for new committees to enforce the association, and they were the largest and most popular yet. Sixty members composed the Philadelphia Committee, which Cumberland County surpassed with eighty-five. Similar-sized committees existed elsewhere. York County created a committee of fifty, and Chester County elected a committee of seventy. To put these numbers in perspective, Cumberland County only had two assembly representatives and its only other powerful office, justice of the peace, was an appointed one. With the committees, over eighty popularly elected people from Cumberland County alone, over double the number of total representatives in the assembly, entered the political world clad in the sovereignty and legitimacy offered by the new Congress.[107]

Furthering the impact, reach, and popularity of these new bodies, the counties were divided into committee districts for the purpose of effective action and election. Such a tactic allowed the committees to have a popular backing that exceeded current institutions.[108] Where Pennsylvanians had to travel to distant county seats to participate in elections for legislators and other elected officials, they now only had to go to a district center or even a central place in their town. The inhabitants of York County, for example, wanted to assure that their committee was elected "in such a Manner, that there is at least one of that Body in each Township of the County."[109] Like York County, the city of Philadelphia's committee had six subdivisions elected locally to regulate the use of scarce articles such as wool and enforced the prohibitions on trade. They inspected ships and their cargoes and looked into all reports of people breaking the articles of association.[110]

Through these committees, traditional political outsiders "were suddenly raised to power." In Chester County, of the seventy committee members only two had been legislators, one of whom hadn't sat in the assembly since 1771 and the other only served for one year. Similarly, in Northampton County, only one out of forty-seven members had held a seat in the legislature in the past, and that was in 1769.[111] Many of these new political participants were political outsiders like the leader of the Black Boys, James Smith, who was elected chairman of Westmoreland's county committee. With such people in control, who "were impatient with any kind of opposition" to their authority, the committee movement gave vent to pent-up animosity toward the provincial government and provided ordinary inhabitants significant power to exercise "an uncontrouled authority over their fellow-citizens."[112]

By the summer and fall of 1775, the committees were pregnant with power, potent politically, and acting as the most important governing mechanism in the province. In September of that year, the city committee published a proclamation stating that it provided "the reality of justice" in the colony. That committee, and no one else, decided who did and did not act "consistent with the peace and welfare of society." Anyone whom the committee judged dangerous to the public welfare, they declared, had no right "to the protection of a community or society" and therefore was "deemed a foe to the rights of British America and unworthy of those blessings" of government.[113] Such statements claimed a power for the committees that exceeded anything granted by the association.

They achieved that expansive authority in part through popular buy-in. Whether because of loyalty to the cause or fear of violence, many people openly accepted the legitimacy of the association and the committees that upheld it. It became rather common for individuals to run ads in the newspapers claiming adherence to the goals of the association or of their innocence if anyone suspected they broke any of the articles. One Philadelphian published an advertisement proclaiming, contrary to rumors, that he did not upon "the arrival of the ships from England this fall" make "it my business to purchase a large quantity of several sorts of Dry Goods, in order to sell them out again at an advanced price."[114] He surely had something to fear. A woman who ran a small shop in the city, for instance, openly "disapproved of the rebellious proceedings of the inhabitants" and had her shop ransacked, her goods carried away, and even her personal clothing stolen by "three different Rebellious Committees." On October 5, 1775, she fled with only the clothes on her back because they "threatened to destroy her house and injure her person."[115]

The association meant much more than just abiding by and enforcing trade restrictions; it also required the active participation of inhabitants to "improve themselves in the military art."[116] By asking colonists to support a potential war with Britain, the chance for which was obviously heightened after the outbreak of actual fighting at Lexington and Concord, the association created a scenario where inhabitants could delineate friends from foes, thus providing a semblance of collective identity wrapped up in the resistance movement. Like the trade regulations, the committees took on responsibility of enforcement. Committees throughout the colony canvased their districts compiling lists of "Associators" and "Non-Associators."[117] Such a move brought many more people under the watchful eye of the committees, thus increasing their coercive strength. In

Bucks County, which had been known for its conservatism in the past, the committee dealt harshly with those who refused to muster or provide monetary backing for the war effort. When a local man refused to associate and spoke out against the committees, the Bucks County Committee quickly deemed him "a disciple of those species of creatures called *Tories*," and he was "formally introduced to a tar barrel, of which he was repeatedly pressed to smell." Realizing his potential fate, the man "thought it prudent to take leave abruptly."[118] Others, rather than fearing the tar bucket, shuddered at the thought of being thrown in "the Common Gaol." In Lancaster, one man was "Double Ironed, and imprisoned for 18 Months" for speaking out against the committees and refusing to associate.[119] Similarly, in Cumberland County, critics of the committees complained of being "seized in the dead of night by order of the usurping Powers, [and] imprisoned."[120]

"Usurping Powers" was an apt description of what was going on. The committees were effectively consolidating governmental powers within themselves. They acted like an official court, hauling people before them, adjudicating their guilt or innocence, and punishing offenders. Some committees even made the county courthouses their official meeting place, thus expanding their aura of legitimacy. What was more, they even had control of the local jails. The deputy governor of the province, John Penn, knew not what to do. He regularly wrote to the secretary of state for North America of the powers these committees held and their threat to legitimate government. Demonstrating his predicament before the outset of war in 1775, Penn related that the city committee arrested and jailed a British major. The officer no more than got off a ship at port when the committee took him into custody, questioned him, and rifled through his papers. The major applied to the deputy governor for his release, which, Penn explained, "hard and illegal as his Confinement was, your Lordship may well imagine it was absolutely out of my power by any Means to afford him in the present disordered Affairs here." Likewise, the major, "very frankly told me he did not expect it, as things were circumstanced."[121] In short, the committees rendered impotent what little government existed in Pennsylvania.

If the provincial government and its supporters challenged such extralegal authority, the committees flexed their muscle and demonstrated that they wielded real power. When Isaac Hunt, a prominent politician and lawyer, attempted to bring a suit in the courts to protest the city committee's seizure of property, the committee reacted. On September 6, 1775, committeemen ripped Hunt from his home and hauled him before the committee at the Coffee House, where they ruled that Hunt "endeavoured to contravene the Association." For his crimes, the committee imitated the punishments meted out by the courts by placing Hunt in "a humble Dung Cart" and parading him through the streets. At each corner block, for nearly two hours, Hunt read out an apology asking "pardon of the public."[122] During Hunt's predicament, "a respected citizen," Dr. John Kearsley, challenged the authority of such punishments. The committee quickly shifted focus to Kearsley, threw him in the cart, and dragged him around the city. Refusing to be cowed, Kearsley tore off his wig and twirled it around while he sang "God Save the King." In response, the committee beat him and sent him to jail wounded, bloodied, and bald where he remained for the last days of his life.[123]

In many ways, Congress often had to keep pace with the committees. It took until October 6, 1775, before Congress legitimized the above activities, resolving that the committees should "arrest and secure every person in their respective colonies, whose going at large may, in their opinion, endanger the safety of the colony, or the liberties of America," a rather wide grant.[124] Such actions made it seem as if "Congress was nothing but the echo of the Committees."[125]

For some, this moment had immense potential. With their collective power, maybe they could "new model their government" by expanding seats in the legislature, setting term limits to undermine a "dangerous" oligarchy, and open the doors of the chamber to the public. While the assembly had "dared to refuse their Constituents" in the past, people now believed they could "seize the present opportunity of redressing our provincial grievances, and let us repair the faults which time and experience have discovered in our constitution, in such a manner, that it may be transmitted safely to the latest posterity."[126]

The assembly, realizing its predicament, attempted to tap into and control the committees by establishing the Committee of Safety, a revolutionary body composed of both members and nonmembers of the assembly from all parts of the province. The Committee of Safety coordinated with other revolutionary committees in propelling the resistance movement forward. However, this body differed from the county committees in that it controlled the executive power of government over the military, thus removing it, forever, from the hands of the Penns. Not only did this new system undercut Penn's authority over the troops, but the assembly used the moment to deny the governor's and the Crown's authority over legislation.[127]

Within this moment lies a critical point: the assembly acted; it created a body that represented more than itself and did away with all vestiges of the Crown in its executive capacity. Moreover, Pennsylvania now had a military power controlled by a new representative body working in tandem with the committees recommended by Congress. If resisting imperial and executive authority constituted the only goal in this moment, then the mechanisms were in place, and therefore Pennsylvanians should have worked within them to complete the task at hand. However, that did not happen. Over the course of the 1760s and 1770s, the assembly faced its own challenges and alienated the people. Although new people came to power over the course of those years, particularly in 1774 when Joseph Galloway retired after his "life was threatened," the legislature still did not provide inclusion in its chamber nor redress the grievances of the people.[128] In return, many Pennsylvanians still despised that body and continued to challenge it; the "House of Assembly" as one author put it, "is part of that power from which we are trying to break away."[129]

The committees served as a significant engine to undermine the authority and legitimacy of the House. In the fall of 1775, the city committee charged many of the legislators with "disaffection" to the cause and moved to "dissolve" the assembly "and substitute a convention" composed of committee representatives to govern the province "in their stead." The committees sought a complete turnover of all that governed in the past and the placement of that power in their hands. Only the impassioned reasoning of John Dickinson, Thomas Mifflin, and Charles Thomson, members of both the city committee and the assembly (though new members), staved off the toppling of the old government.[130] Their about-face struck some as abandonment of the cause, and, what was more, their corruptibility. Dickinson, for example, was charged with trying to ingratiate himself with the Crown to become "a Governor," proving that "interest steals" the most virtuous of hearts. Unsurprisingly, some warned that Dickinson and others should fall like the "*Galloway* rock."[131] For his part, Dickinson felt betrayed by his "unkind countrymen," but, as was pointed out to him, "they did not desert you. You left them."[132]

The winter and spring of 1776 significantly challenged anyone's ability to avoid the dissolution of the government. In January 1776, Thomas Paine, a recent immigrant to Philadelphia from England, published his famous and popular *Common Sense*. In that little book, Paine provided the justifications necessary for a full break with the empire. In plain language, he criticized the whole idea of monarchy, while also calling on the public to wrest control of the colonial governments and place all power in the people. His ideas spoke to colonists everywhere, but particularly in Pennsylvania, where ordinary people advocated yet never actually realized those very designs. By March of 1776, Paine's pamphlet sparked "a terrible wordy war" on "the subject of Independence" and a new responsive government.[133]

The assembly, which controlled the selection of delegates to Congress, rejected Paine's clarion call. Dickinson, for example, now firmly in control of the assembly, could not nor would not envision an America outside the empire and therefore refused to approve any movement toward independence.[134] The stance of the assembly against independence further discredited its authority, and many members of the committees believed they had the assembly right where they wanted it. In a letter from the city committee to the other committees throughout the province, members blasted the assembly as unrepresentative and therefore unreflective of "the sense of this Province." They also argued that the assembly endangered "the safety of this Province."[135]

Combined with Paine's radical ideas, the committee's bold assertions unleashed a firestorm throughout the province. Newspapers teemed with articles branding the government an oligarchy filled with "*unworthy persons*" who treated their offices "as their own property, and deemed it an inheritance to their children." Even the charter did not escape the wrath of angry Pennsylvanians who derided it as "defective," "an imperfect thing," and a "wretched mangled constitution." According to one author, "I object to the present mutilated constitution of Pennsylvania, its tendency to destroy the right of election, and render the exercise of it troublesome, partial and precarious, giving advantage to the profligate and corrupt." Articles in the press castigated the provincial government for failing to uphold "first principles" and "securing the people's liberty." The politics of the 1760s came back to haunt the assembly; it was now a truism that, as one author railed, "we live under a species of government which has always been reprobated by good men as the worst in the world."[136]

In the face of popular antipathy, the assembly again moved to quell dissension and revamp its image. On March 8, 1776, legislators begrudgingly agreed to enlarge membership by seventeen seats, though maintaining the dominance of the eastern oligarchy. They increased the city's seats to four, and the remaining thirteen they gave to the eight back counties. Many of them hoped this alteration would muffle the "Mouths of those violent Republicans belonging to the Committee."[137] The assembly's attempts were too little and too late. It had its supporters, to be sure, but the violent aspersions cast on the assembly by its opponents drowned out their voices. Just a few months earlier, "the infatuated populace" had set fire to the printing house of the *Pennsylvania Mercury*, a newspaper known to be controlled by "friends to government."[138] In any event, belated reforms did not muzzle the committees; those bodies, having tasted the power gained through the resistance effort, refused to give it up and still looked for ways to topple the government.

The assembly's opposition to American independence and the growing importance of Congress provided critical weapons for the committees to achieve that goal. In Congress, the delegations from Massachusetts and Virginia vigorously supported independence and increasingly viewed Pennsylvania as an obstacle to their designs. The goals of the committees and of some members of Congress converged in this moment, producing some rather strange bedfellows. "Fiery independents" in the committees such as Thomas Paine, Timothy Matlack, and Christopher Marshall aligned themselves with the Virginia and Massachusetts delegations to Congress—Richard Henry Lee and John and Samuel Adams. The alliance seems strange; John Adams would later castigate Paine as "a mongrel between Pigg and Puppy, begotten by a wild Boar on a Bitch Wolf."[139] Nevertheless, they needed one another; the delegates and the committee members both sought independence, and they both viewed the Pennsylvania assembly as an impediment they needed to remove.

Lee and the Adamses concocted a plan with the leaders of the committees to dissolve the Pennsylvania government. The congressional delegates would offer a resolution to Congress recommending that any government that did not meet "the exigencies of their affairs" and still operated under "oaths and affirmations" of loyalty to the Crown "should be totally suppressed" and "all the powers of government" should be "exerted under the authority of the people." Meanwhile, if all went as planned in Congress, the committee members would organize a public conference to vote on a popular dissolution of the government and the creation of a convention to form a new one.[140]

Both sides worked fast to accomplish their goals. The delegates to Congress offered the resolution on May 10, and it passed in its final form on May 15. By May 20, the city committee organized a public meeting with between four and five thousand people in attendance, voted in favor of the congressional resolution, and lodged a formal protest against the assembly. They also sent runners to all the county committees, communicating the new resolution and a call for a colony-wide conference. In short order, committee members and others from across the colony convened in early June and voted that the government did not meet the exigencies of their affairs and a convention should be called to form a new government "on the authority of the people."[141] The old leaders were shocked: "A Convention chosen by the people will consist of the most fiery Independents; they will have the whole Executive & Legislative authority in their hands." If the assembly didn't act fast, it would have to "bid adieu to our old happy constitution & peace."[142]

Working on the assumption that the assembly still had power, legislators refused to recognize the authority of the conference or the upcoming convention. They declared, as they had done in 1764 with the unpopular push for royal government, that only the legislature had the right to alter the constitution, and, moreover, its refusal to do so was a popular measure. To demonstrate that popularity, assembly members tried to compete with the committees and canvased for signatures to a remonstrance against the Provincial Conference. With thousands of signatures in hand, legislators claimed popular legitimacy and made public proclamations stating their refusal to alter the government.[143] Such tactics proved futile.

When the public learned they could "settle a form of government for themselves, the rage of the people burst out in protest against their present Assembly."[144] Soon thereafter, the county committees, asserting their position as "Guardians" of the "public welfare," sent instructions to their local legislators demanding they "leave" the chamber if "the continuance of the Assembly" was proposed.[145] Far more menacing, the voluntary battalions throughout the colony mustered, declared the assembly "have no authority," and avowed they would "support the measures now adopted at all hazards, be the consequences what they may."[146] The popular pressure was so immense that some legislators asked public forgiveness, and people who signed the assembly's Remonstrance against the Provincial Conference "repented of their folly." According to Benjamin Rush, "many hundreds who signed it" seized copies of the Remonstrance and "scratched out their names"; still others published advertisements that they "had been cajoled." Apparently, one man was so incensed that he tracked down the person who got him to sign the Remonstrance and "begged him to erase his name" because he was tricked by "d—d lies." In some places, the Remonstrance was publicly burned "as a treasonable libel upon the liberties of America."[147]

When one legislator, James Rankin, refused to leave the assembly and defied his county committee, claiming they "derived no authority from the county in general to command their Representatives," his local committee arrested him.[148] He soon became "convinced of the bad tendency of my past conduct," apologized for injuring "the Committee of York county by sundry public misrepresentations," and begged to be "restored to a good understanding and friendship with my countrymen." Not only did he offer a public apology, but he gave the committee "sufficient surety for his good behaviour in future."[149] By offering surety, which is a legally binding agreement backed by a financial guarantee of compliance, Rankin recognized the legal legitimacy of the committees.

While the committees rose in power, the assembly withered away into insignificance. By early June, the assembly couldn't even maintain a quorum. At one point, only eighteen legislators, a little more than a third of the membership, attended.[150] In stark contrast, the Provincial Conference had over ninety members in attendance, representing all the counties of the province.

That conference nearly completed the revolutionary consolidation of power. Instead of sticking to the tasks it was called on to complete, namely establishing the representative framework of the proposed constitutional convention, members declared that they were "the only representative body of this colony" and proceeded to pass "resolutions" regulating the lives of citizens and usurping governmental authority. In the course of one week, they commanded the citizenry to obtain travel passes from the committees, ordered those same bodies to "examine strangers," called on the counties to muster forty-five hundred men for war, and drew up regulations for how those troops would be mustered, paid, provisioned, and commanded. When it finally addressed how the colony would be represented in the convention, the conference broke with past political practices, giving every county the same number of representatives and expanding suffrage to any male associator over twenty-one who was rated for any kind of tax in the past. While such a move theoretically expanded the vote, the conference also circumscribed potential voters to those who supported the cause, stipulating that any voter, upon request, had to declare by oath or affirmation that he did not hold himself "bound to bear allegiance to George the third." In addition, all elected convention members needed to take a similar oath or affirmation.[151]

By demanding oaths and affirmations, the conference drew on a long-held tradition to announce that the convention represented a sovereign power. Since 1705, the Crown had required colonists to take similar oaths and affirmations for that very purpose. At every election, Pennsylvanians verbally confirmed their status as subjects and voters. Even election inspectors and elected officials had to declare their allegiance to the Crown.[152] Thus oaths and affirmations cut both ways in 1776, and when Congress declared independence in early July, those oaths had a tendency to exclude any Pennsylvanian who desired independence or still sought to remain a British subject. In sum, oaths did not create divisions but rather accentuated battle lines, highlighting two potential ruling powers catering to drastically different bases.

As a result, the Provincial Convention was unlike any other governing body seen before. Dissimilar from the assembly and council, the convention represented the various regional, ethnic, religious, and social interests of Pennsylvania.[153] Most members came from meager backgrounds. They were "Men of small property and learning."[154] As a whole, they were slightly younger than the average legislator, less educated, and new to the governing process. Only 23 percent of the nearly one hundred members had ever held an official position in the old government and only 7 percent had served in the assembly at one time. The majority of them, over 60 percent, came to power through the committee movement.[155]

These political neophytes completed what the Provincial Conference started, effectively destroying the colonial government and concluding the popular consolidation of power. Although tasked with writing a new constitution, the convention took its cue from the conference and set itself up as the sole governing power in the province. Meeting every day but Sunday for over two months, the convention spent much of its time "engaged in the consideration of legislative and executive business." While undertaking that business, it replaced the assembly's Council of Safety with a new executive council to direct the war effort, levied taxes, made continental currency legal tender, established new legal definitions for treason and citizenship, designed punishments for counterfeiting, and set precedents for the treatment of debtors.[156] To enforce its laws and to ensure "proper officers of justice be appointed under the authority of the people only," the convention denied the legal authority of existing judges and justices and appointed new ones in each of the counties. The convention also expanded the power of those officers to imprison "evil minded persons" for "such a time they deem proper."[157] The convention's takeover was so complete that ordinary citizens sent it petitions to fix mundane matters and for relief. Even Congress directed all communications and recommendations to the convention, completely ignoring the assembly—a body that could not achieve a quorum.[158]

By late summer, the colonial assembly finally recognized it had lost the battle and no longer governed Pennsylvania. On September 26, it quietly settled its accounts and dissolved forever. The consolidation of power was complete, and the revolution was in full swing. Rejoicing, many ordinary Pennsylvanians applauded their efforts and looked forward to the creation of government that would "have for its object, not the emolument of one man, or class of men only, but the safety, liberty and happiness of every individual in the community,"[159] a statement that was at once hopeful for the future and critical of the old colonial establishment.

6

"For the Security and Protection of the Community"

Revolutionary State Formation

WHEREAS ALL GOVERNMENT ought to be instituted and supported for the security and protection of the community as such, and to enable the individuals who compose it to enjoy their natural rights, and the other blessings which the Author of existence has bestowed upon man; and whenever these great ends of government are not obtained, the people have a right, by common consent to change it, and take such measures as to them may appear necessary to promote their safety and happiness." This rather lengthy sentence, full of meaning, began the document that would become the governing instrument of a state created by popular forces in the wake of the congressional May 15 resolve. These words were not idle but reflected both the justifications of revolution and a rather general framework for the new government. In one sentence, the members of the Pennsylvania Constitutional Convention condemned the colonial polity and lauded the prospects for the future under a state predicated on the sovereign authority of the people. Their government would offer the basic guarantees and services of government for the "community" rather than any "individual" in a new republican state.[1]

Yet for all this sentence conveys, we know little about the government created in 1776. To be sure, there has not been a dearth of studies exploring the Pennsylvania Constitution. It remains a staple in all histories of the revolution. We have learned through this extensive historiography that Pennsylvanians created a democratic constitution, a "radical manifesto" as one historian terms it, which represented the democratic spirit undergirding the revolutionary movement.² Historians have detailed how this document expanded the suffrage to nearly all white males, erased property qualifications to hold office, and obliterated the powers of the executive. Some have even ridiculed the Pennsylvania Constitution, claiming men ignorant of the science of government drafted the constitution in a moment of passion and therefore it was doomed to failure.³ Historians, then, have provided a rather standard and repeated history of the constitution—it was democratic in the supreme.

Regardless of the sheer number of studies on the constitution, how democracy would provide for the "protection of the community" and "promote the safety and happiness" of the public is far less understood and rarely explained beyond the constitution's expansion of the suffrage and its structuring of the legislative and executive branches. Nevertheless, governance was a key issue for revolutionary reformers, where the safety of the public involved the protection of the people from both tyranny and anarchy, the duality of liberty. In the convention that framed the constitution, members discussed and demanded penal, prison, and judicial reforms. They even set aside space in the constitution to address land policies and the creation of institutions, officers, and laws to eradicate "Vice and Immorality." They debated and instituted such changes in the hopes that their state could secure "the great end and design of all government," the "welfare and safety of the inhabitants."⁴ Writing from the convention, Thomas Smith, a member from Bedford County, saw that creating such a government meant that they had "to clear every part of the old rubbish out of the way and begin upon a clear foundation."⁵

While the constitutional moment started the state formation process, the experience of the war years propelled state building forward in significant directions. After independence, Pennsylvanians faced exigencies, particularly internal political divisions, financial woes, challenges posed by the state's "disaffected" population, and a civil government that initially failed to live up to the lofty expectations of the constitution. The war years demanded more alterations than the constitution provided and a far more authoritative system of governance. Yet the constitution delivered a representative structure that allowed for change. During these years of turmoil, statesmen and citizens worked together to reform the judiciary, the officers that staffed it, and the penal system. They extended state power by regulating the internal dynamics of the economy with new boards, officers, and regulations predicated on the public good of the community. At the same time, they also created a military force and county military officers attached and subordinate to the civil power that served a vital law enforcement and coercive function to implement state tactics and exert state authority at a time of perceived instability. The years 1776 to 1786 were years of profound change in Pennsylvania, when both statesmen and citizens fashioned a representative yet powerful, coercive, and extractive state.

The Constitutional Moment and the Foundation of the State

While not much is known about the debates in the state Constitutional Convention, we do know that the delegates used that forum to address issues of government and governance that were sources of contention, especially for those who stood on and outside the political margins. In the process, they altered Pennsylvania's fundamental laws and embraced a vision of republican governance that placed the needs of the community above Lockean standards of individualism. Both moves created a solid foundation that future officials could build upon as needs demanded during the war.

While most historians of revolutionary Pennsylvania focus on the creation of a unicameral assembly, annual elections, and the expansion of the suffrage in the constitution as the cornerstone of this new American form of democracy, one copied in Vermont and Georgia, these changes made up only a small part of a new system of government. In many ways, the creation of an annually elected unicameral assembly was not that revolutionary. The Frame of Government of 1701 created such a legislature. The framers of the constitution, no doubt influenced by Thomas Paine's argument for unicameral legislatures in *Common Sense*, merely shaped the existing legislative body to fit their own needs and interests.

Other more important constitutional changes came out of the political dialogue that started in the 1760s. During that decade, Pennsylvanians from both eastern and western sections demanded equal representation in the legislature, legislative transparency, and a popular voice in the shaping of public policy. The Constitutional Convention addressed these issues directly in the Declaration of Rights, holding firm to the idea that "all power being originally inherent in, and consequently derived from, the people; therefore all officers of government, whether legislative or executive, are their trustees and servants, and at all times accountable to them." In order to achieve that goal and assure its maintenance in the future, the framers made it an inherent right that "the people" could "assemble together, to consult for their common good, to instruct their representatives, and to apply to the legislature for redress of grievances, by address, petition, or remonstrance." While the majority of Pennsylvania's Declaration of Rights replicated Virginia's Declaration, this resolve was original to Pennsylvania. It drew on experience and past demands for a representative structure where the people could judge and direct public policy.[6]

To assure that citizens played a critical part in the legislative process, the framers also included other popular processes. In four conterminous sections of the constitution, they opened the legislature's doors to the public, declared they would print the votes of every legislator, and avowed that the legislature would provide each proposed piece of legislation for public consideration before it could become the law of the state. Finally, the framers allocated equal representation to each county, which future assemblies would regularly readjust based on population. Beyond the creation of a unicameral assembly, then, the framers of the constitution created a vastly different system of government and representation that offered everyday people, both within and without doors, a greater say.

The framers addressed other problems related to elections and political participation to break the oligarchic nature of the colonial past. Although historians often argue that Pennsylvania's colonial oligarchy symbolized political stability, many contemporaries believed otherwise.[7] For them, the system reflected exclusion and an unrepresentative government that proved unresponsive to the concerns and interests of its constituents. Determined not to allow this "inconvenient aristocracy" from rearing its ugly head again, the framers not only expanded the franchise to all white male taxpayers (and their sons), but they also assured equal access to the ballot box by replicating the tactics of the extralegal committees, creating several voting districts in each county. Such a move, they hoped, would diffuse political power, making it difficult for anyone to manage or deter voting. Moreover, unlike the old oligarchy, the framers viewed legislative turnover as a sign of a healthy government that would, theoretically, always respond to and represent its citizens. In the assembly, no person could serve more than four out of seven years, and no one could serve more than three consecutive years out of seven in the executive branch. Even elected county officers, such as sheriffs, could not serve for more than three consecutive years. Term limits, coupled with the absence of property qualifications to hold office and new voting districts, guaranteed a revolving polity and a greater level of political inclusion.

While many historians have focused on some of the changes outlined above, the constitution offered a far more sweeping transformation of government by altering its governing ideology and the methods of law enforcement.[8] Liberty, the byword of revolution, seemed the perfect catchall phrase that popular writers used to address these issues around the time of the convention. It was that "glorious" idea that assured the "*Safety* of your *Lives* and *Friends*."[9] Yet that safety encompassed more than just the rights and protections of individuals *from* the government. It revolved around the protection of life and the security of property within the social body and, far from elucidating freedom, it emphasized the restriction of the amount of freedom granted to a person in society; it delineated social interactions, upheld collective rights, and required people to know and understand their obligations as individuals in a community. Liberty, then, was a duality. On one side stood freedom of action, on the other, restrictions and restraints enforced by law and government for the "public good." *Salus populi suprema lex est* served as rallying cry of this vision of liberty and government, making it a central truth that, as historian Michael Jan Rozbicki notes, "a single person living on a desert island cannot be said to possess liberty."[10] The positive benefits of law and government, then, and not just their restriction, were central to any conception of liberty. It was absurd to think, one writer proclaimed, that "the Creator formed Man for Society, and that society cannot subsist without regulations, laws, and government; and at the same time to assert, that in spite of all human care to prevent it, every government will degenerate into a tyranny." Government should be, if properly emanating from a body of sovereign people, a necessary good; it was a "daring *blasphemy* of the *divine attributes*" to think otherwise.[11]

The constitution's inclusion of penal reform, prison reform, and the promise to pass laws to prevent vice and immorality speaks to this vision of an activist and beneficial government for "the security and protection of the community." For historians, these constitutional reforms remain an anomaly. For some scholars, these changes represent the ignorance of the framers.[12] Stipulations regarding penal reform and morality laws should have been legislative, not constitutional issues. For other historians, penal and prison reform in the constitution epitomizes the humanitarian side of the Enlightenment and republicanism in the constitutional moment and nothing more.[13] While both interpretations have merit, they don't quite explain why those reforms made their way into the constitution or their significance.

Penal and prison reform demonstrated the centrality of law and governance to the framers' vision of the state's future. In Section 38 of the constitution, the framers stipulated, "The penal laws as heretofore used shall be reformed" and "punishments made in some cases less sanguinary and in general more proportionate to the crimes." Framers based these ideas on the work of an Italian philosopher, Cesare Beccaria, who argued in his famous *Essay On Crimes and Punishments* that an effective administration of justice could never exist with harsh penalties. Under a largely capital punishment system, such as existed in England and the colonies, juries often failed to convict, and criminals repeatedly received pardons. The magnitude of a death sentence frequently mitigated any sort of punishment, placing the entire system in contempt. Punishments proportional to the crimes committed would prove more effective, as juries would no longer fail to convict, and government agents would not issue pardons simply out of pity. Over time, punishment would be certain, citizens would habitually associate crime with punishment, and therefore, "crimes of every kind should be less frequent."[14]

The goals and the governing ideology of the new leaders in Pennsylvania reflected Beccaria's system of criminal justice. Beccaria's plan rested on a social contract theory that placed the good of the community over the individual. Since rational individuals with free will chose to live in a society instead of a state of nature, they also chose to give up some personal liberties in exchange for the safety and comfort of society. Law and the criminal justice system, Beccaria argued, extended and maintained the blessings of society by protecting the community against individuals who challenged the social contract and harmed the personal liberties of others. Since man was rational and therefore predictable, governments could use law to deter individual passions. For example, Beccaria reasoned that all people look out for their own best interest, which may lead to deviant acts against the laws of society. If punishment is uncertain and does not exceed the pleasure one seeks by breaking the law, living in society becomes precarious and dangerous. Therefore, only through proportional punishment, equally and certainly administered, could government deter crime and maintain, uphold, and protect its citizens.[15]

Prison reform worked on a similar rationale. According to Section 39 of the constitution, future legislators would establish houses of correction throughout the state to publicly punish criminals by hard labor. Like penal reform, this system had as its sole purpose the benefit of society. Correctional houses would "deter more effectually from the commission of crimes by continued visible punishments." Through public punishments, citizens could connect a crime with the consequence and thereby learn "the laws of society." In such a system, one Pennsylvanian explained, criminals would become "subjects of abhorrence—lighted beacons for the virtuous to avoid—and living monuments of depravity and unrighteousness."[16] "The punishment of the few" therefore would provide for the "preservation of the many."[17]

As the framers were painfully aware, though, laws made little difference if the government could not enforce them. Under the old government, the problem proved twofold. Population growth and westward expansion hampered the efficiency and purview of the judiciary. In the supreme court, especially, Pennsylvanians argued that without a maintained circuit, inhabitants living outside Philadelphia did not have consistent and inexpensive access to the high court. Moreover, provincial power politics inhibited the judiciary from acting "independently" for the benefit of the whole society. Judges functioned, in the minds of some Pennsylvanians, as either proprietary lackeys or tools of the Crown. In sum, as the pseudonymous "Demophilus" argued, Pennsylvania lacked "distributive justice," where everyone received equitable access to the basic benefits of government untainted by power or prejudice.[18]

Of particular value in understanding the constitution and the influences of the framers are the numerous plans of government for public consumption that claimed to address these governance problems. Although the authors often disagreed as to the makeup of the legislature and the executive, they came together on three crucial points related to judicial reform. First, judges should not be able to hold any other office, civil or military. Second, the legislature should make all salaries fixed and moderate. Third, the state should evenly distribute a "sufficient number of justices" throughout Pennsylvania.[19] They all envisioned jurisdictional districts for officers and courts to allow for easy access to justice. According to one author, judges and courts placed in smaller jurisdictions would relieve "a great hardship, for people in narrow circumstances" who had "to travel far, to have business of so pressing a nature performed for them." Following these plans would, as writers put it, "answer every *good* purpose much better" and "improve its internal police."[20]

Though the framers would leave much of the creation and reform of the judiciary and other law enforcement officers to subsequent assemblies, they did provide changes that followed the suggestions of the authors outlined above. Not only did the framers push for new laws, but they made, as one section of the constitution noted, "provisions . . . for their due execution."[21] For example, the framers made the JP both an elected and an appointed official. Instead of an executive appointing JPs for the entire county, each town, district, or ward would elect two JPs, and the executive would commission one or both of them for seven-year terms. The JPs would have fixed salaries and could not hold any other political office. Importantly, in a brief unexplained segment of Section 30, the framers referred to county districts where each JP would live and work, though they left the mode of election and the carving out of these districts to subsequent assemblies.

On its own, the section on JPs reveals little that is novel or new beyond their popular election. However, when viewed in the light of some of the authors' works discussed above, the section, particularly its reference to "districts," highlights an effort to enhance the "internal police" of the state. According to Demophilus, in order to provide for "distributive justice" each county needed to be broken up into districts for local law enforcement officials. Through the selection of JPs who lived in various sections of a county, a regional system of enforcement could be created. The constitution's inclusion of judicial districts, as will be shown in more detail below, provided for this regional law enforcement system that improved the administration of justice in the state.

The framers also addressed other long-standing concerns with the judiciary, particularly the supreme court. The constitution established that the executive would appoint supreme court judges with fixed salaries for seven-year terms. The constitution also prohibited the judges from holding "any other office civil or military" or "receiv[ing] fees or prerequisites of any kind."[22] In addition, it guaranteed judicial circuits for both oyer and terminer and nisi prius courts, where both local justices of the peace and supreme court judges worked together to provide effective, efficient, timely, and uniform administration of the law. Instead of trying capital cases in the city of Philadelphia and an unreliable circuit court, two JPs with a presiding supreme court judge would hold courts in each county. Under the constitution, then, Pennsylvania had its first fully functioning and regular supreme court circuit, broken up into western and eastern districts, managed by the supreme court judges overseeing local JPs.[23] Such changes were profound. Bedford County, for example, which had only sporadic oyer and terminer courts commissioned randomly by the deputy governors during the colonial period, had, by 1778, quarterly oyer and terminer courts that sat for at least eleven days at a time.[24]

"FOR THE SECURITY AND PROTECTION OF THE COMMUNITY" 175

Ubiquitous land disputes emanating from the rather impractical administration of land and property records constituted another problem related to the dispensation of the law that the framers attempted to rectify. They did away with old archaic forms of landownership, such as entail and other perpetuities. In addition, they altered the land administration by creating a public "register's office for the probate of wills and granting letters of administration." They also created an "office for the recording of deeds." This system replaced the personal officers of the Penns living in Philadelphia with two public offices for each county and city, guided and directed by state law.[25] Reform of the judiciary and land administration in the constitution, initiatives that Pennsylvanians had tried to achieve since the 1750s, reflects the framers' efforts to improve the efficiency and effectiveness of government.

The Constitution of 1776 proved an extremely democratic instrument, more democratic than any other constitution in that revolutionary moment. Nevertheless, its embrace of democracy only sheds light on a part of that document and its significance for the future of the state. The constitution also notably revamped its legal system through its demands for penal and prison reform, establishing public officers for land administration, and the restructuring of the judiciary and other law enforcement officers. The framers, however, only provided a foundation for a government that subsequent assemblies and other civil officers, operating under the constitution, would build upon. Those inaugural officers of the state found they had much to work with, as most of the sections of the constitution about law enforcement officials ended with the stipulation that they could wield "such other powers as may be found necessary by future general assemblies." And the framers granted the legislature the "power to establish all such other courts as they may judge for the good of the inhabitants of the state."[26] Moreover, by predicating the government on the protection of the public welfare, the framers of the constitution gave state officials sweeping powers to construct a state government that would have significant authority over the lives of its citizens.

Years of Profound Change: Creating the Institutions, Officers, and Ideology of State

The constitution only began the state formation process. Responding to colonial inefficiencies and the hefty problems associated with the war, legislators, civil officers, and citizens provided further alterations that increased the institutional strength and overall reach of the state. After the ratification of the constitution, state officials put in place jurisdictional districts for the justices of the peace and defined and enhanced the powers of those officers. They built on and reformed the supreme court, created a stronger military power, and established county officers and three courts. They also formed public offices and separated the duties and defined the powers of others. In addition, citizens and statesmen worked together to develop laws and officials to regulate and shackle the domestic economy and direct commercial development. Likewise, they passed laws that defined citizenship, delineating who was and who was not included in any definition of the political community and ultimately who had the benefits of this new government. Through these changes, citizens and statesmen constructed an infrastructure and embraced a governing ideology predicated on the public welfare that defined their state well into the nineteenth century.

The first elected assembly immediately tackled court reform, deeming it imperative to establish accessible legal structures as soon as possible. Since Congress's May 15 resolve that demolished forever the colonial government, the courts ceased functioning. As of February 1777, the courts remained closed. Though the Pennsylvania Constitutional Convention appointed its own JPs and deputized the Committee of Safety as magistrates, the administration of justice was ephemeral and haphazard at best. Legislators and members of the executive branch, the Supreme Executive Council (SEC), realized that to assure the allegiance of the people, state leaders needed to demonstrate the effectiveness and power of the government for, as the constitution declared, "the common benefit, protection and security of the people."[27]

Despite the fledgling status of the government and the urgency of war, legislators refused to reinstitute the colonial legal system. Continuity would only undermine revolutionaries' arguments for the necessity of independence and a new government. Following the directives of the constitution, they created a regional system of law enforcement, charging the county commissioners and assessors to form judicial districts throughout the state. Each district would have at least one justice of the peace, but if district inhabitants found one justice too few, the SEC would commission more on the application of at least twenty freeholders.[28]

These reforms provided a more equitable geographic distribution of justices in the state. In pre-independence Bucks County, for example, JPs resided in 11 of 28 townships, and 9 of the 17 JPs lived in and around the borough of Bristol, but with the districts, 18 of the 28 townships had JPs, and no town held a majority of the officers. Like Bucks County, Cumberland County's distribution of JPs changed dramatically. In 1775–76, 12 of the 23 townships had JPs. In 1778, JPs resided in all 23 townships. Similar changes occurred in Chester, Lancaster, and Northampton Counties. Where the 18 townships making up the southwestern corner of Chester County shared three JPs before the constitution, they had 9 after its establishment. In Lancaster County, JPs only resided in 10 of the 33 townships prior to 1776, and over 30 percent of them lived in the borough of Lancaster. By 1777, 21 towns had JPs, and no town held a majority of them.[29]

Creating districts also increased the number of JPs in the state. In 1776, there were 202 JPs in the eleven counties. By 1778, the same counties had 249. For many Pennsylvanians, however, this was still not enough. Inhabitants in the town of Easton, Northampton County, petitioned the SEC for "one or more Magistrates" than they already had, and the SEC promptly complied.[30] By 1783, due to the application for more JPs, the number of magistrates increased to 307, an increase of 52 percent in seven years.[31]

By 1790, the number of JPs had increased by 72 percent since 1776, to 348 due to the addition of new counties. State leaders not only created judicial districts in each of the counties for the better administration of justice, but they developed ten counties. Legislators created new counties for the most western regions of the state and at the same time established counties to break up the older sprawling counties of the southeast such as Philadelphia, Chester, Lancaster, and Cumberland. The addition of counties nearly doubled the number of courts, jails, magistrates, sheriffs, undersheriffs, coroners, lieutenants, and sublieutenants, thus providing the infrastructure to better incorporate an extended people into the state and at the same time secure the state's borders.[32]

The creation of judicial districts and counties also proved consequential for the administration of justice. Between 1770 and 1790, criminal prosecutions increased by 57 percent per capita.[33] In Lancaster County, the number of criminal prosecutions more than doubled. In the colonial period the county court heard, on average, thirty-eight cases a year. Between 1778 and 1783, the court averaged about ninety-three cases per year. More significant still, the average remained about the same even after Lancaster County was split in half with the creation of Dauphin County in 1785.[34] In Chester County, while not as dramatic, there was appreciable change. Between 1770 and 1774, the court heard, on average,

1774

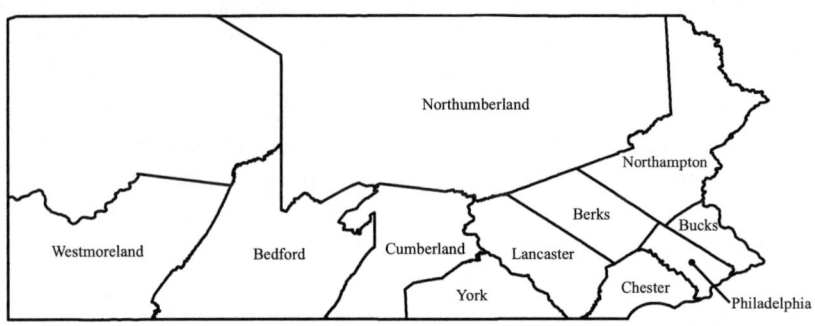

1790

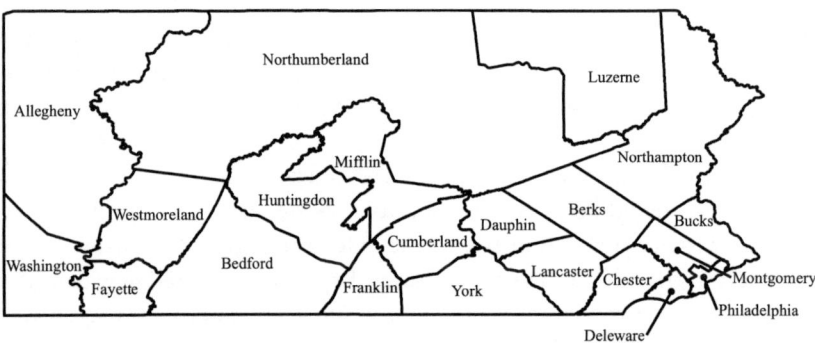

Pennsylvania counties in 1774 and 1790. (Map created by Robert F. Smith using ArcGIS 10.3.1 for Desktop)

sixty-two cases a year. Between 1778 and 1782, the court averaged eighty cases per year.[35] Such an increase, as Thomas Slaughter rightly notes, "bear[s] no obvious relationship to changes in the numbers of people living in the county." While Slaughter points to "heightened sensitivity to disorder" during the revolution as the reason for the increase, institutional development of the state certainly contributed to the increase in the number of cases handled by the county courts.[36]

At the same time as the number of cases increased, the geographic distribution of court cases expanded. Examining the town of origin for criminal cases adjudicated in Chester County between 1740 and 1776 and 1777 and 1790 demonstrates the change. After the districting of JPs and the creation of Delaware County, the uneven geographic distribution of court cases leveled out. The percentage of court cases in the northeastern section of the county dropped from 53 percent to 37 percent. Cases in the northwestern towns increased from 9 percent to 15 percent. West Nottingham, East Nottingham, and Oxford went from 6 percent to 15 percent, and the percentage of cases emanating from the borough of Chester, which dominated the dockets of the colonial period, dropped to just 2 percent.[37] Such changes in the geographic distribution of court cases reflected the goals of Pennsylvanians such as Demophilus who demanded "distributive justice." As a result, Pennsylvanians praised the courts in ways they had never done before. According to one writer, "The Courts at Bedford, Carlisle and York, are held with great regularity and propriety, and more business done in the sessions in a week, than used formerly to be done under the old Constitution."[38]

Not only did legislators create a regional system of law enforcement, but they also created three new courts. In 1778, to deal with maritime law, legislators established a Court of Admiralty, consisting of a judge, a marshal, and several port wardens.[39] The creation this court, because of past imperial control of the admiralty, symbolized the transfer of sovereign authority from the Crown to the state. Another significant step in that direction was the formation of a High Court of Errors and Appeals. In the colonial past, the Crown served as the court of last resort, which, many noted, proved rather impractical and far too expensive, and therefore a "great obstruction of justice." Revolutionaries did away with this "difficult and precarious remedy" and formulated a court of "last resort," superseding in oversight even the supreme court.[40]

Land administration also underwent institutional and judicial development. Legislators created a public land office consisting of three officers—a secretary, a receiver general, and a surveyor general—who commissioned deputies throughout the state. Together, they surveyed land, developed standard forms, gathered preexisting land documents, and housed all records for easy access. Providing for better record keeping did not resolve many of the land controversies plaguing the government. There still existed old colonial disputes and new cases touching caveats, escheats, warrants granted to agree, rights of preemption, and altercations over imperfect titles. However, the public land office gave the state the bureaucratic wherewithal to constitute a court, the Board of Property, dedicated to adjudicating land controversies in an effort to clean up a colonial mess and deal with any future problems. The court also relieved the stressful land disputes placed on the local and high courts.[41]

The supreme court also underwent significant reform during the revolution. Through the hard work of Chief Justice Thomas McKean, the supreme court expanded its reach, became increasingly more efficient in performing its duties, and presented to the public a potent vision of government predicated on the public welfare.[42] McKean, while not legally trained at the Inns of Court in London, nonetheless rose to importance as a jurist in both Delaware and Pennsylvania. Through his experience, he became acutely aware of the problems the judicial system faced and the need for reform. During his first few years as chief justice, he consistently urged for the expansion of personnel so the state court could reach a maximum of efficiency. In 1780, the SEC obliged and appointed another judge. Within three years, McKean redrew the circuit districts. Instead of just a western and eastern district as established by the constitution, he formed four circuit districts running all year around.[43] Jasper Yeates, a lawyer on circuit, was pleased to "find the judges have fixed their Circuit."[44] By 1790, lawyers and suitors praised the court for conducting "Business" so regularly "for many Years past."[45]

While the expansion of state institutions and officers marked an important change in the state, it was a new vision of republican governance, emphasizing as it did the public welfare, that gave those institutions and officers significant power over the everyday lives of citizens. The import of republicanism for the practice of governing in the state is showcased nicely in the decisions of the state supreme court, the state's regulation of the domestic economy during the Revolutionary War, and the debate over the Bank of North America. All three highlight the important ways that citizens and officials came together to create a state that would encourage the "pursuit of happiness" through institutional intervention and an active and energetic use of regulatory power.

In the supreme court, the judges' interpretation of the role of government increased that court's power to enforce and oversee the "supreme law" of the state, even in the most local of spaces. In sum, institutional development went hand in glove with a new governing ideology in the formation of the state. In addresses to jurors and other onlookers, Chief Justice McKean, echoing the constitution's Declaration of Rights, provided a powerful interpretation of government as the protector of the public good that rendered "impracticable," he thought, "unlimited & absolute freedom in Individuals." According to McKean, "Man is a social creature and formed for a social State," and therefore "the end of society is the common interest and welfare of the people associated; this end must of necessity be the supreme law or common standard, by which particular rules of action of the several members of society towards each other are to be regulated; and this can only be obtained by government."[46] Such a relational theory of individual rights, with the government defining and enforcing the mutual obligations inherent in the social being of man, gave the court and the state in general significant authority over the everyday lives of citizens.

Nor was McKean's view an aberration; the other judges stressed a similar vision of governance. George Bryan, president judge of a supreme court circuit district, made it clear in his decisions that "Liberty cannot subsist without public virtue," but such virtue could not exist if the government promoted "private will ... against that of the community." Bryan argued all law had to uphold the "interests of the community," those central "bands of society" against the self-interest of a few.[47] Such self-interest constituted "the very nature of treason ... the most deadly foe to freedom."[48]

This vision of government allowed the supreme court to expand its reach well into the individual lives of the state's inhabitants by adjudicating cases for the crime of murder right down to public nuisance (usually the provenance of the county courts).[49] In those decisions, the court consistently upheld the welfare of society as "a law above all others."[50] When one man "maliciously" killed his *own* horse, the court ruled it a "public wrong," as "every act of a public evil example and against good morals, is an offence indictable by the common law; and this principle affects the killing a horse, as much, at least, as the burning of an empty barn."[51] This expansive vision of the state's purpose put the court in opposition to lawyers who argued the state court had no authority over local and private affairs. Ignoring their criticisms, the high court deemed such crimes as the poisoning of chickens, killing a neighbor's dog, cheating at dice, "deadening and destroying" a neighbor's tree, "fraudulently tearing a promissory note," and breaking a neighbor's window with a rock, indictable public offenses because the "private sufferer was not alone entitled to redress"—the criminal owed the public satisfaction. The court even argued that private property needed to conform to the security of society. Though many early Americans believed the protection of property constituted an essential individual liberty, judges ruled that the government could destroy or confiscate private property for public safety.[52] According to the high court, the public's welfare trumped individual interests.

Other factors, too, contributed to the expanding reach and remit of the supreme court. Over the course of the 1770s and 1780s, Pennsylvanians swamped the legislature with petitions requesting legally sanctioned divorces. Under the Constitution of 1776, divorce law stood on the same footing as before: the assembly, just like the English Parliament, had the sole authority to arbitrate each case. Yet, as before, this proved a cumbersome and haphazard system that cost the legislature as well as citizens time and money.[53] In 1785, the assembly passed a uniform law outlining the circumstances warranting divorce and gave the high court jurisdiction over the law's implementation.[54]

It was in these ways that transformations in the state had the possibility to alter the lives of all people. Divorce law is one important example of this phenomena. In the colonial period, the contours of marriage and divorce were often defined by a given community, but perhaps more so by individual participants. Men and women negotiated their relationships and separated according to their own conception of right and wrong. While legal divorces could be achieved in the colonial period, they were only granted sparingly to a few men who initiated them and, after a royal decree in 1773, ceased altogether. Rather than attempt legal redress, colonial men and women, but particularly women, practiced an informal separation or "self-divorce." While such tactics provided some women the means to escape an abusive husband, the lack of legal remedies and therefor opportunities for subsistence remanded many others to a state of misery. The state's creation of a uniform divorce and alimony law recognized the need for separation, allowing either spouse the ability to achieve a legal divorce without necessarily demonstrating extreme or illicit behavior. According to the law, all that was needed was proof that either spouse had abandoned the marriage for at least four years. Even if separation did not happen previously, either spouse could file for divorce if he or she experienced cruel treatment, adultery, the incapability to reproduce (male impotence or otherwise), or bigamy.

Under this law, between 1785 and 1801 the supreme court heard more than one hundred divorce cases, over 60 percent of them initiated by women, many of whom were granted divorces and alimony.[55] In this way, state law enshrined previous informal practices while also defining the obligations inherent in a marriage and the rules of divorce.[56] Moreover, the law also demonstrates the state's assumption of power over household governance. Divorce, for example, serves as a testament to the loss of patriarchal power, and therefore, through laws and institutions, such as a divorce law providing for alimony, the state increasingly acquired that shifting authority in the revolutionary period, going so far as granting divorces to women whose abusive husbands were "willing to reconcile," the usual method of denying divorces in England because of the patriarchal authority of the male head of household.[57] Such a transfer of power was necessary, as the divorce law indicated, in "every well regulated society." Such a statement almost leaps from the page in its significance. Not long before this moment, Pennsylvania lawmakers would have deemed the informal governance of individual patriarchal households in a community of patriarchal households as the centerpiece of a "well regulated society." But now, in revolutionaries' hands, the state took their place.[58]

The expansion of the state's authority over the lives of Pennsylvanians also meant the continued importance of the common law for the regulation of daily activities and relationships. While that law would shift to fit new social conditions, it still could and did limit the possibilities of transformation. As much as an expansive divorce law challenged immemorial precedents, the common law could just as easily enshrine social positions through variegated rights defined by "office, property, household position, race, gender, infirmity, and age." For women, that meant the retention of statuses as *femme covert* or *femme sole* that designated them as unequal denizens. As became increasingly clear, the state became an active agent in enforcing and preserving such distinctions in an expansive jurisdiction that mitigated the local differences that characterized the decentralized and diverse legal system of the colonial period.[59]

Establishing an overarching divorce law, then, also reflected the state's effort to regulate the social and moral order with some central oversight and uniformity. There are several examples of this goal shaping institutional policy decisions. In the restructuring of the high court, for instance, supreme court judges on circuit presided over county JPs in the hearing of all oyer and terminer cases.[60] The court, in this case, was also a law school. In the same vein, the legislature gave the judges of the supreme court authority over the local judges of the court of common pleas as a "Board of Review" assigned to "guard against plays" and other popular performances that challenged "community standards" and threatened the "good morals" of the entire public.[61] Over the course of 1770s and 1780s, the supreme court had been raised to such a power over the social and moral life of citizens that one critical onlooker noted sarcastically that the president of the state served as the mere "Footman" of the "Chief Justice [who] rides in the Body of the Carriage, and the *People* run whooping and hollowing along side, choak'd with Dust and bespatter'd with Mire."[62]

Though many changes to the governance of the state seem to have come from the top down, ordinary citizens could significantly affect public policy. When citizens felt that the state did not live up to expectations of protecting the public welfare, they used the popular processes guaranteed to them in the constitution to make change. They assembled together, created town meetings and committees, wrote instructions to their delegates, petitioned, and demanded reform. The most well-known demonstration of this fact is the gradual abolition law, where African Americans and antislavery activists articulated their resistance to slavery and achieved a positive statutory response, though limited in scope, as many of the first generation of free blacks still remained in a state of servitude for a proscribed period of twenty-eight years. Nevertheless, as one critic noted, this law's champions had basely ingratiated themselves "with the *people*, in opposition to those who were termed *well born*."[63] Through these actions and events, ordinary Pennsylvanians shaped public policy as well as the power, force, and reach of the state. After all, slavery and the states throughout newly independent America became intimately wedded, making it clear that the states held power over the regulation of labor and the legality of slavery.[64] Similarly, we can see how citizens and their government worked together to enhance state power by regulating the domestic economy during and after the war.

Starting in 1777, the economy of Pennsylvania languished—trade suffered, hard money all but vanished, paper money issued by Congress depreciated, and prices soared. A gallon of molasses that cost two shillings in 1776 cost two hundred shillings in 1779. This economic crisis, while related to rapid depreciation and therefore inflation, also had to do with the market practices of merchants, shopkeepers, and artisans. Many sellers, believing the continental bills useless, refused to deal in them, demanding either high prices or payment in hard currency. Rumors of French fleets carrying specie to the states to buy provisions also pushed some sellers to refuse to trade their goods for any kind of paper money. According to historian Gary Nash, because of this rumor, "overnight, bread was not to be bought at any price."[65]

Many Pennsylvanians deemed these practices "heinously criminal." In the press, anonymous authors issued ominous warnings. "To all FORESTALLERS and RAISERS of the price of GOODS and PROVISIONS" one author wrote, "take notice that a storm is brewing against you."[66] Upset that their "country has been reduced to the brink of ruin by" such "infamous practices," Pennsylvanians demanded the government either take action or "the People" would. In Britain and France, writers argued, "the People have always done themselves justice" in the face of "avaricious forestallers" by breaking open warehouses and appropriating stores for their own use. In some instances, authors cautioned, "the People ... hung up the culprits who have created their distress, without judge or jury." "Hear this and tremble, ye enemies to the freedom and happiness of your country."[67] Strong words indeed.

The state attempted to pacify the public by passing legislation against forestalling and regrating and to assure "fair dealing." Likewise, the SEC issued proclamations against such illicit practices, stating that the government would punish offenders with the full force of the law. Threats through legislation and proclamations proved ineffectual. The assembly only granted powers to justices of the peace, who, already swamped with business, found it difficult to enforce the laws in such unprecedented circumstances.[68] Emerging factional disputes over the constitution further obstructed the ability of the government to act aggressively. By 1779, disagreements over the merits of a bicameral versus a unicameral legislature reached a fever pitch, and some legislators demanded a reconsideration of the constitution before they would take their seats, resulting in days on end where the assembly could not gather a quorum. By May 1779, the assembly adjourned until August, hoping a long break would heal the impasse.

In the interim, depreciation, inflation, and anger deepened. Without the guidance of the assembly, Pennsylvanians saw little recourse. By June 1779, meetings transpired in the city, culminating in the creation of statewide committees to control monopolizers, deter forestallers, and check increasing prices. These bodies, unlike the pre-independence committees, worked under the legal framework of a constitution, particularly the right to assemble for the common good. The state represented the sovereign authority of the people; therefore, members of the committees reasoned, when the government could not counteract "offences against society," it fell to "the community" to take steps "in its own defence, and for its further security." Such "principles of citizenship" made the committees "a necessary appendage to the civil government."[69]

Acting as a supplement to the state, the committees aligned their actions with a popular vision of civil society and public law. According to the city committee, "the social compact in a state of civil society" required "that every right or power claimed or exercised by any man or set of men, should be in subordination to the common good." Since high prices "threatened the whole community," they asserted their right (and by extension the state's right) to control prices as well as punish monopolizers and forestallers whom they deemed dangerous to the public good. This social compact predicated on the welfare of society and the political power of the community associated, they argued, was central to *their* constitution. Therefore, they would "in all cases" carry out their duties in accordance to "JUSTICE and MERCY and the *laws* and *constitution* of our country."⁷⁰

Nevertheless, they recognized that they were only a temporary solution, pledging to disband once the legislature reconvened and "civil government" returned to "its original channel."⁷¹ They most likely felt confident that the assembly would, upon consideration of the situation and popular pressure, establish economic regulations and the means to enforce them. That confidence was buttressed by the fact that many of the committee members were also state officials. Far from representing the "lower sorts" and a class struggle against the encroachments of "laissez-faire principles of political economy," committeemen in the city of Philadelphia and Lancaster, for example, were members of the revolutionary elite.⁷² They were legislators, executive councilors, delegates to the Continental Congress, army officers, justices of the peace, sheriffs, borough burgesses, court clerks, vendue masters, town majors, and county lieutenants and sublieutenants.⁷³ Working together, they convened in courthouses and coffeehouses, set prices, and adjudicated the guilt or innocence of offenders, sometimes with a heavy hand.⁷⁴

Once the assembly reconvened with a quorum on September 9, the committees exited the political scene as suddenly as they entered it. In Lancaster County, the self-styled Committee of Observation and Inspection adjourned itself on September 8, vouching to resume its practices on the first Tuesday in October, yet it never did. Instead, with the legislature back in session, the committee deferred to the assembly's legitimacy, sending the legislators instructions and petitions requesting state action to regulate the domestic economy.⁷⁵

Not everyone shared the committees' faith. Pennsylvania's revolutionary soldiers remained, for good reason, wary of the legislature's willingness to act and, just as important, angry at the economic situation that they believed a few wealthy and disloyal Pennsylvanians helped create. Looking to the city lieutenant, Charles Wilson Peale, the soldiers requested that he use his position to help them punish the people they deemed disloyal offenders. Peale, however, refused to lead the soldiers because he could not comprehend how they would ever come to agree on the individuals to apprehend. Unwilling to be deterred, ordinary soldiers reconstituted the Committee of Privates and paraded through the streets to punish those they deemed the cause of the economic crisis. Culminating on October 4, 1779, the soldiers apprehended a few suspected loyalists and then got into a firefight with some people holed up in the home of James Wilson, an outspoken critic of the state government, in what is now famously called the Fort Wilson riot.[76]

Such violent actions without legal sanction by the city lieutenant placed the state government, especially the executive branch, in a difficult situation. The president of the state, Joseph Reed, while he sympathized with the soldiers and personally hated James Wilson, could not approve their assumption of power. If he did, those Pennsylvanians who openly reviled the state government, particularly the constitution, would use the moment as proof of the government's impotency in the face of "the mob." Riding at the head of a cavalry unit, the president dispersed the crowd of soldiers and sent some to jail. Reed even demanded the arrest of the men inside Wilson's home, who most likely started the fray with the militia in the first place. Such a show of force, Reed and the state legislators agreed, was necessary to achieve "Peace, good order & a due Obedience to Government, on which the Liberty, Happiness & Safety of the Citizens so greatly depend."[77]

While the president asserted state control, the legislature debated the particulars of a new bill to curb illicit market practices and inflation. Four days after Fort Wilson, the assembly passed "An Act for the More Effectually Preventing Engrossing and Forestalling." This act established restrictions on excessive profits and thrust the power of the state into the regulation of all traders and sellers of goods. The new law outlawed selling goods for a gross profit above 25 percent. In addition, the act demanded that everyone accept "ready money," which meant both continental and state paper bills. It also forbade forestalling and regrating, and it expanded the definition of engrossing to include the actions of millers and other manufacturers. Millers, for example, could not "hoard" wheat but must, upon purchase, "manufacture the same into flour" and expose it to sale within six weeks. If they did not, the government would punish them as engrossers, a serious offense for which offenders could be fined up to $5,000, imprisoned for one year, and required to forfeit double the value of the goods sold or offered for sale.[78]

To enforce this act, the assembly created a state officer, the commissioner of trade. The assembly appointed between six and eight of these officers in each county, some of whom had served as members of the recently disbanded price control committees. In the city of Philadelphia, for example, three of the eight commissioners were former committeemen, one of whom, William Henry, served as committee chairman.[79] Granted all the "power and authority of justices of the peace," they could "call all persons before them," issue sentences, and exact fines. They also controlled the licensing of all traders in the state by administering an oath requiring sellers to swear or affirm that they would not make excessive profits, that they would accept "ready money," and that they would not forestall or regrate. This act represented citizens' ability to shape public policy and demonstrated that the state had the power to regulate the domestic economy as public needs and interests demanded. In the early 1780s, when Pennsylvania's economy regained a semblance of normalcy, many citizens judged part of this legislation unnecessary. As before, Pennsylvanians gathered together and petitioned for reform, and the legislature amended part of the law but maintained the state's regulatory authority over illicit market practices such as forestalling, regrating, and engrossing.[80]

The political philosophy of the public welfare espoused by citizens, statesmen, and judges alike gave the state large sweeping powers over the regulation and oversight of the economy. Although historians argue that the "public good" died a quick death in the revolutionary period in the face of commercial interests of emerging capitalists, evidence shows that was not the case.[81] Pennsylvanians, like many other early Americans, understood their economy as a public phenomenon that the state, through public law, shaped and regulated. Such regulatory tactics predicated on a public welfare political and legal philosophy still dominated public law in the first half of the nineteenth century. According to historian William Novak, the sheer volume of "restrictions on economic and social life passed by state and local authorities... suggests that 'regulation' might be a better metaphor for the age than 'contract,' 'the market,' or 'laissez-faire.'"[82]

The struggle over the charter of incorporation for the first Bank of North America in the mid-1780s demonstrates both the longevity of a public welfare philosophy and the power it gave to the state governments over their own internal affairs. Charters of incorporation in the early modern period existed as state entities for public purposes. The first Bank of North America proved no exception to that rule. Pennsylvanians viewed the bank, created in a moment of turmoil and uncertainty, as a public necessity to revive the state's sinking credit and extend its services and capital to the public at large. Mechanics, farmers, shopkeepers, and merchants all stood to benefit from the bank, theoretically, and therefore its incorporation initially received overwhelming support.

When specifics of the bank charter hit the streets, however, some Pennsylvanians expressed concern. The charter gave a significant amount of power to the bank directors without any state oversight. The directors of the bank, some of whom, such as Robert Morris, held powerful congressional and state positions, had the authority to make laws and extend credit as they saw necessary. Nor were the bank directors required to answer to or explain their actions to any governing body.[83] For some Pennsylvanians, the bank charter spelled disaster and repudiated the principles of the constitution and the revolution. According to a group of angry legislators, the bank's charter existed "entirely for the private advantage and emolument of the subscribers." They deemed the bank charter monstrous and potentially threatening to the people because "the government" had "no advantage" in the management or oversight of the bank's affairs.[84] Nevertheless, in the first year or so of the bank's existence, it extended credit rather liberally and at discounts. Though lacking oversight, the bank served its public purpose and therefore remained a popular institution despite a few murmurs.[85]

Popular feeling toward the bank took a drastic turn between 1784 and 1786. Financial difficulties from the war racked both the states and the bank. The bank, due to financial woes, started restricting credit, undermining the credibility and usefulness of the bank in the minds of many citizens and statesmen alike. Almost instantly, the press and the public charged Robert Morris, the bank's innovator, with putting his, the bank directors', and their friends' private interests above everyone else's. Such private interest, writers maintained, undercut a charter of incorporation instituted for public purposes. Though Morris argued such charges were "extraordinary" because he viewed the bank as the *private property* "of the stockholders," the general public and state officials did not.[86] By limiting the extension of credit to a rather small clique of wealthy Philadelphians and Europeans, no matter the necessity during difficult financial times, instantly raised old suspicions of "unequal and partial distribution of public benefits" that would create "distinctions of interest, influence, and power, which lead to the establishment of an aristocracy." With new urgency, Pennsylvanians examined the charter and judged it "destructive to the freedom of the state." As one statesman put it, the bank was "incompatible with the public welfare" because it only "aided" a "handful of our citizens" without any "regulation" by the government.[87] In response, Pennsylvanians petitioned the government for the reform or dismantling of the bank. The assembly, taking into consideration the petitions of the people, by a vote of forty-seven to twenty-one, revoked the charter.[88]

Annulling the charter did not mean that Pennsylvanians opposed commerce or commercial banking. Just a little over three years earlier, Pennsylvanians overwhelmingly supported the bank when it seemed to provide services to a larger constituency, fulfilling the public purposes of a charter. When the bank failed to meet that expectation and the government could do little about it, Pennsylvanians demanded its reform or destruction.[89] One assemblyman noted that at the time of the charter's repeal, the bank had challenged the fundamental law of the state. The state, he argued, was "instituted for the good of society" rather than "for the emolument of any man, family, or set of men." These words, ripped from the Declaration of Rights, prompted the legislator to note that "the bank is inconsistent" with "not only the frame but the spirit of our government."[90]

Citizens and statesmen did not want to destroy the bank entirely. The bank directors' complete control without any oversight was the main concern. To counteract this apparent deficiency, the state moved to reincorporate the bank under a substantially different charter that gave the state the authority to regulate and check the actions and decisions of bank directors. According to legislators, only "under proper regulations" could the government render the bank "useful to the commerce and agriculture of the state." The new charter, then, limited the bank's lifespan to fourteen years (with a renewal option), demanded the directors to report to the SEC any laws, regulations, or ordinances they passed to assure they were in accord with the "laws and constitution" of the state, and outlawed the bank's ability to trade stock to speculate in any "goods, wares, or merchandise." In addition, the state would monitor the financial activity of the directors, all of whom were held accountable individually or collectively as a corporation in any court of law in the state.[91] The charter, in giving the state the power to regulate bank actions and punish the directors, guaranteed, according to one legislator, that "the happiness of the people" would remain "the first law" of the state.[92]

"Happiness," when it came to state intervention, was a relative term, especially for people who resisted state policy or the existence of the state, both of which were prevalent during the Revolutionary War. It was during that conflict that state leaders demonstrated the coerciveness of republican governance. Shifting loyalties, professed neutrality, and even apathy vexed revolutionaries everywhere, pushing them to back regulatory and coercive policies against suspected loyalists to protect "the welfare and happiness of the good people of this commonwealth" who "next under God, entirely depend on the maintaining and supporting the independence and sovereignty of the state."[93] Connecting state sovereignty to the public welfare placed the policy against and treatment of suspected loyalists under the umbrella of state police power. In the process, they centralized the government, forcing once autonomous local institutions, officers, and even citizens to work for unitary purposes in the regulation of the social and moral order of the state.[94]

The republican emphasis on the public welfare, then, had its darker side. Those who refused to accept the authority of the state were excluded from the "benefits of government" and therefore experienced all the force and power the state could muster. Although the remainder of this chapter focuses on the state, loyalists, and the war years, the same language of "protection" and the coercive policy of exclusion embraced in those years continued well into the next century, most energetically expressed against Native peoples when state leaders embarked on a campaign of dispossession to secure the financial security of the state and its narrowly defined "people" but also against anyone who did not fit the state's understanding of its citizens and "acceptable" behavior in their public and private lives.[95]

Attaining Legitimacy and Exerting Power: Deploying the State during a Civil War

Addressing the public on November 14, 1780, President Joseph Reed outlined a fundamental difficulty his state had faced since its inception in September 1776. "To accomplish so great a revolution in so short a time, to subvert an established government, and form a new one, unsupported by habits of obedience and opinion," he opened, "will be allowed no easy task." The state had not experienced a "perfect union"; instead it faced "the disaffection of a considerable number" of people as well as "internal divisions which have subsisted among ourselves." Such circumstances challenged state authority, especially since "government must not only be obeyed, it must be respected."[96]

Reed's statements marked a culmination of sorts. They were the product of the transformation from colony to state, where the old leaders, as John Adams succinctly put, were mowed down "like Grass before the Scythe," which was not an easy transition.[97] Divided loyalties, political dissidence, and a popular questioning of the state's ability to govern brought it to the brink of collapse. James Allen, cut down by the radical scythe, stated bluntly in early 1777, "The Government of this province or *state* as they term it, is truly ridiculous; Not one of the Laws of the Assembly are regarded; No courts open, no justice administered" and "few of the Justices elected thro'out the state accept their offices." Pennsylvania was, Allen believed, "in a state of nature."[98]

Allen's criticisms were not far off the mark. Courts remained closed until late 1777; the old leaders refused to hand over official documents, thus refusing to recognize the transference of sovereignty to the state; and some newly appointed officers snubbed their posts. In Westmoreland County, the deputy prothonotary found that he could not undertake his position because the colonial officer hid the records somewhere in Lancaster. In Northampton County, the inhabitants complained of "great inconveniences" when some of the magistrates refused to accept their posts.[99] In Chester County, civil government collapsed.[100] According to one contemporary, "There are no Justices—no Law—every one seems to do what he listeth—I am surprised that there are not more Murders & Robberies committed for these ever flourish in anarchy and Confusion."[101]

To add to this chaos, the threat of British invasion and the occupation of Philadelphia from September 1777 to June 1778 resulted in fits of anxiety over the state's sovereignty. Beyond the occupation, the war itself presented problems for the new government. The ebb and flow of the war, the dire stakes of the conflict, and the prospects of a British victory shook the foundation of the state. Collecting taxes and mustering troops for the war proved difficult, especially since many Pennsylvanians refused to pledge allegiance to the state, pay their taxes, and march off to war when it seemed "very uncertain upon which side the Victory will fall out."[102] Others, stalwart supporters of the Crown, labeled the new regime "usurpers" and refused to recognize the authority of the state. Even some supporters of the American Revolution insulted the government as "muggletonian" and "tatterdemalion," propped up by a "whimsical ragamuffin constitution."[103] The crumbling of civil authority did not bode well for the state, as some started to assert that the government's "laws are not worth reading."[104] The breakdown of law and authority, coupled with the existence of the disaffected (a term used by many citizens and statesmen to describe those who sided with Britain), the SEC maintained, "would hurt Government considerably."[105]

Such experiences gave cogency and meaning to President Reed's insistence that the government needed to establish its sovereignty. How state leaders attempted to attain that legitimacy is an important part in understanding the formation of the state, particularly how it became what political scientists and sociologists describe as a modern state, which is, at its core, "administrative, legal, extractive, and coercive." Over the course of the late 1770s and early 1780s, the government used each of these four central elements to exert its political and coercive strength over those people deemed disloyal or disorderly and visibly manifested its authority through panoplies of power in state-sanctioned processions and the more macabre spectacles at the gallows. At the same time, the government created offices, institutions, and policies to carry out these goals, enhance its powers, and demonstrate to the public its ability to govern. Taken together, the creation of state infrastructure, both civil and martial, and exhibitions of the coercive authority represent a radical departure from the old colonial polity and thus highlight the transformations of the Revolution.[106]

Requiring inhabitants to profess their loyalty to the state served as a crucial tactic in the quest for legitimacy. In June 1777, the legislature passed an act requiring white male inhabitants over the age of eighteen to abjure the king and vow allegiance to the state. Disloyalty, the assembly concluded, constituted a danger to "the preservation of this State" and therefore threatened "the welfare and happiness of the people."[107] Since the government embodied the sovereign authority of the people, anyone who did not accept its legitimacy endangered the public welfare. "Allegiance and protection," state leaders reasoned, were "reciprocal" and therefore anyone "who will not bear the former are not nor ought to be entitled to the benefits of the latter." Such people existed outside of the community and did not receive the benefits of citizenship. Blurring the lines of public and private in an effort to shape the social and moral order of the state, this policy denied such people the right to vote, hold office, trade, work in a profession such as lawyer or teacher, leave the county, or conduct suits in court, and they had to pay double taxes. State leaders also required all citizens to carry certificates, essentially state identification cards, if traveling to another county or state. They deemed those caught without one "strangers," and if they refused to give an oath to the state on the spot, they were thrown in jail without bail.[108]

The goals were twofold: to force an acknowledgment of the state and to maintain revolutionaries' own conception of the public good. When someone challenged either, state leaders asserted their authority to "protect" the "good people," and mustered the coercive police powers of the state to induce allegiance or remove perceived enemies from the confines of the state.[109] Inhabitants judged disloyal faced state-sanctioned harassment, physical abuse, and destruction of property. They also chanced the confiscation of their estates, long periods of imprisonment, banishment, impressments, and in extreme cases, death. Despite many of the principles ascribed to republican governments, revolutionaries found it relatively easy to do away with equal protection before the law and even individual rights for the sake of "protecting" a narrowly defined "public."

The trial and imprisonment of Samuel Rowland Fisher nicely elucidates this point. In early 1779, officials arrested Fisher for being "inimical" after state agents intercepted a private letter in which Fisher called Pennsylvania a "Province" when, as Chief Justice Thomas McKean was quick to point out, "the Independence of the *States* was so firmly settled."[110] Words mattered when sovereignty was involved, and because of them, state officials were determined to punish Fisher, so much so that the state's attorney and judges coerced the jury to get a conviction. Initially, the jurors refused to declare Fisher guilty of petit treason for the rather innocuous letter, but the heavy-handed judges sent the jurors away without "meat or drink" twice, finally forcing the jurors to state their individual decisions in front of a crowd filled with "the spirit of rage & violence." Unsurprisingly, each found Fisher guilty. With the sought-after verdict in hand, the court sentenced Fisher to imprisonment during the war and ordered the forfeiture of one-half of his "land and tenements, Goods and Chattels."[111]

After his conviction for failing to recognize "the State (as they call it)," Fisher experienced an even uglier side of state coercion that permeated outward, affecting people he knew, and, sometimes, loved. State officials desired his individual submission, but they also wanted to use the opportunity of his sentence to project the power of the state to some of those in Fisher's family, business, and religious networks who still subtly resisted it. The jail served as one important coercive tool to achieve both goals.

The jails in Pennsylvania were deplorable places. Dank and dirty, they exposed inmates to the cold in the winter and extreme heat and disease in the summer. Captain John Smyth, a loyalist in the Queen's Rangers, described his jail cell in Philadelphia, where Fisher was also held, as a "cold vaulted room, without bed, blanket, or straw." During his confinement, Smyth suffered from colic in the winter and dysentery in the summer without the benefit of a physician. He likened "the cruelties practiced" in the Philadelphia jail "to the Spanish inquisition prison." "Death," Smyth complained, "would have been an agreeable deliverance."[112] A group of twenty-seven political prisoners in the Easton jail similarly informed the SEC of their "distress'd situation" on account of their confinement during the "sultry Season of the year." The inmates stated that about thirty of them, in heavy irons, inhabited two small rooms, where they lay in their own filth with little to eat or drink. "One week more such cruel Treatment," the prisoners predicted, "will most certainly reduce us to the Shades of Death and land us in the world of Spirits."[113] Such a fate was not hyperbolic. When investigating the jail in Bethlehem in 1778, the state inspector found that, of the forty prisoners there, "eighteen were reported to me sick this morning, one of which is since dead, & two were buried yesterday."[114]

Capitalizing on these conditions, state officials often visited the jails telling political prisoners, Fisher included, that their suffering would end if they petitioned the government for relief, which meant that they would have to "acknowledge the present rulers." Officials also leveraged the poor health of prisoners to harass family and friends, demanding they too petition the government for their loved one's relief. When Fisher's health "dwindled," state officials punctuated their demands to his family with the rather terrifying question, "Will you be the cause of Sammy's death?" His father, fearful and greatly alarmed, offered to "come and lay in Gaol" in his son's "stead."[115] Individual acts of coercion, as in Fisher's case, often radiated outward, impacting a much larger community.

Fisher's declining health was only one excuse used to harass his family and friends; his continued refusal to recognize the state also justified such actions. State officials ransacked the home of his father, confiscated his only horse, and plundered his barn, clarifying that Fisher's acquiescence would have changed his father's fate. Not yet satisfied, they raided the merchant houses of his friends and even intimidated his sisters, all of whom made their way to the jail and begged Fisher to submit to the state and end their misery. Out of fear for themselves, prominent members of Fisher's Quaker meeting threatened him with disownment if he did not succumb to state demands. As Fisher related in his journal, "I might be disowned as the Society were suffering thro' me." Finally, the state achieved its goal. After almost two years of imprisonment, and fearing he would not "survive the present season," Fisher, his family, and friends petitioned the SEC, and the president released him.[116]

Fisher's experience was not an isolated incident, a fact assured through a slew of laws passed between 1777 and 1779 that increased the coercive capabilities of the state. During those years, the legislature appointed sixty-one "Commissioners of Allegiance," established officers to disarm and confiscate the estates of loyalists, and empowered the members of the SEC to direct every district justice of the peace and newly created county lieutenants and their sublieutenants to "arrest any person or persons within this commonwealth who shall be suspected . . . to be disaffected" for the "the preservation of this state."[117] Out of that list of officers, the county lieutenants proved the most effective in achieving state goals, and the SEC and the legislature routinely drew on them and augmented their power.

At first, state officials only charged the county lieutenants with mobilizing the local militias for war and keeping detailed lists of all white men over the age of eighteen who did or did not muster. By late 1777, faced with an increasingly disloyal countryside, the British occupation of Philadelphia, and the gloomy prospects of the war, legislators included the county lieutenants in their efforts to provide for, as one law was titled, "The Further Security of the Government."[118] Taking their jobs seriously, the county lieutenants traversed their "districts" violently enforcing loyalty to the state. In Northampton County, for example, Lieutenant John Wetzel canvassed his county with the militia, rounding up and jailing all who refused to pledge allegiance. In just the first few days of March 1779, Wetzel and his militia descended on at least three towns and arrested nineteen men "guilty of several transgressions against the interests and liberties of the state." According to Moravian leader John Ettwein, Wetzel had his prisoners bound by the neck and "led through Bethlehem like sheep by a pack of wolves."[119] For Wetzel, such actions were just part of his duty to "force" unwilling inhabitants "to give assurances of their good behavior towards our Laws and the dictates of Government."[120] Wetzel's understanding of his duty as enforcing loyalty to laws and government, rather than some nebulous "cause," highlights the way that loyalty, identity, and state sovereignty, at least from the perspective of state officers, were fundamentally interconnected in the construction of coercive policies and the justification for their violent enforcement.[121]

To protect the county lieutenants from "any Opposition," the executive sent these "Gentlemen acting on publick Authority" assurances that the government would support them against any "Suits in Law," thus further linking them to state goals and assuring that they could carry out the duty of their office using terror and violence with impunity.[122] Executive officers made that guarantee because the legislature passed a law indemnifying all officials acting on the state's behalf regarding "the disaffected."[123] As a result, the county lieutenants made it their "particular study to promote peace and harmony" by "endeavoring to suppress anything that would tend to give our Council or Assembly disturbance or trouble." Anyone who instigated such "trouble," according to county lieutenants such as Wetzel, "merit no Lenity."[124] Armed with substantial and sweeping powers and protected from "Suits in Law," the county lieutenants could and did "every day" terrorize inhabitants "to give assurances of their good behavior" for the "common good and the preservation of government."[125] While some may have viewed the lieutenants as "overzealous & imprudent men," as vice president of the SEC George Bryan conceded, they were also, as he put it, "well meaning."[126]

Bryan viewed the county lieutenants as "well meaning" because they did what the state demanded of them. The SEC routinely sent messages to the county lieutenants to enforce the laws related to the disaffected by any means necessary. President Joseph Reed, for example, instructed County Lieutenant Andrew Boyd to "fully execute" the laws regarding the confiscation of loyalist property, mustering for the militia, and taking the oath of allegiance to the state. Through the lieutenants, Reed hoped that "such Delinquents will find Government sufficiently able & willing to compel them." Reed stipulated that Boyd should use any means at his disposal to force compliance, as the president could not "comprehend the Reason or Propriety of giving the Benefit of Government to those who refuse to contribute to its necessary support."[127] Reed sent similar letters to the other lieutenants, and they, as one lieutenant reported, "excited the Sub-lieutenants all in my power" to enforce the laws by "Execution, Imprisonment or otherwise." Echoing the sentiments of the president, the lieutenant acknowledged that violent coercion was necessary, noting that "nothing but rigor will bring the People into a due compliance" with the law.[128]

The lieutenants made good on such promises because they not only had the power of positive law behind them, but they commanded the militias, linking local citizen-soldiers to state goals in a descending chain of command. According to one critical writer in a loyalist paper, the *Pennsylvania Ledger*, "Every man in the army even to a private centinel is impowered to deprive any person within the state, without any warrant for that purpose, of his liberty, drag him before a magistrate, and if he refuses to take the oath of allegiance and abjuration, he is then to be committed to gaol, there to remain 'till he complies."[129] The civil officers' use of the militia was so effective that one shocked witness in Lancaster County noted that "all persons coming out of their respective Counties, who have not taken the Oath, are clapped up immediately if they refuse swearing. Short Work with the Dissenters!"[130] Many of these people were incarcerated for long durations, often serving open-ended sentences, and spending those years in heavy chains.[131] Nor was this scenario anecdotal: jails throughout the states swelled with political prisoners, so much so that Pennsylvania had to construct new jails, New York resorted to creating prison ships, and Connecticut repurposed an abandoned copper mine, sending the disaffected to cells almost forty yards below ground.[132] For loyalists everywhere, imprisonment was a "Shocking Sentence (Worse than Death)." Another loyalist called jail the "mouth" of "Hell."[133] Such coercive surveillance was a massive undertaking that could not have been achieved without the mobilization of the state's civil and martial authority and a rhetoric that placed equal protection before the law or even individual rights in a subservient position to the public welfare and its instrument, state police power.

While Continental army officers derided the usefulness of the state militia on the battlefield, those units, under the command of the county lieutenants, augmented the power of the state.[134] As one Continental army officer snidely remarked, "I should have staid at home, talked big, been a militia-man, and hunted Tories."[135] Hunting Tories was so central to their service that later in life, recounting their war experience for pensions, militia veterans made it clear that "we ware after the Torys," or, more commonly stated, their main business was "to suppress the Tories." John Hill, for example, drafted into the Bucks County militia on three occasions, noted his "patriotic" service by recounting that he hunted down and apprehended at least eleven "Tories and thieves," was part of a detachment that "killed Thomas Price and Mordecai Wilson—two noted and dangerous [Tory] refugees, with several of their party," and "seized while in the pulpit" a "pretended Methodist Preacher" who was also the leader of the notorious loyalist Doan gang.[136] These men were not just irritated militiamen bent on seeking violent revenge but state actors, under orders, exerting state police power "over awing the malcontents & disaffected."[137]

Acts of "over awing" easily turned into extreme violence. Just outside Philadelphia during the British occupation, for example, County Lieutenant John Lacey, under direction from the SEC to put a "total stop to the insults of the Tories," ordered his men to guard the roads and to "fire upon the villains" bringing goods to the British market. He further ordered his troops to leave the corpses and the goods being carried strewn along the roads so "that they be a warning to others."[138] In the months ahead, the loyalist-controlled *Pennsylvania Ledger* ran stories of "barbarous cruelties" committed by Lacey and his men. One such story recounted how a militia captain stabbed to death a man caught trying to trade goods with the enemy. Another told how the militia punished a man for the same offense by tying a rope around his neck and dragging him behind "a horse in full gallop."[139] Partly because of his brutal tactics, a loyalist militia under General John Simcoe tried to kidnap Lacey, a move that resulted in the bloody Battle of Crooked Billet, where the loyalist militia, no doubt repaying violence in kind, set fire to some of Lacey's troops "while yet alive," and several other Pennsylvania militiamen, shot down in the battle, were found with "near a dozen [postmortem] wounds" made "with cutlasses and bayonets."[140] Unsurprisingly, news of this violence and loyalist militancy increased rather than diminished the state's efforts to suppress opposition.

State-sanctioned torture, destruction, and brutal beatings permeate the historical record of Pennsylvania's revolution. In Philadelphia, militiamen cudgeled people in the streets and hauled them to jail on suspicion of disloyalty. In one instance, the militia fired into the house of a small shopkeeper who refused to take the oath, "wounded and Robb'd his Wife, Cut away her pockets and committed every possible Depredation on his Property." Only his "escape from their bloody search" saved him, but not his wife, from falling "instant victim to their horrid Cruelty."[141] Outside the city, loyalists suffered a similar fate. In the frontier county of Northampton, when the wife and children of a known loyalist under house arrest tried to visit a friend, militiamen "pushed their Bayonets into the Chariot, broke the glass & pierced the chariot in 3 places; during the whole scene my wife begging to be let out & the children screaming." Less than a month earlier, the SEC had directed "a Guard of Soldiers with fixed Bayonets" to officially warn that family not to leave.[142]

Richard Swanwick's family, living in southeastern Chester County, shared a comparable experience, revealing the fear inspired by state action and the violent lengths state actors would go to to achieve obedience and punish the recalcitrant. In 1777, Swanwick fled for his life after he refused to take an oath of allegiance in front of County Lieutenant Andrew Boyd, leaving his small family to pick up the pieces in the process. Not long after Swanwick's escape, Boyd issued orders for the confiscation of his estate and sent a detachment of militia to carry away all movable goods and to obtain the deeds and other papers related to the property. Sensing her vulnerable situation, Richard's wife, Mary, had their slave bury all of the documents. When the militia arrived, Mary refused to divulge the location of the papers, so the militia "tortured" the slave, who, "through pain and fear," disclosed their location.[143] Although the nature of torture the slave endured is unknown, it must have been brutal; the Chester County militia was well known for its cruelty. For example, trying to learn the whereabouts of a man from Goshen Township who defended a fellow loyalist in nearby Delaware and owed over £160 in fines for refusing to muster for the war, the militia burned down his home and interrogated a member of his household by stringing him up and "cutting him down before he was quite dead." At the end of the interview, "while gasping for life, one of them put his musket into his mouth and shot him dead."[144] As revolutionaries everywhere explained, "Exterminating those Direful Wretches [Tories] from amongst us ... protected the People's ... Lives, Liberties and Properties," a connection contingent on the protectionist message that revolutionaries used to buttress the sovereignty of the states during their formative years.[145]

The state capitalized on the collective fear these violent events inspired in popularly attended parades and military reviews. Throughout the state, state leaders used carefully crafted processions of civil and military officers to strike "great terror" into the hearts of Pennsylvania's "internal enemies" as well as provide "comfort and security" for "the good people thereof."[146] Over the course of the war, for example, the president of the SEC commissioned militia and cavalry reviews within the city and counties to project sovereign power. On May 23, 1780, nearly three thousand artillerymen, infantry, and light horsemen paraded through the city to, the president hoped, "afford true delight to every lover of his country, and strike our enemies, both internal and external, with despair."[147]

In a similar vein, after the annual election of state presidents, officials staged elaborate parades to connect the two most potent edifices of state power, the statehouse and the courthouse, with the martial and legal authority of the government. Starting with a speech by the president, a vast array of state officials promenaded from the council chamber on the second floor of the statehouse to the courthouse on Market Street. From 1777 to 1780, the Committee of Councilors increased the number of civil and military officers on display during this parade from eleven to twenty-six.[148] After the election of Joseph Reed in 1780, for example, the procession included twenty-three different state officials in ceremonial dress and carrying their symbols of office. Behind them, a concourse of "citizens" joined, met up with units of militia and cavalry and a detachment of artillery. At the conclusion of the parade, the high sheriff commanded silence as the president, vice president, and Speaker of the House ascended the courthouse steps to proclaim the president "Captain General and Commander in Chief, in and over the Commonwealth of Pennsylvania." Immediately after the announcement, an artillery regiment fired three shots as inhabitants drank toasts to the "Prosperity of the State of Pennsylvania" and "Perdition to all traitors, secret and open."[149]

Bringing this same power of display to the counties, the justices of the supreme court opened the courts of oyer and terminer by parading with a retinue of state officials, both legal and military. Reflecting on the courts of his youth and of his parents' generation, David Paul Brown commented that "with all their professed republican principles," the state "followed and imitated, at no great distance, the example of the judges of the English Court of King's Bench" to "enjoin reverence to the sovereign."[150] When the day came to open a court of oyer and terminer, sheriffs, coroners, county lieutenants, presidents of the court of common pleas, as well as a detachment of cavalry and their captains, met the judges of the supreme court at the county lines and processed them to the courts.[151] When Chief Justice of the Supreme Court Thomas McKean went to Berks County, for example, he and the other judges "were met at the line of the county by the Sheriff and seven other Gentlemen, with white rods" indicating the formality of the endeavor.[152]

While parades displayed the sovereignty of the state in jubilant forms that also capitalized on the threat of coercion and violence, state leaders made the threat of those processions real at the gallows. Although many in power approved such "ideas for the relaxation of part of the Penal Laws" to limit the use of public executions as the constitution mandated, they nonetheless understood the "populace" was "divided" and that "the eyes of many will be upon the Government." Therefore, they argued, "a few examples ought to be made of the more atrocious" enemies of the state.[153] As a result, the state embraced the old penal code with a fervor that seemed, from the perspective of loyalists, "the very extreme of tyranny."[154] Tyrannical or not, adhering to a penal code that ascribed capital punishment for over a dozen crimes was a conscious choice directly related to revolutionaries' efforts to project the power of the state.

Keeping the penal laws intact also allowed the government to conflate disloyalty with criminality. In fact, in the historical record, it is hard to determine if an individual was arrested, jailed, or even executed for an actual crime or if loyalty to the state somehow influenced legal action. After all, high treason was difficult to prove, as the court needed "two sufficient witnesses" of an overt action to surrender "this state or the United States of America into the hands or power of any foreign enemy."[155] State leaders overcame such a difficulty by charging known loyalists with other crimes such as counterfeiting or robbery. James Fitzpatrick, for example, deserted from the American army in 1776, joined the British and fought with them at Brandywine, and then went on to attack, kidnap, and rob state military recruiters and tax collectors. Patriot authorities captured him in 1778 and executed him for burglary and highway robbery—not treason.[156]

Embracing the penal laws, then, provided the state with ample opportunities to prove that it held power over the people within its jurisdiction. During the war years, the state capitalized on those opportunities, publicly executing more people than at any other time in Pennsylvania's history. Between the establishment of state legal institutions in 1777 and the end of the war in 1783, the state executed sixty-eight people. On its own, that number means little, but when compared to the previous ten years, it is striking. Between 1766 and 1775, the colonial government executed less than half that number of people. The *state* government executed more people in just seven years (1777–83) than the colonial government did in the preceding thirty-seven. In fact, Pennsylvania's revolutionary state sent twice as many people to the gallows than the colonial governments of New York, South Carolina, and Massachusetts did between 1765 and 1776 combined—a significant reality considering the urban drama of Boston, the land riots in New York, and the regulation in South Carolina.[157]

A comparison of conviction rates for capital crimes and the use of pardons for two five-year periods, 1771–75 and 1778–82, provides further evidence that the state sought to harness the power of public executions. Between 1771 and 1775, the simple conviction rate for capital crimes was 68 percent. Juries found 86 people guilty out of 126 cases. Between 1778 and 1782, however, the simple conviction rate for capital crimes dropped to 49 percent. Juries found 83 people guilty out of 168 cases. Despite the lower conviction rate, between 1778 and 1782 the state government executed three times as many people as the colonial government did between 1771 and 1775. A comparison of the use of pardons between 1771–75 and 1778–82 reveals how. Where the colonial government issued pardons liberally (between 1771 and 1775, 42 percent of all death warrants resulted in a pardon), the state did not (between 1778 and 1782, only 33 percent of death warrants resulted in a pardon). Focusing on three years, 1778–80, only 25 percent of death warrants resulted in a pardon. Even with a lower conviction rate, then, the state capitalized on the guilty verdicts obtained.[158]

State leaders favored public executions because they offered the large crowd of spectators a potent symbol of the state's authority. In one of the few extant execution day sermons during the revolution, Presbyterian minister Nathan Strong made it clear that public executions proved necessary when "the State is in so critical a situation, that the dishonesty and bad example of a few persons may shake its foundation." From the macabre procession of the condemned to the execution itself, Strong maintained, the public "learn the venerableness of the state" and "our obligations to obedience." "Go not," he warned, to the place of execution "with elevated spirits," for "death is there! Justice and judgment are there! The power of government, displayed in its most awful form, is there!"[159] On the day of an execution, state officials blindfolded, chained, and placed the condemned on a coffin with a noose slung around his or her neck. Large crowds lined the streets as a magistrate and the militia led the condemned with family in tow to the gallows. All the while, drummer and fife filled the air with the rogue's march, a song Pennsylvanians "seemed particularly fond of."[160] Once the condemned made his or her way to the gallows, the crowd heard a sermon like the one preached by Strong that demanded repentance and obedience to the state. During the war the central purpose of the gallows shifted from a space meant to reform the community to a spectacle that projected the state's sovereign power.[161]

State officials even used the few pardons and reprieves they offered with the full intent of capitalizing on this pageantry of death and the majestic power of the state. Using pardons, as Chief Justice McKean argued, constituted a "God-like power, and a God-like virtue," blurring the lines of justice, terror, and mercy all to "create respect to the Rulers" and "endear men to the Government."[162] When the president of the SEC issued a pardon or reprieve, he often directed the sheriff "not to make it known" to the condemned "until he be taken under the gallows."[163] For instance, Lawrence Miller, convicted of sedition, had to watch the execution of his partner, Michael Rosebury, before he received his pardon. According to Reverend William Rogers, "Poor Miller was much agitated at the sight, expecting every moment the same punishment."[164] George Harding, convicted of high treason, or "genuine toryism," as the *Royal Gazette* put it, took the long death march "to the Gallows with a rope about his neck to be hanged."[165] Just as he stepped onto the cart, the magistrate read out his reprieve.[166] Once "delivered from death," Harding offered "sincere thanks to His Excellency the President and Vice President; to the Honorable Council and Court" and to "the public in general."[167] In this case, as in many others, acquiescence to the state's sovereign power was dramatically achieved and further solidified the beneficence of the state, the flipside of the same coercive coin.[168]

In the early years of the state government, officials attempted to counteract challenges to lawful authority and assert state legitimacy through a vigorous exertion of power. They enhanced the government's "internal police" to "protect" citizens, often blurring the lines between public and private in the process. Simultaneously, they put this newfound authority on display through public panoplies of power in the streets, in the courts, and at the gallows. An exploration of the institutions and officers in a newly independent Pennsylvania and their deployment by the state during the war years provides a necessary corrective to a historiography that has described the revolutionary state as little different, beyond democracy, from the old colonial polity. In his work, George David Rappaport, synthesizing a great deal of material on revolutionary Pennsylvania, argued that the state, like the colony, had "too few officials to either administer or coerce its citizens effectively" and proved "weak" in the execution of government services and protections.[169] A more detailed look at the state over the course of the war belies such an interpretation of the post-independence state. Substantially different from the old colonial government, the state could and *did* have the ability to coerce people within its jurisdiction.

Conclusion

New Constitutions and the Persistence of State

SITTING IN THE COUNCIL CHAMBER IN 1785, the president of the state of Pennsylvania, the now eighty-year-old Benjamin Franklin, pondered on the revolution, the power of the state, and the needs for the future prosperity of Pennsylvania. During the Revolutionary War, Franklin decidedly favored the tactics of the day and a state that was forged in crisis. Suppressing the disaffected—their removal and their exclusion from the political structure—were all necessary during a time of uncertainty and war. Franklin even judged the failure of the state to reform its penal laws as stipulated in the constitution as unavoidable in tumultuous times. However, as Franklin saw it, circumstances had changed by 1785. The more dangerous enemies of the state had either died or left the state or had been cowed into obedience or acquiescence or forcibly removed. Independence had been achieved, sovereignty of the people was intact, and nothing, Franklin argued, could now change that. Therefore, laws and coercive tactics that had been "proper or necessary" at "the time and under the circumstances in which they were made" were no longer needed. The revolutionary state was unnecessary and therefore, Franklin and other leaders argued, Pennsylvanians should work together to achieve the laudable goals of the revolution in finishing the formation of a stable, efficient, and effective state.[1]

While Pennsylvanians saw the need to end the revolutionary tactics of the state, such a move in no way meant the principles and goals of the revolution died with it. Pennsylvanians had worked for a system of government in which they had a central place in shaping public policy. They had struggled for inclusion in the political system to offset a past of inefficient and ineffective colonial governance. Pennsylvanians wanted a government that could act with efficiency, effectiveness, and authority to protect the public welfare. They had rebelled and inaugurated their revolution "for the Good Order of Government," and no one would or could give that up. As they had in the early days of the resistance movement, Pennsylvanians sought and demanded a government that met their needs and adapted itself as those needs and interests changed. The authority, usefulness, and necessity of the state government and its constitution would only last as long as it could meet those goals. Such a sentiment was highlighted in the Declaration of Rights. Government was "instituted and supported for the security and protection of the community" and "whenever these great ends of government are not obtained, the people have a right, by common consent to change it."[2] The power of those words would become clear in the late 1780s, when the constitution and those who supported it lost the allegiance and support of a great many of the citizens in the state.

Although historians see the political changes of the 1780s and '90s, the creation of both the US Constitution in 1787 and the new state constitution in 1790, as a Thermidorean reaction that repudiated the revolution that Pennsylvanians and others fought so hard to gain, such an interpretation does not adequately represent the political period, the goals of the revolution, or the continuance of political principles birthed in the revolution.[3] As some of these same historians note, the Constitution of 1776 and the group of politicians who supported it lost considerable popularity and political force in the 1780s. The reasons for that loss crucially demonstrate the persistence of a political logic that favored a governing structure that could, at all times, act efficiently and effectively when needs and interests demanded—that Pennsylvanians worked for the "Good Order of Government," desired its services, and reacted and shifted political allegiance when it did not.

In the years immediately following 1776, the advocates for the 1776 Constitution, styling themselves "Whigs" or "Constitutionalists," gained a broad base of support. They won that backing because they provided the public a clear picture of the future that sharply contrasted with the past. They presented themselves as the champions of the people against a dying and broken system of government that failed to provide for the common good. They offered newly independent Pennsylvanians hope for a future in which the people had a central place in a government where they could always shape public policy and effectuate change. Through such political inclusion, the government would forever uphold the needs and interests of the community. The Constitutionalists solidified their popularity by proving themselves crucial reformers and friends of law and government. They fashioned legal structures and other institutions to meet old demands and new problems. They served as the driving force behind developing a regional system of law enforcement, reform of the supreme court, and creating new courts, laws, and officers in the effort to make the government far more efficient and effective in its ability to offer basic guarantees as stipulated in the vaunted Declaration of Rights.

The Constitutionalists also gained their popularity due to the chicanery of their political opponents. In the immediate years after creating the 1776 Constitution, a powerful group of Pennsylvanians, many of the old political leaders of the past government, sought to maintain the status quo. They detested the state constitution because of its "democratical" notions and its deviation from the past. The "radical scythe" had cut them off from political power, and they resented it. In response, they did everything in their power to stymie the new government. In the early years of the war, these opponents to the constitution realized that they needed to undermine the power of the government to both create and execute laws in order to crush the state at its birth. Nobody, they argued, would support an ineffective government, and therefore they refused to take their local offices if appointed, hand over old documents and records, or to even sit in the legislature, in order to deny the assembly a quorum. Such tactics, however, gained them little popularity and only served to strengthen the attractiveness of the Constitutionalists. In 1779, a year of economic turmoil demanding governmental action, for instance, several assembly members who opposed the new government refused to take their seats, resulting in days and then months of legislative inaction. As a consequence, Pennsylvanians took to the polls at the next general election and ousted many of those members in the support of Constitutionalist candidates.

By the 1780s, political circumstances had changed dramatically. First and foremost, new people controlled the opposition. The leaders of the old opposition had either died, left the state, or retired to political insignificance, leaving the opposition in the hands of new leaders who in no way represented the old. Pennsylvanians such as "revolutionary gadfly" Benjamin Rush, James Wilson, Thomas Mifflin, and Thomas McKean, who supported the government regardless, headed a new oppositional force in the state. Even some Constitutionalist members jumped ship and entered the opposition's ranks, such as radical artisans William Will and Thomas Paine. Unlike the old oppositional group, this new assemblage, labeling themselves Republicans, did away with reactionary tactics and offered, as the Constitutionalists had done, a clear vision for the future of Pennsylvania that upheld the political and governmental goals of the revolution. They presented themselves as the protectors of revolutionary principles, the "Friends to Equal Liberty," and the guardians of the people's constituent powers. They assailed the government under the constitution as precarious, instable, and a threat to the liberty of the people. The constitution could not, they argued, provide for the common good. Republicans advocated replacing the old system with a bicameral legislature, single executive, and independent judiciary that could provide, as Thomas McKean argued, "stability in our laws and permanency in our magistracy" that would make the state "reputable, safe and happy."[4]

This republican structure of government, moreover, did not mean a rejection of the democratic principles of the revolution. Republicans argued that a bicameral legislature would uphold rather than demolish democracy. After 1776, no one could deny the power of the citizenry in the political system and their ability to shape public policy. "It is an insult to the meanest understanding" one Republican argued, for the Constitutionalists to portray the upper house of a bicameral model as "a House of Lords." "They" he argued, would "be chosen by the people & therefore accountable to them, as much as the Assembly are." Such a model, would, Republicans argued, provide for the stability and happiness Pennsylvanians required by enabling an upper house to check the actions of the assembly while still upholding the central elements of popular sovereignty.[5]

The Republican call for stability, order, and maintaining law struck a chord with many Pennsylvanians because of the reality of politics in the 1780s. While the Republicans fashioned themselves as the party of stability, equality, and law, the Constitutionalists entrenched themselves and, to their detriment, used political tactics similar to the opponents of the constitution in the early years of the revolution. Such subterfuge proved a political disaster in the 1770s and remained so in the 1780s. For example, when the Republicans called for further reforms to the judiciary by separating the duties of judges and justices in the county courts, reforming the penal system, and devising further reforms of the supreme court circuit, the Constitutionalists balked. As the opposition had done in the mid-1770s, the Constitutionalists became the party of no and attempted to thwart all Republican agendas, even those that did not directly challenge the constitution and had popular backing. When it seemed the Republicans would gain a point in the House, the Constitutionalists refused to take their seats and therefore denied the assembly a quorum. Political difference had reached such a fever pitch that supreme court judges from the competing parties refused to work together on the same circuits, resulting in several obstructions in the administration of justice.[6] In addition, due to political bickering and legislative upheaval, the assembly passed and repealed laws regularly, furthering a feeling of chaos and confusion in the state.

These political realities had dire consequences for many Pennsylvanians. The assembly's vacillation over legislation to change the location of the Chester County court and jail is an excellent example of that negative impact. Immediately after independence, citizens of the county grumbled to the legislature about the distance they had to travel to get to the courthouse and jail in the borough of Chester and demanded the assembly pass legislation to move these important legal structures to a more central location. Finally in 1780, the assembly passed legislation to remove the court and jail. However, due to internal disagreements the legislators never stipulated where they would move these institutions, and they nominated several persons to carry out this legislation who openly advocated against removal. The issue of removal was so contentious, yet important, that the legislators elected to print for public knowledge each of the representatives' votes for or against the measure.[7] By 1784, inhabitants in Chester, upset at this rather flawed and ineffectual legislation, demanded action and barraged the assembly with angry petitions. The legislature, under new leadership, responded to the petitions by nominating new officers and stipulating the movement of the court and jail to the township of Goshen. Within a few months, inhabitants built the new jail and erected four walls of the court. Yet in the midst of this construction, leadership in the assembly changed hands again, and the legislature, receiving petitions from inhabitants in and around the borough of Chester, repealed the removal bill.

Revocation nearly resulted in bloodshed. The inhabitants erecting the court in Goshen continued construction and refused to adhere to the new law. In response, inhabitants living in and around the borough of Chester formed themselves into a company with a cannon, muskets, rifles, and a barrel of whiskey and marched on Goshen with the intent of "razing the walls of the proposed Court House and jail to the earth." Back at Goshen, citizens armed themselves and turned the courthouse into a rickety fort to repel the invaders. From a dominant position atop an adjoining hill, borough citizens readied to fire their fieldpiece into the ramshackle court. Under siege, the occupants of the courthouse surrendered and agreed to stop construction until the assembly gave further orders. The issue, however, went unresolved for over a year, and citizens again turned to the threat of violence.[8] As this event nicely demonstrates, local legal structures were important for everyday people, and the failure of the assembly to provide stability in its lawmaking threatened those structures and, through that, the peace and harmony of the state.

The chaos bred by political strife over the state constitution, the Constitutionalists' political artifices, and the party line of the Republicans resulted in substantial political changes in the state. Over the course of mid- to late 1780s, the Republicans won sweeping victories at the polls. Much of their victories had to do with the political subterfuge of the Constitutionalists, particularly their abstaining from taking their seats in the house to block the Republican agenda. As a meeting of inhabitants in Northampton put it, "The withdrawing or absenting of any member of assembly, who was sworn to serve his country to the best of his abilities, tends to subvert all order and the fundamental principles of good government and establishes precedents of aristocratic powers, for a minority, to defeat the proceedings of a majority."[9] Similarly, at a meeting in Cumberland County, citizens gathered together and pledged "that the withdrawing or absenting of any member of assembly, in order to defeat any resolution or act of the legislature, is an offence most destructive to good government, and the happiness and true interest of the state." Any member who "is guilty of such desertion and breach of trust," they argued, "is unworthy of the confidence of the people, and unfit to represent them."[10] Citizens were prepared to act on such strong words. When Constitutionalists refused to take their seats, mobs assembled to force them into the chamber. Citizens even threatened to tar and feather the absenting members. Such violent action, one Pennsylvanian argued would "*deter others* from treading in" the steps of these "eighteen or nineteen human asses, who are a disgrace to Pennsylvania."[11] It was a dramatic political reversal that spoke to the needs, interests, and concerns of a citizenry who expected a working government that could enforce the law and provide stability and security for the community. By the end of the 1780s, there was little allegiance left to the 1776 Constitution, its unicameral assembly, or its plural executive.

Over the course of the 1780s, Pennsylvanians displayed their dedication to the revolution and "the Good Order of Government" by mobilizing forces and shifting political allegiance as needs and interests demanded. When the state of Pennsylvania proved incapable of meeting the expectations of the people, Pennsylvanians sought resolutions and supported change. The rather popular support of the US Constitution in Pennsylvania reflected that dedication. According to George Bryan, Pennsylvanians made "very little Bustle" and provided "little or no Opposition" to the ratification of the new federal Constitution. For some Pennsylvanians, the reason for their support was simple. The state proved incapable of protecting the commercial activity of its citizens. Although the state government passed tariffs to promote the domestic economy, particularly for artisans, it could not extend those tariffs to the other states. Foreign goods flowed into the city and hinterland from Delaware, New York, and New Jersey, and there was little the state could do to stop it. Forming a stronger federal government, many thought, promised a concerted system of economic regulation for all the states. Artisans, upon the ratification of the Constitution, marched in celebration parades flying flags and banners that demonstrated this belief in the new union of states. Rope makers, sailmakers, and weavers all marched in step brandishing banners that read, "May commerce flourish," may "industry be rewarded," and importantly, "May government protect us."[12]

Regardless of the ease with which Pennsylvanians ratified the Constitution, many in no way expected or wanted this new federal government to challenge the sovereign authority of the individual states that citizens fought so hard to gain. Antifederalists in Pennsylvania, while they did little to stop ratification, still expressed deep concern about the sovereignty of the state in this new union. In Cumberland County, that apprehension turned to violence as Antifederalists broke up a ratification celebration. Beyond using violence, Antifederalists mobilized in town meetings and conventions, demanding reform of the US Constitution to protect the sovereignty of the state.

On September 3, 1788, Antifederalists held a well-attended convention in Harrisburg that produced several resolutions to amend the constitution. Antifederalists feared that without amendment their liberty would "lie at the discretion of Congress" instead of the state. In the process, Pennsylvanians would lose their constituent powers and their ability to control and shape the internal police of the state, which, they argued, constituted the only guarantee "that order and good government should prevail."[13] Yet, even here, Antifederalists did not oppose the federal Constitution.[14] As ardent Antifederalist William Findley argued, "I wish not to destroy this system. Its outlines are well laid. By amendments it may answer all our wishes."[15] Through amendments, Findley and other Antifederalists sought to preserve the sovereign authority of the states. At the Harrisburg convention, the assembled members made similar declarations that they were "well apprized of the necessity of devolving extensive powers to Congress" and they accepted a "general system of government framed by the late Federal Convention." They mobilized not to resist government but to assure that both the power and authority of their state would remain under a new federal system. They wanted a guarantee that the rights granted under the state constitutions would "remain inviolate" and the states could exercise those "rights of sovereignty which are not by the said Constitution expressly and plainly vested in the Congress." For the members of the convention, who represented a large constituent of Pennsylvanians, it was absolutely necessary that each state maintain the "right of legislation" and any other regulation for "the police and good order" of government.[16]

The actions of the Antifederalists in Pennsylvania and others who expressed concern as to the power of the states in this new union had important consequences for an interpretation of the federal Constitution and the future of the state in Pennsylvania. Even those ardent Federalists who hoped that through the federal Constitution they could fashion a national state conceded that such a vision would never receive popular backing. Federalists had to allay any lingering fears, and by doing so, they offered a vision of the Constitution that was, remarkably, in accord with the thoughts and wishes of the Antifederalists in the state. As a result, Federalists and Antifederalists alike forged a crucial interpretation of the federal Constitution that had lasting significance. In a speech in the statehouse yard, James Wilson, a prominent member of the state Republican Party and ardent Federalist, addressed critical fears that the Constitution was designed to "reduce the State governments to mere corporations and eventually to annihilate them" altogether. According to Wilson, the federal system depended on "their existence" and the "existing union of the States."[17] For Wilson, at least in these early years, the federal Constitution would preserve "the state governments" because "the freedom of the people and their internal good police depends on their [the states] existence in full vigor."[18] According to Wilson and other supporters of the US Constitution, "the powers vested in the federal government are particularly defined, so that each state still retains its sovereignty in what concerns its own internal government." The federal government, writers argued, only protected the sovereign authority of the states "against foreign invasion, and to preserve peace and beneficial intercourse among themselves, and to protect and regulate their commerce with foreign nations." Every other power of government would be "exercised by the sovereign states."[19] The federal Constitution, then, offered the people a fundamental "public good" while preserving the authority of the states and therefore the constituent power of citizens in shaping public policy for their own "good government."[20]

The debate over the federal Constitution also crucially altered state politics by creating a popular dialogue over the value of the state constitution. When Republicans such as James Wilson spoke to the public about "viable" and "stable" state governments, they helped shift popular discussion to the effectiveness of the present state constitution. Moreover, they juxtaposed the frame of the federal Constitution, its bicameral legislature and relatively powerful executive and independent judiciary with Pennsylvania's frame and by doing so, they ultimately unleashed a broad constitutional dialogue.

Over the course of 1788 and 1789, Pennsylvanians kept up a lively debate in the press discussing the merits and deficiencies of the state constitution and its relationship to the goals of the revolution. The opponents of the 1776 Constitution clearly dominated this debate. In the press, Republicans and their supporters produced stinging attacks on the present government. They railed against the practices of the "advocates for the constitution of Pennsylvania" who had denied the citizens of the state their "birthright." Constitutionalists had, Republicans wailed, created great "instability in our laws" and responded with a "sullen No" to all attempts for significant governmental reform, even reforms that did not threaten the frame of government.[21]

Republicans rode the tide of this public discussion of constitutionalism and the deficiencies of the state to push through a popularly elected convention to revise the state constitution. In some ways, however, the sentiments of the times revealed more than a simple tide created by broad discussion of the federal Constitution and its relationship to the states. Experiences over the past several years revealed crucial problems with the state constitution. Even staunch Constitutionalists such as Albert Gallatin conceded that "our Constitution wants some essential amendments," which every "good citizen" should agree with "in order to re-establish peace & harmony in this distracted State."[22] Given a strong majority in the general assembly in favor of amendment, Republicans and some Constitutionalists charged ahead, and on March 24, 1789, by a vote of forty-one to sixteen, resolved to call on the citizens of the state to decide on the merits of a new constitutional convention. Under this resolve, Pennsylvanians had four months in which they could mobilize and create petitions or memorials to state their approval or disapproval of a convention.[23]

By calling on the public, the assembly, particularly the Republicans, upheld the central tenets of their revolutionary settlement, especially when compared to the arguments of the dissenting Constitutionalists. A minority of Constitutionalists in the House argued against calling on the public. They believed a popularly called and elected convention was illegal because the constitution did not allow for any amendment outside a body of its own creation, the Council of Censors.

Such a dissent angered quite a few citizens in the state. It was, one author argued, an "absurdity." The Constitutionalists' argument against a popularly called convention and reform of the constitution, citizens pointed out, threatened the essence of liberty as enshrined in their Declaration of Rights. According to one author, the claims of the Constitutionalist minority limited the "sovereign authority" of the "community" and therefore destroyed "liberty." "The declaration of rights, asserts it as a right of sovereignty in the community 'indubitable, unalienable, and indefeasible, to reform, alter or abolish government,' in such manner, as shall be by that community, (not by any particular council) judged most conducive to the public weal." "The people," he went on "have not alienated this right." The dissent of the Constitutionalist minority, needless to say, alienated an already exasperated citizenry. One angry memorial stated bluntly that "the power of altering the Constitution resides wholly in the PEOPLE, and that they have a right to exercise that power in any way, and at any time, they may judge proper."[24] It was a strange turn of events; the public labeled the champions of the democratic state constitution undemocratic!

By August, calling a constitutional convention proved a foregone conclusion. Writers exposing the "imperfections" of the state constitution dominated the newspapers for the entire spring and summer. "Our very laws themselves want stability" authors argued, because "our single assembly fluctuates like the waves of the sea, and frequently overswells its bounds. What may be done this year, may be undone the next." Moreover, as experience testified, "A discontented minority may break up the house, and put a stop to public business." The constitution as it stood, writers argued, "instead of" promoting "liberty, order and good government," the hallmarks of their revolution, had devolved into "violent factions" where a "few leaders" could "deprive" the people of their right to all "the beneficial advantages of government." Such a government approached "very near to aristocracy" and was therefore "contrary to all republican principles." Although the constitution embraced democracy, it still promoted "the government of the few, and not of the many."[25]

Writers in the public press firmly associated a reform of the state constitution with a continuation of their revolution. Pennsylvanians, according to authors, had begun their revolution for "good government" that protected their rights, liberties, and happiness. It was not a revolution against government but for government, and therefore the 1776 Constitution, while it certainly had its merits, subverted some of the goals of that revolution. "The revolution," Pennsylvanians argued, "is not founded on the idea that government is a necessary evil—but on the reverse, that it is the choicest blessing Heaven ever has bestowed on the human race." The principles of that revolution, writers argued, centered on "improving the condition of human nature" by crafting popular governments and "supporting and strengthening the hands of our civil rulers."[26] Only by approving a convention, writers stated, could the people finally assure "the fundamental principles" of their revolution with "a free and just government."[27]

Connecting the push for a convention with the revolution had a significant impact on the citizens of the state. Pennsylvanians wanted to maintain their democracy and their happiness under an efficient and effective government that could always provide valuable protections and services. By the late 1780s, it was readily apparent that the state constitution as it existed could not guarantee those blessings. As a result, citizens mobilized and sent memorials and petitions to the assembly favoring the calling of a convention. According to one report, "Out of several thousand signers [of petitions], there were none against the measure." "It seems doubtful," the Carlisle Gazette reported, "whether any petitions against a Convention will be presented."[28]

While the editor of the Gazette certainly underestimated the number of Pennsylvanians against a change, he did nonetheless point out the relative silence of opponents to the convention. In the months after the resolve in the assembly, a few Constitutionalists took to the streets, calling on their constituents to mobilize a resistance effort, but nothing transpired. Most of the Constitutionalists reacted rather uninterestedly. William Findley, an ardent Antifederalist and leader of the

Constitutionalist Party, for example, displayed extreme indifference to calling a convention. Instead of rallying his constituents, Findley spent the summer "much in leisure" at his home, because he thought the people would "not exert themselves to oppose the measure."[29] The people's refusal to mobilize against the calling of a convention is significant. Over the course of the revolutionary period, Pennsylvanians were always quick to organize themselves for the sake of opposition; calling price control committees and the Harrisburg convention clearly proves this point. Yet here, when the constitution was in danger, they did little to oppose it. As Findley pointed out, the unwillingness of Pennsylvanians to mobilize against the convention served as a "testimony of want of confidence in" the state constitution.[30] The inaction of Pennsylvanians speaks volumes, and it sounded the death knell of the 1776 Constitution.

A new constitution, however, did not mean the death of democracy or the principles of popular sovereignty. It was not the culmination of a counterrevolution but the continuation of revolutionary principles that allowed the people to assemble to shape public policy and craft governments as they saw fit. The Republican-controlled assembly left calling a convention and electing the representatives for it to the people. Moreover, whatever these representatives created would be served up to the people for public consideration, in which the citizenry would have four months to consider its merits and deficiencies. Meantime, the old constitution and frame would still govern. It was a matter of course that any constitution needed the popular support and backing of the citizens it would govern. Creating constitutions and governments on the authority of the people was a central part and product of the revolution, and no one could refute or take away that central privilege.

In addition, stipulating the popular election of representatives to the convention assured that popular sovereignty would remain a cornerstone of government in Pennsylvania. In the convention both Constitutionalists and Republicans met, debated, and crafted a new government on the authority of the people. Each side, according to William Findley, displayed "the most laudable spirit of accommodation" and, as Albert Gallatin noted, directed their attention to that one supreme "object, that the Representatives should always speak the will of the people."[31] These democratic sentiments, members of the convention argued, undergirded the revolutionary moment and therefore should always remain. Even those Republicans, then, whom many historians view as the enemies of democracy, worked to uphold salient popular aspects of the revolution. The constitution the convention created is expressive of this point. Although the Constitutionalists, often viewed by historians as the sole popular spokesmen, comprised a minority in the convention, the new constitution upheld rather than destroyed democracy. The vaunted Declaration of Rights remained in force with additions, such as a section that banned holding any titles of nobility. In addition, suffrage qualifications remained the same, and although the constitution replaced the plural executive and unicameral assembly with a bicameral legislature and a single executive, the power of election still remained in the people, the suffrage remained the same, and no property qualifications were stipulated to hold office. Moreover, not only was the new governor an elected official but his veto power was significantly circumscribed, as the legislature could, on a two-thirds majority, override his veto. Besides these structural points, the doors of the House remained open, the rights of the people to assembly were guaranteed, and all the votes of the representatives in both houses were to be printed weekly for the people's perusal. The government would remain the protector of the public good, and the people maintained their place in the political system and the right to alter, amend, or abolish the government as they saw fit.[32] The creation of new state constitutions in 1838, 1874, and 1968 reflects that ongoing right and sentiment. In fact, section II of the state constitution of 1968, in place today, maintains the people's "inalienable and indefeasible right to alter, reform or abolish their government in such a manner as they may think proper."[33]

In 1790, as had happened in the Constitutional Convention of 1776, not only did the representatives focus on democratic initiatives, but they sought crucial change in the administration of justice and local legal structures. Pennsylvanians in this moment displayed the same dedication to law, order, and government as they had in the past. Statesmen and citizens alike looked to strengthen their legal structures and make them more efficient and accessible to the people at large. Those institutions and innovations of the revolutionary period that worked, the convention kept. It did not do away with the regional system of law enforcement or the laws and many of the officers created during the war years. Instead, it enhanced, reformed, and further centralized the state's authority through those institutions and officers.

Representatives to the convention and the first legislature under the 1790 constitution furthered the state building process in Pennsylvania by substantially reorganizing the courts and centralizing power. They created five judicial districts to regulate and manage all the courts in the state, regardless of county lines, each presided over by a district president, answerable to the governor. Each district, moreover, was broken down into subdivisions with courts of oyer and terminer, courts of quarter sessions, courts of common pleas, and orphans courts. The district presidents directed and supervised the law enforcement and judicial affairs of each district. They controlled the direction of judges, justices, sheriffs, and coroners. They could issue writs of habeas corpus and certiorari and mobilize the force of the district to put down internal unrest. In addition, the supreme court had to ride a circuit within each district and was under the purview of not only the chief justice but the new district presidents. According to statesmen, such changes would "secure an efficient, safe and *uniform* administration of the laws" and provide for "the Good Order of Government."[34]

When the convention members presented the first draft of the constitution to the public, it sparked instant acclaim. Pennsylvanians printed poems about "Courts refin'd" and the "Happiness" they would feel under this new instrument.[35] In a similar vein, other writers in the press praised the new constitution for producing a government "long unsuccessfully sought after" by developing a "SOCIAL COMPACT founded on the *sole authority of the people*."[36] This new government included the public in its measures and had the institutions capable of maintaining social values and expectations.

At its core, the Constitution of 1790 represented a continuation of the goals of the revolution. Like the 1776 Constitution, it provided a connection of democracy and law, the necessity of government, and the centrality of the state. The state government that existed in 1790 fundamentally deviated from that of the pre-independence era. Over the course of the colonial period, Pennsylvanians clamored for political inclusion because the institutions of government did not meet their needs or their expectations. Representation, the will of the people, and forming efficient and effective government, particularly in improving Pennsylvania's internal police, went hand in hand. Pennsylvanians inaugurated their revolution for "good government" for a "system of government which would effectually provide for the welfare, safety and happiness of our country."[37] Pennsylvanians tried and, many argued, failed to achieve those goals in 1776. For some Pennsylvanians, then, the Constitution of 1790 and the institutions it reformed, created, and enhanced, represented the fulfillment of a revolution for "the Good Order of Government." As one author noted, "To the achievement of a glorious independence and the establishment of an efficient confederation, we have now to add another subject of joy, in the ratification of a system of state government which at once removes every foundation of past deficiencies, and sanctifies every hope for future prosperity."[38] That future, Pennsylvanians expected, promised a government that continued to meet the goal "for which all government was instituted, namely, the advancement of the PUBLIC GOOD."[39]

As hoped for, the importance of the revolution and the kind of state it created continued to shape the minds and decisions of statesmen and jurists well into the nineteenth century. By the 1850s, the state faced popular pushback against policies that "injured" individual citizens for public benefit. Cases inundated the courts as citizens tried to evade the individual impact of state licensing, market regulations, nuisance policies, and the construction of highways, railroads, and canals. In a never-ending series of decisions, though, state justices cited "the revolution" as vesting the state with "sovereign power." And, like revolutionaries, these justices declared that this power allowed the state to "regulate," "supervise," "control," and "police" (even "injure") the lives and property "of an individual for the benefit of the many." Though long superseded by new state constitutions, the justices made clear that in the long "history of jurisprudence" it was the "constitution of 1776" that originally "confirmed these powers."[40]

From our modern vantage point, shrouded as it is with obsessive individualism and popular opinions about the evils of government and regulation, it is hard to imagine such a state, especially one formed by revolutionaries who deemed government "the choicest blessing Heaven ever has bestowed on the human race," rather than a "necessary evil."[41] The efforts to attain that lofty status eluded some, but they nonetheless created a state that people at the time described as "active" and "energetic," taking "care of our Persons, our property, and our reputation, constituting the great field of human concerns."[42] Such was the place and power of the individual states created during the revolution, which had a lasting impact on ordinary citizens for years to come.

NOTES

Abbreviations

APS	American Philosophical Society
CCA	Chester County Archives
CO	Colonial Office Records
CTR	Correspondence of Thomas and Richard Penn with James Hamilton, 1741–1771
HSP	Historical Society of Pennsylvania
JBT	Journals of the Board of Trade
LTP	Letters of Thomas Penn
NYHS	New York Historical Society
PA	*Pennsylvania Archives*
PBF	*The Papers of Benjamin Franklin*
PGW	*The Papers of George Washington*
PHMC	Pennsylvania Historical and Museum Commission
PMHB	*Pennsylvania Magazine of History and Biography*
PPOC	Penn Papers, Official Correspondence
PTJ	*The Papers of Thomas Jefferson, Digital Edition*
PWP	*The Papers of William Penn*
SLP	*The Statutes at Large of Pennsylvania from 1682 to 1809*
TPL	Thomas Penn Letterbook
WLC	William L. Clements Library, University of Michigan

Introduction

1. John Jay to George Washington, June 27, 1786, *PGW*; Washington to Jay, August 15, 1786, *PGW*.
2. Henry Knox to Rufus King, July 15, 1787, as quoted in Bradburn, *The Citizenship Revolution*, 65.
3. George Washington to Alexander Hamilton, July 10, 1787, *PGW*.
4. George Washington to Henry Knox, August 19, 1787, *PGW*.
5. John Adams to Benjamin Rush, February 23, 1813, in Adams, *Old Family Letters*, 447.
6. See such works on the United States Constitution as Wood, *The Creation of the American Republic*; and Beeman, *Plain, Honest Men*. For studies of American nationalism and national identity see Waldstreicher, *In the*

Midst of Perpetual Fetes; Waldstreicher, "Rites of Rebellion, Rites of Assent," 37–61; and Travers, *Celebrating the Fourth*. Since such works, historians have attempted to track that nationalism back to the formation of the First Continental Congress. See Irvin, *Clothed in Robes of Sovereignty*. For works that envision the federal government as a powerful nation-state see Edling, *A Revolution in Favor of Government*; Edling, *A Hercules in the Cradle*; and Griffin, *American Leviathan*. See also Pincus, *The Heart of the Declaration*. While Edling's and Griffin's works describe the creation of the federal Constitution as auguring a strong "leviathan," a nation-state, other scholars convey ambivalence toward such a characterization of the federal government. See, for example, Rothman, "Beware the Weak State," 271–74. A growing and significant body of work has challenged the nationalist interpretation of the Early Republic. Adhering to what David C. Hendrickson terms a "Unionist Paradigm," these scholars emphasize the federal rather than national character of the United States after the ratification of the Constitution. See Hendrickson, *Peace Pact*; Bradburn, *The Citizenship Revolution*; and Max M. Edling, "The Legislative Output of Congress under the Washington Administration, 1789–1797," working paper in the author's possession.

7. In part, the emphasis on continuity, in this capacity, has its origins in the early Whig history of the United States by George Bancroft, who saw the birth of the United States in the planting of the first English colonies. Robert E. Brown continued this view with a bit more circumspection, finding the origin of a middle-class democracy in the colonial rather than the revolutionary period. The force of continuity took on new importance through a focus on the assemblies and their rise, suggested by Charles Mclean Andrews in his annual message to the AHA in 1926 and given renewed emphasis by Jack P. Greene and John Philip Reid in the latter half of the twentieth century. Bancroft, *History of the United States of America*; Brown, *Middle-Class Democracy*; Andrews, "The American Revolution"; Boorstin, *The Genius of American Politics*; Greene, *The Quest for Power*; Greene, "Political Mimesis"; Reid, *In Defiance of the Law*. See also Roney, "1776, Viewed from the West." Even for those historians who see change in the revolution, particularly social change, they often accept the idea that the states, besides becoming more politically inclusive, were institutionally and functionally the same as their colonial predecessors. See, for example, Wood, *The Radicalism of the American Revolution*. We can also see this view of governmental continuity in the work of historians exploring the social and economic character of the American Revolution, such as Woody Holton and Michael McDonnel. Holton, *Forced Founders*; McDonnell, *The Politics of War*. For an excellent introduction to the historiography of the American Revolution, see Griffin, introduction to *Between Sovereignty and Anarchy*. See

also Lynd and Waldstreicher, "Free Trade, Sovereignty, and Slavery"; and McDonnell and Waldstreicher, "Revolution in the *Quarterly?*"
8. Franklin, *Cool Thoughts*, 8.
9. Galloway, *The Speech*, 64.
10. Thomas Gage to John Reid, June 24, 1765, Thomas Gage Papers, American Series, vol. 38, WLC.
11. Marietta and Rowe, *Troubled Experiment*, 4. See also Murrin, "Political Development"; Wolf, *Urban Village*; and Tully, *Forming American Politics*.
12. Tomlins, *Law, Labor, and Ideology*, 47; Appleby, Jacob, and Jacob, introduction to *The Origins of Anglo-American Radicalism*, 7, 11; Zuckerman, *Peaceable Kingdoms*, 85; Roney, *Governed by a Spirit of Opposition*.
13. The state as an area of study has achieved revitalized interest among political scientists, sociologists, and historians. This new interest has sparked studies that explain the state less as an "area within which economic interest groups or normative social movements contended or allied with one another to shape the making of public policy decisions" and more as an independent actor. Building off the theories of Max Webber and Otto Hintze, political scientists and sociologists have begun to describe the state as an "administrative, legal, extractive, and coercive organization" that controls "territories and people" with the basic goal to "maintain control and order." Such a vision, while abstract, provides a way to understand "the State" as a fundamental actor, one made up of a wide spectrum of people and police powers that affected and was affected by the governed. Skocpol, "Bringing the State Back In," 7–9. See also Nozick, *Anarchy, State, and Utopia*; Krohn-Hansen and Nustad, *State Formation*; Huntington, *Political Order in Changing Societies*, 12; and Goldstone, "Toward a Fourth Generation of Revolutionary Theory," 146. The literature on state formation and its relationship to revolutions has had a substantial impact on European historiography, particularly scholarship on the English Civil War and the Glorious Revolution. See for example, Hindle, *The State and Social Change in Early Modern England*; Gilmour, *Riot, Risings and Revolution*; Brewer, *The Sinews of Power*; and Pincus, *1688*. State formation has also had an impact on the study of the French Revolution. See for example, Sewell, "The French Revolution and the Emergence of the Nation Form"; and Bossenga, "Origins of the French Revolution."
14. State formation in early America is also a growing avenue of study, much of it informed by the work of John Brewer and emphasizing the development of the federal government after the Constitution. These works show that in key areas, such as war and diplomacy, the federal government certainly exercised considerable power, but such a focus does not support a view of the early federal government as a national state that presaged the Lochner era. In response David C. Hendrickson argues that we need to bring

"the state system back in" and explore the ways that the states came into being and were governed. Due to that call, historians are starting to look at the individual states and their broad powers. In some ways resurrecting the early works of Oscar and Mary Handlin as well as Louis Hartz, who searched in vain for a clear "liberal tradition" in the revolution or, rather, the revolutionary origins laissez-faire, scholars such as William Novak, Steve Pincus, Gary Gerstle, and Brian Murphy have highlighted the astounding reach and remit of the states, particularly in their ability to regulate the domestic economy as well as the public and at times private lives of their citizens. In their work, it is clear that the states were endowed, as Gary Gerstle succinctly puts it, "with a scope of authority more capacious in many respects than that which inhered in the central government itself." For a good overview of the literature on state formation in the Early Republic, see the forum "Taking Stock of the State in Nineteenth-Century America," *Journal of the Early Republic* 38, no. 1 (2018): 61–118. See also Hendrickson, "Bringing the State System Back In," 113–49. For the individual states, see Handlin and Handlin, *Commonwealth*; Hartz, *The Liberal Tradition in* America; Novak and Pincus, "Revolutionary State Formation," 138–55; Gerstle, *Liberty and Coercion*, 17–88; and Murphy, *Building the Empire State*.

15. Understanding the rise and importance of the states in the revolutionary era also helps bridge the gap between the literatures on eighteenth- and nineteenth-century American governance. Historians of the American Revolution and Early Republic often focus on national identity and policy, whereas historians of nineteenth-century law, governance, and politics stress the autonomy and power of the states, creating a disconnect and interesting contradictions that need to be addressed. For the importance of the states in the nineteenth century, see Paludan, "The American Civil War Considered as a Crisis in Law and Order."; Keller, *Affairs of State*; Campbell, *The Growth of American Government*; Novak, *The People's Welfare*; and Pearson, "A New Birth of Regulation."

16. In her dissertation, Heather Schwartz unearthed over 130 plans to reform the empire. Schwartz, "Re-Writing the Empire."

17. Pearl, "Franklin's Turn," 117–39.

18. See, for example, two pieces of synthesis that nicely encapsulate prevailing interpretations of the "Imperial Crisis": Christie, *Crisis of Empire*; and Yirush, "The Imperial Crisis." While they all disagree over the exact political ideology espoused in the years before independence, historians such as Edmund Morgan, Bernard Bailyn, and Jack Greene see the constitutional question as a paramount and singular moment that destabilized a rather stable political system that existed in the years preceding 1763. Morgan and Morgan, *The Stamp Act Crisis*; Bailyn, *The Ideological Origins of the American Revolution*; Greene, *The Constitutional Origins of the American Revolution*.

19. Historians of the revolutionary South and New England have come to similar conclusions about the importance of law and legal institutions for the lives of ordinary people. As Laura F. Edwards demonstrates, local legal institutions in colonial and revolutionary North and South Carolina had an impact on the lives of not only adult white male property owners but also the propertyless, women, slaves, and servants. Similarly, Michael Bellesiles argues that ordinary folk on the frontier of New England viewed legal structures as "essential to their economic survival and the security of their communities." The broad expanse of the law, particularly its enforcement, was important to the lives and liberties of a large segment of a given population. Similar to the revolutionary South and New England, law and its enforcement affected the everyday lives of Pennsylvania's inhabitants whether through direct interaction or their responses to its inadequacies. Edwards, *The People and Their Peace*; Bellesiles, "The Establishment of Legal Structures on the Frontier," 906.
20. For this expansive definition of governance as more than just philosophy of governmental powers, see Novak, *The People's Welfare*, 8–10; and Jensen, "Government, the State, and Governance," 379–85.
21. McCusker and Menard, *The Economy of British America*, 54.
22. Burnaby, *Travels through the Middle Settlements*, 86.
23. For the movement of people, see Bailyn, *Voyagers to the West*, 7–28.
24. Burnaby, *Travels through the Middle Settlements*, 86. Historians often focus on the Seven Years' War in North America and the fiscal response to it as the lynchpin of the "Imperial Crisis," but such a focus does not take into consideration how that war exacerbated an ongoing debate about how the empire and the individual colonies were governed. That debate touched off conflict in the early 1760s that had a lasting impact on all conversations about governance and state formation in the years to come. For the importance of the Seven Years' War, see Gipson, "The American Revolution as an Aftermath of the Great War for the Empire"; Anderson, *Crucible of War*; and Calloway, *The Scratch of a Pen*.
25. For North Carolina, see Kars, *Breaking Loose Together*. For South Carolina, see Brown, *The South Carolina Regulators*; and Klein, *Unification of a Slave State*, 47–77. For New York, see Countryman, *A People in Revolution*, 36–71. For New Jersey, see McConville, *These Daring Disturbers of the Public Peace*, 223–44. For Virginia, see Ward, *Breaking the Backcountry*, 255–61; and Crawford, "A Frontier of Fear," 1–29.
26. Alan Tully has produced this argument in various forms. See, for instance, his work *Forming American Politics*; and *William Penn's Legacy*. See also his essay "Quaker Party and Proprietary Polices." Richard Ryerson makes a similar argument in *The Revolution Is Now Begun* and in his essay "Portrait of a Colonial Oligarchy." Tully's and Ryerson's interpretations of the

stability of colonial past due to the popularity of the oligarchic assembly and its place in the revolution has become the standard political narrative for Pennsylvania, leading one work of synthesis to label the "popular and Oligarchic political behavior" in colonial Pennsylvania a "paradox." Beeman, *The Varieties of Political Experience*, 204–42.
27. McCusker and Menard, *The Economy of British America*, 203.
28. "A Petition from Sundry Inhabitants from Bucks County," 1753, PA, 8:4:3558.
29. Petition of Bucks County Inhabitants, *Votes and Proceedings of the Assembly*, January 3, 1764, PA, 8:7:5408.
30. "A Petition from a Number of the Inhabitants on the East and West Branches of the River Susquehanna," January 14, 1772, PA, 8:9:6749.
31. "A New Song, in High Vogue," 1.
32. *Declaration and Remonstrance of the distressed and bleeding Frontier Inhabitants of the Province of Pennsylvania*, in Dunbar, *The Paxton Papers*, 104.
33. Thomas Gage to John Reid, June 24, 1765, Thomas Gage Papers, American Series, vol. 38, WLC.
34. Depositions, in Brown, *Archives of Maryland*, 32:315–26.
35. John Penn to Thomas Penn, March 16, 1765, LTP, Reel 9.
36. Franklin, *Cool Thoughts*, 7.
37. Galloway, *The Speech*, 51.
38. For the royal veto, see chapter 3. For the interpretation of salutary neglect, see Henretta, *Salutary Neglect*.
39. Goldstone, "Rethinking Revolutions"; Goldstone, "Toward a Fourth Generation of Revolutionary Theory," 146; Goldstone, *Revolution and Rebellion in the Early Modern World*, 1–62.
40. John Winthrop to John Adams, June 1, 1776, *The Adams Papers Digital Edition*; John Adams to Benjamin Hichborn, May 19, 1776, *The Adams Papers Digital Edition*.
41. Thomas Smith to Arthur St. Clair, August 22, 1776, in St. Clair, *The St. Clair Papers*, 1:374.
42. Declaration of Independence, 1.
43. "Pennsylvania's 1776 Constitution," in Thorpe, *The Federal and State Constitutions*, 5:3091.
44. "An Act for the Further Security of the Government," *SLP*, 9:238; "An Act to Empower the Supreme Executive Council and Justices of the Supreme Court to Apprehend Suspected Persons, and to Increase the Fines to which Persons are Liable, for Neglecting to Perform their Tour of Militia Duty," October 10, 1779, in *SLP*, 9:440–42.
45. The term "internal police" became far more prevalent in the writings of colonists in the years preceding independence, particularly during the spring and summer of 1776 as colonists debated why and how to create

new constitutions and governments. See, for example, the publications of the anonymous Demophilus, "To the worthy Inhabitants of the Province of Pennsylvania," *Pennsylvania Packet*, May 20, 1776; and Demophilus, *The Genuine Principles of the Ancient Saxon, or English Constitution*.

46. Tomlins, *Law, Labor, and Ideology*, 35–59. See also Gerstle, *Liberty and Coercion*, 55–86.
47. Due to excellent new studies that show how the war accentuated racial othering and exclusive and coercive official policy, this book attempts to show how those changes were emblematic of overarching change in the governing philosophy of revolutionaries and the states they commanded. For new work on race and the war, see Parkinson, *The Common Cause*; and Spero, *Frontier Country*.
48. For a fresh look at the reintegration of loyalists and how it shaped the memory of the revolution, particularly erasing its violence, see Brannon, *From Revolution to Reunion*.
49. See, for instance, William J. Novak's work on the nineteenth-century states. Novak challenges the historical vision of the "weak" American state by highlighting the power of the individual states, places that have been treated as local appendages of a "weak" national state. Once freed from a nationally centered interpretation, the individual states come into focus as powerful entities defying popular myths, a status, I would argue, that was achieved by and through the American Revolution. See Novak, "Public Economy and the Well-Ordered Market"; and Novak, *The People's Welfare*. See also Novak, "The Myth of the 'Weak' American State."
50. Thomas Jefferson, "First Annual Message to Congress, December 8, 1801," in *PTJ*.
51. Franklin, *Cool Thoughts*, 7.

1. "Perfect Strangers"

1. Muhlenberg, *Journals*, 1:122.
2. Smolenski, *Friends and Strangers*, 2.
3. George Michel Weiss to Herman Bethold Hoedmaker, October 1, 1752, quoted in Schwartz, "Mixed Multitude," 146.
4. *Bethlehem Diary*, August 30–September 10, 1742, quoted in Schwartz, "Mixed Multitude," 83.
5. "Diary of a Voyage from Rotterdam," 17.
6. Sachse and Falckner, "The Missive of Justus Falckner," 218.
7. Ester Werndtlin, 1736, in "Documents in Swiss Archives Relating to Emigration to American Colonies in the Eighteenth Century," *American Historical Review* 22, no. 1 (1916): 124, translated in Schwartz, "A Mixed Multitude," 85.

8. Isaac Norris Sr. to Joseph Pike, October 28, 1728, in "Isaac Norris Sr. Letterbook, 1716–1730," Norris Family Papers, 1742–1860, HSP.
9. Governor George Thomas to Conrad Weiser, February 26, 1742, in Thomas, "Some Selections from the Peters Papers," 454.
10. "A Petition from a Number of the Inhabitants on the East and West Branches of the River Susquehanna," January 14, 1772, *PA*, 8:9:6749.
11. When people like Falckner bemoaned the lack of "order," they did not mean only the hierarchal structure that characterized the Old World, as historians often suggest. Order was more than just a social distinction; it was at the core of a belief that life was made up and framed by rules, regulations, and laws that governed and sometimes circumscribed the interactions of people with each other and with the community for the benefit of all. For jurisprudential theorists such as Locke or Hooker, order was synonymous with law. As Hooker explained in his *Of the Laws of Ecclesiastical Polity*, "two foundations" bore "up public societies—the one, a natural inclination, whereby all men desire sociable life and fellowship; the other an order expressly or secretly agreed upon, touching the manner of their union living together. The latter is that which we call the law of the common weal, the very soul of the politic body." Order, then, from a legal standpoint defined and "framed man's outward action, so that they be no hindrance unto the common good for which societies are instituted." Richard Hooker, *Of the Laws of Ecclesiastical Polity*, ed. Christopher Morris (Eugene, OR: Wipf and Stock, 2003), 188.
12. Penn, *An Address to Protestants of all Persuasions*, 40.
13. Roney, *Governed by a Spirit of Opposition*, 47–49. See also Smolenski, *Friends and Strangers*, 65, 80–90.
14. Although my focus is on the countryside, Jessica Roney has shown some of the same processes at work in the creation of the city of Philadelphia as people on the ground refashioned and outright contested Penn's ideals. Roney, *Governed by a Spirit of Opposition*, 11–37. See especially her description of Penn's imagined "Central Square" with what Philadelphians, needed, wanted, and, ultimately, created.
15. For the importance of neighborliness for colonial governance see Smith, *The Freedoms We Lost*, 47–85.
16. Penn, *A Further Account of the Province of Pennsylvania and its Improvements*, 12:263–64.
17. Wolf, *Urban Village*, 125.
18. Kain and Baigent, *The Cadastral Map in the Service of the State*, 288–99.
19. Lemon, *The Best Poor Man's Country*, 50. See also Smolenski, *Friends and Strangers*, 61.
20. Petition of Richard Prichard to Court of Quarter Sessions, 1734, in *History of Chester County, Pennsylvania*, 210.

21. Ibid.; Richard Pike to William Peters, April 24, 1742, in Chester County Miscellaneous Papers, 1684–1847, vol. 1, HSP.
22. See for example the maps of Pennsylvania's counties in Frantz and Pencak, *Beyond Philadelphia*, 3, 25, 48, 68. See also Futhey and Cope, *History of Chester County*, 336.
23. Nash, *Quakers and Politics*, 89.
24. William Penn to James Harrison, October 4, 1685, in Nash, *Quakers and Politics*, 100.
25. Lokken, *David Lloyd*, 202–3.
26. John Penn to Thomas Penn, December 13, 1766, Reel 9, LTP.
27. Thomas Penn to Richard Hockley, February 2, 1754, LTP, Reel 8.
28. Cohen, "William Allen," 44.
29. Cohen, "William Allen," 69–75; Craig W. Horle, "William Allen," in Horle et al., *Lawmaking and Legislators in Pennsylvania*, 233.
30. Craig W. Horle, "William Allen," in Horle et al., *Lawmaking and Legislators*, 233.
31. William Allen to Thomas Penn, March 8, 1767, LTP, Reel 9; William Allen to Evan Patterson, William Allen Letter Book, April 20 and December 23, 1754, Shippen Family Papers, HSP.
32. Kain and Baigent, *The Cadastral Map in the Service of the State*, 288. See also Libecap, Lueck, and O'Grady, "Large Scale Institutional Changes," 1–37.
33. Samuel Blunston to Thomas Penn, August 13, 1734, quoted in Lemon, *Best Poor Man's Country*, 111.
34. Chester County Court of Quarter Sessions Dockets, November 26, 1728, and May 29, 1744.
35. Futhey and Cope, *History of Chester County*, 210.
36. Munger, *Pennsylvania Land Records*, xxix.
37. Mary Sayre to Jasper Yeates, August 15, 1769, Jasper Yeates Papers, 1733–1876, Series 2, Box 7, Folder 1, HSP.
38. Mittelberger, *Journey to Pennsylvania*, 67.
39. Wolf, *Urban Village*, 56.
40. Jasper Yeates to Duncan Campbell, Lancaster, January 22, 1771, Burd-Shippen Family Papers, Reel 2, Folder 39, PHMC.
41. Lemon, *Best Poor Man's Country*, 102.
42. Mittelberger, *Journey to Pennsylvania*, 106.
43. Muhlenberg, *Journals*, 1:151, 136, 388.
44. "Petition to the Council of Maryland," June 24, 1769, in Brown, *Archives of Maryland*, 32:321–22. This episode of neighborly violence is discussed further in chapter 4.
45. Muhlenberg, *Journals*, 1:136.
46. McCusker and Menard, *The Economy of British America*, 203.

47. Mancini, Bowen, and Martin, "Community Social Organization," 572.
48. Sampson, "Linking the Micro- and Macrolevel Dimensions of Community Social Organization."
49. McCusker and Menard, *The Economy of British America*, 204.
50. William Allen to Evan Patterson, November 5, 1753, "William Allen Letter Book," Shippen Family Papers, HSP.
51. John Pemberton to Israel Pemberton Jr., August 11, 1750, quoted in Schwartz, *"Mixed Multitude,"* 201.
52. Mittelberger, *Journey to Pennsylvania*, 118–19.
53. Moraley, *The Infortunate*, 73–75; Thomson, "Franklin County One Hundred Years Ago," 318.
54. Lemon, *Best Poor Man's Country*, 55.
55. Isaac Norris to Joseph Pike, June 22, 1724, "Isaac Norris, Sr. Letterbook, 1716–1730," Norris Family Papers, 1742–1860, HSP.
56. Lemon, *Best Poor Man's Country*, 57. Private owners, particularly absentee land speculators, often worked through provincial officials and granting powers of attorney to remove squatters by force. See, for instance, the power of attorney granted to William Peters by Richard Pike in 1742 to remove "Irish Incroachers" from Pikeland township in Chester County. Richard Pike to William Peters, April 24, 1742, in Chester County Miscellaneous Papers, 1684–1847, vol. 1, HSP.
57. Richard Peters, "The Report of Richard Peters, Esq; Secretary of the Province of Pennsylvania, of the proceedings against sundry Persons settled in the Unpurchased Part of the Province Aforesaid," *PA*, 8:4:3325–26.
58. Ibid., 8:4:3324.
59. Isaac Norris Sr. to Joseph Pike, October 28, 1728, Isaac Norris Letterbook, Norris Family Papers, 1742–1860, HSP.
60. Shephard, *History of Proprietary Government in Pennsylvania*, 49.
61. "The Humble Petition of Andrew Dunlap," 1735, correspondence, original secretary of state, CO 5/1233, British National Archives.
62. Ibid.; "Richard Peters to Proprietors, Concerning Dunlap," 1735, *PA*, 2:7:191–92.
63. "Humble Petition of Andrew Dunlap," 175.
64. "Richard Peters to Proprietors, Concerning Dunlap," 1735, *PA*, 2:7:191–92. Dunlap was still fighting for his right to the land claimed by Black in 1764. See "A Petition from Andrew Delap [Dunlap]," January 17, 1764, *PA*, 8:7:5520–22.
65. Dunaway, "Pennsylvania as an Early Distributing Center of Population," 136.
66. Edward Shippen to Lawrence Williams, December 17, 1734, Burd-Shippen Family Papers, Reel 2, Folder 1, PHMC.
67. *Minutes of the Provincial Council of Pennsylvania*, 7:253.
68. Thomson, "Franklin County One Hundred Years Ago," 323.

69. Kars, *Breaking Loose Together*, 21.
70. Lemon, *Best Poor Man's Country*, 155, 239n71; Ball, "Dynamics of Population and Wealth."
71. "A Petition from a Number of the Inhabitants on the East and West Branches of the River Susquehanna," January 14, 1771, *PA*, 8:8:6748–49.
72. Penn, *A Further Account of the Province of Pennsylvania and its Improvements*, 12: 263–64.
73. See, for instance, contract between John Wade and John Heinkel, March 10, 1762, Jasper Yeates Family Papers, Reel 1, B, Legal Papers, Folder 1, PHMC. See also Robert Parke to Mary Valentine, October 1725, in "Original Letters and Documents."
74. Simler, "Tenancy in Colonial Pennsylvania," 554.
75. Affidavit of Charles Grantham, November 17, 1758, in Chester County Miscellaneous Papers, 1684–1847, vol. 1, HSP.
76. Lydon, "Philadelphia's Commercial Expansion," 402–4.
77. Schweitzer, *Custom and Contract*; Egnal, "The Economic Development of the Thirteen Continental Colonies," 198–209.
78. Lemon, *Best Poor Man's Country*, 168; Bushman, *The Refinement of America*, 3–29; Breen, *The Marketplace of Revolution*, 33–71.
79. Guenther, "Berks County," 69.
80. Simler, "The Landless Worker," 167.
81. Tax Records for 1756 and 1775, CCA.
82. Quoted in Ball, "Dynamics of Population and Wealth," 625.
83. Simler, "The Landless Worker," 163–99.
84. Simler, "Tenancy in Colonial Pennsylvania," 549.
85. Robert Parke to Mary Valentine, October 1725, in "Original Letters and Documents."
86. Moraley, *The Infortunate*, 318.
87. Simler, "The Landless Worker," 177.
88. Franz, *Paxton*, 121–58.
89. Wolf, *Urban Village*, 76–79.
90. Franz, *Paxton*, 125. Tax data for Chester County was compiled from the tax records located at the Chester County courthouse. With some variations, my analysis of Chester County mobility follows the methods used by Franz and Wolf. Like Franz, I tracked the number of those individual taxpayers moving in and out of each township. However, where Franz assumed that nonconsecutive appearances signified mobility, I judged it as an error in tax recording. It seems rather unlikely that a taxpayer, a landholder no less, would sell his property only to return later to buy it back. When I found a nonconsecutive appearance, I added the taxpayer back to the preceding lists, though there were very few such cases. In addition, my calculation of mobility percentages uses two high and low per-decade

mortality estimates of 15 percent and 10 percent, both of which are rather conservative estimates. Even with instituting these changes, my findings and Franz's are very similar. For a fuller account of mobility in Chester County see Pearl, "For the Good Order of Government," 53–84.
91. Muhlenberg, *Journals*, 1:141–42.
92. Ibid., 1:176.
93. Ibid., 1:141–42.
94. St. Michael's manifesto, January 1753, quoted in Wolf, *Urban Village*, 220.
95. Franz, *Paxton*, 121.
96. Penn, *A Further Account of the Province of Pennsylvania and its Improvements*, 12: 263–64.
97. Boss, "The Development of Social Religion," 578.
98. Voltaire, *Philosophical Dictionary*, 106.
99. Montesquieu, *The Spirit of the Laws*, part 5, book 24, chapter 2, 460.
100. Benjamin Franklin to unknown, December 13, 1757, *PBF*, 7:293.
101. For the importance of ministers in the revolutionary era see McBride, *Pulpit and Nation*.
102. Muhlenberg, *Journals*, 1:72.
103. Ibid., 1:161.
104. Ibid., 1:174.
105. Grubb, "German Immigration to Pennsylvania," 417.
106. Glatfelter, "The Eighteenth Century German Lutheran and Reformed Clergymen in the Susquehanna Valley," 58.
107. Ibid., 61.
108. The data on Lutheran and Reformed clergymen can be found in Glatfelter, "The Colonial Pennsylvania German Lutheran and Reformed Clergymen," 230–34.
109. The ratio is calculated using the number of ministers serving in Pennsylvania according to Glatfelter's data and the number of Lutheran and German Reformed congregations supplied in Stark and Finker, "American Religion in 1776," table 4 and table 5, 48–49.
110. Muhlenberg, *Journals*, 1:128.
111. Ibid., 1:75.
112. Ibid., 1:91.
113. Ibid., 1:92.
114. Wokeck, "German and Irish Immigration to Colonial Philadelphia," 128–33.
115. Muhlenberg, *Journals*, 1:186–87.
116. Ibid., 1:358.
117. Ibid., 1:504.
118. Ibid., 1:491.
119. Ibid., 1:538.

120. Mittelberger, *Journey to Pennsylvania*, 56.
121. Sachse and Falckner, "The Missive of Justus Falckner, of Germantown."
122. Michael Schlatter to Thomas Penn, June 12, 1750, PPOC, HSP.
123. Lodge, "The Crisis of the Churches in the Middle Colonies," 202.
124. Perry, *History of the Church*, 111.
125. Reverend Alex Howie to the secretary of the SPG, July 20, 1732, in Perry, *History of the Church*, 178–79.
126. See, for instance, Reverend John Humphreys to the secretary of the SPG, October 24, 1718, in Perry, *History of the Church*, 117.
127. Reverend Griffith Hughes to secretary of the SPG, March 2, 1734, in Perry, *History of the Church*, 188–89.
128. "Some Account of the Missions in Pennsylvania, delivered at a Convention of the Clergy of that Province at Philadelphia," May 2, 1760, in Perry, *History of the Church*, 311–16.
129. Thomas Barton to the secretary of the SPG, December 21, 1759, in Perry, *History of the Church*, 282–83; Reverend Craig to the secretary of the SPG, July 6, 1761, in Perry, *History of the Church*, 330.
130. Thomas Barton to the secretary of the SPG, July 6, 1761, in Perry, *History of the Church*, 328.
131. Reverend Craig to the secretary of the SPG, July 27, 1760, in Perry, *History of the Church*, 290–91.
132. William Bird and Others, "To the Venerable Society for Propagating the Gospel in Foreign Parts," 1760, in Perry, *History of the Church*, 288–89. See also "A Petition from the Missionary and Vestry of the English Church in the Town of Reading," January 14, 1765, PA, 8:7:5703–4.
133. Mittelberger, *Journey to Pennsylvania*, 62.
134. Quoted in Broderick, "Pulpit, Physics, and Politics," 56.
135. Lodge, "Crisis of the Churches in the Middle Colonies," 201.
136. Fishburn, "Gilbert Tennent," 40.
137. Beatty, *A Sermon Preached in Woodbury*, 39.
138. Wokeck, "German and Irish Immigration," 137.
139. The number of churches and pastors in Chester County can be found in Futhey and Cope, *History of Chester County*, 248–54, and in Ashmead, *History of Delaware County*. For the lack of ministers during the 1720s and '30s see Griffin, "The People with No Name," 598.
140. Griffin, "The People with No Name," 599.
141. Quotes of John Craig and *Minutes of the Presbyterian Church in America, 1706–1788* in Griffin, "The People with No Name," 598.
142. Quote of *Minutes of the Presbyterian Church in America* in Griffin, "The People with No Name," 599.
143. Fishburn, "Gilbert Tennent," 31–49.
144. *An Examination and Refutation of Mr. Gilbert Tennent's Remarks*, 13–14.

145. Butler, *Awash in a Sea of Faith*, 164–93.
146. Bonomi, *Under the Cope of Heaven*, 8.
147. Lodge, "Crisis of the Churches in the Middle Colonies," 199.
148. Lambert, "'Pedlar in Divinity.'"
149. Labaree, "The Conservative Attitude toward the Great Awakening," 336.
150. Isaac Norris Letterbook, 1729–56, 70–71, HSP.
151. *South Carolina Gazette*, August 30, 1742.
152. Quoted in Schwartz, "Mixed Multitude," 123.
153. Muhlenberg, *Journals*, 1:75–76. See also *A Protestation of the Several Members of the Protestant Lutheran and Reformed Religions*; Count Zinzendorf, "Memorandum," *Pennsylvania Gazette*, August 26, 1742. For disturbances in Lancaster see the fracturing of the Lutheran Church over Reverend Nyberg in 1746 in Muhlenberg, *Journals*, 1:111.
154. Muhlenberg, *Journals*, 1:76.
155. Resolution of the German Reformed Coetus on the Case of Rev. Mr. Rothenbuhler, June 18, 1763, in *Minutes and Letters of the Coetus of the German Reformed Congregations in Pennsylvania*, 218–19. Also published in *Pennsylvania Gazette*, June 23, 1763, and "The Rejoinder by the Coetus," *Pennsylvania Gazette*, August 18, 1763.
156. Frederick Rothenbuhler, "To the Public," August 4, 1763, *Pennsylvania Gazette*.
157. This was not a singular occurrence. The Lutheran and Reformed churches split over ministers quiet often. The Lutheran church split over Reverend Nyberg in 1746, Carl Rudolph in 1747, and Reverend Handschun in the 1750s. Similarly, the Reformed Church divided over Rev. Casper Stover in 1747 and Michael Schlatter in 1750 and again in 1752.
158. Muhlenberg, *Journals*, 1: 654.
159. Muhlenberg, *Journals*, 1:650.
160. *South Carolina Gazette*, August 30, 1742.
161. Richard Hockley to Bernard Hannington, June 8, 1740, Richard Hockley Letterbook, 1739–42, 20, Quaker Collection, Haverford College.

2. "For Want of Power"

1. A Petition from divers Inhabitants of Berks County, January 29, 1761, PA, 8:6:5182.
2. Ibid.
3. Dianna DiIllio, "John Potts," in Horle et al., *Lawmaking and Legislators in Pennsylvania*, 1098.
4. Guenther, "Berks County," 71.
5. "A Petition from divers Inhabitants of Berks County," January 29, 1761, PA, 8:6:5182. For the importance of a public economy to early Americans see Novak, "Public Economy and the Well-Ordered Market."

6. "A Petition from a Number of the Inhabitants on the East and West Branches of the River Susquehanna," January 14, 1772, *PA*, 8:9:6749.
7. Tully, *Forming American Politics*, 258. See also Wolf, *Urban Village*, 177; Newcomb, *Franklin and Galloway*; Newcomb, *Political Partisanship in the American Middle Colonies*; Lemon, *Best Poor Man's Country*; Marietta and Rowe, *Troubled Experiment*; and Hutson, *Pennsylvania Politics*. For a differing interpretation of frontier political ideology and political experience at odds with those of the East see Kozuskanich, "For the Security and Protection of the Community"; Kozuskanich, "Falling under the Domination Totally of Presbyterians," 298; Spero, "Creating Pennsylvania"; Griffin, *American Leviathan*; and Kenny, *Peaceable Kingdom Lost*.
8. *Pennsylvania Gazette*, May 27, 1756.
9. *Pennsylvania Chronicle*, July 24, 1769.
10. Logan, *The Charge Delivered from the Bench*, 3–4.
11. Goodlet, *A Vindication of the Associate Synod*, 7.
12. Logan, *The Charge Delivered from the Bench to the Grand Inquest*, 4–5, 13. See also Keith, *A Letter to his Majesty's Justices of the Peace*; Carmichael, *A Self-Defensive War*; and Smith, *A Wheel in the Middle of a Wheel*, 12–13, 16–17.
13. Logan, *The Charge Delivered from the Bench*, 3–4, 7–8.
14. Chew, *The Speech of Samuel Chew*, 5.
15. Ibid.; Logan, *The Charge Delivered from the Bench to the Grand Inquest*, 17–18.
16. Chew, *The Speech of Samuel Chew*, 6.
17. Goodlet, *A Vindication of the Associate Synod*, 8–9.
18. Logan, *The Charge Delivered from the Bench*, 4.
19. *Pennsylvania Journal*, January 25, February 1, February 22, and March 1, 1759.
20. *Pennsylvania Journal*, February 22, March 8, and March 15, 1759.
21. *Pennsylvania Gazette*, July 22, 1736.
22. *American Weekly Mercury*, March 23, 1721. See also Davies, *Religion and Public Spirit*, 7.
23. Novak, *The People's Welfare*, 42.
24. Logan, *The Charge Delivered from the Bench*, 4, 17.
25. Carmichael, *A Self-Defensive War*, 19.
26. *American Weekly Mercury*, September 27, 1733.
27. Ibid.
28. Logan, *The Charge Delivered from the Bench*, 14.
29. Logan, *The Latter Part of the Charge*, 1.
30. Carmichael, *A Self-Defensive War*, 11.
31. *Pennsylvania Gazette*, May 23, 1754.
32. Tennent, *The Late Association for Defence*, 17, 19.
33. As Jessica Roney importantly points out, most early Americans grappled with questions about governance "not through the articulation of

highbrow political rhetoric but in the day-to-day operations of community life." Roney, *Governed by a Spirit of Opposition*, 2.
34. See Herrup, *The Common Peace*; and Hindle, *The State and Social Change*, 23–25.
35. Muhlenberg, *Journals*, 1:136; Courtney Case File, 1760, Chester County Quarter Sessions Papers, CCA. If a particular person wished to receive some compensation for the destruction caused by fire, he or she did not look to the courts of justice but attempted, if indeed necessary, to request relief from the assembly. See Petition of John Gemmel, Derry Township, Cumberland, February 4, 1771, *PA*, 8:8:6627–28.
36. For Lancaster see Slaughter, "Interpersonal Violence in a Rural Setting," 98–123. For Chester County, see Chester County Court of Quarter Sessions Dockets, CCA. For Bedford see Records of the County Governments, Bedford County, Quarter Sessions Dockets, book 1, PHMC.
37. For an excellent description of community hostility to fornication and bastardy and its relationship to law in early America see Pagan, *Anne Orthwood's Bastard*.
38. While the offenses highlighted above make up a large proportion of cases brought before the quarter sessions, the crime of assault was one of the most prevalent crimes prosecuted and punished in the courts. In Lancaster County between 1729 and 1776, 39 percent of all cases coming before the court were for assault. In Chester County between 1740 and 1776, assault made up 29 percent of the cases. In Bedford County from its creation in 1771 to 1776, 37 percent of cases were for assault. Slaughter, "Interpersonal Violence in a Rural Setting," 100. Chester County Court of Quarter Sessions, Dockets, 1733–42, 1742–59, A and B, CCA; Records of the County Governments, Bedford County, Quarter Sessions Dockets, book 1, PHMC.
39. Goodlet, *Vindication of the Associate Synod*, 10.
40. Grand Inquest for the City of Philadelphia, 1729–30?, in John William Wallace Collection of Ancient Records of Philadelphia, 1702–1847, HSP.
41. *American Weekly Mercury*, December 21, 1733.
42. Barton, *Conduct of the Paxton-Men*, 33.
43. Schweitzer, *Custom and Contract*, 84; Lydon, "Philadelphia's Commercial Expansion, 1720–1739," 401–18; Appleby, "Commercial Farming and the 'Agrarian Myth,'" 833–49; Doerflinger, *A Vigorous Spirit of Enterprise*; Salinger, "To Serve Well and Faithfully," 23, 69, 152; Egnal, "The Economic Development of the Thirteen Continental Colonies," 199, 202, 217.
44. See, for instance, the Bucks County petition in *PA*, 8:4:3238.
45. See, for instance, the petition from Germantown on January 12, 1773, in *PA*, 8:8:6910–11.
46. Petitions in *PA*, 8:5:3871–72, 3884.

47. Tanner petition in *PA*, 8:8:6640–41.
48. "A Petition from a Number of Inhabitants on the Western Side of the River Schuylkill," 1749, *PA*, 8:4:3257.
49. "A Petition from a Number of the Inhabitants of the County of Philadelphia, residing on and near the River Schuylkill," January 9, 1767, *PA*, 8:7:5949.
50. "A Petition from a Number of Freeholders, and others, residing near the River Schuylkill, February 1, 1770, *PA*, 8:7:6093, 6491–92.
51. Ibid. A "great Number of the Inhabitants of the County of York, living near the River Connewago," and "a Number of Inhabitants of the River Leheigh" in Northampton County made a similar argument about dams and mills as obstructions detrimental to the public good. See three petitions of York County Inhabitants, January 9, 1771, *PA*, 8:8:6593–94. See also a petition from "a Number of Inhabitants of the River Leheigh" in Northampton County, January 23, 1771, *PA*, 8:8:6607–8. Lancaster County inhabitants near the Conestoga Creek made a similar argument in late 1773 in their petition in *PA*, 8:8:7053–54. See also petitions from Philadelphia and Chester in January 1774, *PA*, 8:8:7056. By these various petitions it is readily apparent that people on the frontier as well as in the East shared common assumptions that individual aspirations should give way to the needs of the community.
52. "An Act to Regulate the Fishery in the River Schuylkill," February 21, 1767, *SLP*, 7:80.
53. "An Act for Making the River Schuylkill Navigable and for the Preservation of the Fish in the Said River," March 14, 1761, *SLP*, 6: 96; "A Supplement to the Act, Entitled 'An Act for Making the River Schuylkill Navigable and for the Preservation of the Fish in the Said River,'" February 26, 1773, *SLP*, 8:327–30.
54. "A Petition from a Number of Inhabitants of the Counties of Berks, Philadelphia and Chester," January 16, 1768, *PA*, 8:7:6092; "A Petition from Sundry Inhabitants near the River Schuylkill," January 19, 1768, *PA*, 8:7:6100.
55. Similar circumstances plagued the enforcement of other regulations for the public welfare during the colonial period. See, for instance, the complaints made by Lancaster County inhabitants about the failure to enforce hunting laws, "A Petition from divers Inhabitants of the County of Lancaster," January 5, 1773, *PA*, 8:8:6904.
56. Meredith case file, 1747, Chester County Quarter Sessions Papers, CCA.
57. Chester County Quarter Sessions Dockets, May 1747–February 1748, Docket Book, 1742–59, CCA.
58. *Pennsylvania Packet*, June 10, 1776.
59. McCusker and Menard, *The Economy of British America*, 203.
60. "An Act for Establishing Courts of Judicature in this Province," May 22, 1722, *SLP*, 3:298–309.

61. Percentages of the total petitions are as follows: internal improvements 4 percent, taxes (for and against) 4 percent, land policy (reform of) 2 percent, public health regulations 2 percent. There were also petitions that requested a reform of the poor laws, 2 percent; equal representation in the legislature, 3 percent; lotteries, 2 percent; liberty of conscience, 1 percent; and debtor legislation, 1 percent. The remainder of the petitions focused on particular grievances relegated to a certain time and place, such as complaints against the British billeting troops or enlisting servants during King George's War and the Seven Years' War, which made up 3 percent of all petitions.
62. Quoted in Franz, *Paxton*, 32.
63. Wood, "The Town Proprietors of Lancaster," 346–68; petition from Chester and Patrick Gordon quoted in in Mombert, *An Authentic History of Lancaster County*, 111–16.
64. Petitions in *PA*, 8:7:5843–44, 5872–73, 5874, 5902.
65. "A petition from Sundry Inhabitants from Bucks County," 1753, *PA*, 8:4:3558; "Several Petitions from the Justices of Chester County," March 1, 1757, *PA*, 8:6:4543; "Petition of Bucks County Inhabitants," January 3, 1764, *PA*, 8:7:5408; "A Petition of Divers Inhabitants of Lancaster County," February 10, 1764, *PA*, 8:7:5397.
66. Jasper Yeates to Sarah Yeates, July 22, 1772, Jasper Yeates to Sarah Yeates, July 22, 1773, Jasper Yeates Papers, Series 1, Box 1, APS; "A Petition, from Bernard Dougherty, in Behalf of the Inhabitants of Bedford Settlement, and divers Townships in the Western Part of Cumberland County," January 18, 1769, *PA*, 8:7:6319–20.
67. Richard Peters Jr. to Jasper Yeates, October 15, 1764, Jasper Yeates Papers, 1733–1876, Series 2, Box 7, Folder 1, HSP.
68. See *Continuance Docket #11*, Northampton County Quarter Sessions Dockets, Northampton County Court House.
69. In Bedford County, between 1771 and 1776, 56 percent of people indicted failed to attend trial. Just as revealing, only 26 percent of cases were settled in the term in which they were entered on the dockets. The average case in Bedford, at least for those actually settled, remained on the dockets for at least three terms, and some over two years. Records of the County Governments, Book 1, PHMC.
70. "A Petition from a Considerable Number of Inhabitants of Bedford County," March 10, 1771, *PA*, 8:8:6819.
71. Richard Peters Jr. to Jasper Yeates, September 5, 1766, Jasper Yeates Papers, 1733–1876, Series 2, Box 7, Folder 3, HSP.
72. Jasper Yeates to Joseph Shippen, August 2, 1768, Burd-Shippen Family Papers, Reel 2, Folder 38, PHMC.
73. Richard Peters Jr. to Jasper Yeates, October 15, 1764, Jasper Yeates Papers, 1733–1876, Series 2, Box 7, Folder 1, HSP. For a definition of matters of

fact, matters of law, and *communis error facit jus* see *Black's Law Dictionary*, 5th ed., ed. Joseph R. Nolan et al., (Minnesota: West, 1979), 883, 532, 254.

74. "A Petition, from Bernard Dougherty, in Behalf of the Inhabitants of Bedford Settlement, and divers Townships in the Western Part of Cumberland County," January 18, 1769, *PA*, 8:7:6319–20.
75. Richard Baird to Jasper Yeates, February 23, 1770, Jasper Yeates Family Papers, Reel 1, PHMC.
76. William Allen to Thomas Penn, March 8, 1767, PPOC, 10:94–98; Supreme Court Dockets, 1753–1799, vol. 1, HSP. For the best analysis of the supreme court, specifically the problems associated with a circuit court, see Rowe, *Embattled Bench*, 97–118.
77. Thomas Penn to James Hamilton, February 25, 1751, CTR vol. 1, Box 1, APS.
78. Edward Shippen Jr. to Edward Shippen Sr., September 17, 1761, Burd-Shippen Family Papers, Reel 2, Folder 35, PHMC.
79. *PA*, 8:7:5582–83.
80. Edward Shippen to Governor Morris, February 17, 1756, Burd-Shippen Family Papers, Reel 2, Folder 2, PHMC; "A Petition from the Inhabitants of the Path Valley, Auckwick and Tuscarora," January 28, 1768, *PA*, 8:7:6121.
81. "A Petition from Sundry Inhabitants of Bucks County," 1753, *PA*, 8:4:3558; "Petition from a Considerable number of the Inhabitants of Chester County," 1754, *PA*, 8:5:3626-–27; "Petition from sundry Inhabitants of the County of Lancaster," 1754, *PA*, 8:5:3635; "A Petition from the County of Cumberland signed by Upwards of Twelve Hundred Inhabitants of Said County," 1764, *PA*, 8:7-5580-81; "A Petition from Sundry Freeholders of Bucks," January 9, 1767, *PA*, 8:7:5949; "Petition, signed by a great number of freemen, inhabitants of the County of Bucks," January 12, 1767, *PA*, 8:7:5952; "A Petition from a Number of the Inhabitants of the County of Chester," January 13, 1767, *PA*, 8:7:5954; "Eleven Petitions from the County of Cumberland, in Substance the same with those from Bucks and Chester, concerning the Judges of the Supreme Courts riding the Circuit into the several Counties of this Province," January 13, 1767, *PA*, 8:7:5955
82. "A Petition from Sundry Inhabitants of Bucks County," 1753, *PA*, 8:4:3558.
83. William Allen to Thomas Penn, March 8, 1767, PPOC, 10:94–98.
84. Marietta and Rowe, "Violent Crime," 45.
85. Deposition of John Philip De Haas, September 26, 1770, *Colonial Records*, 9:682–83. See also Kenny, *Peaceable Kingdom Lost*, 221–22; *PA*, 8:8:6628–31. Even once a prisoner was successfully conveyed to Philadelphia, it did not guarantee the court would be able to proceed, as many "evil-disposed" persons commonly made their escape due to the "Badness of Materials and Workmanship" of the Philadelphia jail. *PA*, 8:8:6924.
86. Deposition of John Philip De Haas, September 26, 1770, *Colonial Records*, 9:682–83.

87. Marietta and Rowe, "Violent Crime," 45.
88. Goebel and Naughton, *Law Enforcement in Colonial New York*, 135. See also Conley, "Doing It by the Book," 257–98; and Albert, *History of the County of Westmoreland*, 294–95.
89. Edward Shippen Jr. to Edward Shippen Sr., Philadelphia, September 20, 1764, Burd-Shippen Family Papers, Reel 2, Folder 36, PHMC.
90. Illick, *Colonial Pennsylvania*, 208. In the assembly, for example, between 1757 and 1775 well over 50 percent of members had established kinship ties with other members. See Horle et al., *Lawmaking and Legislators*, figure 7, p. 141.
91. Hanna, *Benjamin Franklin and Pennsylvania Politics*, 207n6.
92. Edward Shippen to Joseph Shippen, November 17, 1759, Burd-Shippen Papers, Series 1, Box 2, APS. See also Bockelman, "Local Politics in Pre-Revolutionary Lancaster County," 45–74; and Bockelman, "Continuity and Change," 166–67.
93. John Penn to Lynford Lardner, Esq., March 18, 1740, in *Letters and Papers Relating Chiefly to the Provincial History of Pennsylvania*, 194; Dr. William Shippen to his brother, Judge Edward Shippen of Lancaster, Pennsylvania, July 17, 1776, *PMHB* 44 (1920): 286.
94. See, for instance, Jerome Wood's description of the intrigue involved in the creation of the county seat in Lancaster County. Wood, *Conestoga Crossroads*, 4–6.
95. Bockelman, "Continuity and Change," 97–104. For biographical data for justices of the peace for Bucks County see Davis, *The History of Bucks County*. Davis's county history was of significant use in determining the residences of justices of the peace not included in Bockelman's study for 1775–76. My number of justices of the peace and Bockelman's number are slightly different. Bockelman used justices appointed *dedimus potestatem*, which did not make these men, like Gilbert and Isaac Hicks, full-time justices of the peace. A *dedimus potestatem* was a special appointment for a singular event or use. This type of commission was often used to appoint a person to take a written deposition when no commissioned justice resided close enough or if the justices in the county were unwilling. For a list of commissioned officers for the counties up to 1776 see "Provincial Officers" in *PA*, 2:9:691–818. For Bucks County JPs, see pages 768–69.
96. "Petition of Sundry Inhabitants of Bucks County," 1743, *PA*, 8:4:2869.
97. Bockelman, "Continuity and Change," appendix X: Taxables—Bucks County, 315.
98. Ibid., 109–15.
99. Ibid., 150–59, 318.
100. *Provincial Tax List for 1775*, CCA.
101. James Burd, Docket Book for 1764, Burd-Shippen Papers, Series 1, Box 5, APS.

102. Muhlenberg, *Journals*, 1:247.
103. William Allen to Thomas Penn, March 8, 1767, LTP, Reel 9.
104. Lemon, *The Best Poor Man's Country*, 134, 259n27.
105. Muhlenberg, *Journals*, 1:223, 503.
106. Lemon, *Best Poor Man's Country*, 270n74.
107. Muhlenberg, *Journals*, 1:128.
108. Herrup, *The Common Peace*, 55.
109. This geographic distribution remained similar throughout the period discussed, 1740–76. Between 1740 and 1768, like the later years, the towns on the northeastern side of the Brandywine Creek held 59 percent of the JPs in the county.
110. Data compiled from a combination of the Chester County Quarter Sessions Dockets, Docket Books, 1733–42, 1742–59, A and B, the extant indictment files, and the tax records all located at CCA. The clerk did not record the town of origin for every defendant in the docket books. However, a combination of indictment files, which mostly included the town of origin and the tax records, though more difficult, helped supply many of the missing towns. Out of 2,276 cases before the court of quarter sessions I was able to identify the residences of 2,019 defendants. The residences of women, unless the dockets specified or there were indictment files, could not be ascertained. Luckily, the clerk noted most of the residences for the defendants in the docket books.
111. Lewis Ourry to James Hamilton, August 26, 1763, Burd-Shippen Papers, Series 1, Box 3, APS. See also Ourry to Hamilton, October 12, 1763, Burd-Shippen Papers, Series 1, Box 3, APS.
112. "A Petition, from Bernard Dougherty, in Behalf of the Inhabitants of Bedford Settlement, and divers Townships in the Western Part of Cumberland County," January 18, 1769, *PA*, 8:7:6319–20.
113. Marietta and Rowe, *Troubled Experiment*, 108. For the mangled body see *American Weekly Mercury*, May 20, 1742.
114. Jasper Yeates to Mark Grime, Lancaster, December 22, 1764, Burd-Shippen Family Papers, Reel 2, Folder 36, PHMC.
115. "New Year's Verse," *Pennsylvania Gazette*, December 27, 1739.
116. *American Weekly Mercury*, June 15, 1738.
117. Common people in the North Carolina Piedmont, as Marjoleine Kars argues, had the same dedication to the rule of law and held the same belief that unscrupulous officers, caring very little for the people's concerns, were just as much a threat to liberty as ordinary criminals. Kars, *Breaking Loose Together*, 134–35.
118. *PA*, 8:8:6604.
119. Department of the Interior, "William Moore House (Moore Hall)," in *Historic American Buildings Survey* (Washington, DC: GPO, 1959), 8.

120. *PA*, 8:6:4850.
121. *Ibid.*, 8:6:4850, 4852, 4845.
122. Ibid., 8:6:4847–50, 4853. Significantly, many of the inhabitants' petitions against Moore, in both the language used and the scenarios they decried, mirrored the grievances of inhabitants of the Granville District in North Carolina in the years preceding the North Carolina Regulation, particularly George Sims's "Nutbush Address." The similarity of grievances in eastern Chester County and backcountry North Carolina nicely represents the pervasiveness of political and social tensions in colonial society beyond either the frontier or individual colonies. See Troxler, *Farming Dissenters*, 23–25.
123. *PA*, 8:6:4520.
124. Governor William Denny to Assembly, January 24, 1758, *PA*, 8:6:4714; see also "The Report of the Committee of Grievances," February 23, 1757, *PA*, 8:6:4537–40.
125. James Hamilton to Assembly, February 13, 1760, *PA*, 4:3:15.
126. Ibid., 8:6:4841–42.
127. Ibid.
128. Ibid. Moore's docket book simply lists cases adjudicated, not indicating, obviously, fraud or extortion. William Moore, Docket Book, William Moore Papers, 1764–77, HSP.
129. Moore, *A Preface to a Memorial Delivered to the Assembly*, 1–4.
130. "Governor Denny and Council to William Moore, Esq," *Pennsylvania Gazette*, August 31, 1758.
131. *PA*, 8:6:4839. In 1775, inhabitants of Chester County resumed their complaints against the arbitrary proceedings of Judge Moore. See petitions from John Williamson, Jesse Jones, William Lewis, and William Reece, February 21, 1775, *PA*, 8:9:7188.
132. Dove, *Labour in Vain*; Sansom, *The Diary*, 68.
133. For the use of "Black-Moore" in English culture, particularly in terms of race and identity see Neill, "'Mullatos,' 'Blacks,' and 'Indian Moors,'" 361–74. See also Jordan, *White over Black*, 34–35.
134. Dove, *Labour in Vain*.
135. Pritchard, "Gaius Verres and the Sicilian Farmers."
136. Dill, *Roman Society from Nero to Marcus Aurelius*, 12.
137. Dove, *Labour in Vain*.

3. The "Stupendous Machine"

1. A.B., "Dear Ned," *Pennsylvania Gazette*, May 4, 1738.
2. Ibid.
3. Ibid.

4. Ryerson, *The Revolution Is Now Begun*, 8–9.
5. Bradburn, "The Eschatological Origins of the English Empire."
6. Sarson, *British America*, 19–45.
7. Brown, "Violence and the American Revolution," 85; Ubbelohde, *The American Colonies and the British Empire*, 13–37.
8. Webb, "William Blathwayt, Imperial Fixer," 3, 7.
9. Webb, "'The Peaceable Kingdom,'" 180.
10. "At the Committee of Trade & Plantations in the Council-Chamber," January 22, 1680/1 in *PWP*, 2:57.
11. Webb, "Peaceable Kingdom," 181.
12. North, *The Lives of the Right Hon. Francis North*, 1:316.
13. Webb, "Peaceable Kingdom," 183–84.
14. In Ireland, for example, all the courts of the King's Bench served as the court of last resort. This became a crucial constitutional issue in the eighteenth century, especially during the 1770s. See for example Wilson, *Considerations on the Nature and Extent of the Legislative Authority of the British Parliament*, 22; Egerton, "The Seventeenth and Eighteenth Century Privy Council in Its Relations with the Colonies."; and Webb, "Peaceable Kingdom," 183.
15. "Chief Justice North's Memorandum on William Penn's Draft Chapter," January 1681, in *PWP*, 2:59.
16. Webb, "William Blathwayt, Imperial Fixer," 7.
17. Webb, "Peaceable Kingdom," 186–89.
18. Dickerson, *American Colonial Government*, 31.
19. Hall, "The House of Lords, Edward Randolph, and the Navigation Act of 1696," 498.
20. *Journal of the House of Lords* (London, 1767–1830), 15:619.
21. *House of Lords Manuscripts*, 414.
22. William Penn to Sir William Trumbull, January 14, 1697, in *PWP*, 3:476.
23. Spotswood et al., "The Case of the Proprietor of Pensilvania &C., About the Appointing a New Deputy-Governor," 209.
24. Board of Trade to Patrick Gordon, Esq., Deputy Governor of Pennsylvania, September 8, 1730, JBT, CO 5/1294, 15–18, British National Archives.
25. Board of Trade to the Right Honorable the Lords of the Committee of His Majesty's Most Honorable Privy Council, February 21, 1739, JBT, CO 5/1294, 115–18, British National Archives.
26. John Penn to Governor Gordon, May 3, 1730, TPL, vol. 8, Reel 1, HSP.
27. Instructions to James Hamilton, July 1748, JBT, CO 5/1248, 267–81, 285–350, British National Archives.
28. The most infamous and politically explosive instruction of this kind was the "Additional Instruction" for paper money bills sent to Deputy Governor George Thomas in August 1740, which embroiled the four governors

succeeding Thomas and the assembly in factious disputes for over fifteen years.
29. See, for instance, Hutson, *Pennsylvania Politics*, 12.
30. Thomas Penn to James Hamilton, July 13, 1749, CTR, APS.
31. Thomas Penn to Richard Peters, 1754, TPL, vol. 4, Reel 1, HPS.
32. Thomas Penn to Governor Morris, May 10, 1755, LTP, Reel 8; Thomas Penn to James Hamilton, July 13, 1752, CTR, APS.
33. Thomas and Richard Penn to James Hamilton, June 5, 1752, CTR, APS.
34. Thomas and Richard Penn to James Hamilton, July 10, 1762, CTR, APS.
35. Thomas Penn to Richard Peters, 1754, TPL, vol. 4, Reel 1.
36. Thomas Penn to Richard Peters, September 27, 1755, TPL, vol. 5, Reel 2, HSP. Deputy Governor Thomas's diligent submission of political accounts to the home government was not an aberration. The Original Correspondence of the Secretaries of State from 1740 to 1775 is filled with descriptions of Pennsylvania politics scrawled by the several deputy governors. Original Correspondence of the Secretaries of State, CO 5/1233 and 1234, British National Archives.
37. The Memorial of Henry Popple on behalf of Colonel George Thomas of Antigua, to Council of Trade and Plantations, May 12, 1738, Headlam and Newton, *Calendar of State Papers, Colonial Series*, 39:83.
38. Governor George Thomas to the Duke of Newcastle, November 26, 1741, CO 5/1234, 146–47, British National Archives.
39. "Additional Instruction to George Thomas, esq; Deputy Governor of his Majesty's Province of Pennsylvania in America, or to the Commander in Chief of his Majesty's said Province for the Time Being," presented to the Assembly by Governor Hamilton in 1753, *PA*, 8:4:3576–77.
40. Richard Hockley to Thomas Penn, August 3 and 4, 1754, LTP, Reel 8, HSP.
41. *Minutes of the Provincial Council*, September 14, 1741, 497.
42. Governor Thomas to Assembly, August 17, 1742, *PA*, 8:4:2773.
43. Governor Morris to Assembly, January 7, 1755, *PA*, 8:5:3844.
44. Governor Morris to Assembly, March 31 and April 1, 1755, *PA*, 8:5:3874.
45. "Sir Dudley Ryder's Opinion," November 30, 1753, *PA*, 8:5:3789.
46. Thomas Penn to Richard Peters, January 1755, TPL, vol. 4, Reel 1, HSP.
47. Board of Trade to the Committee of Privy Council for Plantation Affairs, May 30, 1755, JBT, CO 5/1295, 163–81, British National Archives.
48. George Bryan's Letterbook, February 1758, Papers of George Bryan, Library of Congress.
49. Ibid., July 5, 1758.
50. Ibid., April 26, 1764.
51. Marietta, *The Reformation of American Quakerism*, 150–68.
52. Wainwright, "Governor William Denny," 179.

53. *SLP,* 5:543–44.
54. Thomas Penn to Richard Hockley, December 11, 1759–January 18, 1760, TPL, vol. 6, Reel 2, HSP; Thomas Penn to Benjamin Chew, April 11, 1760, TPL, vol. 6, Reel 2, HSP; Wainwright, "Governor William Denny," 172.
55. Richard Peters to Thomas Penn, October 2, 1756, Richard Peters Letter Book, quoted in Wainwright, "Governor William Denny," 175.
56. Truxes, *Defying Empire,* 93.
57. George Bryan to unknown, July 5, 1758, George Bryan's Letterbook, Papers of George Bryan, Library of Congress.
58. Thomas Penn to Richard Peters, January 12, 1760, Thomas Penn Papers, vol. 6, Reel 2, HSP.
59. Robert Hunter Morris to John Penn, date unknown, Simon Gratz Autograph Collection, Box 15, Folder 18, HSP; Richard Hockley to Thomas Penn, April 21, 1759, LTP, Reel 8, HSP; Isaac Norris to Benjamin Franklin, April 12, 1759, *PBF,* 8:326–27; Norris to Franklin, July 31, 1759, *PBF,* 8:420; Richard Peters to Thomas Penn, November 22, 1756, LTP, Reel 8, HSP.
60. Isaac Norris to Benjamin Franklin, August 22, 1759, *PBF,* 8:429–30.
61. *Minutes of the Provincial Council,* 333, 362, 376.
62. Isaac Norris to Benjamin Franklin, August 22, 1759, *PBF,* 8:429.
63. Thomas Graeme to Thomas Penn, June 6, 1760, LTP, Reel 8.
64. Commission for Joseph Breintnal, October 6, 1735, *PA,* 3:8:36.
65. Commission for "William Allen, for Chief Justice, Etc," September 24, 1750, *PA,* 3:8:703.
66. The five bills considered as altering the structure of the courts are as follows: "An Act for Establishing Court of Judicature in this Province," February 28, 1710 (vetoed by the Crown); "An Act for Establishing the Courts of General Quarter Sessions in this Province," May 28, 1715 (vetoed by the Crown); "An Act for Establishing the Several Courts of Common Pleas in this Province," May 28, 1715 (vetoed by the Crown); "An Act for the Better Ascertaining the Practice of the Courts of Judicature in this Province," May 28, 1715 (vetoed by the Crown); "An Act for Establishing Courts of Judicature in this Province," May 22, 1722 (never considered by the Crown).
67. Edward Shippen Sr. to Edward Shippen Jr., October 24, 1749, Burd-Shippen Family Papers, Reel 2, Folder 1, PHMC.
68. "A Supplement to the Act, Entitled 'An Act for Establishing Courts of Judicature in this Province,'" *SLP,* 6:462–65; Edward Shippen Sr. to Edward Shippen Jr., November 17, 1759, Burd-Shippen Papers, Series 1, Box 2, 1757–59, APS.
69. Galloway, *A Letter to the People of Pennsylvania; Occasioned by the Assembly's Passing that Important Act, for Constitution the Judges of the Supreme Courts and Common-Pleas, During Good* BEHAVIOUR, 1:249–55.

70. "An Act for Recording of Warrants and Surveys, and for Rendering the Real Estates and Property within this Province more secure," July 7, 1759, *SLP,* 5:448–55.
71. Richard Hockley to Thomas Penn, April 21, 1759, LTP, Reel 8, HSP.
72. Lynford Lardner to Thomas Penn, December 15, 1759, LTP, Reel 8, HSP.
73. Thomas Graeme to Thomas Penn, June 6, 1760, LTP, Reel 8, HSP.
74. William Allen to David Barclay and Sons, February 9, 1760, William Allen Letterbook, Shippen Family Papers, HSP.
75. Benjamin Franklin to Isaac Norris, June 9, 1759, *PBF,* 8:396.
76. Isaac Norris to Benjamin Franklin, July 31 and August 22, 1759, *PBF,* 8:420–21, 8:428–29.
77. Thomas Penn to James Hamilton, June 27, 1760, TPL, vol. 6, Reel 2, HSP.
78. Benjamin Franklin to Isaac Norris, January 14, 1758, *PBF,* 7:360–62.
79. Thomas Penn to Richard Peters, January 12, 1760, TPL, vol. 6, Reel 2, HSP.
80. Thomas Penn to James Hamilton, May 24, 1760, TPL, vol. 6, Reel 2, HSP.
81. Thomas Penn to James Hamilton, May 10, 1760, TPL, vol. 6, Reel 2, HSP.
82. Thomas Penn to James Hamilton, December 8, 1759, TPL, vol. 6, Reel 2, HSP.
83. Thomas Penn to Richard Peters, April 11, 1760, TPL, vol. 6, Reel 2, HSP.
84. Thomas Penn to Richard Peters, June 9, 1760, TPL, vol. 6, Reel 2, HSP.
85. Thomas Penn to Richard Peters, May 10, 1760, TPL, vol. 6, Reel 2, HSP.
86. Thomas Penn to James Hamilton, March 8, 1760, CTR, APS.
87. Thomas Penn to James Hamilton, March 8, 1760, TPL, vol. 6, Reel 2, HSP.
88. JBT, CO 5/1295, 296–97, 315, British National Archives; *Journal of the Commissioners for Trade and Plantations,* 64:109; Thomas Penn to Richard Peters, June 9, 1760, TPL, vol. 6, Reel 2, HSP.
89. *Journal of the Commissioners for Trade and Plantations,* 67:110.
90. JBT, June 24, 1760, CO 5/1295, 312, British National Archives.
91. Ibid., 327, 357, 374–79, 401–2, 407–8, British National Archives.
92. Thomas Penn to James Hamilton, May 24, 1760, TPL, vol. 6, Reel 2, HSP.
93. Thomas Penn to James Hamilton, June 6, 1760, TPL, vol. 6, Reel 2, HSP.
94. Thomas Penn to James Hamilton, June 27, 1760, TPL, vol. 6, Reel 2, HSP.
95. JBT, June 24, 1760, CO 5/1295, 405–6, 411–13, British National Archives.
96. William Franklin to Joseph Galloway, June 16, 1760, *PBF,* 9:123.
97. Thomas Penn to James Hamilton, June 6, 1760, TPL, vol. 6, Reel 2, HSP.
98. Thomas Penn to James Hamilton, July 5, 1760, TPL, vol. 6, Reel 2, HSP.
99. James Hamilton, "A Message from the Governor to the Assembly," February 8, 1762, *SLP,* 6:491–93.
100. William Allen to the House, April 11, 1761, *PA,* 8:6:5239.
101. Foulke, "A Memorandum," 407–9.

102. Ibid.; *PA*, 8:6:5255–76; "Minutes of the Provincial Council," *Colonial Records*, 8:673–74.
103. Thomas Penn to Robert Hunter Morris, November 15, 1760; Thomas Penn to Richard Peters, November 15, 1760, TPL, vol. 6, Reel 2, HSP. See also Governor Francis Bernard to the Lords of Trade, February 25, 1760, March 22, 1760, and Copy of the Minutes of the Supreme Court of New Jersey on the Claim of Mr. Morris to resume the Office of Chief Justice, March 22, 1760 in *Archives of the State of New Jersey*, 1:9:209–18.
104. Labaree, *Royal Government in America*, 395–97.
105. Circular Instruction of Crown in Labaree, *Royal Instructions to British Colonial Governors*, 1:367–68.
106. Labaree, *Royal Government in America*, 399.
107. Thomas Penn to James Hamilton, March 6, 1762, CTR, APS. See also Penn to Hamilton, April 25, 1762, CTR, APS.
108. James Hamilton to Assembly, February 15, 1763, SLP, 6:530. See also *PA*, 8:6:5401–2.
109. William Allen to Thomas Penn, March 8, 1767, PPOC, 10:94–98, HSP.
110. "An Act to Amend the Act, Entitled 'An Act for Establishing Courts of Judicature within this Province,'" May 20, 1767, SLP, 7:107–10; "The Council's Amendment to the Bill (not included in the Bill)," SLP, 7:386.
111. John Penn to Thomas Penn, April 29, 1767, LTP, Reel 9, HSP.
112. William Allen to Thomas Penn, March 8, 1767, PPOC, 10:94–98, HSP.
113. William Allen to Thomas Penn, March 8, 1767, PPOC, 10:94–98; William Allen to Thomas Penn, April 5, 1767, LTP, Reel 9, HSP.
114. John Penn to Thomas Penn, April 29, 1767, LTP, Reel 9, HSP.
115. Pennsylvania Assembly Committee of Correspondence to Richard Jackson and Benjamin Franklin, in *PBF*, 14:285.
116. Thomas Penn to Richard Peters, February 10 and April 8, 1758, TPL, vol. 6, Reel 2, HSP.
117. Governor Penn to Assembly, May 26, 1769, *PA*, 8:7:6391.
118. Assembly to Richard Jackson and Benjamin Franklin, October 17, 1767, *PA*, 8:7:6070.

4. "When the Thunder of the Law Sleeps"

1. Isaac Hunt to Benjamin Franklin, May 21, 1766, *PBF*, 13:279.
2. Hunt, *A Continuation of the Exercises, in Scurrility Hall*, 7.
3. Bryan to unknown, March 10, 1764, George Bryan's Letterbook, Papers of George Bryan, Library of Congress.
4. According to sociologist Jack Goldstone, a state crisis happens when citizens begin to conceive of their government as fundamentally "ineffective, unjust, and obsolete." Goldstone, "Rethinking Revolutions"; Goldstone,

"Toward a Fourth Generation of Revolutionary Theory," 146; Goldstone, *Revolution and Rebellion in the Early Modern World*, 1–62.
5. Lazarus Stewart, "Narrative of Lazarus Stewart," in Day, *Historical Collections of the State of Pennsylvania*, 278.
6. Vaughan, "Frontier Banditti and the Indians," 6.
7. For more information on the groups not discussed in this chapter, especially the "Fair Play Men," see, George D. Wolf, *The Fair Play Settlers of the West Brach Valley, 1769–1784: A Study of Frontier Ethnography* (Harrisburg: Pennsylvania Historical and Museum Commission, 1969); Marcus Gallo, "'Fair Play Has Entirely Ceased, and Law Has Taken Its Place': The Rise and Fall of the Squatter Republic in the West Brach Valley of the Susquehanna River, 1768–1800," *PMHB* 136, no. 4 (2012): 405–34. For an excellent new book on the Black Boys, see Spero, *Frontier Rebels*.
8. Narrative of Matthew Smith, in Day, *Historical Collections of the State of Pennsylvania*, 279–80.
9. John Elder to Governor John Penn, January 27, 1764, in Sprague, *Annals of the American Pulpit*, 3:78.
10. Merrell, *Into the American Woods*, 284–88, 290–91; Calloway, *The Scratch of a Pen*, 77–79; Silver, *Our Savage Neighbors*, 179–81; Kenny, *Peaceable Kingdom Lost*; Spero, "Creating Pennsylvania," 222–31.
11. Tennant, *The Late Association for Defence*, 8–19.
12. Elder, "A booklet of notes for sermons and prayers of Rev. John Elder," Elder Collection, MG 070, Dauphin County Historical Society. For a recent investigation of the political thought of Pennsylvania's frontier dwellers see Kozuskanich, "Falling under the Domination Totally of Presbyterians." See also Kozuskanich, "For the Security and Protection of the Community." In these works, Kozuskanich nicely sums up the community-oriented political philosophy of frontier inhabitants. However, Kozuskanich often downplays the place and importance of religion in forming, disseminating, and sustaining a "public welfare" "man in society" vision of civil society. Nevertheless, Kozuskanich provides an important interpretation, one that seriously challenges the work of past historians such as Thomas Slaughter who portray an individualistic antigovernment political philosophy dominating the frontier.
13. Goodlet, *A Vindication of the Associate Synod*, 11. My emphasis.
14. Tennant, *The Late Association for Defence*, 18–19.
15. McClenchan, *A Letter, from a Clergyman in Town*, 5.
16. Elder, booklet of notes, Elder Collection, MG 070, Dauphin County Historical Society.
17. Montgomery, *A Sermon Preached at Christiana Bridge and Newcastle*, 28.
18. Carmichael, *A Self-Defensive War*, 20.

19. For more on the intersection of religion and politics on the frontier see Pearl, "'Our God and Our Guns'"; and Pearl, "Pulpits of Revolution."
20. Unknown correspondent, Fort Augusta, December 20, 1756, *Edward Shippen Thompson Collections*, Reel 1, Folder 4, PHMC.
21. John Armstrong to Major James Burd, Carlisle, May 29, 1756, *Edward Shippen Thompson Collections*, Reel 1, Folder 4, PHMC.
22. Extract of a Letter from Fort Bedford, February 28, 1764, in *Pennsylvania Gazette*, March 8, 1764.
23. See for example account of Joseph Sturges, November 26, 1755, Timothy Horsfield Papers, Box 1, Piece 55, APS.
24. Silver, *Our Savage Neighbors*, 78, 83, 126–27.
25. Silver, *Our Savage Neighbors*, 56–58.
26. Rev. John Elder to James Hamilton, October 25, 1763, in Boyd, *The Susquehanna Company Papers*, 2:277.
27. Muhlenberg, *Journals*, 1:388–89.
28. Petition to Governor Hamilton, Aug 17, 1763, Timothy Horsfield Papers, Box 1, Piece 475, APS.
29. Meeting of Inhabitants from Philadelphia and Chester, November 19, 1755, *PA*, 8:5:4157–58.
30. Muhlenberg, *Journals*, 1:388–89.
31. James Martin to William Parsons, March 8, 1756, Timothy Horsfield Papers, Box 1, Piece 107, APS.
32. John Elder to Richard Peters, November 1755, in Dunbar, *The Paxton Papers*, 9–10.
33. Robert Hunter Morris to Assembly, April 13, 1756, *PA*, 8:5:4221.
34. Smith, *A Brief View*, 52. See also Galloway, *A True and Impartial State of the Province of Pennsylvania*, 143–45.
35. William Moore to Robert Hunter Morris, November 23, 1755, *Colonial Records*, 6:729. Inhabitants from Lancaster also targeted both the assembly and the governor in their threats to march on Philadelphia. See "Minutes of the Provincial Council," April 13, 1756, *Colonial Records*, 7:87.
36. Smith, *A Brief View*, 88.
37. Merrell, *Into the American Woods*, 284–85.
38. Hutcheson, *A System of Moral Philosophy*, 1:110.
39. Merrell, *Into the American Woods*, 286.
40. John Elder to Governor John Penn, January 27, 1764, in Sprague, *Annals of the American Pulpit*, 3:78.
41. Quoted in Merrell, *Into the American Woods*, 286.
42. John Elder to Colonel Shippen, February 1, 1764, in Parkman, *The Conspiracy of Pontiac*, appendix E, 2:347–48.
43. Stewart, "Narrative of Lazarus Stewart," 280.
44. *Declaration and Remonstrance*, in Dunbar, *The Paxton Papers*, 104.

45. Stewart, "Narrative of Lazarus Stewart," 280.
46. *Declaration and Remonstrance*, in Dunbar, *The Paxton Papers*, 101; Deposition of Felix Donolly in Parkman, *Conspiracy of Pontiac*, appendix E, 2:343–44.
47. "Extract from a Remonstrance presented to John Penn," February 24, 1764, in Day, *Historical Collections of the State of Pennsylvania*, 279; *Declaration and Remonstrance*, in Dunbar, *The Paxton Papers*, 108.
48. *Declaration and Remonstrance*, in Dunbar, *The Paxton Papers*, 104.
49. See petitions sent to the assembly between March 23 and May 25, 1764, in PA, 8:7:5581–5610.
50. John Armstrong to George Croghan, March 26, 1765, quoted in Spero, "Creating Pennsylvania," 262.
51. For the North Carolina Regulators, see Kars, *Breaking Loose Together*. For more on the Black Boys, see Spero, *Frontier Rebels*; Dowd, *War under Heaven*, 208–9; Bouton, *Taming Democracy*, 43–45.
52. Vaughan, "Frontier Banditti and the Indians," 6.
53. Smith, *Remarkable Occurrences*, 106–11.
54. Ibid., 111–13.
55. Edward Shippen Jr. to Edward Shippen Sr., September 20, 1764, Burd-Shippen Family Papers, Reel 2, Folder 36, PHMC.
56. Smith, *Remarkable Occurrences*, 111–13.
57. Ibid., 108.
58. Sir William Johnson to Thomas Gage, April 12, 1765, CO 5/83, 403, British National Archives.
59. Ibid.
60. Instructions to George Croghan, December 30, 1764, Thomas Gage Papers, American Series, vol. 29, WLC.
61. Thomas Gage to Henry Bouquet, March 20, 1765, Thomas Gage Papers, American Series, vol. 32, WLC.
62. Thomas Gage to George Croghan, March 30, 1765, Thomas Gage Papers, American Series, vol. 33, WLC.
63. Henry Bouquet to Thomas Gage, March 29, 1765, Thomas Gage Papers, American Series, vol. 33, WLC.
64. Thomas Gage to Henry Bouquet, March 20, 1765, Thomas Gage Papers, American Series, vol. 32, WLC.
65. John Penn to Thomas Gage, March 22, 1765, Thomas Gage Papers, American Series, vol. 32, WLC.
66. The Address of the Inhabitants of Cumberland County to the Governor, March 1765, in Bouquet, *The Papers of Henry Bouquet*, 6:777–79.
67. Sir William Johnson to Lords of Trade, January 16, 1765, CO 5/66, 197, British National Archives.
68. Smith, *Remarkable Occurrences*, 109.

69. Conrad, *From Terror to Freedom*, 143–44; PA, 2:9:808, 2:2:521–22; Will of Robert Callender, July 26, 1776, Irvine-Newbold Family Papers, Series 1, Box 11, Folder 1, HSP.
70. Deposition of James Maxwell, April 3, 1765, Thomas Gage Papers, American Series, vol. 38, WLC. To prevent any confusion, the depositions of James Maxwell and Richard Brownson both state that the gunpowder and lead were located in William Maxwell's barn. William Maxwell was James Maxwell's father, who lived with his son. In his deposition, James states that his "home" was also "his fathers."
71. Deposition of William Smith, April 3, 1765, Thomas Gage Papers, American Series, vol. 38, WLC.
72. A Petition from the Inhabitants of the Great Cove and Conecocheague in the County of Cumberland, September 17, 1763, PA, 8:6:5437–38; Assembly's Response, PA, 8:6:5440; A Petition from David Scott, of the Great Cove in Cumberland County, January 11, 1764, PA, 8:7:5509–11.
73. Deposition of Robert Allison, March 10, 1765, Cumberland County Quarter Sessions, in Thomas Gage Papers, American Series, vol. 32, WLC. There are two depositions by Robert Allison in the Thomas Gage Papers; in the second deposition Allison confirmed that he was taking private trade goods. See Deposition of Robert Allison, Cumberland County Quarter Sessions, April 1, 1765, Thomas Gage Papers, American Series, vol. 38, WLC; Robert Callender to Colonel Bouquet, March 11, 1765, Thomas Gage Papers, American Series, vol. 32, WLC.
74. Deposition of James Maxwell, April 3, 1765, Thomas Gage Papers, American Series, vol. 38, WLC; Deposition of Richard Brownson, April 3, 1765, Thomas Gage Papers, American Series, vol. 38, WLC.
75. Smith, *Remarkable Occurrences*, 109.
76. Deposition of William Smith, Esq, April 3, 1765, Thomas Gage Papers, American Series, vol. 38, WLC. For inquisition see Papers of the Governors, PA, 4:3:300–301.
77. Extract of a Letter from _____ to Mr. Croghan, 1768, Thomas Gage Papers, American Series, vol. 75, WLC.
78. Thomas Gage to John Reid, June 9, 1765, Thomas Gage Papers, American Series, vol. 37, WLC.
79. Deposition of James Maxwell, April 3, 1765, Thomas Gage Papers, American Series, vol. 38, WLC.
80. Smith, *Remarkable Occurrences*, 110.
81. Advertisement, Thomas Gage Papers, American Series, vol. 37, WLC.
82. John Ross to Benjamin Franklin, May 20, 1765, PBF, 12:138.
83. Deposition of James Maxwell and Deposition of Richard Brownson, April 3, 1765, Thomas Gage Papers, American Series, vol. 38. WLC.

84. George Croghan to Lieutenant Colonel Wilkins, March 20, 1768, Thomas Gage Papers, American Series, vol. 75, WLC.
85. Lieutenant Charles Grant to Thomas Gage, August 24, 1765, *PA*, 1:4:232.
86. John Reid to Thomas Gage, June 1, 1765, Thomas Gage Papers, American Series, vol. 37, WLC; Deposition of Lieutenant Grant, 1765, *PA*, 1:5:220–22.
87. Bouton makes this same point. See Bouton, *Taming Democracy*, 44–45.
88. John Reid to Thomas Gage, June 4, 1765, Thomas Gage Papers, American Series, vol. 37, WLC.
89. Ibid.
90. John Reid to Thomas Gage, June 1, 1765, Thomas Gage Papers, American Series, vol. 37, WLC.
91. Ibid.
92. Thomas Gage to John Penn, July 5, 1765, Thomas Gage Papers, American Series, vol. 39, WLC.
93. The longevity of the movement is shocking, as James Smith had not been part of the regulation since at least June 1766. Although many histories focus solely on Smith's involvement, his absence and the continued resistance of the Black Boys speaks to the overwhelming popularity and scope of the regulation. For the activity of the Black Boys in 1768 see, for example, Lieutenant Colonel Wilkins to Thomas Gage, March 11, 1768, Thomas Gage Papers, American Series, vol. 75, WLC.
94. Anonymous letter to George Croghan, 1768, Thomas Gages Papers, American Series, vol. 75, WLC.
95. Deposition of Robert Allison, April 1, 1765, Thomas Gage Papers, American Series, vol. 38, WLC. For Allison's earlier deposition before Justice Alricks, less than a month earlier, see Deposition of Robert Allison, March 10, 1765, Thomas Gage Papers, American Series, vol. 32, WLC.
96. Deposition of Richard Brownson, April 3, 1765, Thomas Gage Papers, American Series, vol. 38, WLC.
97. John Penn to Thomas Gage, June 28, 1765, Thomas Gage Papers, American Series, vol. 38, WLC.
98. John Penn to Thomas Penn, March 16, 1765, LTP, Reel 9, HSP.
99. Deposition of James Doltin, April 1769, Jasper Yeates Family Papers, Reel 1, B, Legal Files, Folder 2, PHMC. This deposition corroborates evidence in Smith's *Remarkable Occurrences* of an assault on Fort Bedford, an event historians, such as Gregory Evans Dowd and Patrick Spero, question actually took place. Spero argues that the attack on Fort Bedford "has yet to be verified by historians." See Gregory Evans Dowd, *War under Heaven*, 208–9; and Spero, "Recreating James Smith at the Pennsylvania State Archives," 478.
100. Extract of a letter from Fort Bedford, August 2, 1769, *Pennsylvania Journal*, August 17, 1769; extract of a letter from Fort Bedford, September 21, 1769, *Pennsylvania Gazette*, September 28, 1769.

101. Extract of letters from Fort Bedford, September 21 and September 28, 1769, *Pennsylvania Gazette*.
102. Smith, *Remarkable Occurrences*, 121–22.
103. *Pennsylvania Gazette*, November 2, 1769.
104. *Pennsylvania Gazette*, October 5, 1769.
105. *Pennsylvania Gazette*, October 5, 1769; Smith, *Remarkable Occurrences*, 123.
106. Smith, *Remarkable Occurrences*, 122.
107. *Pennsylvania Journal*, October 25, 1769; *Pennsylvania Gazette*, November 2, 1769.
108. Smith, *Remarkable Occurrences*, 130; public address of William Smith, October 16, 1769, in *Pennsylvania Gazette*, November 2, 1769.
109. Thomas Gage to John Reid, June 24, 1765, Thomas Gage Papers, American Series, vol. 38, WLC.
110. John Penn to Horatio Sharpe, February 4, 1769, in Brown, *Archives of Maryland*, 32:262.
111. Jasper Yeates to James Burd, Lancaster, September 8, 1768, Burd-Shippen Family Papers, Reel 2, Folder 38, PHMC.
112. Chester County Quarter Sessions Dockets, Docket Book A, 1759–69, CCA.
113. Petition to Chester County, Quarter Sessions Papers, in Brown, *Archives of Maryland*, 32:321–24.
114. Chester County Quarter Sessions Dockets, 1723–33, 1733–42, 1742–59, and Docket Books A and B, CCA.
115. Petition to Chester County Quarter Sessions Papers, in Brown, *Archives of Maryland*, 32:322.
116. Case File Carmichael et al., November 1768, Chester County Quarter Sessions Papers, CCA; Deposition of William Reynolds, Prudence Reynolds, Daughter Reynolds, and Elisha Reynolds, June 24, 1769, in Brown, *Archives of Maryland*, 32:315–26; Jasper Yeates to James Burd, September 8, 1768, Burd-Shippen Family Papers, Reel 2, Folder 38, PHMC.
117. Indictment File McGarrigan et al., August 1763, Chester County Quarter Sessions Papers, CCA.
118. *King v. John Harris et al.*, Chester County Quarter Sessions Papers, May 1762, CCA.
119. Indictment File Wiley et al., Chester County Quarter Sessions Papers, August 1768, CCA.
120. Deposition of Prudence Reynolds, in Brown, *Archives of Maryland*, 32: 319.
121. Petition to Chester County Quarter Sessions Papers, in Brown, *Archives of Maryland*, 32:321–24.
122. Case File Reynolds et al., August 1765, Chester County Quarter Sessions Papers, CCA.
123. Alexander Johnston to unknown, Indictment Files Reynolds et al., Chester County Quarter Sessions Papers, CCA.

124. Case File Carmichael et al., Chester County Quarter Sessions Papers, November 1768, CCA; Deposition of William Reynolds, in Brown, *Archives of Maryland*, 316–19.
125. Case File Carmichael et al., November 1768, Chester County Quarter Sessions Papers, CCA; Deposition of William Reynolds, Prudence Reynolds, Daughter Reynolds, and Elisha Reynolds, June 24, 1769, in Brown, *Archives of Maryland*, 32:315–26.
126. Comparison of the names on the petition with the 1768 tax lists for Chester County reveals the social and economic heterogeneity of the signers and signifies that this episode did not reflect class antagonism that historians often associate with civil unrest and extralegal action. The petitioners from West Nottingham, for example, represented the top as well as bottom of the tax lists. The median acreage of the signers was one hundred acres; they owned on average two horses, three and a half cattle, and ten sheep; and only two of the petitioners owned servants. For the town as a whole, the median acreage of taxable inhabitants was one hundred, and they owned on average two horses, three cattle, six sheep, and one servant. Tax Lists for 1768 in *PA*, 3:11:422–26.
127. Case File Carmichael et al., November 1768, Chester County Quarter Sessions Papers, CCA.
128. Jasper Yeates to James Burd, September 8, 1768, Burd-Shippen Family Papers, Reel 2, Folder 38, PHMC; Jasper Yeates to Duncan Campbell, September 8, 1768, Burd-Shippen Family Papers, Reel 2, Folder 38, PHMC.
129. *Porcupine's Gazette and United States Daily Advertiser*, March 11, 1797.
130. *Philadelphia Gazette*, December 8, 1800.

5. "Usurping Powers"

1. Smith, *Remarkable Occurrences*, 121.
2. Becker, *The History of Political Parties in the Province of New York*, 5. Historians such as Richard Ryerson, David Hawke, and recently Ken Owen portray the revolution as the result of immediate concerns that had little to do with the past. Hawke is the most forward with such an interpretation, as he argues that "Pennsylvanians did not care much about politics" and generally liked the government as it existed. Hawke does not even address the earlier period of Pennsylvania's history. Ryerson, on the other hand, does project backward into the 1760s, but he disassociates the provincial political dialogue of the 1760s with the overall resistance effort and therefore, much like Hawke, provides an argument that centers on the events surrounding the Imperial Crisis and the standard interpretation of the revolution's constitutional causes. Owen builds on Ryerson, exploring the place of popular political mobilizations in revolutionary Pennsylvania

and the creation of a "political community." He is largely unconcerned with how the colonial past dramatically affected the formation and focus of that community. Historians who focus on the economic origins of the American Revolution such as Steven Rosswurm and Terry Bouton, on the other hand, have long seen the revolution as a conflict for both home rule and who should rule at home. Yet their focus on economic determinism as the driving force behind revolution misses salient issues related to governance, local law, local control, and the place of political representation that drove the anger and eventual alienation of many Pennsylvanians, both ordinary people and the elites. Historians of the frontier have moved the conversation in important directions. Patrick Griffin, Patrick Spero, and Nathan Kozuskanich demonstrate the significance of internal politics and local governance, particularly as it relates to defense initiatives and Native American policy, to the causes and consequences of the American Revolution. Ryerson, *The Revolution Is Now Begun*; Hawke, *In the Midst of a Revolution*; Owen, *Political Community in Revolutionary Pennsylvania*; Rosswurm, *Arms, Country, and Class*; Bouton, *Taming Democracy*; Griffin, *American Leviathan*; Spero, *Frontier Country*, Kozuskanich, "For the Security and Protection of the Community."

3. Goldstone, *Revolution and Rebellion in the Early Modern World*, 1–62.
4. Goldstone, "Toward a Fourth Generation of Revolutionary Theory."
5. Ibid., 149–50.
6. Benjamin Franklin to Richard Jackson, February 11, 1764, *PBF*, 11:76; John Penn to the Assembly, January 3, 1764, *Colonial Records*, 9:109.
7. Dowd, *War under Heaven*, 196.
8. "A Petition from the County of Cumberland signed by Upwards of Twelve Hundred Inhabitants of Said County," 1764, *PA*, 8:7:5581–5610.
9. Barton, *A LETTER from a GENTLEMAN*, 9, 33, 34.
10. Ibid., 33.
11. Franklin, *Cool Thoughts*, 5–6.
12. Ibid., 7.
13. Olson, "The Pamphlet War over the Paxton Boys," 33.
14. Benjamin Franklin to Isaac Norris, September 16, 1758, *PBF*, 8:157.
15. *Votes and Proceedings of the House of Representatives of the Province of Pennsylvania*, *PA*, 8:7:5595.
16. *An Address to the Freeholders and Inhabitants of the Province of Pennsylvania*, 11–12.
17. *The Plot. By Way of a Burlesk*, 1–2.
18. Hunt, *A Humble Attempt at Scurrility*, 41. Hunt makes another crucial statement about judicial tenure on page 42 of the same satire: "This, this is he, who scruples not to go; Upon the Bench, *durante placito*; For well he knows, he scarce an Hour should sit; If the Law was *quam bene gesserit*."

Like many other politicians and citizens supporting the assembly, the problem with the administration of justice had little to do with legal structures but more to do with the tenure of office, which allowed judges to sit on the bench whether they did their job or not.

19. Ibid., 25.
20. *Lucifer's Decree, after a Fray*, 1–7.
21. *The Plot. By Way of a Burlesk*, 5. See also Hutson, *Pennsylvania Politics*, 159.
22. Galloway, *The Speech*, 82, 51, 62, 64.
23. Ibid., 66, 67, 77.
24. Ibid., 67. See also *The Scribler*, 1–25.
25. Dickinson, *A Reply to a Piece called the Speech of Joseph Galloway*, 20.
26. Williamson, *Plain Dealer Number II*, 11.
27. Galloway, *The Speech*, 69–73.
28. Dickinson, *A Reply to a Piece called the Speech of Joseph Galloway*, 20.
29. Williamson, *The Plain Dealer: Or Remarks on Quaker Politics, Number III*, 21.
30. Dickinson, *A Speech Delivered*, 28.
31. *Pennsylvania Journal*, January 10, 1765.
32. See, for example, the discussion of the literature in Roney, *Governed by a Spirit of Opposition*, 161–62. See also Newcomb, *Franklin and Galloway*, 105–13.
33. George Grenville to William Knox, August 15, 1768, William Knox Papers, vol. 1, Folder 33, WLC.
34. *Pennsylvania Journal*, October 24, 1765.
35. Dickinson, *The Late Regulations Respecting the British Colonies*, 19. See also Jasper Yeates to Richard Peters Jr., May 14, 1765, Burd-Shippen Family Papers, Reel 2, Folder 36, PHMC; Jasper Yeates to Edward Shippen, October 21, 1765, Burd-Shippen Family Papers, Reel 2, Folder 36, PHMC.
36. Dickinson, *Friends and Countrymen*, 1–2.
37. *Pennsylvania Journal*, September 20, 1764.
38. *Six Arguments Against Chusing Joseph Galloway*, 1; *To the Freeholders and Electors of the City and County of Philadelphia*, 1–2.
39. Biddle, *To the Freeholders and Electors*, 1; Richard Peters Jr. to Jasper Yeates, September 6, 1766, Jasper Yeates Papers, 1733–1876, Series 2, Box 7, Folder 3, HSP.
40. John Hughes to John Penn, October 8, 1765, and John Hughes to John Swift, Alexander Barclay, and Thomas Graeme, November 5, 1765, Pennsylvania Stamp Act and Non-Importation Resolution Collection, vol. 1, Folder 1, APS; Deborah Franklin to Benjamin Franklin, September 22 and October 9, 1765, *PBF*, 12:270, 299.
41. Dickinson, *Friends and Countrymen*, 2.

42. *Observations on the late Epitaph*, 4.
43. Philanthropos, *The Universal Peace-Maker*, 6. See also Edward Shippen Jr. to Edward Shippen Sr., September 10, 1765, Burd-Shippen Family Papers, Reel 2, Folder 37, PHMC.
44. *Observations on the late Epitaph*, 5–6.
45. Franklin, "Remarks on a Late Protest," *Pennsylvania Journal*, November 22, 1764.
46. Horle et al., *Lawmaking and Legislators*, 3:130–32.
47. Franklin, *The Autobiography*, 95.
48. Nash, "Up from the Bottom in Franklin's Philadelphia," 57–83.
49. Dinkin, *Voting in Provincial America*, 9–10.
50. Jasper Yeates to James Burd, September 17, 1769, Burd-Shippen Family Papers, Reel 2, Folder 38, PHMC.
51. Dinkin, *Voting in Provincial America*, 56, 44, 158–59, 80.
52. Ibid., 56, 158–59.
53. *Anmerkungen uber ein noch nie Erhoert* (Germantown, 1764), 2.
54. Galloway, *The Speech*, 25.
55. Ibid., 81–82.
56. *Observations on the late Epitaph*, 4.
57. *Advertisement and Not a Joke*, 1.
58. Historians such as Benjamin Newcomb, James Hutson, and Alan Tully, because they write and think of this new opposition as a party, have deemed them generally unsuccessful and unpopular with the community at large. By coming to terms with the fact that the party mentality historians have fashioned for them does not reflect the reality of what existed, we can begin to see the importance of what was happening. Popular forces were turning and moving in the province but lacked the collectivity and purpose of action that a party would offer to effect real change.
59. Bouton, *Taming Democracy*, 45.
60. "The Circular Letter and Articles of 'Some Gentlemen of the Presbyterian Denomination,' in the Province of Pennsylvania," March 24, 1764, in Hanna, *The Scotch-Irish*, 2:4–5.
61. Although Terry Bouton deems these committees "gentry-led," their ranks were still filled with political outsiders who did not have a forceful say in the politics of the province. These committees filled a critical void for a politicized people. It gave them entry into the political system; though not direct, it was entry nonetheless. For the place of artisans in these groups see Olton, *Artisans for Independence*, 33–47. The dichotomy of elite versus popular or "ordinary folk" in the resistance effort in extralegal committees, as Olton shows, does not adequately explain popular involvement over the period 1765–76.
62. Petitions in *PA*, 8:7:5691–5798.

63. Circular Letter of Gilbert Tennent, Francis Alison and John Ewing, relating to making Pennsylvania a Royal Province, March 30, 1764, in Documents Relating to the Province of Pennsylvania and to the American Revolution, no. 26, APS.
64. "A Petition from the County of Cumberland," March 23, 1764, *PA*, 8:7:5582–83; see also petition from "Divers Freemen" in Berks County, September 11, 1764, *PA*, 8:7:5626.
65. "A Petition from a Number of the Inhabitants of the City of Philadelphia," February 25, 1764, *PA*, 8:7:5557–58. See also "Petition from Divers Inhabitants of Berks County, May 16, 1764," *PA*, 8:7:5597–98; *A Tradesman's Address to his Countrymen*, 1. These issues had been raised before. See "Petition from Sundry Inhabitants from Bucks County," 1745, *PA*, 8:4:3030; and "Petition from Sundry Inhabitants of Chester," 1747, *PA*, 8:4:3132.
66. Quincy, "Journal of Josiah Quincy," 49:476.
67. Samuel Wharton to William Franklin, September 29, 1765, Benjamin Franklin Papers, APS.
68. Newcomb, *Franklin and Galloway*, 100–104.
69. For a thorough analysis of the Wyoming controversy see Moyer, *Wild Yankees*.
70. Frederick Haldimand to Lord Dartmouth, November 3, 1773, in Davies, *Documents of the American Revolution*, 6:238.
71. MacGregor, "The Ordeal of John Connolly," 164–66.
72. Rowe, "The Frederick Stump Affair," 259–88. In this work, Rowe provides an excellent description of the Stump affair and how it challenged the government both legally and popularly. Nevertheless, Rowe downplays the place of popular animosity toward the supreme court and its refusal to ride a circuit to ensure that all trials were "fair," meaning adjudicated by a "jury of peers," in the rescue of Stump and Ironcutter. This animosity had a great deal to do with the rescue. See, for example, Edward Shippen to James Tilghman, February 2, 1768, Burd-Shippen Family Papers, Reel 2, Folder 38, PHMC.
73. A Letter to the Governor from the Assembly, February 5, 1768, *PA*, 8:7:6136.
74. Quoted in Konkle, *George Bryan*, 86.
75. Joseph Galloway to Benjamin Franklin, March 10, 1768, *PBF*, 15:71.
76. Jasper Yeates to Joseph Swift, March 1, 1768, Burd-Shippen Family Papers, Reel 2, Folder 37, PHMC.
77. Jasper Yeates to Duncan Campbell, March 15, 1768, Burd-Shippen Family Papers, Reel 2, Folder 37, PHMC.
78. Jasper Yeates to Joseph Burd, February 28, 1768, Burd-Shippen Family Papers, Reel 2, Folder 37, PHMC; Jasper Yeates to Duncan Campbell, September 8, 1768, Burd-Shippen Family Papers, Reel 2, Folder 38, PHMC.

79. *Pennsylvania Chronicle*, February 8 and February 15, 1768.
80. Assembly to Deputy Governor, February 18, 1768, *PA*, 8:7:6088, 6179.
81. Thomas Wharton to Benjamin Franklin, March 29, 1768, *PBF*, 15:88.
82. "A Petition from a Number of the Inhabitants on the East and West Branches of the River Susquehanna," January 14, 1772, *PA*, 8:9:6749; "A Petition from a Number of the distressed Persons, Inhabitants of the County of Northampton," January 31, 1772, *PA*, 8:9:6777; "A Petition from a Considerable Number of the Inhabitants of Bedford County," March 10,1772, *PA*, 8:9:6819; "The Petition of the Inhabitants of Northumberland County," December 14, 1773, *PA*, 8:9:7042; "A Petition from the Managers of the Alms-house and House of Employment, Over-seers of the Poor, and Others," January 11, 1774, *PA*,8:9:7061; "A Remonstrance and Petition from a great Majority of the Inhabitants settled in the back Parts of the County of Lancaster, and also the Inhabitants of the Part of Berks adjacent thereto," January 11, 1774, *PA*, 8:9:7062. That criminals could easily escape was a common theme in not only the petitions but even casual comments in journals and diaries. See for example Muhlenberg, *Journals*, 1:136.
83. Jasper Yeates to Duncan Campbell, September 8, 1768, February 13 and December 9, 1769, Burd-Shippen Family Papers, Reel 2, Folder 38, PHMC.
84. *Pennsylvania Chronicle*, August 22, 1768.
85. Committee of Tradesmen to Franklin quoted in Egnal, *A Mighty Empire*, 257.
86. Lover of Liberty and a Mechanic's Friend, *To the Free and Patriotic Inhabitants of the City of Philadelphia and the Province of Pennsylvania*, 1.
87. *A Riddle*.
88. *Pennsylvania Gazette*, September 27, 1770.
89. *A German Freeholder*, 1; *To the Tradesmen, Farmers, and Other Inhabitants of the City and County of Philadelphia*, 1.
90. Dickinson et al., *Fellow Citizens and Countrymen*, 1.
91. Joseph Galloway to Benjamin Franklin, September 27, 1770, *PBF*, 17:228.
92. Olton, *Artisans for Independence*, 53.
93. Joseph Galloway to Benjamin Franklin, October 12, 1772, *PBF*, 19:330.
94. Joseph Reed quoted in Thayer, *Pennsylvania Politics and the Growth of Democracy*, 154.
95. Jensen, *The Founding of a Nation*, 431.
96. Olton, *Artisans for Independence*, 57.
97. *Pennsylvania Chronicle*, September 27, 1773.
98. Maier, *From Resistance to Revolution*, 225–26.
99. Jensen, *The Founding of a Nation*, 287, 312–13.
100. Thomson, "Early Days," 413–17.
101. Thomson, "Early Days," 417; *Pennsylvania Packet*, July 18, 1774.
102. Thomson, "Early Days," 416–17.

103. *Rivington's New-York Gazetteer*, July 28, 1774.
104. Willing held a seat in 1764 and 1765, and Dickinson had only held a seat once since the heady days of 1764 in 1770.
105. Minutes of Public Meeting, Instructions, and Assembly response in *Rivington's New York Gazetteer*, July 28, 1774.
106. Irvin, *Clothed in Robes of Sovereignty*, 20–24.
107. "The New Committee of Sixty Elected," November 22, 1774, in Force, *American Archives*, 4:1:330; *Pennsylvania Journal*, January 11 and January 18, 1775; *Pennsylvania Packet*, December 12 and December 28, 1774.
108. See, for instance, election rules posted in *Pennsylvania Gazette*, November 9 and November 16, 1774.
109. Minutes of York County Committee, *Pennsylvania Gazette*, December 28, 1774.
110. See for example "Proclamation of Committee of Observation and Inspection in the City of Philadelphia," *Pennsylvania Packet*, December 19, 1774.
111. Comparison of Committee Lists from 1775, in Horle et al., *Lawmaking and Legislators*, vol. 3.
112. Thomson, "Early Days," 421.
113. *Pennsylvania Packet*, September 25, 1775.
114. *Pennsylvania Packet*, December 19, 1774.
115. Memorial of Elizabeth Webster, American Loyalist Claims, Series II, AO 13/72, British National Archives.
116. *Pennsylvania Packet*, May 10, 1775; *Articles of Association in Pennsylvania*, 1–2.
117. *Extracts from the Votes and Proceedings of the Committee of Observation of Lancaster*, 1.
118. *Pennsylvania Gazette*, May 10, 1775.
119. Memorial of George Weidell, American Loyalist Claims, Series II, AO 13/72, British National Archives.
120. Memorial of Rev. Daniel Batwell, American Loyalist Claims, Series II, AO 13/70B, British National Archives.
121. John Penn to Lord Dartmouth, undated, CO 5/1300, British National Archives.
122. Graydon, *Memoirs*, 127; Marshall, *Extracts from the Diary of Christopher Marshall*, 41; Hunt, *The Autobiography of Leigh Hunt*, 17–18.
123. Graydon, *Memoirs*, 125–26; Hunt, *The Autobiography of Leigh Hunt*, 18. For both the Hunt and Kearsley affair see Rosswurm, *Arms, Country, and Class*, 47.
124. "In the Committee of October 7th 1775," in Minute Book of the Committee of Safety, July 3, 1775–July 22, 1776, in Records of Pennsylvania's Revolutionary Governments, 1775–1790, Reel 1, 3, PHMC.
125. *Pennsylvania Evening Post*, March 9, 1776.

126. *Pennsylvania Journal*, September 27, 1775; *Pennsylvania Packet*, November 20, 1775.
127. John Penn to Lord Dartmouth, September 5, 1775, CO 5/1300; John Penn to Lord Dartmouth, October 2, 1775, CO 5/130, British National Archives.
128. Memorial of Joseph Galloway, American Loyalist Claims, Series II, AO 13/102, British National Archives.
129. *Pennsylvania Evening Post*, May 21, 1776.
130. Thomson, "Early Days," 421–22.
131. *Pennsylvania Journal*, December 6, 1775.
132. Charles Thomson to John Dickinson, August 16, 1776, in Dickinson, *The Life and Times of John Dickinson*, 210.
133. Joseph Reed to Charles Pettit, March 30, 1776, in Reed, *Life and Correspondence of Joseph Reed*, 1:182.
134. Instructions to the Delegates, November 9, 1775, in Force, *American Archives*, 4:3:1792.
135. *Pennsylvania Evening Post*, March 9, 1776.
136. *Pennsylvania Packet*, April 22 and April 29, 1776; *Pennsylvania Gazette*, May 15, 1776; *Pennsylvania Evening Post*, March 9, 1776; *Pennsylvania Packet*, June 10, 1776.
137. Joseph Shippen to Edward Shippen, March 12, 1776, Shippen Family Papers, Box 7, HSP.
138. Memorial of Enoch Story, American Loyalist Claims, Series II, AO 13/72, British National Archives.
139. John Adams quoted in Hawke, *In the Midst of a Revolution*, 111.
140. Ibid., 112–14.
141. William Bradford Jr., "Memorandum Book and Registrar for the Months of May and June 1776," Bradford Family Papers, HSP; *Pennsylvania Gazette*, June 12, 1776.
142. Allen, "Diary of James Allen," 187.
143. *Pennsylvania Gazette*, June 12, 1776.
144. Clitherall, "Extracts from the Diary," 470.
145. *Pennsylvania Journal*, May 22 and June 12, 1776.
146. "Meeting of the Associators of the first battalion of Chester County," June 10, 1776, in Force, *American Archives*, 4:6:786. See also *Pennsylvania Evening Post*, June 1 and June 6, 1776; *Pennsylvania Gazette*, June 12 and June 19, 1776.
147. Benjamin Rush to Julia Rush, June 1, 1776, in Rush, *Letters of Benjamin Rush*, 1:101; *Pennsylvania Journal*, June 12, 1776.
148. *Pennsylvania Gazette*, June 12, 1776.
149. Force, *American Archives*, 5:1:221.
150. PA, 8:8:7540.
151. Proceedings of the Provincial Conference, June 20–21, 1776, PA, 2:3:561–63.

152. "An Act to Ascertain the Number of Members of Assembly and to Regulate the Election, January 12, 1705–6," *SLP*, 2:212–21.
153. Ireland and Bockelman, "Internal Revolution," 142–44.
154. *Pennsylvania Ledger*, October 12 and October 26, 1776; Sarah Yeates to Jasper Yeates, September 14, 1776, Jasper Yeates Papers, HSP.
155. Data on convention members compiled from Egle, "The Constitutional Convention of 1776." Data on assembly and council in Ryerson, *The Revolution Is Now Begun*, 71.
156. Minutes of the Convention of 1776, *PA*, 3:10:753–84.
157. *SLP*, 9:13–18.
158. *PA*, 8:8:7586; see also Selsam, *The Pennsylvania Constitution of 1776*, 152–53.
159. Morton et al., "The Pennsylvania Provincial Conference of 1776," 325.

6. "For the Security and Protection of the Community"

1. "Pennsylvania's 1776 Constitution," in Thorpe, *The Federal and State Constitutions*, 5:3081.
2. In his book, Kenneth Owen shows how this constitution continued and legitimized a popular sovereignty that Pennsylvanians would use both within and outside the political system. Where extralegal movements were illegitimate under the colonial government, they were not after 1776. See Owen, *Political Community in Revolutionary Pennsylvania*, 8.
3. This interpretation has had a long history. Starting with J. P. Selsam's 1936 work, *The Pennsylvania Constitution of 1776: A Study in Revolutionary Democracy*, historians have consistently portrayed the framers as unlearned and therefore producing a problematic constitution with many flaws and therefore doomed to failure. Historians such as Theodore Thayer, David Hawke, and Charles Olton have largely affirmed the stance of Selsam. See Thayer, *Pennsylvania Politics and the Growth of Democracy*; Hawke, *In the Midst of a Revolution*; Olton, *Artisans for Independence*.
4. "Pennsylvania's 1776 Constitution," in Thorpe, *The Federal and State Constitutions*, 5:3081, 3082, and 3091.
5. Thomas Smith to Arthur St. Clair, August 22, 1776, in St. Clair, *The St. Clair Papers*, 1:374.
6. "Pennsylvania's 1776 Constitution," in Thorpe, *The Federal and State Constitutions*, 5:3082, 3084.
7. See, for instance, Tully, *Forming American Politics*; and Tully, *William Penn's Legacy*.
8. J. P. Selsam's work, *The Pennsylvania Constitution*, for instance, remains the most thorough examination of the Constitution of 1776 to this date. In that work, Selsam completely disregarded any changes to the legal structures of the state in the constitution, arguing that there was "no distinct

difference between the province and commonwealth." Selsam, *The Pennsylvania Constitution*, 199.
9. Rusticus, *Liberty*, 26.
10. Rozbicki, *Culture and Liberty in the Age of the American Revolution*, 3.
11. Demophilus, *Pennsylvania Packet*, February 12, 1776.
12. Hawke, *In the Midst of a Revolution*, 184–95. J. P. Selsam made a similar argument. See Selsam, *The Pennsylvania Constitution*, 169–204.
13. In his work *The Counter-Revolution in Pennsylvania*, Robert Brunhouse characterizes penal reform as "enlightened" and emblematic of westerners' and working-class easterners' liberal character. Douglas M. Arnold and G. S. Rowe argue similarly. See Arnold, *A Republican Revolution*, 226; Rowe, *Thomas McKean*, 234–37. See also Meranze, *Laboratories of Virtue*, 79–86.
14. Beccaria, *An Essay on Crimes and Punishments*, 14.
15. See Monachesi, "Pioneers in Criminology"; Darnton, "In Search of the Enlightenment"; De Pauley, "Beccaria and Punishment"; and Funston and Funston, "Cesare Beccaria and the American Founding Fathers."
16. *The Freeman's Journal; or, The North-American Intelligencer*, August 31, 1785.
17. *Pennsylvania Evening Herald*, January 25, 1785.
18. Demophilus and other eighteenth-century writers in Pennsylvania often used the term "distributive justice" in relationship to the structure of the legal system and its capacity to allocate its resources equitably and effectively to the whole society. Modern philosophers and sociologists, however, often use this term to explain the distribution of economic resources in society, channeling "distributive justice" into a Marxian framework. For the purposes here, "distributive justice" is used in the context that contemporaries wrote about it and its relationship to the development of legal structures. For modern interpretations of "distributive justice" see Fleischacker, *A Short History of Distributive Justice*.
19. *Four Letters on Interesting Subjects*, 18.
20. Ibid. 18; Demophilus, *The Genuine Principles of the Ancient Saxon, or English Constitution*, 39–40. See also *An Essay of a Frame of Government for Pennsylvania*, 14.
21. "Pennsylvania's 1776 Constitution," in Thorpe, *The Federal and State Constitutions* Section 45.
22. Ibid., Section 23.
23. Ibid., Sections 22–30. See also Rowe, *Embattled Bench*, 129.
24. "Expences for a Court of Oyer and Terminer in Bedford after 1778–1780," in Pennsylvania Counties, Miscellaneous Records, 1701–1901, Box 1, Folder 4, Bedford County Collection, HSP.
25. "Pennsylvania's 1776 Constitution," in Thorpe, *The Federal and State Constitutions*, Section 34. See also Fox, "The Prothonotary."
26. Ibid., Section 26.

27. Ibid., Section 5.
28. "An Act Directing the Mode and Times of Electing Justices of the Peace for the City of Philadelphia, and the Several and Respective Counties in this Commonwealth, and for other Purposes therein Mentioned," February 5, 1777, *SLP*, 9:41–45; "A Supplement to 'An Act Directing the Mode and Times of Electing Justices of the Peace for the City of Philadelphia, and the Several and Respective Counties in this Commonwealth, and for other Purposes therein Mentioned,'" March 5, 1777, *SLP*, 9:73–75.
29. Bockelman, "Continuity and Change," 97–104. Bockelman's work on post-independence JPs ends in 1777, as he was attempting to determine if local officials, like assembly members, had an immediate transformation in their ethnic-religious makeup and whether they held offices before independence. However, elections for JPs did not end in some counties until 1778, which increased the number of JPs. There were also additions in 1779, 1781, 1782, and 1783 due to the application from several districts for more JPs. An incomplete list of local officers commissioned under the 1776 Constitution is located in *PA*, 2:3:667–794. Unlike the list of commissions during the colonial period, the justices commissioned *dedimus potestatem* are listed separately. Nevertheless, this list is incomplete, and the *Minutes of the Supreme Executive Council* must be used in tandem for appointments. Because of Bockelman's focus on 1776–77, my number and distribution of JPs and Bockelmen's are significantly different.
30. "Petition of upwards of Twenty Freeholders of the Town & Township of Easton," August 6, 1777, *Colonial Records*, 11:260.
31. These totals were determined by comparing "Officers of the State of Pennsylvania in the Revolution and Under the 1776 Constitution," *PA*, 2:3:667–794, with Bockelman's "Continuity and Change" as well as the *Minutes of the Supreme Executive Council* located in the *Colonial Records*.
32. Washington (1781) added 3 JPs, Fayette (1783) added 4, Montgomery (1784) added 6, Franklin (1784), added 4, Dauphin (1785) added 3, Luzerne (1786) added 6, Huntingdon (1787) added 4, Allegheny (1788) added 3, Delaware (1789) added 2, and Mifflin (1789) added 5. The number of additional justices, it should be noted, were in addition to those JPs already holding commissions in the districts before they became part of the new counties.
33. Similarly, comparing the number of indictments for capital crimes for the years 1763–75 and 1778–90 (excluding 1776 and 1777 due to court closings), indictments increased from an average of twenty-four indictments between 1763 and 1775 to an average of fifty-five indictments between 1778 and 1790, a 130 percent increase. Controlling for population, capital indictments increased by 54 percent per capita. The per capita increase is based on data graciously supplied by G. S. Rowe and Jack Marietta and an estimate of linear population growth based on table 9.4 in McCusker and

Menard, *The Economy of British America*, 203; and Carter et al., *Historical Statistics of the United States, Earliest Times to the Present*. I am greatly indebted to G. S. Rowe and Jack Marietta for their kindness in responding to numerous emails and sending me their database of capital cases. To calculate the 57 percent per capita increase in criminal prosecutions, I used the number of indictments from Marietta and Rowe, *Troubled Experiment*, 46, table 2.5, with a calculation of linear population growth.

34. Slaughter, "Interpersonal Violence in a Rural Setting," 100.
35. Chester County Quarter Sessions Dockets, Docket Books, 1733–42, 1742–59, A, B, and C, CCA.
36. Slaughter, "Interpersonal Violence in a Rural Setting," 120, 100.
37. Data compiled for this paragraph are from the Chester County Quarter Sessions Dockets, Docket Books, 1733–42, 1742–59, A, B, and C, CCA; the extant indictment files and the tax records are all located at the Chester County Historical Society. The court clerk did not record the town of origin for every defendant in the docket books. Therefore, I tracked the names of the defendants in the quarter sessions dockets with the indictment files, which mostly had the town of origins, and on the rare occasion when both indictment file and dockets did not list a town, I used the tax records to determine the place of residence.
38. Robert Galbraith to President Thomas Wharton, May 16, 1778, *PA*, 1:6:511–12.
39. "An Act for Establishing a Court of Admiralty," September 9, 1778, *SLP*, 9:277–83.
40. "An Act for Erecting an High Court of Errors and Appeals," February 28, 1780, *SLP*, 10:52–58.
41. "An Act for Establishing a Land Office, and for other Purposes Therein Mentioned," April 9, 1781, *SLP*, 10:308–14; "An Act to Vest Certain Powers in the President of the State, Together with the Other Officers Therein Named, and for other Purposes therein Mentioned," April 5, 1782, *SLP*, 10:408–11.
42. McKean was not the SEC's first choice. The SEC offered Joseph Reed the position, but due to the influence of his friends, such as Robert Morris, the famous financier, and his growing desire to enter the Continental army and serve under Washington, Reed turned down the post.
43. Edward Burd to unknown, March 14, 1786, Burd-Shippen Family Papers, Reel 1, Folder 13, PHMC. In this letter, Burd nicely lays out the circuit routes and the judges who presided over them.
44. Jasper Yeates to Edward Burd, October 3, 1784, Burd-Shippen Family Papers, Reel 1, Folder 12, PHMC.
45. Jasper Yeates to Edward Burd, February 27, 1790, Burd-Shippen Family Papers, Reel 2, Folder 43, PHMC.

46. Thomas McKean, "Notes of Charges Delivered to Grand Juries," Papers of Thomas McKean, Box 12, HSP. See also McKean, *A Charge Delivered to the Grand-Jury at York*, 13.
47. *Commonwealth v. Dyer*, May 25, 1787, and *Commonwealth v. Well*, November 13, 1788, Papers of George Bryan, Box 4, HSP.
48. George Bryan to Joseph Reed, November 7, 1780, Papers of Joseph Reed, NYHS.
49. *Respublica v. Caldwell*, September 1785, in *Reports of Cases*, 1:155.
50. *Respublica v. Sparhawk*, 1788, in *Reports of Cases*, 1:357–63.
51. *Respublica v. Teischer*, July 1788, in *Reports of Cases*, 1:334–38.
52. *Commonwealth v. Wade*, September 1786, in *Reports of Cases*,1:337; *Respublica v. Sweers*, April 1779, in *Reports of Cases*,1: 41–42.
53. Between 1777 and 1785, the legislature received thirty-five petitions for divorce, requiring special committees, inquiries, and the creation of individual legislation for each request, many of which the assembly denied. As one historian points out, the number of petitions for divorce in this period was "unprecedented." See Meehan, "Not Made Out of Levity," 446.
54. "An Act Concerning Divorces and Alimony," September 19, 1785, *SLP*, 12:94–99.
55. Meehan, "Not Made Out of Levity," 455.
56. Lyons, *Sex among the Rabble*, 14–58, 199–200.
57. Meehan, "Not Made Out of Levity," 458–59. We can see the shifting of authority from the patriarchal household to the state in the works of historians such as Elaine Forman Craine and Irene Q. and Richard D. Brown. See Craine, *Witches, Wife Beaters, and Whores*, especially, 84–118. See also Brown and Brown, *The Hanging of Ephraim Wheeler*.
58. "An Act Concerning Divorces and Alimony," 12:94.
59. Novak, "The Legal Transformation of Citizenship in Nineteenth-Century America," 105. See also Bradburn, *Citizenship Revolution*, 51–53.
60. Constitution, Sections 22–30. See also Rowe, *Embattled Bench*, 129.
61. *Laws of the Thirteenth General Assembly . . . Second Sitting* (Philadelphia, 1789), 14–15. For a fuller description of this board, see Rowe, *Embattled Bench*, 325.
62. Francis Hopkinson to Thomas Jefferson, September 28, 1785, in *PTJ*.
63. A Philadelphia "Tory," quoted in Nash, *Forging Freedom*, 61.
64. Quintana, *Making a Slave State*, 48–88.
65. Nash, *The Unknown American Revolution*, 312.
66. *Pennsylvania Evening Post*, August 30, 1777.
67. *Pennsylvania Packet*, December 10, 1778.
68. Pennsylvanians criticized these rather lethargic and ineffective attempts, demanding the creation of institutions and officers to vigorously enforce the law and relieve the great burden placed on JPs. See for example the articles in the *Pennsylvania Gazette*, April 7, 1779.

69. "The Address of the Committee of the City and Liberties of Philadelphia, to their Fellow-Citizens throughout the United States," *Pennsylvania Packet*, June 24, 1779.
70. *Pennsylvania Packet*, May 27, 1779.
71. Ibid.; "In Committee," *Pennsylvania Packet*, June 12, 1779.
72. For depictions of the committees as a lower-class mobilization see Nash, *Unknown American Revolution*, 311; Rosswurm, *Arms, Country, and Class*, 185–87; Brunhouse, *The Counter Revolution in Pennsylvania*, 70–71; and Olton, *Artisans for Independence*, 85. Kenneth Owen, on the other hand, makes an important distinction between these committees and class antagonism. According to Owen, the committees deferred to the legitimacy of the legislature and deemed their actions a legitimate response to the exigencies of the time. See Owen, *Political Community in Revolutionary Pennsylvania*, chapter 2.
73. For example, in the city committee, thirteen of thirty-three members held an official position in the state government. In Lancaster, ten of twenty held offices in the civil government. For membership in the city committee, see *Pennsylvania Packet*, May 27, 1779. For membership in the Lancaster County Committee see *Pennsylvania Packet*, July 3, 1779.
74. The best account of the interworking of the committees is in Christopher Marshall's diary. Marshall, *Extracts from the Diary of Christopher Marshall*, 222.
75. Marshall, *Extracts from the Diary of Christopher Marshall*, 230. For petitions, see *Minutes of the Third General Assembly*, 122–28.
76. "Abstract from the Life of Charles Wilson Peale, written by himself some years past," undated, Papers of Joseph Reed, NYHS; "Philip Hagner's Account of the Fort Wilson Riot," undated, Papers of Joseph Reed, NYHS.
77. Draft of a speech by Joseph Reed, October 10, 1779, Papers of Joseph Reed, NYHS.
78. "An Act for the More Effectually Preventing Engrossing and Forestalling, For the Encouragment of Commerce and the Fair Trader, and for Other Purposes Therein Mentioned," October 8, 1779, *SLP*, 9:421–32.
79. See the list of officers for the city in the "Act for the More Effectually Preventing Engrossing" and the list of committee members in *Pennsylvania Packet*, May 27, 1779.
80. Olton, *Artisans for Independence*, 89–92; "An Act to Repeal Divers Acts of Assembly of this Commonwealth Herein After Mentioned, For Preventing Forestalling and Regrating, and for the Encouragement of Fair Dealing; and an Act Entitled 'An Act to Permit the Making of Whiskey and Other Spirits from Rye, Barley, or The Malt Made Thereof, Under Certain Restrictions Therein Mentioned'; and to Prohibit the Distilling any Whiskey or Other Spirits From Any other Grain, Meal, Malt or Flour," March 22, 1780, *SLP*, 10:175–76.

81. This is a crucial argument made by both Rosswurm and Bouton in their work on revolutionary Pennsylvania. Drawing on the work of E. P. Thompson, Rosswurm sees a competing dialectic at play in Pennsylvania. As Thompson found in eighteenth-century England, Rosswurm argues that the "political economy of self interest," what Thompson called the "new political philosophy of Adam Smith," had sway over state politicians and therefore left the maintenance of a "political economy of the public good" to futile extralegal activities carried out by the "lower sorts." Rosswurm, *Arms, Country, and Class*, 194–99; Bouton, *Taming Democracy*, 100–103. Gordon Wood also makes this argument in *Creation of the American Republic*. According to Wood, the "public good" as a political philosophy lost considerable popularity and force in the 1780s to the private interest and commercial pursuits of many Americans. See Wood, *The Creation of the American Republic*, 415–16.
82. Novak, "Public Economy and the Well-Ordered Market," 2–3. In this essay, Novak makes a crucial point: "These regulatory ideas and laws-in-action are out-of-synch only with the historical constructs and chronologies that have marginalized them" (3).
83. "An Act to Incorporate the Subscribers to the Bank of North America," April 1, 1782, *SLP*, 10:406–8.
84. Legislators quoted in Rappaport, *Stability and Change*, 143.
85. For the popularity of the bank in these initial years see Olton, *Artisans for Independence*, 90–91.
86. Speech of Robert Morris in the General Assembly, March 30, 1786, in *Debates and Proceedings . . . Annulling the Charter of the Bank*, 36.
87. Colbert, "Strictures on the Bank and on a Paper Currency," *Pennsylvania Packet*, March 31, 1785; Speech of John Smilie in the General Assembly, March 29, 1786, in *Debates and Proceedings . . . Annulling the Charter of the Bank*, 25.
88. Rappaport, *Stability and Change*, 190.
89. Ibid.
90. Speech of William Findley in the General Assembly, March 31, 1786, in *Debates and Proceedings . . . Annulling the Charter of the Bank*, 65.
91. "An Act to Revive the Incorporation of the Subscribers to the Bank of North America," March 17, 1787, *SLP*, 12:412–16.
92. John Smilie quoted in Rappaport, *Stability and Change*, 207.
93. "An Act for the Further Security of the Government," *SLP*, 9:238.
94. Police power, or "internal police," as revolutionaries termed it, is a key instrument of state sovereignty, as it is often used to restrict private rights for the public benefit and can do so, under the language of "protection," by regulating the morals, health, safety, and property of citizens. Revolutionary state leaders used the language of "protection" to justify not only

coercive policies toward the "disaffected" but the creation of institutions and officers to enforce those policies, providing important precedents for a broad use of police powers to regulate the moral and social order of the individual states well into the twentieth century. Importantly, William Novak explains that the "triumph" of police power as a "legal terminology" was the main factor in individual states' efforts in the nineteenth century to "centralize the disparate powers of states and localities." Novak, *The People's Welfare*, 13. However, I would argue that the development and triumph of police powers occurred during the revolution, led by state leaders who used it to justify and enforce regulatory policies regarding the "disaffected."

95. Blaakman, "Speculation Nation," 171–89; Pearson, "A New Birth of Regulation," 432–34; Novak, "Public Economy and the Well-Ordered Market."
96. *Pennsylvania Gazette*, November 15, 1780.
97. John Adams to Abigail Adams, July 10, 1776, *The Adams Papers*, 42.
98. Allen, "Diary of James Allen," 282, 191.
99. Brunhouse, *The Counter-Revolution in Pennsylvania*, 36.
100. Warden, "The Infamous Fitch," 382.
101. Colonel Thomas Hartley to James Wilson, December 22, 1776, quoted in Selsam, *The Pennsylvania Constitution*, 239.
102. George Kriebel, for example stated bluntly that he would not abjure his allegiance to the king "for the present time" as "it is so uncertain upon what side God Almighty will bestow the Victory." George Kriebel's Declaration, 1777, *PA*, 1:5: 432–33. See also Molovinsky, "Tax Collection Problems in Revolutionary Pennsylvania," 253–59.
103. *Pennsylvania Packet and General Advertiser*, September 10, 1778.
104. Marshall, *Extracts from the Diary of Christopher Marshall*, 123.
105. Thomas Wharton Jr. to John Morris, August 2, 1777, *PA*, 2:3: 99.
106. Skocpol, "Bringing the State Back In," 7. Similarly, Steve Pincus argues that in the creation of a modern state, particularly during a revolution, state officials modify and develop state infrastructure in an attempt to attain state legitimacy. Moreover, Pincus contends that the modification and development of the modern state is not only predicated on the exigencies during the moment of creation but is rooted in long-term grievances of the populace. The formation of the state, then, serves a twofold purpose: state actors are at once translating long-held grievances into revolutionary action while also using these tools of the state to exert authority and suppress political dissidence in the quest for state legitimacy. See Pincus, *1688: The First Modern Revolution*, 1–10, 30–45.
107. "An Act for the Further Security of the Government," April 1, 1778, *SLP*, 9:404; "A Further Supplement to the Test Laws of this State," October 1, 1779, *SLP*,, 9:238.

108. "An Act Obliging the Male White Inhabitants of this State to Give Assurance of Allegiance to the Same and for Other Purposes Therein Mentioned," June 13, 1777, *SLP*, 9:110.
109. "An Act to Empower the Supreme Executive Council and Justices of the Supreme Court," *SLP*, 9:440–42.
110. Fisher, "Journal of Samuel Rowland Fisher," 149.
111. Ibid., 163–68; Thomas McKean to Sarah McKean, July 26, 1779, in *Letters of Delegates to Congress*, 13:294.
112. Smyth, "Narrative," 160–63.
113. "Petition from 27 people in the Easton Jail," 1784, Lancaster County Petitions Folder, Miscellaneous Documents, 1682–1800, HSP.
114. Lewis Nicola to President Wharton, January 22, 1778, *PA* 1:6:198.
115. Fisher, "Journal of Samuel Rowland Fisher," 176, 179, 183, 189, 279.
116. Ibid., 185, 439; Samuel Rowland Fisher, Clemency File, Records of Pennsylvania's Revolutionary Governments, 1775–1790, Reel 37, piece 326, PHMC.
117. "An Act to Empower the Supreme Executive Council of this Commonwealth to provide for the Security thereof in Special Cases where no Provision is Already Made by Law," September 6, 1777, *SLP*, 9:138–40; "Attainder of Divers Traitors if they Render not Themselves by a Certain Day and for Vesting their Estates in this Commonwealth and for more Effectually Discovering the Same and for Ascertaining and Satisfying the Lawful Debts and Claims Thereupon," March 6, 1778, *SLP*, 9:201–15; "An Act for the Further Security of Government," April 1, 1778, *SLP*, 9:238–45; "A Supplement to the Act, Entitled 'An Act for the Further Security of the Government,'" September 10, 1778, *SLP*, 9:284–86; "A Further Supplement to the Act, Entitled 'An Act for the Further Security of the Government,'" December 5, 1778, *SLP*, 9: 303–8; "An Act to Empower the Supreme Executive Council and Justices of the Supreme Court," *SLP*, 9: 440–42.
118. In the law establishing oaths of allegiance, the lieutenants and their deputies were given the power to disarm those who refused. By the end of the following year, the county lieutenants served directly at the command of the president of the SEC, which, as President Wharton pointed out, "multiplied the business of the Lieutenants." Thomas Wharton, "Circular Letter," August 28, 1777, in Documents Relating to the Province of Pennsylvania and to the American Revolution, no. 41, APS.
119. Ettwein, "A Short Account," 192–93.
120. Lieutenant John Wetzel to President Wharton, May 25, 1778, *PA*, 1:6:551–52.
121. For more on Wetzel, see Fox, *Sweet Land of Liberty*, 73–96.
122. Joseph Reed to John Piper, July 24, 1779, *PA*, 1:8:578.

123. "An Act to Empower the Supreme Executive Council of this Commonwealth to provide for the Security thereof in Special Cases where no Provision is Already Made by Law," September 6, 1777, *SLP*, 9:138–40.
124. John Wetzel to President Wharton, May 25, 1778, *PA*, 1:6:551–52.
125. Joseph Reed to John Piper, July 24, 1779, *PA*, 1:8:578; John Wetzel to President Wharton, May 25, 1778, *PA*, 1:6:551–52.
126. George Bryan to John Thorne, May 25, 1778, *PA*, 2:3:170.
127. Joseph Reed to Andrew Boyd, June 7, 1779, *PA*, 1:7:471.
128. Bartram Galbraith to Joseph Reed, September 4, 1779, *PA*, 1:7:679–80.
129. *Pennsylvania Ledger*, April 22, 1778.
130. Jasper Yeates to James Burd, September 4, 1777, Burd-Shippen Family Papers, Reel 2, Folder 40, PHMC.
131. Marietta and Rowe, *Troubled Experiment*, 186.
132. For the incarceration of the disaffected, see Jones, "The Rage of Tory-Hunting," 730–42; and Miller, *Dangerous Guests*, 125–51.
133. Loyalist prisoners quoted in Brown, *The Good Americans*, 142.
134. For the view of the militia by Continental army officers see Cox, *A Proper Sense of Honor*, xvi. As John Shy explained, historically "the militia enforced law and maintained order." Add to this point that mustering for militia service during the Revolutionary War, whether drafted or voluntary, was a political choice—a demonstration of allegiance to neighbors and officials—and you get a powerful force of men who could continue to demonstrate their fidelity by rooting out the disloyal. Shy, *A People Numerous and Armed*, 237.
135. Graydon, *Memoirs*, 323.
136. William Denniston, Revolutionary War Pension Files, W2924, National Archives; Jacob Van Artsdalen, Revolutionary War Pension Files, W3894, National Archives ; George Simmers, Revolutionary War Pension Files, S22511, National Archives; John Hill, Revolutionary War Pension Files, W5298, National Archives.
137. James Fulton, Revolutionary War Pension Files, S22779, National Archives. All too often historians depict the militia as uncontrolled individuals, harassing the disaffected for their own ends rather than as an institution of the state carrying out policy. As a result, the militia and "the mob" or "the crowd" have been improperly intertwined. Such a critique does not mean that individual militiamen did not partake in violent crowd action—they certainly did. The Fort Wilson riot is a crucial reminder of that fact. Nonetheless, it should be noted that the militia involved in that riot sought to make their actions legitimate by first taking their ideas to the county lieutenant, Charles Wilson Peale. In any event, their subsequent actions do not make every act of violence carried out by the militia

illegitimate or, rather, outside official sanction. For an example of the conflation of violence carried out by the militia and crowds see Ousterhout, *A State Divided*, 178. See also Smith, "The Attack on Fort Wilson"; Alexander, "The Fort Wilson Incident of 1779"; and Slaughter, "Crowds in Eighteenth-Century America."

138. Council to John Lacey, March 12, 1778, *PA*, 1:6:361; General Lacey's Orders to his Scouting Party, March 19, 1778, in Hazard, *The Register of Pennsylvania*, 3:308.

139. *Pennsylvania Ledger*, March 25, 1778. See also *Pennsylvania Ledger*, March 21, April 22, and May 16, 1778.

140. John Lacey to John Armstrong, May 7, 1778, in Hazard, *The Register of Pennsylvania*, 3:343–44.

141. Lawrence Fegan, American Loyalist Claims, Series II, AO 13/102, 514, British National Archives.

142. Allen, "Diary of James Allen," 195–96. See also "Warrant to Arrest Certain Persons," 1777, *PA*, 2:5:478.

143. Richard Swanwick, American Loyalist Claims, Series II, AO 13/72, British National Archives; Richard Swanwick to Captain Henry, June 15, 1778, *PA*, 2:3:182–83; "Forfeited Estates, Estate of Richard Swanwick," *PA*, 6:12:210–11.

144. "State of Accounts of the County Lieutenants During the War of the Revolution, 1777–1789," *PA*, 3:2:264; *Pennsylvania Ledger*, April 25, 1778.

145. "The Humble Petition of Sundry Persons of Distinguished Attachment to the Independence of this and the United States," 1780, William Lenoir Papers, Southern Historical Collection, Wilson Library, University of North Carolina at Chapel Hill, Box 31. Thank you to Matthew Spooner for providing me this petition along with many other helpful suggestions.

146. *Pennsylvania Packet*, April 8, 1778.

147. Dorland et al., "The Second Troop of Philadelphia Cavalry," *PMHB* 45, no. 3 (1921): 265; *Pennsylvania Gazette*, May 31, 1780.

148. *Minutes of the Supreme Executive Council, Colonial Records*, 12:539. For an example of the change, compare the procession at the election of Thomas Wharton on March 6, 1777, with the procession after the election of Joseph Reed in November 1780. See *Pennsylvania Evening Post*, March 6, 1777, and *Pennsylvania Gazette*, November 15, 1780.

149. *Pennsylvania Gazette*, November 15, 1780.

150. Brown, *The Forum*, 326, 328.

151. *Pennsylvania Mercury*, October 20, 1786.

152. Thomas McKean to Sarah McKean, May 10, 1779, Box 6, Folder 2, HSP; Brown, *The Forum*, 327.

153. General John Armstrong to Vice President George Bryan, July 4 and September 10, 1778, *PA* 1:6:663, 744.

154. Allen, "Diary of James Allen," 285.

155. "An Act Declaring What Shall be Treason and What Other Crimes and Practices Against the State Shall be Misprison of Treason," *SLP,* 9:46.
156. Warden, "The Infamous Fitch," 376–87.
157. Figures based on "Executions in the United States, 1608–2002: The Espy File" from the Death Penalty Information Center, Inter-university Consortium for Political and Social Research. Some of the executions for Pennsylvania are missing in this database, and I included those missing executions found in the Pennsylvania newspapers as well as those not listed but included in Teeters, "Public Executions in Pennsylvania," 85–164.
158. The data in this paragraph are based on a combination of a database of oyer and terminer cases that G. S. Rowe and Jack Marietta graciously supplied and table 3.2 of their work *Troubled Experiment,* 76. The discrepancy in the numbers (pardons versus actual executions) is due to reprieves and stays of execution that never turned into pardons but nonetheless did not result in executions.
159. Strong, *The Reason and Design of Public Punishments,* 14, 17.
160. Smyth, "Narrative," 160.
161. While Louis P. Masur argues that community reform was the ultimate goal of public executions, the focus on spectacle, the lack of publications expressing the last dying words of the condemned (unless they thanked state leaders), and the call for penal reform in the constitution that was based on the belief that sanguinary punishments did not mitigate crime or reform criminals and the community suggest that state power was the more prominent aspect of public executions in the early years of the state government. See Masur, *Rites of Execution,* 25–50.
162. Thomas McKean to William A. Atlee, June 5, 1778, in *Letters of Delegates to Congress,* 10:32–33.
163. *Minutes of the Supreme Executive Council, Colonial Records,* 5:31.
164. William Rogers, "Journal of Rev. William Rogers, 1779," *PA,* 2:15: 262.
165. *Royal Gazette* (New York), May 8, 1779; Fisher, "Journal of Samuel Rowland Fisher," 167.
166. Fisher, "Journal of Samuel Rowland Fisher," 167.
167. *Pennsylvania Packet,* May 4, 1779.
168. *Pennsylvania Gazette,* May 5, 1779. See also *Minutes of the Supreme Executive Council, PA,* 1:12:149, 458.
169. Rappaport, *Stability and Change,* 132.

Conclusion

1. Benjamin Franklin and the Pennsylvania Supreme Executive Council to the Pennsylvania General Assembly, November 11, 1785, *PBF* (unpublished series), http://www.franklinpapers.org.

2. "Pennsylvania's 1776 Constitution," in Thorpe, *The Federal and State Constitutions*, 5:3081.
3. See for example, Brunhouse, *The Counter-Revolution in Pennsylvania*; Bouton, *Taming Democracy*; and Holton, *Unruly Americans and the Origins of the Constitution*. Kenneth Owen challenges the sustainability of the counterrevolution thesis. According to Owen, popular extralegal mobilization had been a crucial factor in the revolution and Pennsylvania's political settlement. Neither the US Constitution nor the 1790 state constitution challenged the place of this "political toolkit" in early American politics. Owen's argument is an excellent start in any attempt at dismantling this long-held historical argument. Although Owen excellently portrays the persistence of extralegal politics in Pennsylvania, he often divorces the political cause of these movements from the political and governmental goals of the revolution beyond popular sovereignty. Not only did Pennsylvanians mobilize as an expression of their belief in and reliance on popular sovereignty, but they used this "political toolkit" to force governmental change in an effort to enhance and modify the governance of the state to meet their expectations of a government that could provide for the security and protection of the community. These were central goals in the early years of the revolution and continued to be a mainstay in the politics of Pennsylvania throughout the eighteenth century. Nevertheless, Owen's work has critically informed my understanding of the importance of popular sovereignty and political inclusion in the revolutionary moment and to the development of American politics, both national and state. Owen, *Political Community in Revolutionary Pennsylvania*.
4. Thomas McKean to John Adams, April 30, 1787, quoted in Rowe, *Thomas McKean*, 243. See also *Pennsylvania Journal*, February 3, 1779, and July 7, 1784.
5. Speech of Cadwallader Colden, in Owen, *Political Community in Revolutionary Pennsylvania*, 117.
6. *Journal of the Council of Censors*, HSP; Council of Censors, *An Address of the Council of Censors to the Freemen of Pennsylvania*, 1; *A Candid Examination of the Address of the Minority of the Council of Censors to the People of Pennsylvania*, 13–16, 30–33; Jasper Yeates to James Burd, March 8, 1790, Burd-Shippen Family Papers, Reel 1, Folder 15. According to Yeates, Benjamin Rush and George Bryan, who rode together on the same circuit, refused to work with one another. As a result, the circuits in York, Cumberland, and Northumberland were stopped up. Yeates argued, "Will not the Suitors of Northumberland clamor if their Causes are hung up another Year without either Rhime or Reason?"

7. *Minutes of the First Session, of the Fourth General Assembly*, March 14, 1780, 225.
8. Ashmead, *Historical Sketch of Chester*, 55–56; Martin, *Chester and Its Vicinity*, 190–92. For the legislation see "An Act to Enable William Clingan, Thomas Bill, John Kinkead, Roger Kirk, John Sellers, John Wilson, and Joseph Davis to Build a New Court House and Prison in the County of Chester and Sell the Old Court House and Prison in the Borough of Chester," March 20, 1780, *SLP*, 10:143–44; "A Supplement to an Act," *SLP*, 11:276–78; and "An Act to Suspend An Act of General Assembly," March 30, 1785, *SLP*, 11:535–37.
9. "At a Meeting of Sundry Respectable Inhabitants of the County of Northampton, October 22, 1787," in *American Museum*, 2:394.
10. "A Meeting of the Inhabitants of the Borough of Carlisle, in the County of Cumberland," October 30, 1787, in *American Museum*, 2:393.
11. *Freeman's Journal*, September 26, 1787; *Independent Gazetteer*, October 2, 1787.
12. See Olton, *Artisans for Independence*, 117.
13. "The Petition of the Subscribers Freemen of the County of Franklin," *Carlisle Gazette*, January 30, 1788.
14. Maier, *Ratification*, 424.
15. Jensen, *Ratification of the Constitution by the States*, 2:459; see also 462–64.
16. Petition of Harrisburg Convention, September 3, 1788, in Wakelyn, *Birth of the Bill of Rights*, 1:49–51.
17. Speech of James Wilson, *Pennsylvania Packet*, October 10, 1787.
18. James Wilson at the Constitutional Convention, June 7, 1787, in *Secret Proceedings*, 107.
19. "Observations on the New Federal Constitution," *Pennsylvania Packet*, April 4, 1789.
20. Speech of James Wilson, *Pennsylvania Packet*, October 10, 1787. Debates over the Constitution, particularly over the sovereignty of the states against the national state envisioned by the Federalists, would be an enduring struggle throughout the United States. In Pennsylvania, frontiersmen resisted the Federalist agenda of crafting a national state in the Whiskey Rebellion. Throughout the state, democratic societies, ethnic associations, and a new political party structure also resisted and ultimately defeated the Federalist agenda. The gubernatorial election of Thomas McKean over James Ross, according to Douglas Bradburn, was the "first victory in the Republican 'Revolution of 1800'" that represented "a complete rejection of the Federalist vision of the national state." See Bradburn, *Citizenship Revolution*, 230–32. For the Whiskey Rebellion see Slaughter, *The Whiskey Rebellion*, 207.

21. *Pennsylvania Evening Herald,* October 17, 1787; "A Citizen of Franklin County," *Carlisle Gazette,* June 24, 1789; "The Memorial of the Subscribers," *Carlisle Gazette,* July 15, 1789; "Philadelphia," *Carlisle Gazette,* September 9, 1789. Pennsylvanians expressed similar criticisms of the government dating back to at least 1784. See Council of Censors, *An Address of the Council of Censors to the Freemen of Pennsylvania; A Candid Examination of the Address of the Minority of the Council of Censors to the People of Pennsylvania; An Alarm.*
22. Albert Gallatin to Alexander Addison, October 7, 1789, quoted in Burrows, *Albert Gallatin and the Political Economy of Republicanism,* 1:256.
23. Resolve in Assembly, March 28, 1789, in *Carlisle Gazette,* April 8, 1789; Tench Coxe to James Madison, March 24, 1789, *Papers of James Madison.*
24. "A Citizen of Franklin County," *Carlisle Gazette,* June 24, 1789; "The Memorial of the Subscribers," *Carlisle Gazette,* July 15, 1789.
25. "The Friends of Harmony," *Pennsylvania Packet,* April 29, 1789; *Federal Gazette,* October 6, 1788; "Lucius, Northumberland County to the People, No II," *Federal Gazette,* April 30, 1789.
26. *Pennsylvania Mercury,* March 11, 1790.
27. "The Friends of Harmony," *Pennsylvania Packet,* April 29, 1789; *Federal Gazette,* October 6, 1788; "Lucius, Northumberland County to the People, No II," *Federal Gazette,* April 30, 1789.
28. *Carlisle Gazette,* September 9, 1789.
29. William Findley to George Bryan, August 3, 1789, Papers of George Bryan, Box 3, HSP.
30. Findley, "William Findley: An Autobiographical Letter," *PMHB* 5, no. 4 (1881): 446.
31. William Findley quoted in Caldwell, *William Findley,* 206; Albert Gallatin quoted in Cachia-Riedl, "Albert Gallatin and the Politics of the New Nation," 13.
32. Constitution of Pennsylvania, 1790, in Thorpe, *Federal and State Constitutions,* 5:3092–3103.
33. "The Constitution of the Commonwealth of Pennsylvania," 1968, *Pennsylvania General Assembly,* https://www.legis.state.pa.us/cfdocs/legis/LI/consCheck.cfm?txtType=HTM&ttl=00&div=0&chpt=1.
34. "An Act to Establish the Judicial Courts of This Commonwealth in Conformity to the Alterations and Amendments in the Constitution," April 13, 1791, *SLP,* 14:110–20.
35. *Freeman's Journal,* December 23 and December 30, 1789.
36. *Freeman's Journal,* January 5, 1791.
37. "Lucius, Northumberland County to the People, No II," *Federal Gazette,* April 30, 1789.
38. "Friends and Fellow Citizens," *Freeman's Journal,* September 18, 1790.

39. *Freeman's Journal*, January 5, 1791.
40. *Soohan v. The City of Philadelphia*, 1859, in Casey and Harris, *Pennsylvania State Reports*, 30:18; *Commonwealth v. Ickhoff*, 1859, in Casey and Harris, *Pennsylvania State Reports*, 30:81; *O'Conner v. Pittsburgh*, 1851, in Casey and Harris, *Pennsylvania State Reports*, 18:189; *Downing v. McFadden*, 1851, in Casey and Harris, *Pennsylvania State Reports*, 18:338.
41. *Pennsylvania Mercury*, March 11, 1790.
42. Jefferson, "First Annual Message to Congress," in *PTJ*.

BIBLIOGRAPHY

Manuscripts
American Philosophical Society
Benjamin Franklin Papers, 1642–1841
Burd-Shippen Papers
Correspondence of Thomas and Richard Penn with James Hamilton, 1741–1771
Documents Relating to the Province of Pennsylvania and to the American Revolution
Jasper Yeates Papers
Peale-Sellers Family Collection
Pennsylvania Stamp Act and Non-Importation Resolution Collection
Shippen Family Papers
Timothy Horsfield Papers

British National Archives
American Loyalist Claims
Colonial Office Records
Journals of the Board of Trade
Original Correspondence of the Secretaries of State

Chester County Archives
Chester County Quarter Sessions Dockets
Chester County Quarter Sessions Papers
Chester County Provincial Tax Records
Chester County Quarter Sessions Indictment Files

Dauphin County Historical Society
Elder Collection

Historical Society of Pennsylvania
Bedford County Collection
Bradford Family Papers, 1620–1906
Chester County Miscellaneous Papers, 1684–1847
Irvine-Newbold Family Papers
Jasper Yeates Papers, 1733–1876

John William Wallace Collection of Ancient Records of Philadelphia, 1702–1847
Journal of the Council of Censors
Lancaster County Petitions, Miscellaneous Documents 1682–1800
Letters of Thomas Penn
Norris Family Papers, 1742–1860
Papers of George Bryan, 1756–1829
Papers of Thomas McKean, 1757–1792
Penn Family Papers
Pennsylvania Counties, Miscellaneous Records, 1701–1901
Shippen Family Papers
Simon Gratz Autograph Collection, 1517–1925
Smith Family Papers, 1728–1846
Supreme Court Dockets, 1753–1799
Thomas Penn Letterbook
William Moore Papers, 1764–1777

Library of Congress
Papers of George Bryan

National Archives
Revolutionary War Pension Files

New York Historical Society
Papers of Joseph Reed

Northampton County Courthouse
Northampton County Quarter Sessions Dockets

Pennsylvania Historical and Museum Commission, State Archives
Burd-Shippen Family Papers
Edward Shippen Thompson Collections
Jasper Yeates Family Papers
Records of the County Governments, Bedford County, Quarter Sessions Dockets
Records of Pennsylvania's Revolutionary Governments, 1775–1790

Quaker Collection, Haverford College
Richard Hockley Letterbook

William L. Clements Library, University of Michigan
Thomas Gage Papers
William Knox Papers

Newspapers and Magazines

American Museum, or Repository of Ancient and Modern Fugitive Pieces
American Weekly Mercury
Carlisle Gazette
Federal Gazette
Freeman's Journal; or, The North-American Intelligencer
Independent Gazetteer
Pennsylvania Chronicle
Pennsylvania Evening Herald
Pennsylvania Evening Post
Pennsylvania Gazette
Pennsylvania Journal
Pennsylvania Ledger: Or the Philadelphia Market-Day Advertiser
Pennsylvania Mercury
Pennsylvania Packet
Philadelphia Gazette
Porcupine's Gazette and United States Daily Advertiser
Rivington's New-York Gazetteer
South Carolina Gazette

Pamphlets, Broadsides, and Other Publications

An Account of the Robberies Committed by John Morrison. Philadelphia, 1751.
An Address to the Freeholders and Inhabitants of the Province of Pennsylvania. Philadelphia, 1764.
Advertisement and Not a Joke. Philadelphia, 1764.
An Alarm. Philadelphia, 1784.
Articles of Association in Pennsylvania, for the Defence of American Liberty. Philadelphia, 1775.
Barton, Thomas. *Conduct of the Paxton-Men*. Philadelphia, 1764.
———. *A* LETTER *from a* GENTLEMAN *in One of the Frontier Counties to His Friend in Philadelphia*. Philadelphia, 1764.
Beatty, Charles. *A Sermon Preached in Woodbury*. Philadelphia, 1752.
Beccaria, Cesare. *An Essay on Crimes and Punishments*. Charleston, SC, 1777.
Biddle, James. *To the Freeholders and Electors*. Philadelphia, 1765.
Burnaby, Andrew. *Travels through the Middle Settlements in North America: In the Years 1759 and 1760. With Observations Upon the State of the Colonies*. London, 1775.
A Candid Examination of the Address of the Minority of the Council of Censors to the People of Pennsylvania. Philadelphia, 1784.
Carmichael, John. *A Self-Defensive War*. Philadelphia, 1775.

Chew, Samuel. *The Speech of Samuel Chew, Esq.* Philadelphia, 1741.
Council of Censors. *An Address of the Council of Censors to the Freemen of Pennsylvania.* Philadelphia, 1784.
———. *Religion and Public Spirit: A Valedictory Address to the Senior Class, Delivered in Nassau Hall.* New York, 1761.
Debates and Proceedings of the General Assembly of Pennsylvania, On the Memorials Praying A Repeal of the Law Annulling the Charter of the Bank. Philadelphia: Mathew Carey, 1786.
Demophilus. *The Genuine Principles of the Ancient Saxon, or English Constitution.* Philadelphia, 1776.
Dickinson, John. *Friends and Countrymen.* Philadelphia, 1765.
———. *The Late Regulations Respecting the British Colonies.* Philadelphia, 1765.
———. *A Reply to a Piece called the Speech of Joseph Galloway, Esquire.* Philadelphia, 1764.
———. *A Speech Delivered in the House of Assembly of the Province of Pennsylvania, May 24th, 1764.* Philadelphia, 1764.
Dickinson, John, et al. *Fellow Citizens and Countrymen.* Philadelphia, 1772.
Dove, David James. *Labour in Vain: No 1. Or, An Attempt to Wash the Black-Moor White.* Philadelphia, 1758.
An Essay of a Frame of Government for Pennsylvania. Philadelphia, 1776.
An Examination and Refutation of Mr. Gilbert Tennent's Remarks. Philadelphia, 1742.
Extracts from the Votes and Proceedings of the Committee of Observation of Lancaster. Lancaster, PA, 1775.
Four Letters on Interesting Subjects. Philadelphia, 1776.
Franklin, Benjamin. *Cool Thoughts on the Present Situation of Our Public Affairs. In a Letter to a Friend in the Country.* Philadelphia, 1764.
Galloway, Joseph. *A Letter to the People of Pennsylvania; Occasioned by the Assembly's Passing that Important Act, for Constitution the Judges of the Supreme Courts and Common-Pleas, During Good* BEHAVIOUR. Philadelphia, 1760.
———. *The Speech of Joseph Galloway, Esq.* London, 1764.
———. *A True and Impartial State of the Province of Pennsylvania.* Philadelphia, 1759.
A German Freeholder. Philadelphia, 1770.
Goodlet, John. *A Vindication of the Associate Synod.* Philadelphia, 1767.
Hunt, Isaac. *A Continuation of the Exercises, in Scurrility Hall.* Philadelphia, 1765.
———. *A Humble Attempt at Scurrility.* Philadelphia, 1765.
Hutcheson, Francis. *A System of Moral Philosophy.* London, 1755.
Keith, William. *A Letter to his Majesty's Justices of the Peace.* Philadelphia, 1718.
Logan, James. *The Charge Delivered from the Bench.* Philadelphia, 1723.

———. *The Charge Delivered from the Bench to the Grand Inquest, at a Court of Oyer and Terminer and General Goal-Delivery*. Philadelphia, 1736.
———. *The Latter Part of the Charge Delivered from the Bench to the Grand Inquest, at a Court of Oyer and Terminer and Gaol Delivery*. Philadelphia, 1733.
Lover of Liberty and a Mechanic's Friend. *To the Free and Patriotic Inhabitants of the City of Philadelphia and the Province of Pennsylvania*. Philadelphia, 1770.
Lucifer's Decree, after a Fray. Philadelphia, 1765.
McClenchan, William. *A Letter, from a Clergyman in Town*. Philadelphia, 1764.
McKean, Thomas. *A Charge Delivered to the Grand-Jury at York*. Lancaster, PA, 1778.
Minutes of the First Session, of the Fourth General Assembly of the Commonwealth of Pennsylvania. Philadelphia, 1780.
Minutes of the Third General Assembly of the Commonwealth of Pennsylvania. Philadelphia, 1779.
Montgomery, Joseph. *A Sermon Preached at Christiana Bridge and Newcastle*. Philadelphia, 1775.
Moore, William. *A Preface to a Memorial Delivered to the Assembly*. Philadelphia, 1757.
"A New Song, in High Vogue in Northampton County." Easton, PA, 1771.
Observations on the late Epitaph, In a Letter from a Gentleman in the Country to his Friend in Philadelphia. Philadelphia, 1764.
Penn, William. *An Address to Protestants of all Persuasions; More Especially the Magistracy and Clergy; for the Promotion of Virtue and Charity*. London, 1679.
———. *A Further Account of the Province of Pennsylvania and its Improvements, for the Satisfaction of those that are Adventurers, and enclined to be so*. London, 1685. In *Original Narratives of Early American History*, vol. 12, edited by J. Franklin Jameson, 259–78. Charlottesville: University of Virginia Press, 1912.
Philanthropos. *The Universal Peace-Maker or Modern Author's Instructor*. Philadelphia, 1764.
Philo-Pennsylvania. *To the Freemen of the Province of Pennsylvania*. Philadelphia, 1773.
The Plot. By Way of a Burlesk. Philadelphia, 1764.
A Protestation of the Several Members of the Protestant Lutheran and Reformed Religions in the City of Philadelphia, jointly Concerned in the Lease of their Meeting-House in Arch-Street, about the late Commotion which happened on Sunday the 18th of July 1742. Philadelphia, 1742.
A Riddle. Philadelphia, 1770.
Rusticus. *Liberty: A Poem*. Philadelphia, 1768.
The Scribler: Being a Letter from a Gentleman in Town to his Friend in the Country Concerning the Present State of Public Affairs. Philadelphia, 1764.

Six Arguments Against Chusing Joseph Galloway. Philadelphia, 1766.
Smith, James. *An Account of the Remarkable Occurrences in the Life and Travels of Col. James Smith*. Lexington, KY, 1799.
Smith, Robert. *A Wheel in the Middle of a Wheel: Or, On Harmony and Connexion of Various Acts of Divine Providence. A Sermon Delivered before the second Rev. Presbytery of New Castle*. Philadelphia, 1759.
Smith, William. *A Brief View of the Conduct of Pennsylvania for the Year 1755*. London, 1756.
Strong, Nathan. *The Reason and Design of Public Punishments*. Hartford, CT, 1777.
Tennent, Gilbert. *The Danger of an Unconverted Ministry*. Philadelphia, 1740.
———. *The Late Association for Defence encouraged or The Lawfulness of a Defensive War Represented in a Sermon Preach'd at Philadelphia*. Philadelphia, 1748.
To the Freeholders and Electors of the City and County of Philadelphia. Philadelphia, 1764.
To the Tradesmen, Farmers, and Other Inhabitants of the City and County of Philadelphia. Philadelphia, 1770.
A Tradesman's Address to his Countrymen. Philadelphia, 1772.
Williamson, Hugh. *Plain Dealer Number II*. Philadelphia, 1764.
———. *The Plain Dealer: Or Remarks on Quaker Politics, Number III*. Philadelphia, 1764.
Wilson, James. *Considerations on the Nature and Extent of the Legislative Authority of the British Parliament*. Philadelphia, 1774.

Other Printed Primary Sources

Adams, John. *The Adams Papers Digital Edition*. Edited by C. James Taylor. Charlottesville: University of Virginia Press, Rotunda, 2008–19.
———. *Old Family Letters*. Edited by Alexander Biddle. Philadelphia, 1892.
Allen, James. "Diary of James Allen, Esq., of Philadelphia, Counselor-at-Law, 1770–1778." *Pennsylvania Magazine of History and Biography* 9, nos. 2, 3 and 4 (1885–86): 176–96, 278–96, 424–41.
Archives of the State of New Jersey. Edited by Frederick W. Ricord and William Nelson. Newark, NJ: Daily Advertiser, 1885.
Bouquet, Henry. *The Papers of Henry Bouquet*. Edited by Louis M. Waddell. Harrisburg: Pennsylvania Historical and Museum Commission, 1994.
Boyd, Julian P., ed. *The Susquehanna Company Papers*. Ithaca, NY: Cornell University Press, 1962.
Brown, David Paul. *The Forum: Or, Forty Years of Full Practice at the Philadelphia Bar*. Philadelphia: R. H. Small, 1856.
Brown, William Hand, ed. *Archives of Maryland: Proceedings of the Council of Maryland*. Baltimore: Maryland Historical Society, 1912.

Casey, Joseph, and George Harris, ed. *Pennsylvania State Reports: Cases Decided by the Supreme Court of Pennsylvania*. Philadelphia, 1858, 1859.
Clitherall, James. "Extracts from the Diary of Dr. James Clitherall, 1776." *Pennsylvania Magazine of History and Biography* 22, no. 4 (1898): 468–74.
Colonial Records. Edited by Samuel Hazard. Harrisburg, PA: Theo. Fenn, 1851.
Davies, K. G., ed. *Documents of the American Revolution, 1770–1783*. Colonial Office series. Shannon: Irish University Press, 1972.
Day, Sherman, ed. *Historical Collections of the State of Pennsylvania*. Philadelphia: George W. Gorton, 1843.
"Diary of a Voyage from Rotterdam to Philadelphia in 1728." Translated by Julius F. Sachse, *Pennsylvania German Society*. Lancaster, PA, 1909.
Dickinson, John. *The Life and Times of John Dickinson, 1732–1808*. Edited by Charles J. Stillé. Philadelphia: Historical Society of Pennsylvania, 1891.
Dorland, W. A. Newman, David Snyder, Abraham Duffield, Casper Dull, Joseph Reed, Wm. Dean, William Coats, and George Smith. "The Second Troop of Philadelphia Cavalry." *Pennsylvania Magazine of History and Biography*, 47, 48 and 49, nos. 1, 2, 3 and 4 (1921): 75–94, 163–91, 270–84, 357–75.
Dunbar, John R., ed. *The Paxton Papers*. The Hague: Martinus Nijhoff, 1957.
Ettwein, John. "A Short Account of the Disturbances in America and of the Brethren's Conduct and Suffering in this Connection." In *John Ettwein and the Moravian Church during the Revolutionary Period*, edited by Kenneth Gardiner Hamilton, 188–97. Bethlehem, PA: Times Publishing, 1940.
Findley, William. "William Findley of Westmoreland, Pa., Author of 'History of the Insurrection in the Western Counties of Pennsylvania.': An Autobiographical Letter." *Pennsylvania Magazine of History and Biography* 5, no. 4 (1881): 440–50.
Fisher, Samuel Rowland. "Journal of Samuel Rowland Fisher, of Philadelphia, 1779–1781." *Pennsylvania Magazine of History and Biography* 41, nos. 2, 3 and 4 (1917): 145–97, 274–333, 399–457.
Force, Peter, ed. *American Archives*. Washington, DC, 1837.
Foulke, Samuel. "A Memorandum Kept by Samuel Foulke of the Pennsylvania Assembly in 1761–1762." *Pennsylvania Magazine of History and Biography* 8, no. 4 (1884): 407–13.
Franklin, Benjamin. *The Autobiography of Benjamin Franklin*. Edited by Peter Conn. Philadelphia: University of Pennsylvania Press, 2005.
———. *The Papers of Benjamin Franklin*. Edited by Leonard W. Labaree, William B. Willcox, Claude A. Lopez, Barbara B. Oberg, and Ellen K. Cohn. New Haven, CT: Yale University Press, 1959–2018
Gibson, James E., John Morton, John Hancock, Daniel Roberdeau, Henry Haller, Charles Shoemaker, Joseph Heister, Mark Bird, and Thomas McKean. "The Pennsylvania Provincial Conference of 1776." *Pennsylvania Magazine of History and Biography* 58, no. 4 (1934): 312–41.

Graydon, Alexander. *Memoirs of His Own Time*. Philadelphia: Lindsay and Blackston, 1846.
Hazard, Samuel, ed. *The Register of Pennsylvania Devoted to the Preservation of Facts and Documents and Every Other Kind of Useful Information Respectibe the State of Pennsylvania*. Philadelphia: Wm. F. Geddes, 1829–33.
Headlam, Cecil and Arthur Percival Newton, eds. *Calendar of State Papers Colonial, America and West Indies*. Vol. 39. London: His Majesty's Stationary Office, 1930.
House of Lords Manuscripts, 1695–1697. London: Eyre and Spottiswoode, 1903.
Hunt, Leigh. *The Autobiography of Leigh Hunt*. New York: Harper and Brothers, 1850.
Jefferson, Thomas. *The Papers of Thomas Jefferson Digital Edition*. Edited by Barbara B. Oberg and J. Jefferson Looney. Charlottesville: University of Virginia Press, Rotunda, 2008.
Jensen, Merrill, ed. *Ratification of the Constitution by the States: Pennsylvania*. Madison: State Historical Society of Wisconsin, 1976.
Journal of the Commissioners for Trade and Plantations from January 1759 to December 1763. London: His Majesty's Stationery Office, 1935.
Labaree, Leonard W., ed. *Royal Instructions to British Colonial Governors, 1670–1776*. New York: D. Appleton, 1935.
Letters and Papers Relating Chiefly to the Provincial History of Pennsylvania with some Notices of the Writers. Edited by Thomas Balch. Philadelphia: Crissy and Markley, 1855.
Letters of Delegates to Congress, 1774–1789. Edited by Paul Hubert Smith and Ronald M. Gephart. Washington, DC: Library of Congress, 1976.
Madison, James. *The Papers of James Madison Digital Edition*. Edited by J. C. A. Stagg. Charlottesville: University of Virginia Press, Rotunda, 2010.
Marshall, Christopher. *Extracts from the Diary of Christopher Marshall*. Edited by William Duane. Albany, NY: Joel Munsell, 1877.
Minutes and Letters of the Coetus of the German Reformed Congregations in Pennsylvania, 1747–1792. Philadelphia: Reformed Church Publication Board, 1903.
Minutes of the Provincial Council of Pennsylvania, Colonial Records. Harrisburg, 1851.
Mittelberger, Gottlieb. *Journey to Pennsylvania in the Year 1750 and Return to Germany in the Year 1754*. Translated and Edited by Carl T. Eben. Philadelphia: John Jos. McVey, 1898.
Montesquieu, Charles de Secondat. *The Spirit of the Laws*. Edited by Anne M. Cohler, Basia Carolyn Miller, and Harold Samuel Stone. Cambridge: Cambridge University Press, 1989.
Moraley, William. *The Infortunate: The Voyage and Adventures of William Moraley, Indentured Servant*. Edited by Susan E. Klepp and Billy G. Smith. Philadelphia: Pennsylvania State Press, 2005.

Muhlenberg, Henry Melchior. *The Journals of Henry Melchior Muhlenberg.* Edited and translated by T. G. Tappert and J. W. Doberstein. Philadelphia: Lutheran Historical Society, 1942.

"Original Letters and Documents." *Pennsylvania Magazine of History and Biography* 5, no. 3 (1881): 349–50.

Penn, William. *The Papers of William Penn.* Edited by Richard S. Dunn and Mary Maples Dunn. Philadelphia: University of Pennsylvania Press, 1982.

Pennsylvania Archives. Edited by Samuel Hazard, John Blair Linn, William Henry Egle, George Edward Reed, and Thomas Lynch Montgomery. Harrisburg, PA: Printer to the State, 1852–1935.

Perry, William Stevens, ed., *Papers Relating to the History of the Church in Pennsylvania, 1680–1778.* Privately printed, 1871.

Quincy, Josiah. "Journal of Josiah Quincy, Junior, 1773." *Proceedings of the Massachusetts Historical Society* 49 (1916): 455–80.

Reed, Joseph. *Life and Correspondence of Joseph Reed.* Edited by William Bradford Reed. Philadelphia: Lindsay and Blakiston, 1847.

Reports of Cases Ruled and Adjudged in the Courts of Pennsylvania before and since the Revolution. Edited by Alexander J. Dallas. New York: Banks and Brothers, 1889.

Rush, Benjamin. *Letters of Benjamin Rush.* Edited by L. H. Butterfield. Princeton, NJ: Princeton University Press, 1951.

Sachse, Julius Friedrich, and Justus Falckner. "The Missive of Justus Falckner, of Germantown, Concerning the Religious Condition of Pennsylvania in the Year 1701." *Pennsylvania Magazine of History and Biography* 21, no. 2 (1897): 216–23.

Sansom, Hannah Callender. *The Diary of Hannah Callender Sansom: Sense and Sensibility in the Age of the American Revolution.* Edited by Susan E. Klepp and Karin Wulf. Ithaca, NY: Cornell University Press, 2010.

Secret Proceedings and Debates of the Convention Assembled at Philadelphia, in the Year 1787, for the Purpose of Forming the Constitution of the United States of America. Albany, NY: Websters and Skinners, 1821.

Smyth, John Ferdinand Dalziel. "Narrative or Journal of Capt. John Ferdinand Dalziel Smyth of the Queen's Rangers." *Pennsylvania Magazine of History and Biography* 39, no. 2 (1915): 143–69.

Spotswood, Alexander, John Gray, Edward Jeffreys, John Baskett, Micajah Perry, and Robert Carey, eds. "The Case of the Proprietor of Pensilvania &C., About the Appointing a New Deputy-Governor." *Pennsylvania Magazine of History and Biography* 39, no. 2 (1915): 201–15.

Sprague, William B., ed. *Annals of the American Pulpit.* New York: Robert Carter and Brothers, 1858.

The Statutes at Large of Pennsylvania from 1682 to 1809. Edited by Robert L. Cable. Harrisburg, PA: Legislative Reference Bureau, 2001.

St. Clair, Arthur. *The St. Clair Papers: The Life and Public Services of Arthur St. Clair*. Edited by William Henry Smith. Cincinnati: Robert Clarke, 1882.

Thomas, Governor George. "Some Selections from the Peters Papers in the Library of the Historical Society of Pennsylvania." *Pennsylvania Magazine of History and Biography* 29, no. 4 (1995): 451–66.

Thomson, Alexander. "Franklin County One Hundred Years Ago." *Pennsylvania Magazine of History and Biography* 8, no. 3 (1884): 311–18.

Thomson, Charles. "Early Days of the Revolution in Philadelphia." *Pennsylvania Magazine of History and Biography* 2, no. 4 (1878): 411–23.

Thorpe, Francis Newton, ed. *The Federal and State Constitutions*. Washington, DC: Government Printing Office, 1909.

Voltaire, Francois-Marie Arouet. *Philosophical Dictionary*. Part 1. Kessigner, 2003.

Wakelyn, Jon L., ed. *Birth of the Bill of Rights: Encyclopedia of the Antifederalists*. Westport, CT: Greenwood, 2004.

Washington, George. *The Papers of George Washington Digital Edition*. Charlottesville: University of Virginia Press, Rotunda, 2008.

Secondary Sources

Albert, George D. *History of the County of Westmoreland, Pennsylvania, with Biographical Sketches of Many of the Pioneers and Prominent Men*. Philadelphia: L. H. Everts, 1882.

Alexander, John K. "The Fort Wilson Incident of 1779: A Case Study of the Revolutionary Crowd." *William and Mary Quarterly*, 3rd ser., 31, no. 4 (1974): 589–612.

Anderson, Fred. *Crucible of War: The Seven Years' War and the Fate of Empire in British North America, 1754–1766*. New York: Vintage Books, 2001.

Andrews, Charles M. "The American Revolution: An Interpretation." *American Historical Review* 31, no. 2 (1926): 219–32.

Appleby, Joyce. "Commercial Farming and the 'Agrarian Myth' in the Early Republic." *Journal of American History* 68 (1982): 833–49.

Appleby, Joyce, James Jacob, and Margaret Jacob. Introduction to *The Origins of Anglo-American Radicalism*, 1–22. Edited by James Jacob and Margaret Jacob. London: Allen and Unwin, 1984.

Arnold, Douglas M. *A Republican Revolution: Ideology and Politics in Pennsylvania, 1776–1790*. New York: Garland, 1989.

Ashmead, Henry Graham. *Historical Sketch of Chester, on Delaware*. Chester: Republican Steam Printing House, 1883.

———. *History of Delaware County, Pennsylvania*. Philadelphia: L. H. Evert, 1884.

Bailyn, Bernard. *The Ideological Origins of the American Revolution*. Enlarged ed. Cambridge, MA: Belknap, 1992.

———. *Voyagers to the West: A Passage in the Peopling of America on the Eve of the Revolution*. New York: Vintage Books, 1988.

Ball, Duane. "Dynamics of Population and Wealth." *Journal of Interdisciplinary History* 6, no. 4 (1976): 621–44.

Becker, Charles Lotus. *The History of Political Parties in the Province of New York, 1760–1776*. Madison: University of Wisconsin Press, 1968.

Beeman, Richard R. *Plain, Honest Men: The Making of the American Constitution*. New York: Random House, 2009.

———. *The Varieties of Political Experience in Eighteenth Century America*. Philadelphia: University of Pennsylvania Press, 2004.

Bellesiles, Michael A. "The Establishment of Legal Structures on the Frontier: The Case of Revolutionary Vermont." *Journal of American History* 73, no. 4 (1987): 895–915.

Blaakman, Michael A. "Speculation Nation: Land and Mania in the Revolutionary American Republic, 1776–1803." PhD diss., Yale University, 2016.

Bockelman, Wayne. "Continuity and Change in Revolutionary Pennsylvania." PhD diss., Northwestern University, 1969.

———. "Local Politics in Pre-Revolutionary Lancaster County." *Pennsylvania Magazine of History and Biography* 97, no. 1 (1973): 45–74.

Bonomi, Patricia. *Under the Cope of Heaven: Religion, Society, and Politics in Colonial America*. New York: Oxford University Press, 1986.

Boorstin, Daniel Joseph. *The Genius of American Politics*. Chicago: University of Chicago Press, 1958.

Boss, Ronald I. "The Development of Social Religion: A Contradiction of French Free Thought." *Journal of the History of Ideas* 34, no. 4 (1973): 577–89.

Bossenga, Gail. "Origins of the French Revolution." *History Compass* 5, no. 4 (2007): 1294–1337.

Bouton, Terry. *Taming Democracy: "The People," the Founders, and the Troubled Ending of the American Revolution*. New York: Oxford University Press, 2007.

Bradburn, Douglas. *The Citizenship Revolution: Politics and the Creation of the American Union, 1774–1804*. Charlottesville: University of Virginia Press, 2009.

———. "The Eschatological Origins of the English Empire." In *Early Modern Virginia: Reconsidering the Old Dominion*, edited by Douglas Bradburn and John C. Coombs, 15–48. Charlottesville: University of Virginia Press, 2011.

Brannon, Rebecca. *From Revolution to Reunion: The Reintegration of the South Carolina Loyalists*. Columbia: University of South Carolina Press, 2016.

Breen, T. H. *The Marketplace of Revolution: How Consumer Politics Shaped American Independence*. New York: Oxford University Press, 2004.

Brewer, John. *The Sinews of Power: War, Money, and the English State, 1688–1783*. New York: Alfred A. Knopf, 1989.

Broderick, Francis L. "Pulpit, Physics, and Politics: The Curriculum of the College of New Jersey, 1746–1794." *William and Mary Quarterly*, 3rd ser., 6, no. 1 (1949): 42–68.

Brown, Irene Q., and Richard D. Brown. *The Hanging of Ephraim Wheeler: A Story of Rape, Incest, and Justice in Early America.* Cambridge, MA: Harvard University Press, 2003.

Brown, Robert E. *Middle-Class Democracy and the Revolution in Massachusetts, 1691–1780.* Ithaca, NY: Cornell University Press, 1955.

Brown, Richard M. *The South Carolina Regulators.* Cambridge, MA: Belknap, 1963.

———. "Violence and the American Revolution." In *Essays on the American Revolution*, edited by Stephen G. Kurtz and James H. Hutson. Chapel Hill, 81–120. Chapel Hill: University of North Carolina Press, 1973.

Brown, Wallace. *The Good Americans: The Loyalists in the American Revolution.* New York: William Morrow, 1969.

Brunhouse, Robert L. *The Counter-Revolution in Pennsylvania, 1776–1790.* Harrisburg: Pennsylvania Historical Commission, 1942.

Burrows, Edwin G. *Albert Gallatin and the Political Economy of Republicanism, 1761–1800.* New York: Garland, 1986.

Bushman, Richard. *The Refinement of America: Persons, Houses, Cities.* New York: Vintage Books, 1992.

Butler, Jon. *Awash in a Sea of Faith: Christianizing the American People.* Cambridge, MA: Harvard University Press, 1990.

Cachia-Riedl, Markus Claudius. "Albert Gallatin and the Politics of the New Nation." PhD diss., University of California, Berkeley, 1998.

Caldwell, John. *William Findley from West of the Mountains: A Politician in Pennsylvania, 1783–1791.* Gig Harbor, WA: Red Apple, 2000.

Calloway, Collin G. *The Scratch of a Pen: 1763 and the Transformation of North America.* New York: Oxford University Press, 2006.

Campbell, Ballard C. *The Growth of American Government: Governance from the Cleveland Era to the Present.* Bloomington: Indiana University Press, 1995.

Carter, Susan B., Scott Sigmund Gartner, Michael R. Haines, Alan L. Olmstead, Richard Sutch, and Gavin Wright. *Historical Statistics of the United States: Earliest Times to the Present.* Millennial ed. New York: Cambridge University Press 2006.

Christie, Ian R. *Crisis of Empire: Great Britain and the American Colonies, 1754–1783.* New York: Edward Arnold, 1966.

Cohen, Norman. "William Allen: Chief Justice of Pennsylvania, 1704–1780." PhD diss., University of California, 1966.

Conley, John A. "Doing It by the Book: Justice of the Peace Manuals and English Law in Eighteenth Century America." *Journal of Legal History* 6, no. 3 (1958): 257–98.

Conrad, W. P. *From Terror to Freedom in the Cumberland Valley.* Chambersburg, PA: Robson and Kaye, 1976.

Countryman, Edward. *A People in Revolution: The American Revolution and Political Society in New York, 1760–1790*. New York: W. W. Norton, 1989.

Cox, Caroline. *A Proper Sense of Honor: Service and Sacrifice in George Washington's Army*. Chapel Hill: University of North Carolina Press, 2004.

Craine, Elaine Forman. *Witches, Wife Beaters, and Whores: Common Law and Common Folk in Early America*. Ithaca, NY: Cornell University Press, 2011.

Crawford, B. Scott. "A Frontier of Fear: Terrorism and Social Tension along Virginia's Western Waters, 1742–1775." *West Virginia History* 2 (2008): 1–29.

Darnton, Robert. "In Search of the Enlightenment: Recent Attempts to Create a Social History of Ideas." *Journal of Modern History* 43, no. 1 (1971): 113–32.

Davis, W. W. H. *The History of Bucks County, Pennsylvania: From the Discovery of the Delaware to the Present Time*. Doylestown. PA: Democrat Book and Job Office, 1876.

De Pauley, W. C. "Beccaria and Punishment." *International Journal of Ethics* 35, no. 4 (1925): 404–12.

Dickerson, Oliver Morton. *American Colonial Government, 1696–1765: A Study of the British Board of Trade in Its Relation to the American Colonies, Political, Industrial, Administrative*. Cleveland: Arthur H. Clark, 1912.

Dill, Samuel. *Roman Society from Nero to Marcus Aurelius*. New York: Macmillan, 1905.

Dinkin, Robert J. *Voting in Provincial America: A Study of Elections in the Thirteen Colonies, 1689–1776*. Westport, CT: Greenwood, 1977.

Doerflinger, Thomas M. *A Vigorous Spirit of Enterprise: Merchants and Economic Development in Revolutionary Philadelphia*. Chapel Hill: University of North Carolina Press, 1986.

Dowd, Gregory Evans. *War under Heaven: Pontiac, the Indian Nations & the British Empire*. Baltimore: John Hopkins University Press, 2002.

Dunaway, Wayland F. "Pennsylvania as an Early Distributing Center of Population." *Pennsylvania Magazine of History and Biography* 55, no. 2 (1931): 134–69.

Edling, Max M. *A Hercules in the Cradle: War, Money, and the American State, 1783–1867*. Chicago: University of Chicago Press, 2014.

———. *A Revolution in Favor of Government: Origins of the U.S. Constitution and the Making of the American State*. Oxford: Oxford University Press, 2003.

Edwards, Laura F. *The People and Their Peace: Legal Culture and the Transformation of Inequality in the Post-Revolutionary South*. Chapel Hill: University of North Carolina Press, 2009.

Egerton, H. E. "The Seventeenth and Eighteenth Century Privy Council in Its Relations with the Colonies." *Journal of Comparative Legislation and International Law* 7 (1925): 1–16.

Egle, William H. "The Constitutional Convention of 1776: Biographical Sketches of Its Members." *Pennsylvania Magazine of History and Biography*

3–4, no. 1–4 (1879–80): 3: 96–101, 194–201, 319–30, 438–46; 4: 89–98, 225–33, 361–72.

Egnal, Marc. "The Economic Development of the Thirteen Continental Colonies, 1720–1775." *William and Mary Quarterly*, 3rd ser., 32, no. 2 (1975): 191–222.

———. *A Mighty Empire: The Origins of the American Revolution*. Ithaca, NY: Cornell University Press, 1988.

Fishburn, Janet F. "Gilbert Tennent, Established 'Dissenter.'" *Church History* 63, no. 1 (1994): 31–49.

Fleischacker, Samuel. *A Short History of Distributive Justice*. Cambridge, MA: Harvard University Press, 2005.

Fox, Francis F. "The Prothonotary: Linchpin of Provincial and State Government in Eighteenth-Century Pennsylvania." *Pennsylvania History* 59, no. 1 (1992): 41–53.

———. *Sweet Land of Liberty: The Ordeal of the American Revolution in Northampton County, Pennsylvania*. University Park: Pennsylvania State University Press, 2000.

Frantz, John B., and William Pencak. *Beyond Philadelphia: The American Revolution in the Pennsylvania*. University Park: Pennsylvania State University Press, 1998.

Franz, George W. *Paxton: A Study of Community Structure and Mobility in the Colonial Pennsylvania Backcountry*. New York: Garland, 1989.

Funston, Janet, and Richard Funston. "Cesare Beccaria and the American Founding Fathers." *Italian Americana* 3, no. 1 (1976): 72–92.

Futhey, J. Smith, and Gilbert Cope. *History of Chester County, Pennsylvania, with Genealogical and Biographical Sketches*. Philadelphia: Louis H. Everts, 1881.

Gerstle, Gary. *Liberty and Coercion: The Paradox of American Government from the Founding to the Present*. Princeton, NJ: Princeton University Press, 2015.

Gilmour, Ian. *Riot, Risings and Revolution: Governance and Violence in Eighteenth-Century England*. London: Pimlico, 1993.

Gipson, Lawrence Henry. "The American Revolution as an Aftermath of the Great War for the Empire, 1754–1763." *Political Science Quarterly* 65 (1950): 86–104.

Glatfelter, Charles H. "The Colonial Pennsylvania German Lutheran and Reformed Clergymen." PhD diss., Johns Hopkins University, 1952.

———. "The Eighteenth Century German Lutheran and Reformed Clergymen in the Susquehanna Valley." *Pennsylvania History* 20, no. 1 (1953): 57–68.

Goebel, Julius, and T. R. Naughton. *Law Enforcement in Colonial New York: A Study in Criminal Procedure, 1664–1776*. Montclair, NJ: Patterson Smith, 1970.

Goldstone, Jack A. "Rethinking Revolutions: Integrating Origins, Processes, and Outcomes." *Comparative Studies of South Asia, Africa and the Middle East* 29, no. 1 (2009): 18–32.

———. *Revolution and Rebellion in the Early Modern World*. Berkeley: University of California Press, 1991.

———. "Toward a Fourth Generation of Revolutionary Theory." *Annual Review of Political Science* 4 (2001): 140–55.

Greene, Jack P. *The Constitutional Origins of the American Revolution*. Cambridge: Cambridge University Press, 2011.

———. "Political Mimesis: A Consideration of the Historical and Cultural Roots of Legislative Behavior in the British Colonies in the Eighteenth Century." *American Historical Review* 75, no. 2 (1969): 337–60.

———. *The Quest for Power: The Lower Houses of Assembly in the Southern Royal Colonies, 1689–1776*. Chapel Hill: University of North Carolina Press, 1963.

Griffin, Patrick. *American Leviathan: Empire, Nation, and Revolutionary Frontier*. New York: Hill and Wang, 2007.

———. Introduction to *Between Sovereignty and Anarchy: The Politics of Violence in the American Revolution*. Edited by Patrick Griffin, Robert G. Ingram, Peter S. Onuf, and Brian Schoen, 1–20. Charlottesville: University of Virginia Press, 2015.

———. "The People with No Name: Ulster's Migrants and Identity Formation in Eighteenth-Century Pennsylvania." *William and Mary Quarterly*, 3rd ser., 58, no. 3 (2001): 587–614.

Grubb, Farley. "German Immigration to Pennsylvania, 1709 to 1820" *Journal for Interdisciplinary History* 20, no. 3 (1990): 417–36.

Guenther, Karen. "Berks County." In *Beyond Philadelphia: The American Revolution in the Pennsylvania Hinterland*, edited by John B. Frantz and William Pencak, 67–84. University Park: Pennsylvania State University Press, 1998.

Hall, Michael G. "The House of Lords, Edward Randolph, and the Navigation Act of 1696." *William and Mary Quarterly*, 3rd ser., 14, no. 4 (1957): 494–515.

Handlin, Oscar, and Mary Handlin. *Commonwealth: A Study of the Role of Government in the American Economy- Massachusetts, 1774–1861*. Cambridge, MA: Belknap, 1947.

Hanna, Charles Augustus. *The Scotch-Irish: Or, the Scot in North Britain, North Ireland, and North America*. New York: G. P. Putnam's Sons, 1902.

Hanna, William S. *Benjamin Franklin and Pennsylvania Politics*. Stanford, CA: Stanford University Press, 1964.

Hawke, David Freeman. *In the Midst of a Revolution*. Philadelphia: University of Pennsylvania Press, 1961.

Hendrickson, David C. "Bringing the State System Back In: The Significance of the Union in Early American History, 1763–1865." In *State and Citizen: British America and the Early United States*, edited by Peter Thompson and Peter S. Onuf, 113–49. Charlottesville: University of Virginia Press, 2013.

———. *Peace Pact: The Lost World of the American Founding*. Lawrence: University Press of Kansas, 2003.

Henretta, James A. *Salutary Neglect: Colonial Administration under the Duke of Newcastle*. Princeton, NJ: Princeton University Press, 1972.

Herrup, Cynthia B. *The Common Peace: Participation and the Criminal Law in Seventeenth-Century England*. Cambridge: Cambridge University Press, 1987.

Hindle, Steve. *The State and Social Change in Early Modern England, 1550–1640*. New York: Palgrave, 2002.

Holton, Woody. *Forced Founders: Indians, Debtors, Slaves, and the Making of the American Revolution in Virginia*. Chapel Hill: University of North Carolina Press, 1999.

———. *Unruly Americans and the Origins of the Constitution*. New York: Hill and Wang, 2007.

Horle, Craig W., Marianne S. Wokeck, Jeffrey L. Scheib, David Haugard, Joy Wiltenberg, Joseph S. Foster, and Rosalind J. Beiler, eds. *Lawmaking and Legislators in Pennsylvania: A Biographical Dictionary*. Harrisburg: Commonwealth of Pennsylvania House of Representatives, 2005.

Huntington, Samuel P. *Pennsylvania Politics, 1746–1770: The Movement for Royal Government and Its Consequences*. Princeton, NJ: Princeton University Press, 1972.

———. *Political Order in Changing Societies*. New Haven, CT: Yale University Press, 2006.

Illick, Joseph E. *Colonial Pennsylvania: A History*. New York: Scribner, 1976.

Ireland, Owen S., and Wayne Bockelman. "The Internal Revolution in Pennsylvania: An Ethnic-Religious Interpretation." *Pennsylvania History* 41, no. 2 (1974):124–59.

Irvin, Benjamin H. *Clothed in Robes of Sovereignty: The Continental Congress and the People Out of Doors*. Oxford: Oxford University Press, 2011.

Jensen, Laura S. "Government, the State, and Governance." *Polity* 40 (2008): 379–85.

Jensen, Merrill. *The Founding of a Nation: A History of the American Revolution, 1763–1776*. Indianapolis: Hackett, 1968.

Jones, Cole T. "'The Rage of Tory-Hunting': Loyalist Prisoners, Civil War, and the Violence of American Independence." *Journal of Military History* 81 (2017): 719–46.

Jordan, Winthrop. *White over Black: American Attitudes Toward the Negro, 1550–1812*. Chapel Hill: University of North Carolina Press, 1968.

Kain, R. P. J., and Elizabeth Baigent. *The Cadastral Map in the Service of the State: A History of Property Mapping*. Chicago: University of Chicago Press, 1992.

Kars, Marjoleine. *Breaking Loose Together: The Regulator Rebellion in Pre-Revolutionary North Carolina*. Chapel Hill: University of North Carolina Press, 2002.

Keller, Morton. *Affairs of State: Public Life in Late Nineteenth Century America.* Cambridge: Belknap, 1977.

Kenny, Kevin. *Peaceable Kingdom Lost: The Paxton Boys and the Destruction of William Penn's Holy Experiment.* New York: Oxford University Press, 2009.

Klein, Rachel N. *Unification of a Slave State: The Rise of the Planter Class in the South Carolina Backcountry, 1760–1808.* Chapel Hill: University of North Carolina Press, 1990.

Konkle, Burton A. *George Bryan and the Constitution of Pennsylvania, 1731–1791.* Philadelphia: William J. Campbell, 1922.

Kozuskanich, Nathan Ross. "'Falling under the Domination Totally of Presbyterians': The Paxton Riots and the Coming of the Revolution in Pennsylvania." In *Pennsylvania's Revolution*, edited by William Pencak, 7–35. University Park: Pennsylvania State University Press, 2010.

———. "'For the Security and Protection of the Community': The Frontier and the Makings of Pennsylvania Constitutionalism." PhD diss., Ohio State University, 2005.

Krohn-Hansen, Christian, and Knutt G. Nustad, *State Formation: An Anthropological Perspective.* London: Pluto, 2005.

Labaree, Leonard W. "The Conservative Attitude toward the Great Awakening." *William and Mary Quarterly*, 3rd ser., 1, no. 4 (1944): 331–52.

———. *Royal Government in America: A Study of the British Colonial System before 1783.* New Haven, CT: Yale University Press, 1930.

Lambert, Frank. "'Pedlar in Divinity': George Whitefield and the Great Awakening, 1737–1745." *Journal of American History* 77, no. 3 (1990): 812–37.

Lemon, James. *The Best Poor Man's Country: A Geographical Study of Early Southeastern Pennsylvania.* New York: W. W. Norton, 1972.

Libecap, Gary D., Dean Lueck, and Trevor O'Grady. "Large Scale Institutional Changes: Land Demarcation within the British Empire." *NBER Working Paper no. 15820* (2010): 1–37.

Lodge, Martin E. "The Crisis of the Churches in the Middle Colonies, 1720–1750." *Pennsylvania Magazine of History and Biography* 95, no. 2 (1971): 195–220.

Lokken, Roy N. *David Lloyd, Colonial Lawmaker.* Seattle: University of Washington Press, 1959.

Lydon, James D. "Philadelphia's Commercial Expansion, 1720–1739." *Pennsylvania Magazine of History and Biography* 91, no. 4 (1967): 401–18.

Lynd, Stoughton, and David Waldstreicher. "Free Trade, Sovereignty, and Slavery: Toward an Economic Interpretation of American Independence." *William and Mary Quarterly*, 3rd ser., 68, no. 4 (2011): 597–630.

Lyons, Clare A. *Sex among the Rabble: An Intimate History of Gender and Power in the Age of Revolution, Philadelphia, 1730–1830.* Chapel Hill: University of North Carolina Press, 2006.

MacGregor, Doug. "The Ordeal of John Connolly: The Pursuit of Wealth through Loyalism." In *The Other Loyalists: Ordinary People, Royalism, and the Revolution in the Middle Colonies, 1763–1787*, edited by Joseph S. Tiedemann, Eugene R. Fingerhut, and Robert W. Venables, 161–78. Albany: State University of New York Press, 2009.

Maier, Pauline. *From Resistance to Revolution: Colonial Radicals and the Development of American Opposition to Britain, 1765–1776*. New York: Vintage Books, 1972.

———. *Ratification: The People Debate the Constitution, 1787–1788*. New York: Simon and Schuster, 2010.

Mancini, Jay A., Gary L. Bowen, and James A. Martin. "Community Social Organization: A Conceptual Linchpin in Examining Families in the Context of Communities." *Family Relations* 54, no. 5 (2005): 570–82.

Marietta, Jack D. *The Reformation of American Quakerism, 1748–1783*. Philadelphia: University of Pennsylvania Press, 1984.

Marietta, Jack D., and G. S. Rowe. *Troubled Experiment: Crime and Justice in Pennsylvania, 1682–1800*. Philadelphia: University of Pennsylvania Press, 2006.

———. "Violent Crime, Victims, and Society in Pennsylvania, 1682–1800." *Pennsylvania History* 66 (1999): 24–54.

Martin, John Hill. *Chester and Its Vicinity: Genealogical Sketches of Some Old Families*. Philadelphia, 1877.

Masur, Louis P. *Rites of Execution: Capital Punishment and the Transformation of American Culture, 1776–1865*. New York: Oxford University Press, 1989.

McBride, Spencer. *Pulpit and Nation: Clergymen and the Politics of Revolutionary America* Charlottesville: University of Virginia Press, 2016.

———. *These Daring Disturbers of the Public Peace: The Struggle for Property and Power in Early New Jersey*. Ithaca, NY: Cornell University Press, 1999.

McCusker, John J., and Russell R. Menard. *The Economy of British America, 1607–1789*. Chapel Hill: University of North Carolina Press, 1985.

McDonnell, Michael. *The Politics of War: Race, Class, and Conflict in Revolutionary Virginia*. Chapel Hill: University of North Carolina Press, 2007.

McDonnell, Michael, and David Waldstreicher. "Revolution in the *Quarterly*? A Historiographical Analysis." *William and Mary Quarterly*, 3rd ser., 74, no. 4 (2017): 633–66.

Meehan, Thomas R. "Not Made Out of Levity: Evolution of Divorce in Early Pennsylvania." *Pennsylvania Magazine of History and Biography* 92 (1968): 441–64.

Meranze, Michael. *Laboratories of Virtue: Punishment, Revolution and Authority in Philadelphia, 1760–1835*. Chapel Hill: University of North Carolina Press, 1996.

Merrell, James H. *Into the American Woods: Negotiators on the Pennsylvania Frontier*. New York: W. W. Norton, 1999.

Miller, Ken. *Dangerous Guests: Enemy Captives and Revolutionary Communities during the War for Independence.* Ithaca, NY: Cornell University Press 2014.

Molovinsky, Lemuel. "Tax Collection Problems in Revolutionary Pennsylvania." *Pennsylvania History* 47, no. 3 (1980): 253–59.

Mombert, J. J. *An Authentic History of Lancaster County.* Philadelphia: J. E. Barr, 1869.

Monachesi, Elio. "Pioneers in Criminology. IX, Cesare Beccaria (1738–1794)." *Journal of Criminal Law, Criminology, and Police Science* 46, no. 4 (1955): 439–49.

Morgan, Edmund S., and Helen M. Morgan. *The Stamp Act Crisis: Prologue to Revolution.* Chapel Hill: University of North Carolina Press, 1953.

Moyer, Paul B. *Wild Yankees: The Struggle for Independence along Pennsylvania's Revolutionary Frontier.* Ithaca, NY: Cornell University Press, 2007.

Munger, Donna Bingham. *Pennsylvania Land Records: A History and Guide for Research.* Wilmington, DE: Scholarly Resources, 1991.

Murphy, Brian Philips. *Building the Empire State: Political Economy in the Early Republic.* Philadelphia: University of Pennsylvania Press, 2015.

Murrin, John. "Political Development." In *Colonial British America: Essays in the New History of the Early Modern Era,* edited by Jack P. Greene and J. R. Pole, 408–56. Baltimore: Johns Hopkins University Press, 1984.

Nash, Gary B. *Forging Freedom: The Formation of Philadelphia's Black Community, 1720–1840.* Cambridge, MA: Harvard University Press, 1988.

———. *Quakers and Politics: Pennsylvania 1681–1726.* Boston: Northeastern University Press, 1993.

———. *The Unknown American Revolution: The Unruly Birth of Democracy and the Struggle to Create America.* New York: Penguin Books, 2006.

———. "Up from the Bottom in Franklin's Philadelphia." *Past & Present* 77 (1977): 57–83.

Neill, Michael. "'Mullatos,' 'Blacks,' and 'Indian Moors': Othello and Early Modern Constructions of Human Difference." *Shakespeare Quarterly* 49, no. 4 (1998): 361–74.

Newcomb, Benjamin H. *Franklin and Galloway: A Political Partnership.* New Haven, CT: Yale University Press, 1972.

———. *Political Partisanship in the American Middle Colonies, 1700–1776.* Baton Rouge: Louisiana State University Press, 1995.

North, Roger. *The Lives of the Right Hon. Francis North.* London: George Bell and Sons, 1890.

Novak, William J. "The Legal Transformation of Citizenship in Nineteenth-Century America." In *The Democratic Experiment: New Directions in American Political History,* ed. Meg Jacobs, William J. Novak, and Julian E. Zelzer, 85–119. Princeton, NJ: Princeton University Press, 2003.

———. "The Myth of the 'Weak' American State." *American Historical Review* 113, no. 3 (2008): 752–72.

———. *The People's Welfare: Law & Regulation in Nineteenth-Century America.* Chapel Hill: University of North Carolina Press, 1996.

———. "Public Economy and the Well-Ordered Market: Law and Economic Regulation in 19th Century America." *Law and Social Inquiry* 18, no. 1 (1993): 1–32.

Novak, William J., and Steven Pincus. "Revolutionary State Formation: The Origins of the Strong American State." In *State Formations: Global Histories and Cultures of Statehood*, edited by John L. Brooke, Julia C. Strauss, and Greg Anderson, 138–55. Cambridge: Cambridge University Press, 2018.

Nozick, Robert. *Anarchy, State, and Utopia.* New York: Basic Books, 1974.

Olson, Alison. "The Pamphlet War over the Paxton Boys." *Pennsylvania Magazine of History and Biography* 123, no. 1 (1999): 31–55.

Olton, Charles S. *Artisans for Independence: Philadelphia Mechanics and the American Revolution.* Syracuse, NY: Syracuse University Press, 1975.

Ousterhout, Anne M. *A State Divided: Opposition in Pennsylvania to the American Revolution.* New York: Greenwood Press, 1987.

Owen, Kenneth. *Political Community in Revolutionary Pennsylvania, 1774–1800.* Oxford: Oxford University Press, 2018.

Pagan, John Ruston. *Anne Orthwood's Bastard: Sex and Law in Early Virginia.* New York: Oxford University Press, 2003.

Paludan, Philip S. "The American Civil War Considered as a Crisis in Law and Order." *American Historical Review* 77, no. 4 (1972): 1013–34.

Parkinson, Robert G. *The Common Cause: Creating Race and Nation in the American Revolution.* Chapel Hill: University of North Carolina Press, 2016.

Parkman, Francis. *The Conspiracy of Pontiac and the Indian War after the Conquest of Canada.* Lincoln: University of Nebraska Press, 1994.

Pearl, Christopher. "For the Good Order of Government: The American Revolution and the Creation of the Commonwealth of Pennsylvania, 1740–1790." PhD diss., Binghamton University, 2013.

———. "Franklin's Turn: Imperial Politics and the Coming of the American Revolution." *Pennsylvania Magazine of History and Biography* 136, no. 2 (2012): 117–39.

———. "'Our God and Our Guns': Religion and Politics on the Revolutionary Frontier." *Pennsylvania History* 85, no. 1 (2018): 58–89.

———. "Pulpits of Revolution: Presbyterian Political Thought in the Era of the American Revolution." *Journal of Presbyterian History* 95 (2017): 4–17.

Pearson, Susan J. "A New Birth of Regulation: The State of the State after the Civil War." *Journal of the Civil War Era* 5 (2015): 422–39.

Pincus, Steve. *The Heart of the Declaration: The Founders' Case for an Activist Government.* New Haven, CT: Yale University Press, 2016.

———. *1688: The First Modern Revolution.* New Haven, CT: Yale University Press, 2009.

Pritchard, R. T. "Gaius Verres and the Sicilian Farmers." *Historia Zeitschrift* 20, no. 3 (1971): 224–38.
Quintana, Ryan A. *Making a Slave State: Political Development in Early South Carolina*. Chapel Hill: University of North Carolina Press, 2018.
Rappaport, George David. *Stability and Change in Revolutionary Pennsylvania: Banking, Politics, and Social Structure*. University Park: Pennsylvania State University Press, 1996.
Reid, John Philip *In Defiance of the Law: The Standing Army Controversy, the Two Constitutions, and the Coming of the American Revolution*. Chapel Hill: University of North Carolina Press, 1981.
Roney, Jessica Choppin. *Governed by a Spirit of Opposition: The Origins of American Political Practice in Colonial Philadelphia*. Baltimore: Johns Hopkins University Press, 2014.
———. "1776, Viewed from the West." *Journal of the Early Republic* 37 (2017), 655–700.
Rosswurm, Steven. *Arms, Country, and Class: The Philadelphia Militia and the "Lower Sort" during the American Revolution*. New Brunswick, NJ: Rutgers University Press, 1987.
Rothman, Adam. "Beware the Weak State." *William and Mary Quarterly*, 3rd ser., 64, no. 2 (2007): 271–74.
Rowe, G. S. *Embattled Bench: The Pennsylvania Supreme Court and the Forging of a Democratic Society, 1684–1809*. Newark: University of Delaware Press, 1994.
———. "The Frederick Stump Affair, 1768, and Its Challenge to Legal Historians of Early Pennsylvania." *Pennsylvania History* 49, no. 4 (1982): 259–88.
———. *Thomas McKean: The Shaping of American Republicanism*. Boulder: Colorado Associated University Press, 1978.
Rozbicki, Michal Jan. *Culture and Liberty in the Age of the American Revolution*. Charlottesville: University of Virginia Press, 2011.
Ryerson, Richard Alan. "Portrait of a Colonial Oligarchy: The Quaker Elite in the Pennsylvania Assembly, 1729–1776." In *Power and Status: Officeholding in Colonial America*, edited by Bruce C. Daniels, 106–35. Middletown, CT: Wesleyan University Press, 1986.
———. *The Revolution Is Now Begun: The Radical Committees of Philadelphia, 1765–1776*. Philadelphia: University of Pennsylvania Press, 1978.
Salinger, Sharon V. *"To Serve Well and Faithfully": Labour and Indentured Servants in Pennsylvania, 1682–1800*. Cambridge: Cambridge University Press, 1987.
Sampson, Robert J. "Linking the Micro- and Macrolevel Dimensions of Community Social Organization." *Social Forces* 70, no. 1 (1991): 43–64.
Sarson, Steven. *British America, 1500–1800: Creating Colonies, Imagining an Empire*. London: Hodder Arnold, 2005.

Schwartz, Heather. "Re-Writing the Empire: Pans for Institutional Reform in British America, 1643–1788." PhD diss., Binghamton University, 2011.

Schwartz, Sally. *"Mixed Multitude": The Struggle for Toleration in Colonial Pennsylvania*. New York: New York University Press, 1987.

Schweitzer, Mary M. *Custom and Contract: Household, Government, and the Economy in Colonial Pennsylvania*. New York: Columbia University Press, 1987.

Selsam, J. P. *The Pennsylvania Constitution of 1776: A Study in Revolutionary Democracy*. Philadelphia: University of Pennsylvania Press, 1936.

Sewell, William H. "The French Revolution and the Emergence of the Nation Form." In *Revolutionary Currents: Nation Building in the Transatlantic World*, edited by Michael A. Morrison and Melinda Zook, 91–125. New York: Rowman and Littlefield, 2004.

Shephard, William Robert. *History of Proprietary Government in Pennsylvania*. New York: Columbia University Press, 1896.

Shy, John. *A People Numerous and Armed: Reflections on the Military Struggle for American Independence*. Ann Arbor: University of Michigan Press, 1990.

Silver, Peter. *Our Savage Neighbors: How Indian War Transformed Early America*. New York: W. W. Norton, 2008.

Simler, Lucy. "The Landless Worker: An Index of Economic and Social Change in Chester County, Pennsylvania, 1750–1820." *Pennsylvania Magazine of History and Biography* 114, no. 2 (1990): 163–99.

———. "Tenancy in Colonial Pennsylvania: The Case of Chester County." *William and Mary Quarterly*, 3rd ser., 43, no. 4 (1986): 542–69.

Skocpol, Theda. "Bringing the State Back In: Strategies of Analysis in Current Research." In *Bringing the State Back In*, edited by Peter B. Evans, Dietrich Rueschemeyer, and Theda Skocpol, 1–24. Cambridge: Cambridge University Press, 1985.

Slaughter, Thomas P. "Crowds in Eighteenth-Century America: Reflections and New Directions." *Pennsylvania Magazine of History and Biography* 115, no. 1 (1991): 3–34.

———. "Interpersonal Violence in a Rural Setting: Lancaster County in the Eighteenth Century." *Pennsylvania History* 58, no. 2 (1991): 98–123.

———. *The Whiskey Rebellion: Frontier Epilogue to the American Revolution*. New York: Oxford University Press, 1986.

Smith, Barbara Clark. *The Freedoms We Lost: Consent and Resistance in Revolutionary America*. New York: New Press, 2010.

Smith, C. Page. "The Attack on Fort Wilson." *Pennsylvania Magazine of History and Biography* 78, no. 2 (1954): 177–88.

Smolenski, John. *Friends and Strangers: The Making of a Creole Culture in Colonial Pennsylvania*. Philadelphia: University of Pennsylvania Press, 2010.

Spero, Patrick. "Creating Pennsylvania: The Politics of the Frontier and the State, 1682–1800." PhD diss., University of Pennsylvania, 2009.
———. *Frontier Country: The Politics of War in Early Pennsylvania*. Philadelphia: University of Pennsylvania Press, 2016.
———. *Frontier Rebels: The Fight for Independence in the American West, 1765–1776*. New York: W. W. Norton, 2018.
———. "Recreating James Smith at the Pennsylvania State Archives." *Pennsylvania History* 76, no. 4 (2009): 474–83.
Stark, Rodney, and Roger Finker. "American Religion in 1776: A Statistical Portrait." *Sociological Analysis* 49, no. 1 (1988), 35–55.
Teeters, Negley K. "Public Executions in Pennsylvania: 1682–1834." *Journal of the Lancaster Historical Society* 64, no. 2 (1960): 85–164.
Thayer, Theodore. *Pennsylvania Politics and the Growth of Democracy, 1740–1776*. Harrisburg: Pennsylvania Historical and Museum Commission, 1953.
Tomlins, Christopher L. *Law, Labor, and Ideology in the Early American Republic*. Cambridge: Cambridge University Press, 1993.
Travers, Len. *Celebrating the Fourth: Independence Day and the Rites of Nationalism in the Early Republic*. Amherst: University of Massachusetts Press, 1999.
Troxler, Carole Watterson. *Farming Dissenters: The Regulator Movement in Piedmont North Carolina*. Raleigh: Office of Archives and History, North Carolina Department of Cultural Resources, 2011.
Truxes, Thomas M. *Defying Empire: Trading with the Enemy in Colonial New York*. New Haven, CT: Yale University Press, 2008.
Tully, Alan. *Forming American Politics: Ideals, Interests, and Institutions in Colonial New York and Pennsylvania*. Baltimore: Johns Hopkins University Press, 1994.
———. "Quaker Party and Proprietary Polices: The Dynamics of Politics in Pre-Revolutionary Pennsylvania, 1730–1775." In *Power and Status: Officeholding in Colonial America*, edited by Bruce C. Daniels, 75–105. Middletown, CT: Wesleyan University Press, 1986.
———. *William Penn's Legacy: Politics and Social Structure in Provincial Pennsylvania, 1726–1755*. Baltimore: Johns Hopkins University Press, 1977.
Ubbelohde, Carl. *The American Colonies and the British Empire, 1607–1763*. Arlington Heights, IL: Harlan Davidson, 1968.
Vaughan, Alden T. "Frontier Banditti and the Indians: The Paxton Boys' Legacy, 1763–1775." *Pennsylvania History* 51, no. 1 (1984): 1–29.
Wainwright, Nicholas B. "Governor William Denny in Pennsylvania." *Pennsylvania Magazine of History and Biography* 81, no. 2 (1957): 170–98.
Waldstreicher, David. *In the Midst of Perpetual Fetes: The Making of American Nationalism, 1776–1820*. Chapel Hill: University of North Carolina Press, 1997.

---. "Rites of Rebellion, Rites of Assent: Celebrations, Print Culture, and the Origins of American Nationalism." *Journal of American History* 82, no. 1 (1995): 37–61.
Ward, Matthew C. *Breaking the Backcountry: The Seven Years' War in Virginia and Pennsylvania, 1754–1765.* Pittsburgh: University of Pittsburgh Press, 2008.
Warden, Rosemary S. "'The Infamous Fitch': The Tory Bandit, James Fitzpatrick of Chester County." *Pennsylvania History* 62 (1995): 376–87.
Webb, Stephen Saunders. "'The Peaceable Kingdom': Quaker Pennsylvania in the Stuart Empire." In *The World of William Penn*, edited by Richard S. Dunn and Mary Maples Dunn, 173–94. Philadelphia: University Pennsylvania Press, 1986.
---. "William Blathwayt, Imperial Fixer: From Popish Plot to Glorious Revolution." *William and Mary Quarterly*, 3rd ser., 25, no. 1 (1968): 3–21.
Wokeck, Marianne S. "German and Irish Immigration to Colonial Philadelphia." *Proceedings of the American Philosophical Society* 133, no. 2 (1989): 128–33.
Wolf, Stephanie Grauman. *Urban Village: Population, Community, and Family Structure in Germantown, Pennsylvania, 1683–1800.* Princeton, NJ: Princeton University Press, 1976.
Wood, Gordon. *The Creation of the American Republic: 1776–1787.* New York: W. W. Norton, 1969.
---. *The Radicalism of the American Revolution.* New York: Alfred A. Knopf, 1992.
Wood, Jerome H. *Conestoga Crossroads: Lancaster, Pennsylvania, 1730–1790.* Harrisburg: Pennsylvania Historical and Museum Commission, 1979.
---. "The Town Proprietors of Lancaster, 1730–1790." *Pennsylvania Magazine of History and Biography* 96, no. 3 (1972): 346–68.
Yirush, Craig B. "The Imperial Crisis." In *The Oxford Handbook of the American Revolution*, edited by Edward G. Gray and Jane Kamensky, 85–102. Oxford: Oxford University Press, 2013.
Zuckerman, Michael. *Peaceable Kingdoms: New England Towns in the Eighteenth Century.* New York: Alfred A. Knopf, 1970.

INDEX

Adams, John, 1–2, 162, 191
Adams, Samuel, 162
admiralty courts, 137, 179
Allen, Andrew, 58
Allen, James, 58, 191–92
Allen, William, 16, 20, 23, 58–59; as Chief Justice, 54–56, 60, 89, 96, 98–99, 122, 134
Allison, Robert, 119
American Revolution, influences on: consolidation of power, 129–30, 151–66; mobilization for change, 129, 139–51, 155; politicization of grievances, 129–39
Armstrong, John, 114
Aubrey, Laetitia Penn, 16

Baird, Richard, 54–55
Baker, Francis, 124, 125–26
Bank of North America, 188–90
Barton, Thomas, 131–33
Battle of Crooked Billet, 199
Baynton, Wharton, and Morgan, 112–13, 114–15
Beccaria, Cesare, 172
Black, John, 22
Black Boys, 5–6, 102, 111–22, 127, 128
Blathwayt, William, 73, 74, 75
Bouquet, Henry, 113, 114–15
Boyd, Andrew, 197, 199
Breintnal, Joseph, 87
British Empire: Board of Trade, 6–7, 76, 78, 81, 84, 87, 91–98; Committee of Trade and Plantations, 74; House of Commons, 65; House of Lords, 77, 208; imperial policies of, 71–95, 116–17, 147–48; Parliament, 3–4, 6, 65, 73, 76–77, 128; Privy Council, 6–7, 61, 74, 75–76, 78, 84, 87, 91, 93–95
Brown, David Paul, 201
Brownson, Richard, 119
Bryan, George, 82–83, 101, 142, 146, 181, 197, 211, 274n6
Buhlman, Frederick, 56
Burd, James, 59, 60

Callender, Robert, 114–15, 116, 117, 120
Campbell, George, 111–12
Carl, John, 66
Carmichael, John (minister), 104
Carmichael, John (vigilante), 125, 126
Carolinas, 4, 23, 73, 76–77, 111, 152, 202, 241n117, 242n122
Cavenah, John, 125, 126
Charles II, 73, 86, 87
Chew, Samuel, 42
civil libertarianism, 41
class and politics, 140–41, 146, 149–50, 170, 186, 257n61, 267n72
Coercive Acts, 153
Coleman, William, 98–99
College of New Jersey, 33–34
Committee of Safety, 159, 176
committees of correspondence, 143, 152, 154
common pleas, court of: colonial, 51, 88; state, 183, 201, 218
Conestoga Massacre, 109
Connecticut, 76, 146–47, 148, 198
Constitutional Convention, 1–2, 9, 128, 169–69, 176, 217
Continental Congress, 151, 153–55, 159, 162–65, 186
Coxe and Company, 14–15
Croghan, George, 112–15, 118, 119

303

Davenport, James, 35, 36
"Dear Ned" (A.B.), 70–71
Declaration of Independence, 7–8
Declaration of Rights, 169–70, 180, 190, 206, 207, 214, 217
De Haas, John Philip, 57
Delaware, 76
Demophilus (pseudonym), 173, 174
Denny, William, 85–86, 89, 91, 121
Dickinson, John, 136, 137–38, 142, 148, 154, 155, 160–61
Dickinson, Jonathan, 33–34
"distributive justice," 134, 173, 174, 179, 263n18
divorce law, 182–83
Dunlap, Andrew, 22
Dunmore, John Murray, Earl of, 146

Elder, John, 103, 104, 106–7, 108
Ettwein, John, 196
Evans, Rowland, 146
Everhart, Christian, 64

Falckner, Justus, 12
Findley, William, 211–12, 215–16
Fisher, Samuel Rowland, 194, 195
Fitzpatrick, James, 202
Fleeson, Plunket, 146
Forrestor, Alexander, 91
Fort Wilson riot, 186–87
Foulke, Samuel, 96
France, 4, 105
Franklin, Benjamin, 83, 86, 93, 94–95, 146, 205; on Judiciary and Land Records Acts, 90; on Paxton Boys, 103, 132; on the "rabble," 140; on religion, 28; on weakness of local government, 2, 6, 133–34, 136, 138
Franklin, William, 94–95

Gage, Thomas, 2, 6, 109, 111–16, 122
Gallatin, Albert, 213, 216
Galloway, Joseph, 2, 6, 10, 83, 88, 94, 96, 141–42, 146; on lower classes, 151; opposition to, 152–55; retirement of, 160; royal takeover proposal and, 133–38, 147–48
Gamble, James, 125
George II, 87
George III, 136, 164
Georgia, 169
Gerock, John Siegfried, 31
Gibson, James, 110, 131
Goddard, William, 148
Goodlet, John, 42
Gordon, Patrick, 80
Grant, Charles, 116, 117–18
Grantham, Charles, 24
Great Awakening, 27, 35–38
Grenville, George, 137
Grotius, Hugo, 106

Halifax, George Montagu-Dunk, Earl of, 79, 82, 90, 91, 97
Hamilton, Andrew, 123
Hamilton, James, 51, 58–59, 79, 80, 87, 95, 96, 98
Harding, George, 203
Hardy, Josiah, 97
Harris, John, 124
Henry, William, 187
Hill, John, 198
Hillsborough, Wills Hill, Viscount of, 147
Holmes, John, 114, 120
Howie, Alexander, 32
Hughes, Griffith, 32–33
Hughes, John, 138
Humphreys, Samuel, 64
Hunt, Isaac, 101, 158–59, 255n18
Hutcheson, Francis, 108

Illinois Country, 112, 114
Imperial Crisis, 3–4
Ironcutter, John, 147, 148

James I, 73
James II, 73
Jaucourt, Louis de, 11

INDEX

Jay, John, 1–2
Jefferson, Thomas, 9
Johnson, William, 113, 115
Judiciary and Land Records Acts, 89–92, 95, 96
justices of the peace (JPs), 56–64, 86–87, 114, 174, 176–77, 183, 264n29

Kearsley, John, 159
Keppele, Henry, 146
Knox, Henry, 1–2
Kriebel, George, 269n102

Lacey, John, 198–99
Lamb, Matthew, 91
La Mothe le Vayer, François de, 28
land policies, 13–19, 21–23, 175, 179
Lee, Richard Henry, 162
Lemon, James, 18, 60–61
Logan, James, 42, 44
Log College, 33
lotteries, 43
loyalists, wartime treatment of, 186–87, 190–91, 194, 195, 197–202
loyalty oaths, 193, 196, 199, 270n118

Marshall, Christopher, 162
Maryland, 23, 73, 74, 76–77, 122, 126–27
Massachusetts, 73, 76, 153, 202
Matlack, Timothy, 162
Maxwell, James, 114, 115–16, 117, 119, 251n70
McKean, Thomas, 180–81, 194, 201, 203, 207–8
McKnight, John, 114
Mercer, George, 105
Mifflin, Thomas, 153–54, 160, 207
Miller, Lawrence, 203
Mittelberger, Gottlieb, 17, 20
Montesquieu, Charles-Louis de Secondat, 11, 28
Moore, William, 64–68, 89
Moraley, William, 21, 25
Moravian Brethren, 12–13, 37

Morris, Robert Hunter, 80–82, 85, 86, 87, 97, 189
Muhlenberg, Henry Melchior, 11, 18–19, 26, 28–31, 38, 60–61

Native Americans, 4, 9, 73, 105–6, 112, 191; in Pennsylvania, 5, 12, 16, 20, 21, 102, 107–10, 113–15, 147
Navigation Acts, 74, 76
Neel, Matthew, 53–54
New Jersey, 4, 76, 97
New York, 4, 73, 76, 198, 202
Norris, Isaac, Sr., 21, 22, 86, 90, 96
North, Francis, 74–75

"order" concept, 12, 228n11
orphans court, 59, 218
Ourry, Lewis, 62

Paine, Thomas, 160–61, 162, 169, 208
Parke, Robert and Thomas, 25
Parker, Joseph, 151
patronage, 15–16
Pawling, Henry, 146
Paxton, Thomas, 120
Paxton Boys, 10, 102–3, 109–11, 112, 127, 130–33
Peale, Charles Wilson, 186–87, 271n137
penal system, 9, 168, 171–72, 175, 201–2, 205, 208
Penn, Anne Allen, 58
Penn, John, 6, 15, 58, 78–79, 99, 111, 113, 115–16, 119, 122, 126–27, 158, 159
Penn, Thomas, 16, 51, 79, 82, 85, 86, 89–100
Penn, William, 10, 11, 12, 27, 38, 71, 72–75, 77, 81, 90–91; land policy of, 13–17, 19, 21
Penn, William, Jr., 16
Pennsylvania: Charter (of 1701) for, 65, 71, 81–82, 90–92; coercive powers of, 192–204; colonial era in, 11–38, 72–83; constitution of, 9, 152, 167–75, 182, 206–7, 213–18; county map of, 178; economic issues in, 24–25, 47–49,

Pennsylvania (*continued*)
111–15, 154, 184–85, 187–88, 211; faction in, 72, 84, 107, 122, 131, 133–34, 185; Frame of Government of, 169; German immigrants in, 29–30, 66, 81; government formation in, 2–3, 4–7, 9–10, 71–72; government inadequacies in, 70–72, 95–103, 106, 108–12, 126–27, 129–39, 148–49, 153, 161; land prices in, 20–21, 23; legal system in, 43–46, 48–67, 87, 88–89, 96–99, 109, 176–84, 201, 217–18; military in, 51, 84, 101, 108–9, 135–36, 160, 168–69, 186–87, 196, 197–203; mobility and tenancy in, 19–27; occupation of Philadelphia in, 192; policing and criminal justice system in, 8–9, 41, 50–52, 56, 101–2, 124, 171–73, 194–95, 202–4; population growth in, 19–21, 50, 52, 89; post-revolution era in, 205–19; religion in, 12–13, 15, 19–20, 27–38; royal takeover proposal in, 133–38, 142, 147–48; Scots-Irish immigrants in, 34–35, 104; suffrage in, 140–41, 168
Pennsylvanicus (pseudonym), 43
Peters, Richard, 21–22, 59, 85
Peters, Richard, Jr., 54
petitioning, 46–47, 48–52, 63, 65, 72, 110, 131, 139, 144, 149
Pike, Joseph, 14–15
police powers, 8–9, 268n94. *See also under* Pennsylvania
Pontiac's War, 105, 107, 112, 131
Porter, Reese, 116
Porter, Robert, 124, 125–26
Porter, Stephen, 126
Potts, John, 40
Pownall, John, 79, 91, 97
Pratt, Charles, 92
Proclamation of 1763, 112, 114
Presbyterians, 142, 143
price control committees, 186, 187, 216
public executions, 201–3, 273nn157–58, 273n161

public welfare philosophy (*salus populi suprema lex est*), 41–48, 57, 104, 131–32, 171, 176, 180–85, 188, 190–91, 193–94, 268n81
Pugh, James, 45

Quakers, 7, 10, 19–20, 38, 107, 110; elite status of, 5, 12–13, 68–69, 71–72, 83, 87–88; pacifism of, 108, 135
quarter sessions, courts of, 45, 51, 53, 88, 218; assault cases before, 236n38; JPs and, 61

Ralph, James, 149
Randolph, Edward, 76–77
Rankin, James, 164
Reed, James, 40
Reed, Joseph, 153–54, 187, 191, 192, 197, 200, 265n42
Reid, John, 118
religion and governance, 11–12, 27–38, 73, 103–4, 143, 146
representation issues, 144–45, 149, 154, 170
republicanism, 8, 155, 169, 171, 180
Reynolds, William, and family, 123–27
Rhoads, Samuel, 146
Rhode Island, 74, 76
Rogers, William, 203
Rothenbuhler, Frederick, 37–38
Rush, Benjamin, 1, 163, 207, 274n6
Ryder, Dudley, 82

Saget, Mary, 46
Seven Years' War, 5, 85, 105, 107, 114, 131, 225n24
Sharpe, Horatio, 122
Sheehays, 108
Shippen, Edward, 23, 59
Shippen, Edward, Jr., 59
Shippen, Joseph, 59
Simcoe, John, 199
slavery, 9, 123, 184; gradual abolition of, 184
Smith, James, 111, 112, 115, 117–22, 128, 156, 252n93

Smith, Matthew, 103, 110, 131
Smith, Thomas, 168
Smith, William, 115, 116, 117, 121
Smyth, John, 194
Society for the Propagation of the Gospel in Foreign Parts (SPG), 32, 33
Sock, Will, 107–8
Stamp Act, 137–38, 143–44
"state crisis" concept, 7, 103, 127, 129, 247n4
state governance: dominance of, 3; formation of, 2–3, 167–204, 192–93, 269n106; inadequacies of, 2, 4–5, 7, 128–29; "internal police" of, 8–9, 52, 173–74, 204, 211, 218, 226n45, 268n94; opposition to power of, 1–2; US Constitution and, 212–13, 275n20
Stewart, Lazarus, 56–57, 103, 108–9
Strettle, Amos, 146
Strong, Nathan, 203
Stump, Frederick, 147, 148
Supreme Court, 54–56, 87, 89, 96–99, 121–22, 131, 173; as oyer and terminer court, 96, 121, 174, 183, 201, 218; state reforms of, 110, 174, 176, 179–82, 201, 207, 208–9, 218
Supreme Executive Council (SEC), 176–77, 180, 185, 190, 192, 194–200
Swanwick, Richard and Mary, 199–200

Tea Act, 152, 153
Tennent, Gilbert, 35–36, 38, 45, 104
Tennent, William, 33

Thomas, George, 12, 80, 87
Thomson, Charles, 153–54, 160
Townshend Acts, 143–44, 152

US Constitution, 1, 206, 211–13, 274n3

Vatel, Emerich de, 106
Vermont, 169
vigilantism, 6, 101–4, 109, 111–12, 115–22, 124–27, 129
Virginia, 4, 23, 73, 76, 102, 146–47, 152, 170
Voltaire, 11, 28

Washington, George, 1–2
Webb, James, 149
Wetzel, John, 196, 197
Wharton, Samuel, 146
Whitefield, George, 16, 35–36, 38
Will, William, 207
William, Duke of Cumberland, 85
William III, 76
Willing, Thomas, 146, 155
Wilmot, Henry, 92
Wilson, James, 155, 187, 207, 212–13
Wilson, Mordecai, 198

Yeates, Jasper, 18, 53, 62, 127, 148, 180
"yellow wigs," 102, 125–27
Yorke, Charles, 92

Zinzendorf, Nikolas Ludwig von, 36–37

RECENT BOOKS IN THE SERIES
Early American Histories

Conceived in Crisis: The Revolutionary Creation of an American State
Christopher R. Pearl

Redemption from Tyranny: Herman Husband's American Revolution
Bruce E. Stewart

Experiencing Empire: Power, People, and Revolution in Early America
Patrick Griffin, editor

Citizens of Convenience: The Imperial Origins of American Nationhood on the U.S.-Canadian Border
Lawrence B. A. Hatter

"Esteemed Bookes of Lawe" and the Legal Culture of Early Virginia
Warren M. Billings and Brent Tarter, editors

Settler Jamaica in the 1750s: A Social Portrait
Jack P. Greene

Loyal Protestants and Dangerous Papists: Maryland and the Politics of Religion in the English Atlantic, 1630–1690
Antoinette Sutto

The Road to Black Ned's Forge: A Story of Race, Sex, and Trade on the Colonial American Frontier
Turk McCleskey

Dunmore's New World: The Extraordinary Life of a Royal Governor in Revolutionary America—with Jacobites, Counterfeiters, Land Schemes, Shipwrecks, Scalping, Indian Politics, Runaway Slaves, and Two Illegal Royal Weddings
James Corbett David

Creating the British Atlantic: Essays on Transplantation, Adaptation, and Continuity
Jack P. Greene

The Evil Necessity: British Naval Impressment in the Eighteenth-Century Atlantic World
Denver Brunsman

Early Modern Virginia: Reconsidering the Old Dominion
Douglas Bradburn and John C. Coombs, editors